Guide to
Community Action

Guide to Community Action

A SOURCEBOOK FOR CITIZEN VOLUNTEERS

By Mark S. Matthews

HARPER & BROTHERS   PUBLISHERS
NEW YORK

To the millions of Americans
who are creating
a design for democracy
through volunteer cooperative action
in all the communities of America

CONTENTS

P R E F A C E

THIS BOOK is for you—one of an estimated 100,000,000 Americans who are members of volunteer groups working for better communities, with objectives such as better schools, more efficient government, a more healthful and safer environment, a more careful use of natural resources, or more adequate opportunities for recreation and cultural growth.

The idea for *Guide to Community Action* had its beginnings during my association with one of the largest and most active of organizations dedicated to community service. In conferring with civic leaders in hundreds of towns and cities, I found that few local groups working for community betterment were utilizing the experience of other groups, or were aware of the great wealth of advisory and material assistance that is available—without charge or at a nominal cost—from hundreds of sources.

This book, therefore, has two major purposes: to suggest program and project ideas which may be adapted to meet needs in your community, and to let you know what kind of help is available and where you can get it.

Strong citizen groups are essential for effective volunteer action. Part I of *Guide to Community Action* offers suggestions for attracting and holding members, making meetings interesting and worth while, financing activities, developing a continuing leadership, and securing and maintaining public approval.

Part II describes the major fields of group interest. It reviews problems faced by most towns and cities. It suggests how to determine needs, offers procedures which have worked, and presents activity ideas based upon reports of citizen achievement in the major community-service areas.

In the development of the book thousands of programs in representative towns and cities have been studied for ideas that would be of value to all types of volunteer groups—ranging from those with

ix

a formal organization and continuing programs, to those made up of neighbors informally associated for a limited purpose. Other preparation included exhaustive surveys of the kinds of assistance available to citizens in communities. National associations, foundations, universities, government agencies, corporations, unions, and other groups are conducting extensive research in all areas of living, and are discovering new, more effective approaches to the complex problems arising from rapid changes in our society. They depend upon local citizens to implement their programs. The assistance they offer includes background information, detailed manuals of instruction, program guides, films and other audio-visual aids, public education materials, and consultant services.

While this book has been written for all citizens interested in better communities, I feel that its suggested blueprint for democratic action should be of special interest to those who have an official or professional concern for community living. These may include school administrators and teachers, churchmen, charity and welfare personnel, government officials, business executives, public relations consultants, and labor leaders. *Guide to Community Action* presents an over-all view of community needs and suggests how these individuals can contribute to volunteer action. It furnishes information, ideas, and points of view essential for good relations with the public. It suggests methods by which churches, schools, private agencies, government departments, and business and industrial concerns may cooperate with citizen groups. Ideas for citizen action may be useful in the development of their own programs.

The author is grateful to the thousands of local organizations that have contributed information, and to the great national associations, foundations, government agencies, corporations, and unions that have made possible the descriptions of services and material help available.

MARK S. MATTHEWS

Greenwich, Connecticut
March 1, 1954

INTRODUCTION
Volunteer Action in the Community

THE SECOND half of the twentieth century finds the United States with a civilization in which its people enjoy material and spiritual advantages and opportunities without parallel in all the history of mankind. Economists and political scientists have failed to account for the emergence of this civilization in terms of material and geographic advantage. It is the thesis of *Guide to Community Action* that its uniqueness must be attributed to a heritage of freedom which has made possible the full utilization of the creative energy of its citizens in voluntary association on the community level.

In the formative years of the nation, as economic, political, social, and cultural concerns grew, local societies had a corresponding growth. Many, with common interests in better community living, developed into national federations.

By 1830, the association of citizens to promote their own welfare was such an outstanding American phenomenon that it excited special comment from Alexis de Tocqueville, a visitor from France. This observant admirer of early American democracy declared, ". . . in the United States associations are established to promote public order, commerce, industry, morality and religion, for there is no end which the human will, seconded by the collective exertions of individuals, despairs of attaining."

In summing up his observations of the total effect of American volunteer organizations, Tocqueville commented, "The most natural privilege of man, next to the right of acting for himself, is that of combining his exertions with those of his fellow creatures, and of acting in common with them. . . ."

Today millions of Americans are "combining their exertions" through affiliation with great federated groups dedicated to bold and vigorous action to create an increasingly better community living for all. These "exertions" are making communities safer and more healthful places in which to live and work and play. They are making possible the steady amelioration of the condition of those whose material and personal resources are inadequate for a decent standard of living. They are re-emphasizing the moral, ethical, and spiritual values in living. They are making steady progress, with the resourcefulness and vigor that only free men acting in concert can have, toward the solutions of problems in all the areas suggested by this book.

The strength of our democracy is largely dependent upon the quality of leadership that emerges from this free association of individuals with common ideals and purposes. Men and women characterized by leadership qualities, skills, and knowledges do not appear full-fledged in a community, state, or nation. Frequently they are average individuals who have grown to leadership stature through the practice of leadership in cooperative effort. Through group action they have received the human-relations understandings and skills necessary to achieve personal success, and to make important contributions to their community, state, and nation.

Recognition of the value of such training is emphasized by the attitude that schools, the professions, business, and industry take toward affiliation with volunteer groups. In the evaluation of students for college entrance and for job placement, club participation and other extracurricular activities which develop an ability to get along with others and to lead are given an emphasis once reserved for scholastic achievement. Both business and industry, in self-interest, give weight to volunteer-group membership when they employ executive and supervisory personnel, and often encourage affiliation and participation by allowing time from the job, and by paying membership dues. The Armed Forces find in the membership background of officer candidates evidence of leadership ability and experience.

In addition to enabling individuals to make important contributions to our democracy, and to achieve material success, organization training and practice bring other rich personal returns. There is the extension of self in an ever-widening circle of friendship. There is the fulfillment of personality, integrated in service to others. And, finally, there is the strengthening of character as the developing leader responds to the challenge that he exemplify the highest ideals of the group. Millions are finding the great truth known to philosophers since recorded time: true happiness and peace of mind can come only when there is a reaching out and an identification of self with others. And modern psychology buttresses this ancient philosophic insight with the generally accepted premise that true selfhood, with its wholeness of personality, is possible only through sympathetic inter-relations with others.

In activities such as those suggested in this book, individuals become aware of their potentialities for achievement, and discover values and goals common to all men. They achieve human dignity in a devotion to a high ideal. Real security comes with the feeling of belonging. Accomplishment that is concrete and measurable in the recognition of other men and women leads to greater and greater accomplishment. Personality thrives in a climate which encourages creativity.

It is hoped that the following record of achievement and the outline of problems which still remain unsolved will stimulate people in communities to even greater effort; that the accounts of successful organization experience will help citizens realize their full capacities for service; and that the utilization of the best knowledge and technical assistance now available in every field will help in discovering and solving the problems which communities now face. It is only by experimentation in the laboratory of the community that we can gain the knowledge that will be needed to keep pace with the even more complex problems that America may face in the future.

PART I

An Effective Community Organization

CHAPTER 1

Membership, Officers, and Committees

MOST COMMUNITY organizations are concerned with securing and maintaining an adequate, active membership; developing capable officers and committeemen; and building an efficient administrative structure. Some of the successful practices followed by typical groups are described in this chapter.

MEMBERSHIP

Many community organizations today find it difficult to secure and maintain adequate and active membership rolls in the face of increasing community demands on the time and effort of citizens, and the appeal of readily available diversions such as the automobile, radio, and television. In some groups, the problem is one of periodic replacement. In others, the need is for a continuing expansion to furnish additional personnel for service to the community, or to meet increasing costs of operation. In all there is the task of assimilating new members, and of holding the active interest of old members.

The particular methods by which a group solves these complex problems will, of course, depend on the character of the organization and its purposes. Some rely almost entirely on year-round, informal recruitment through individual member contacts, with officers or a membership committee furnishing direction and supervision. Others engage in carefully organized, widely publicized, and intensively conducted membership drives. Varying methods, formal and informal, are used in assimilating and holding members.

THE MEMBERSHIP COMMITTEE. Usually a standing committee has charge of membership procurement and maintenance. Such a group should be composed of those especially interested in membership problems, who also have a wide acquaintance in the community.

In most organizations, the chairmanship of the membership committee is an important post. To give it added prestige and to facilitate a correlation of membership efforts with other organization activities, a member of the board of directors or an officer is often selected. He has the responsibility of clearly defining and implementing the committee's purposes, which typically include the following:

1. Maintaining membership to the limits prescribed by the bylaws or dictated by organization requirements, through long-range planning and direction, and by special promotion efforts.
2. Recommending to the board of directors changes in membership policy, record forms, membership privileges, and other practices.
3. Assimilating new members.
4. Encouraging attendance at meetings and general participation in organization activities.

COMPOSITION OF THE MEMBERSHIP. Even though the nature and purposes of an organization limit members to those with particular interests, the membership committee may often strengthen the group through securing a cross section of the community so that many points of view are represented. In some situations, a better geographic distribution may be desirable. Perhaps younger men or women are needed to balance the conservative influence of older members. In other cases, the service program may be made more effective through the addition of individuals with special talents. Generally speaking, a good prospect is an individual who is acceptable under the bylaws of the organization, interested in the objectives of the group, and able to help achieve them.

Part of the solution of the membership problem of some organizations may lie in giving membership a community value and prestige through admission requirements. While artificial barriers are to be avoided, a prospect is more interested in joining if he knows an honor and privilege are conferred with membership.

Members who sponsor applicants undertake a serious responsibility and should feel strictly accountable to the board of directors or membership committee, not only for the general worthiness of those whom they propose, but also for their rapid and thorough assimilation. Some organization bylaws provide that the sponsored applicant be endorsed by two or more other members.

Sponsorship forms should provide for all the information necessary to act on a prospect's qualifications: his full name, date of birth, residence and business addresses, telephone numbers, occupation, church group, and other present and former organization affiliations.

YEAR-ROUND PROCUREMENT. The organization that can make membership procurement a year-round effort has certain advantages over those that must resort to intensive drives. It can, for example, exercise greater discrimination in the choice of applicants, give more careful attention to the assimilation of new members, and avoid the printing, clerical, and other costs sometimes necessary in large-scale campaigns.

The most important factor in the success of a continuing effort is the influence of individuals in an organization. Ask members to consider the membership qualifications of their friends and acquaintances. If particularly desirable prospects cannot be reached by members, try to arrange introductions through mutual acquaintances.

The reputation of an organization for interesting meetings and worth-while activities is a major influence in membership building. The extent of this influence depends mainly on the effectiveness of public relations and publicity measures, such as those suggested in Chapter 4.

The formal approach through a letter to prospects is appropriate for some organizations. Although the style and content are determined largely by the character of the organization, the letter usually describes the organization's membership, its purposes, the advantages and privileges of being associated with it, and plans for the immediate future. Ideally, the letter should be a personal one, written with a particular individual's interests in mind.

Desirable applicants are not those who join for the sake of joining, or to help an individual or a campaign team fill its quota, but rather those who are sold on the idea that membership is worth while. Such prospects may be interested through a brochure that describes the organization's history, purposes, and ideals; points out its accomplishments, its record of growth, and its challenge for the future; shows the applicant how he can participate in worth-while current organization activities; and suggests other personal advantages that can be obtained from membership.

The introduction of prospects to the organization may take the form of an invitation to a luncheon or other meeting. Many groups plan special guest night programs.

A hospitality committee may contribute to the membership effort by including among its duties that of welcoming and entertaining new arrivals in the community. They are an important source of prospects.

Some organizations expand the membership committee into clubs, or form groups outside the committee, which meet regularly at luncheons to plan membership procurement and to entertain prospects. Often membership in such groups is restricted to individuals who have secured two or more members. To continue as a member in good standing, the individual sometimes must meet a quota for each quarter, half, or full year.

MEMBERSHIP DRIVE. The short drive has important advantages: enthusiasm, difficult to sustain throughout the year, can be effectively aroused for the relatively short period of a few weeks; incentive devices such as contests and prizes can be utilized more fully; the concentration of attention on the membership problem for a few meetings permits scheduling of programs free from this distraction for the balance of the year; more satisfactory induction proceedings can be planned for groups than for individuals; a formal assimilation program is more practical with large groups; and through the publicity accompanying a drive, the community learns more about the organization, its purposes, and its ideals.

The planning and direction of a membership campaign may be the responsibility of the membership committee, or of a group composed of officers, representatives of key standing committees, and individuals appointed from the membership at large.

Before the campaign can be organized, several questions should be considered. How many additional members are needed or desired? How many workers will be required? During what time of the year is a membership campaign usually most successful? How can workers be most effectively organized? How long will it take to set up the campaign machinery and to approach the number of prospects chosen?

Most important as a preliminary task is the drawing up of a master list of eligible persons to be approached. It is often helpful to ask each member to submit a list of five prospects.

Even though some groups have no membership limits, adoption of a definite number of new members as a campaign goal, and assigning of specific quotas to groups and individuals furnish a challenge for workers to put forth their best efforts. The number to be aimed at in any campaign will, of course, depend on your organization need, the extent of the prospect list, and man power available for the drive.

To guard against the loss of morale that results from too wide a margin between anticipated and actual results, the quota should be fixed at a figure that the group can reasonably expect to meet. Review the results of campaigns of other years and of recent drives by other community groups with comparable memberships, and the general economic and other community influences that might affect membership in organizations such as yours.

Membership may be appreciably increased through periodic competition. The group is sometimes divided into two or more teams. At the end of several weeks the team obtaining the greatest number of new members is given a dinner by the others. Similar contests can be conducted as "baseball" or other games, with new members counted as hits and runs, and failure to secure members within given time limits as strike-outs. Individuals may compete for prizes such as hard-to-get tickets for sporting events or the theater. An interesting stunt used by some groups is to give an individual the responsibility of caring for a live duck or guinea pig. When he has secured a new member he may pass on his charge to the member with the poorest score.

Useful for the planning and direction of future drives and for the operation of a continuing, year-round procurement program is a careful evaluation of campaign experience. Did the quotas fixed offer sufficient challenge or were they too high? Did the drive reveal leadership abilities useful in the organization's administration and community activities program? What changes in organization, methods of personnel instruction, procedures, and techniques would perhaps have brought better results? How effective were incentives such as prizes for team performances? How fully were all publicity media used? What general public relations needs were noted?

In some large organizations, an intensive campaign for new members is also a major fund-raising effort. Chapter 3 offers further suggestions of interest to those planning for membership procurement.

ASSIMILATION. Many individuals join community organizations with slight knowledge or appreciation of what membership entails. The process of assimilation should have its beginning when the prospect first receives information about the purposes and ideals of the organization, and should be concluded only when he joins in the group efforts to further them. An organization has the responsibility, usually through the membership committee or officers, of carefully directing this process.

Specifically, an assimilation program might aim at helping the newcomer to develop friendly relations with other members; acquire a knowledge and appreciation of the history, structure, purposes, and ideals of the organization; join in group social and recreational activities; and participate in meeting activities and service projects to the limits of his capacities.

The first meeting the new member attends is important in that he receives there his first impression of the group. This impression may affect his association with other members for a long period and even, in some cases, determine whether or not complete assimilation is possible.

The president might send a letter of welcome inviting him to a premeeting luncheon or dinner with his sponsor, the officers, and the members of the board of directors. Arrangements should be made to introduce him to as many members as possible, before and at the meeting. Have all members wear badges or tags with their names, and identify the new member by giving him a badge of distinctive color. Formally present the new member in the course of the meeting.

Organizations often facilitate assimilation by providing each new member with a kit of materials, including such items as his lapel button and membership card, a pamphlet giving essential information about the national and local organization; the ritual, if any; a roster of members and officers; and copies of the national publication and local bulletin.

A special indoctrination meeting of new members with a program of quizzes, discussion, and questions and answers based on an organization handbook is sometimes scheduled. A formal course in organization affairs is offered by some groups. Conducted under the direction of an officer, it has regular sessions and study assignments; uses textbooks, charts, and other visual aids; and is climaxed by graduation ceremonies at which diplomas or certificates are presented. A few large national organizations conduct home study courses for their members.

Early assimilation is encouraged when the new member receives an assignment to a working group as soon as possible after his induction. Some organizations maintain personnel records and use counseling and guidance techniques in placing members on committees according to their special interests and abilities.

MAINTAINING AN ACTIVE MEMBERSHIP. As important to a vigorous organization as securing and assimilating new members is the maintenance of an active, interested membership through a varied program of service and meeting activities, the recognition of individual achievement, and the development of an *esprit de corps.*

A board of directors makes an important contribution to a strong membership when its policy emphasizes the rights and responsibilities inherent in organization affiliation. Membership rights might include the following: to retain an independence of thought and opinion, to have the best leadership available in the organization, to participate at meetings in accordance with the rules of parliamentary procedure, to take part in the determination of policy to the fullest extent permitted by the constitution and bylaws, to be protected against unreasonable or arbitrary assessment or other action on the part of the organization administration, to enjoy all the privileges that membership implies, to participate in organization activities to the limit of the individual's capacity, and to share in the opportunty for leadership training and practice.

Specific rights conferred by membership should be complemented by the assumption of certain parallel responsibilities by the individual: to distinguish in his public utterances between personal opinion and attitudes and organization policies, to refrain from using the fact of his membership as a pressure approach in his business relations with other members, to attend meetings and to participate in activities to the limit of his ability, to strengthen the bonds of organization fellowship, to understand and appreciate ritual and symbols when they are a part of meeting procedure, and to exemplify the highest ideals of his organization in his relations with others in the community.

There is an interdependence between attendance and good meeting programs that suggests the chicken-or-the-egg conundrum. Which comes first? Members will not turn out for dull meetings; interesting meetings often depend on large attendances. Close cooperation between a membership or attendance committee and the program committee seems to be the answer. Often responsibility for programming and for attendance is placed in the same committee.

Organizations sometimes encourage attendance by awarding door prizes. Some have a special attendance-prize fund to which each member contributes. Others purchase prizes from regular organization funds.

Various methods of choosing the door-prize winner are practicable. An effective method is to assign numbers or distribute tickets for a drawing to be held at the next meeting, thus encouraging consecutive attendance.

Competition may stimulate attendance. Divide the membership into two groups. At the end of each quarter have the group with the poorer attendance entertain the other at dinner.

Sometimes organizations impose a humorous forfeit for tardiness or successive absences. Some make each individual his brother's keeper by pairing him with another member. The member who cannot account for the whereabouts of his fellow member is subjected to a penalty, usually a light fine or the performance of an amusing skit.

Attendance can also be stimulated by recognizing perfect records as worth-while achievements. Organizations feature such items in the local bulletin or in national publications, confer honorary titles, grant special privileges, present special lapel buttons, automobile emblems, or membership cards. The names of attendance record holders often are conspicuously posted on a chart that also shows at a glance the attendance record of the group as a whole.

Personal telephone calls might be made to members who have been absent two consecutive meetings. Often this show of interest alone leads members to make a special effort to be present. Telephone calls have other advantages, too, in that they may reveal the illness of a member or the fact that he has not been receiving notices of meetings.

Recognition of the achievement of individuals can take many forms. For example, officers and committee chairmen in their informal relations with members as well as in their official capacities at meetings and in reports can emphasize individual contributions. The publicity chairman can see that the accomplishments of individuals are given due notice in the bulletin, the national publication, and local news releases. Awards and scrolls can be presented. Formal resolutions recognizing outstanding service can be offered.

In some groups, length of active membership is ceremoniously honored at an old-timers dinner. Special pins and other devices are used to distinguish the five-, ten-, and twenty-year members. Other groups have special classes or degrees of membership based on length of membership, special knowledge of the organization, and distinguished service. These individuals are often given important roles in rituals, and privileged places at meetings.

The effectiveness of any group organized for action depends on the development and maintenance of an *esprit de corps*—that comradely spirit that holds members together for a common purpose. *Esprit de corps* is not something that has to do only with the assimilation of new members; it is to be worked for as a characteristic of the group as a whole. The following procedures have proved practical:

1. Urge everyone to take part in the social and recreation program. Occasionally make refreshments and a social hour a part of meeting programs.

2. Devise ways by which the entire membership can have the benefits of the thinking and planning of policy makers. Good group relations demand that officers and members understand one another's points of view.

3. Use the bulletin as a means of making members better acquainted with one another. Feature human interest stories and personal items.

4. Mark the occasion of a member's securing a new job or a promotion, his engagement or marriage, with a congratulatory letter from the president and an announcement at a meeting.

5. Provide a suggestions system to solicit ideas about how to further fellowship or improve morale generally.

6. Show the hospitalized or the confined-at-home member that his fellow members are concerned about him by a resolution, "get well" cards, gifts, and regular visits by groups and individuals.

7. Encourage everyone to wear his lapel button, or display his automobile emblem.

8. Investigate underlying causes of poor attendance and resignations.

9. Impress on the membership the significance of the ritual and symbols. Standing as they do for the important concepts and ideals of the group, they help the individual to identify himself with each of his fellow members and with the organization as a whole.

OFFICERS, DIRECTORS, AND COMMITTEES

The efficient organization is one with an administrative structure that makes possible the smooth functioning of its activities. How many officers, directors, and committees are required, and their relationship to one another and the membership depend on the special purposes of the group, its size, and the range of its activities.

Committees are of two kinds—standing and special. Standing committees are appointed for a purpose that requires their continuous functioning; for example, those having to do with membership, finance, and programs. Special committees perform specific tasks not included in the work of standing committees. When their special purposes are achieved, such committees are dissolved.

ELIGIBILITY FOR OFFICE. Most eligible as officer candidates are those who have demonstrated qualities of leadership in organization activities, and have won the regard of the community. Important too is an extensive knowledge of the group's relation to the state and national organization, its history, objectives, and ideals. Those who aspire to organization leadership should have the time to devote to organization interests.

Some groups, through an informal apprenticeship system or formal training program, prepare members for positions of responsibility. In other groups, one office is considered a stepping stone to the next.

PROCEDURE FOR ELECTING OFFICERS AND DIRECTORS. The methods by which candidates are nominated are usually prescribed by the bylaws, or in the absence of such explicit provisions are determined by custom or through a motion offered at a meeting. The motion may provide for nominations from the floor or by a committee.

The common practice of nominating from the floor tends to develop the feeling that the selections are those of the group as a whole. While the procedure appears to be more democratic, it has these shortcomings: the selection may not be discriminating; members may be nominated who, though able, may not wish to serve; time is spent while members decline; too many candidates make it difficult for any one to get a majority; sometimes, through improper use of a motion to close the nominations, capable members are kept from the list.

Nominating by a special committee is more desirable, as it usually results in a more carefully drawn slate. In naming such a committee, the presiding officer should avoid choosing members who may be candidates for office.

Nominating committees usually choose but one candidate for each office. Multiple choices for any one office may, in effect, eliminate able members from consideration for other posts. This limitation does not apply, however, to nominations for the board of directors, for which it is often the practice to offer at least two candidates for each vacancy.

A motion delegating responsibility for nominations to a committee does not bar additional nominations from the floor. When committee nominations are reported, they are handled as if they had come directly from the floor. The chair should ask if there are any further nominations before declaring nominations closed.

The announcement of a nominating committee's slate in advance of the election date permits a proper consideration of the candidates, and time for support for other members to develop. Of the various methods of electing officers—by voice vote, show of hands, or secret ballot—usually fixed in the bylaws, the secret ballot gives members the greatest freedom in choosing. Organizations that find it difficult to get substantial meeting attendance sometimes arrange for balloting by mail. Most organizations do not permit voting by proxy.

OFFICERS' DUTIES AND RESPONSIBILITIES. The principal duties and responsibilities of officers are briefly summarized below.

The president has many responsibilities. As a member of the board of directors, he exerts an important influence in the determination of policies and procedures, and in initiating activities through participation in the drawing up of meeting agenda in conference with other board members, officers, and committee heads. As presiding officer, he has the task of disposing of the agenda. A working knowledge of parliamentary law, the essentials of which are offered in Appendix B, usually is necessary.

Specific presidential duties and responsibilities at meetings include making sure reports and other materials are available; opening the meeting at the proper time; holding to the order of business, clearly presenting each item and expediting action; maintaining a reasonable adherence to parliamentary procedure; and refraining from taking sides in a debate, or, when participation is necessary, stepping down in favor of a vice-president or other officer. The president usually appoints all committee chairmen and committee members.

In general, the president is responsible—directly, or through the officers and standing or special committees—for carrying out the wishes of the members as expressed in motions or resolutions. This necessitates periodic checks on committee progress and correlation of the work of officers and committees. In large organizations, some of this responsibility is delegated to other officers or to a salaried executive.

The president usually represents his organization in important programs and projects undertaken with other community groups. He is expected to attend organization conferences and conventions and to arrange for reports to the membership. As chief officer, he is often considered the organization's representative in community affairs. As such, he must realize that his public statements often are taken as official organization policy.

Depending on the size and the scope of its activities, an organization may have one or several vice-presidents. Duties include presiding at meetings in the absence of the president and acting for him in other capacities. When there is more than one vice-president, each is responsible to the president for some particular area of organization activity, such as administration or service, and is sometimes referred to in order of succession as first vice-president, second vice-president, and so forth.

The duties of a secretary in most organizations may be divided into two categories: those having to do with official correspondence, and those having to do with the keeping and presenting of all necessary records. In some organizations, there are a corresponding secretary and a recording secretary.

A corresponding secretary's duties are usually limited to the writing of communications having to do with the official business of the organization as a whole, in most cases at the direct order of the membership, the president, or the board of directors. Such correspondence includes letters to state and national headquarters and other organization groups; notes of thanks, congratulations, sympathy, and condolence; and motions and resolutions that the membership has expressly ordered forwarded to outside individuals and organizations. He receives all such organization correspondence and confers with other officers and the board about its inclusion in meeting agenda.

The duties of a recording secretary are to keep the minutes; take attendance; register votes; read the minutes of the previous meeting; read all letters, papers, and documents when called on to do so by the presiding officer; and file all official documents, such as copies of minutes and committee reports.

The treasurer receives all funds, deposits them in a manner approved by the organization, and pays out funds as stipulated by the bylaws.

The treasurer should stand ready to make a detailed report at any time, although usually such a report is required only annually or semiannually. Customarily, at each regular business meeting, the treasurer gives a summarized report of the financial status of the organization as affected by transactions since the last meeting, which would include a statement of the balance reported at the previous meeting, receipts and expenditures for the period, and the balance on hand.

Additional offices maintained by some organizations include that of a sergeant at arms, whose general function includes arranging the meeting place, assuring the comfort and convenience of members, and escorting late comers to seats; a historian, concerned with recording important events; a parliamentarian; and a counsel, whose duties include giving advice on legal matters and assisting in the drafting of resolutions.

THE BOARD OF DIRECTORS. The board of directors or board of governors is often referred to as an executive board. Among its functions are those of initiating and correlating activities, holding the organization to the purposes and ideals embodied in the constitution, approving the agenda for meetings, and acting for the whole group between meetings.

The board has no inherent power, but derives authority and duties from the constitution and bylaws and the will of the organization membership. Members of the board are usually elected. Its composition usually includes three or more from the organization membership, and the officers. Often membership on the board is staggered so that it may maintain a continuity of policy. The bylaws of many organizations provide that the president shall preside at board meetings. In other groups, this duty is performed by the immediate past-president, or a board chairman is elected.

STANDING AND SPECIAL COMMITTEES. Through committees, the work and responsibility of an organization may be divided among a maximum number of qualified members. It is through these groups that an organization functions. Committees create ideas and plans for meeting consideration, and they are given jobs to be carried out and reported on to the membership.

Some advantages of committee action over total membership

action include more time for the study of problems; greater opportunity for members to exchange ideas; more effective use of experience and professional and expert help from the membership and from outside individuals, through conferences and interviews; and greater liberty in discussion than would be possible at a general meeting.

While committees should include as large a part of the membership as is practicable, only those interested and able should be named, especially to key groups, and the number should be kept small enough for efficient functioning.

Standing committees are listed in the bylaws and are added to from time to time by amendment, as organization activities change or expand. Essential to most groups are the administrative committees having to do with membership, programs, public relations, and finance. Other administrative standing committees useful for some groups are resolutions, house, and hospitality. Service committees, such as those charged with recreation and health programs, are other important typical standing committees, the functioning of which is suggested in other chapters.

In many organizations, all resolutions must be presented for approval to a resolutions committee to avoid duplication and to make certain that form and style are in accordance with good usage. The committee may rewrite or otherwise edit resolutions, but it may not block them or act on them. Approved resolutions are made part of the agenda, to be read by their sponsors or the chairman of the resolutions committee.

In organizations that have permanent meeting places or clubhouses, a house committee is charged with such duties as maintenance of the building, grounds, and equipment; supervision of employees; and enforcement of the rules governing the use of facilities.

Special committees are named whenever the organization finds the time too short to explore a problem fully or to work out a solution, when it needs more data, or when a small group is required to carry out its will. Such committees may be created by a motion to refer. The motion may permit the presiding officer to determine the committee's size and its chairman. It should define precisely the committee's purpose and powers.

Sometimes a question before a meeting is too complex, or time is too limited, or an issue is not clearly defined for membership action. A committee may be named to consider further and report at the next meeting. In the course of discussion, the need for additional data often leads to the formation of such a committee. Its authority is limited to the gathering of information, although it may recommend action. A committee to carry out a special project, such as a banquet, would have the authority to make all necessary arrangements, committing the organization to the limits specified in the motion which created it.

COMMITTEE ORGANIZATION AND PROCEDURE. The president, in choosing a committee, may specify its chairman, or leave the selection of a chairman to the committee members themselves. In some organizations, the first individual named to a committee by the presiding officer is, traditionally, its chairman. In others, a temporary chairman is appointed until the election of a permanent chairman and a secretary at the first committee meeting.

Although committee procedure is usually informal, the chairman has all the responsibilities of a presiding officer, and may have recourse to parliamentary law in the event of serious disagreement, or to expedite committee business.

The following suggestions may be helpful in directing committee work:

1. Be sure each member has a clear conception of the committee's purpose and limitations.

2. Schedule meetings well in advance; fix the meeting time and place to suit the convenience of as many members as possible.

3. Include a copy of the agenda in the notice of the committee meeting.

4. Open meetings promptly.

5. Keep organization officers and the board of directors informed. Prepare progress reports for presentation to the membership.

6. Delegate responsibility for details.

7. See that each committee member has an assignment, and check on his progress and results.

8. Use the principles and techniques of group-discussion leadership described in Chapter 2.

9. Be prepared to accept the decisions of the group.

10. Confer with the chairman of the public relations or publicity committee about the public relations value of the work the committee is doing, and about giving recognition to the accomplishments of committee members.

Committee reports are written by the chairman from minutes kept by the secretary of the committee. Ordinarily they are signed by the chairman only. When important action is suggested, or when matters having to do with club policy or finances are involved, it is customary for the report to carry the signatures of all committee members. The signed report is presented to the organization's recording secretary to be placed upon the agenda of a regular meeting.

Whether or not minority reports are to be presented depends on custom, an agreement reached at the start of a committee's work, or on how close a decision was reached on an important controversial matter. A report approved by a small majority might properly call for a minority report to do justice to two points of view. The assembly then could take action on a motion to substitute the minority for a majority report.

TRAINING FOR LEADERSHIP. Organizations maintain formal training programs and make other planned efforts to develop leadership among members.

Officers and committee chairmen can influence this development of members by demonstrating leadership qualities and techniques; conducting meetings in accordance with the rules and principles of parliamentary procedure; displaying in their official and unofficial actions an enthusiasm for leadership in community service worthy of emulation; and choosing some guest speakers with a regard for their value as demonstrators of effective techniques.

Officers, chairmen, and the leadership training committee have the important responsibility of encouraging wide membership participation in activities, of recognizing and guiding those who show ability, and of furnishing opportunities for their growth.

Practical measures for meeting this responsibility are the following:

1. Planning a varied program to permit the widest possible participation. Include discussion groups and forums, which afford especially effective practice.

2. Utilizing business personnel techniques to discover special aptitudes and interests, and to fit the right members into the right projects.

3. Keeping a record of project participation as a check on the effectiveness of the training program. Aim at 100 per cent participation in service.

4. Recognizing leadership achievement, as an incentive for its development, by featuring individuals at meetings, in press releases and the house organ, and by making awards.

5. Rotating committee chairmen.

6. Encouraging members to attend conventions and conferences.

7. Urging individuals to volunteer for service in organizations such as the Red Cross and the Community Chest, and to take an active interest in municipal government.

8. Organizing a speakers' bureau.

9. Making available information about institutes, university extension courses, and local adult education opportunities designed to develop executive, sales, and general leadership ability through practice.

SOURCES OF AID

The national headquarters of most community organizations furnish local groups with information and suggestions about administrative structure; membership procurement and assimilation; the selection of officers and committees, and their duties. Representative sources of other aid include the following:

Adult Education Association of the United States, 743 North Wabash Ave., Chicago 11, Ill. Publishes *Adult Leadership* monthly except August. Nominally priced reprints suggest answers to questions such as these: How can you get people interested in joining your organization? How can meeting attendance be improved? How can members be encouraged to participate?

Boy Scouts of America, 120 West 42nd St., New York 36, N. Y. Maintains about 450 local councils throughout the country. Aids community groups and institutions in organizing Scout units. Films, slides, and instruction manuals are available from the National Council.

Boys' Clubs of America, 381 Fourth Ave., New York 16, N. Y. Provides pamphlets and handbooks about how to organize a Boys' Club, secure quarters and equipment, and participate in an activities program. Regional offices have free loan motion pictures.

Camp Fire Girls, Inc., 16 East 48th St., New York 17, N. Y. Provides publications, training courses, and assistance in organizing Camp Fire Girl units. Source of leaflets for sponsors.

Girl Scouts of the U.S.A., 155 East 44th St., New York 17, N. Y. Publishes *Blue Book of Girl Scout Policies and Procedures*. Includes advice for sponsoring groups and a catalogue of publications.

Haiman, Franklyn S., *Group Leadership and Democratic Action*, New York: Houghton Mifflin Company, 1951. A discussion of leadership which strikes a balance between theory and practice. Against a background of scientific-philosophic analysis, the book describes the attitudes and skills needed in democratic leadership, and suggests some approaches to the development of those attitudes and skills.

Hegarty, Edward J., *How to Run a Meeting*, New York: McGraw-Hill Book Company, Inc., 1947. The chapter "Making New Members Feel at Home" offers useful assimilation suggestions.

Hurley, Marvin, ed., *Chamber of Commerce Administration*, Chicago: National Institute for Commercial and Trade Organization Executives, 832 First National Bank Building, Chicago, Ill., 1947; revised edition, 1951. Outstanding work in the field of organization administration. Useful to many community groups as a guide to the solution of their membership, officer, and committee problems.

Library Research Service, *Encyclopaedia Britannica*, 20 North Wacker Drive, Chicago 6, Ill. Pamphlet *Women's Interests and Cultural Activities* includes sections on how to organize a club, how to conduct a meeting, methods of voting, duties of officials, and the constitution and bylaws.

National C.I.O. Community Services Committee, 1776 Broadway, New York 19, N. Y. Has information about training programs for union and community leadership.

National Publicity Council for Health and Welfare Services, 257 Fourth Ave., New York 10, N. Y. Publications include the booklet *Making Committees Effective*. Covers types and functions of committees; getting organized; planning for meetings; discussion proceedings; and the writing of minutes, reports, and recommendations.

Sarachan, Harman A., *Campaigning for Members*, New York: The Association Press, 1949. Intended primarily as a handbook for the planning and direction of membership and fund-raising campaigns such as those of the Y.M.C.A. and Y.M.H.A., the book has ideas adaptable to other organizations which procure members through community-wide campaigns.

Sturgis, Alice F., *Parliamentary Procedure*, New York: McGraw-Hill Book Company, Inc., 1950. Has a section describing the method of setting up a new organization, the qualifications and duties of officers, the organization and functioning of committees, the rights of members, and methods and procedures in voting.

CHAPTER 2

Meetings

IMPORTANT FOR organization success are meetings that consistently interest members and contribute to group and individual purposes. Suggestions for assuring such meetings are here offered.

PROGRAM PLANNING

The records of many successful organizations demonstrate the value of a tentative calendar drawn up early in the year. The Minneapolis Junior Chamber of Commerce, for example, attributed tripled membership participation in organization activities, over 300 new members, and a record number of successful projects to the adoption of a detailed year-round program plan.

Before deciding on any schedule of meetings, however tentative, a program committee might check on the previous year's activities to determine those most popular; talk informally with board members, officers, committee heads, and others; ask members to choose from a list of program possibilities; and discuss ideas at a regular meeting.

Some programs, such as those required by the bylaws or those that have become traditional, are musts in most organizations. Those related to national holidays or the observances of special days, weeks, or months are planned for particular times. In cooperation with project committees, meetings in support of service activities then are scheduled. With these programs decided, carefully balanced and varied offerings are chosen.

Try to give your meetings a continuity. Many groups choose a theme or a series of themes, to which programs are related. Often speakers or films suggest a series of logical and worth-while follow-up events. For example, a speaker or film on UNESCO might be followed by a luncheon invitation to exchange students in the area.

Once a tentative schedule has been approved, major changes should not be made without careful consideration. This is especially important when program plans have been given wide publicity and are

21

the result of much preparational effort on the part of committeemen. Resist pressure by individuals and groups to squeeze an activity of limited interest into an already full meeting time schedule. On the other hand, an unusual program opportunity may be lost by adoption of a calendar so set as to prevent a change of plans.

Provide for late speakers or entertainers, last-minute cancellations, the failure of a film to arrive, or other eventualities by having membership or community talent in reserve.

MEETING ACTIVITIES

So varied and overlapping are the purposes of community organization meetings, and the kinds of activities designed to meet them, that a logical classification seems impracticable. The following is intended only to suggest types of programs that have proved successful.

SPEAKERS. Budgets for outside speakers usually are limited. Before turning to the commercial agencies for talent, exhaust the resources of your own group and the community. Survey the membership for hobbyists, for authorities in the fields currently of interest to the members, for those who have had unusual experiences, who have traveled recently, or who have attended organization conferences or conventions, and for those whose professions, businesses, or occupations furnish interesting speech material.

The chief of police might give a talk on crime-detection methods; the superintendent of schools, on the relation of school and community; a clergyman, on religion and everyday living; the editor of the local paper, on a newspaper's responsibility to its readers. Outstanding sportsmen, actors, and artists might talk and give demonstrations in their fields.

Other sources of speaking talent are various volunteer agencies, associations, and foundations, whose special interests coincide with some of the purposes of your organization. Public officials are interested in talking about their programs before community groups. Among them are heads of municipal government, legislators, and representatives of state and federal agencies. Frequently the success of their programs depends on the support of groups such as yours. The faculties of colleges and universities in the area are excellent sources of lecturers on topics of current interest.

Some national business and industrial organizations offer lecture and demonstration programs without cost, or assist in the programming of meetings by furnishing discussion plans and materials. Ask their local representatives for information.

Music. Music can be a valuable part of your meeting program. Provide copies of old favorites and currently popular songs for group singing. The choruses of some old-time favorites are available on slides and in animated motion pictures. Canvass the membership for directing and accompanying talent. Ask members to practice and present an all-music meeting. Some clubs have developed excellent voice and instrument groups.

The music departments of schools and colleges, and music clubs welcome invitations to present their soloists and voice groups, bands, and orchestras. Ask them to give previews of parts of concerts, operettas, and other musicales.

Youth Programs. Members of youth organizations often are invited to luncheons or meetings. Leaders of a sponsored group may be asked to tell about their activities. The high school debating group may present a panel discussion, the stamp club may exhibit and talk about the collections of its members, or the nature-study club may discuss the wildlife in the area. Perhaps the high school science club can adapt a science show to the time and place of your meeting. Invite contest winners to deliver their prize-winning speeches or essays, or to exhibit their posters or paintings.

Programs in Support of Community Activities. Each chapter of Part II of this book, covering an important aspect of community living, suggests ideas and materials for meetings. Effective project action depends on general membership support and on the ready recognition of committee and individual service achievement. Committees may be supported through speakers, demonstrations, films, and exhibits. Some meetings may be devoted to activities that directly contribute to the work of service committees. Feature reports on the progress or results of their projects.

Special Observances. Holidays and other national and local special days, weeks, and months, such as Independence Day, National Citizenship Day, Fire Prevention Week, and Cancer Control Month, are occasions worthy of organization observance. Appendix A lists some national occasions, with the names and addresses of sponsoring organizations that offer valuable advisory and material help.

Traditional Affairs. Annual, traditional affairs such as a Get

Acquainted or New Members meeting early in the year help new and old members to know one another quickly. Some groups hold an annual Bosses' Night. Ladies' Day, Husbands' Day, Sons' Day, and Daughters' Day programs have proved popular. Frequently scheduled is Recognition Day to honor individuals who have been of outstanding service to the community. The installation of officers may be an occasion for the recognition of members who have distinguished themselves in organization affairs.

INTERORGANIZATION ACTIVITIES. Representatives of other organizations or entire memberships may be invited as guests or to cosponsor programs. Such meetings often serve as effective first steps to cooperative intergroup community service. Opportunities for unusual professional programs—and their costs—may be shared by scheduling them for several or joint meetings.

STUNTS. Stunts encourage good fellowship and enliven meetings. Popular are "gridiron" sessions, at which members, local officials, or other prominent personages are "roasted" in burlesques or parodies of their community roles; "old hat" meetings for women's groups, in which each member appears with a hat from another fashion era or with one that is worn for a humorous effect; mock trials of members or others in public life; tall-story contests; meetings directed by wives or husbands; impromptu joke sessions; skits; and membership or interorganization quiz programs.

Many groups traditionally stage a short stunt of a broadly humorous nature as a preliminary to the serious part of each meeting. Sometimes a special committee is given this responsibility.

FIELD TRIPS. Businesses, industries, radio and television stations, newspapers, museums, private institutions, and municipal departments frequently offer guided tours as a public relations measure. Luncheon, demonstration, and lecture arrangements often are made for community organizations.

THE SUMMERTIME PROGRAM. Many groups make a special effort to maintain membership ties through the summer months. Even if regular meetings are impractical, informal social events such as clambakes, picnics, excursions, and beach parties may prove popular.

MEMBERSHIP INTERESTS

Successful meeting schedules provide for the inclusion of features that help members meet everyday problems of living, and satisfy their intellectual, cultural, social, and other interests.

LITERATURE. Talks by authors and critics may be popular. Prepare for an author's talk by making copies of his work available to the membership. Consult local bookshops about a joint sponsorship of a visit of a successful author under the auspices of his publisher. Such a feature could be used to arouse interest in establishing a book-circulating plan. Schedule review and discussion sessions. Members may be encouraged to read their own creative writing to the group.

CONSUMER EDUCATION. So varied and persistent are newspaper, magazine, radio, and television appeals to buy, and so confusing the claims for competing products and services, that programs aimed at helping members to become intelligent consumer buyers are of practical value. Material for study-discussion groups is available in books, periodicals, government and private agency consumer research literature, and films. Many manufacturers offer information, materials, visual aids, and demonstrations that help the buyer make wise choices. Local merchants and teachers of consumer education may be secured as lecturers.

FOOD PREPARATION AND SERVING. Programs having to do with preparing and serving food, and arranging table service and decoration are favorites among women's groups. Many schedule talks by homemaking teachers, nutrition experts, and representatives of kitchen appliance manufacturers or sales concerns. Others present exhibits of table service and decoration in cooperation with local shops. Cake, candy, and other cooking contests are popular. Unusual or historically interesting recipes and cookbooks make interesting exhibits. With the aid of the local newspaper, a utility company, or an appliances dealer, a cooking class may be organized for members and other townspeople.

FAMILY LIVING. Among the major concerns of most people are problems involved in family living. Speakers and study-discussion groups on subjects such as education for marriage; physical, intellectual, and spiritual growth through family living; and the life adjustment of young people meet commonly felt needs. Arrange talks by a marriage counselor, a psychiatrist, a school guidance head, an educator, a clergyman. Organize discussion groups using material available from child welfare agencies, mental hygiene associations, government bureaus, schools, churches, and youth-service organizations. Consider joint meetings with the local P.T.A. and other groups with a special interest in family life. Arrange for visits to child and family centers, and to nursery schools.

FASHIONS. Professional designers and the fashion editors of newspapers and magazines often are available as speakers. Offer your meeting place, an audience, models, and background music to shops willing to show their clothes. Adapt the show to current local interests. Such an affair might have a wide appeal if several shops cover such fashions as evening, sports, spectator, country, and city wear. Include accessory shops such as those featuring gloves, shoes, jewelry, and cosmetics.

Novelty fashion shows have been very successful. Your group might present Fashions of Yesterday and Today, featuring the Gibson Girl or the Flapper, costumes for which might be available in the homes of members. A showing of unusual hair-do's with a demonstration by a hair style expert is an interesting variation of this type of program. Arrange displays of striking fashion photographs from current magazines, and stills used in motion-picture promotion.

Your members might canvass the community for authentic costumes of other peoples. Ask members of nationality groups to model them. Such a program would be particularly appropriate as an observance of United Nations Day.

GARDENING. Gardening offers an infinite variety of program ideas. Arrange talks and demonstrations by commercial growers, garden shops, tree-care experts, the parks superintendent, the county agriculture agent, and faculty members of agricultural schools and colleges. Among interesting topics are the culture of unusual flowers and plants, methods of plant propagation, house plants, glass culture, flower arrangements, miniature gardens, landscape architecture, garden statuary and pools, and attracting birds to the garden.

A showing of the products of members' vegetable and flower gardens would be interesting. Consider a community garden show. Commercial growers and estate garden supervisors are often willing to arrange visits to their gardens and greenhouses. Organize a community garden tour. Devote a meeting to arranging flowers or making corsages. Collect material and practice arranging winter bouquets. As an early spring feature, your group might present an exhibit of garden equipment and supplies available from local merchants.

HOBBIES. Most hobbyists are eager to talk about and show their collections, or to demonstrate their skills. Stage a membership show of hobbies; offer awards in such categories as "most unusual" and "most effectively presented." Sponsor such a project for the community.

HOME REPAIRS. Most men are interested in knowing how to make simple repairs about the home. Organization programs include instruction and demonstrations in procedures such as refinishing furniture, replacing a broken pane of glass, replacing faulty wiring, and eliminating floor squeaks.

INTERIOR DECORATION. Local decorators, and furniture, fabrics, paint, and wallpaper shops may be willing to arrange demonstrations and exhibits for your group. Ask members to talk about their interior decoration interests. Plan tours of unusual homes. Visit museums and restorations in a study of period decoration. Some homemaking magazines have program guides and offer advisory services. Ask the librarian for help in compiling a bibliography for study and discussion. Collect magazine and other picture material for display.

JEWELRY. Talks about precious and semiprecious stones, jewelry, and other ornaments, their origins and their processing, may be arranged through local merchants. In some instances, jewelers may wish to present showings during meetings.

PAINTINGS. An exhibit of oils, water colors, and other art work of members and others in the community is usually well attended. Children's art efforts appeal to adults. Ask the schools to arrange for a showing. Owners of art objects usually welcome an opportunity to exhibit them. Arrange for an amateur or professional artist to present a one-man show. An antique shop, an artists' supplies shop, or a local gallery might sponsor an exhibit. Some museums, galleries, and art schools in large cities maintain traveling shows. Good copies of classic and contemporary paintings are available at most libraries or through commercial dealers.

PERSONAL FINANCE. Discussions of personal-finance problems are well attended. Ask a banker, insurance broker, lawyer, businessman, or a business-education teacher to talk to your group. Of general interest are subjects such as drawing up a personal and family budget, investments, the financing of homes and cars, insurance, personal liability at home and in the community, income and inheritance tax laws, and the making of a will.

FORMAL INSTRUCTION. Among other self-improvement programs that have been presented successfully as lectures or formal courses are leadership training, public speaking, salesmanship, merchandising, memory training, group-discussion techniques, human relations, personality development, and physical culture. Local and state adult education departments frequently offer help in presenting courses in subjects such as painting, ceramics, creative writing, music appreciation, and consumer education. A course in effective speech is offered in Appendix D.

THE USE OF MOTION PICTURES

A study of P.T.A.'s showed that twice as many people attended meetings when films were used, the Film Council of America reports. Chiefly responsible for this development are the thousands of free-loan and nominal-rental 16 mm pictures produced by business, industry, government, and national agencies and associations. Industry alone has produced over 150,000, many of which may be borrowed by community groups for the cost of shipping. In one year, corporations spent an estimated $60,000,000 on films.

The entertainment and educational qualities of most of these productions are excellent. Advertising tie-ins usually are presented in an unobjectionable fashion. Many are offered as a public service, with a trailer announcement of the sponsor the only direct promotion.

Some nontheatrical 16 mm sponsored pictures, The Wall Street Journal declares, rival in elaborateness and popularity the hits of the commercial theater. The DuPont Story, for example, with a cast of 225 and 91 sets, cost $455,000 to produce. Unfinished Rainbow, the story of aluminum, has played to audiences totaling over 30,000,000. Big Idea, a film on Americanism sponsored by Swift and Company, has attracted attendances totaling over 5,000,000. In one year, 7,000,000 persons viewed Ford pictures. Since 1934, the Chrysler Corporation estimates, over 50,000,000 have attended showings of its free-loan films.

At a nominal cost, your meeting programs may include films to entertain, provide background and develop support for service activities, and raise the level of motion picture appreciation among members.

Most programs to meet the cultural and other interests of members, suggested in this chapter, may feature or include motion pictures.

There are many excellent free-loan and low-rental titles in fields such as fiction, travel, sports, literature, art, drama, family living, fashions, home repairs, and consumer education.

FILM FORUMS AND DISCUSSIONS. Motion pictures have given new life to meetings featuring the discussion of contemporary problems. They present background material, identify issues, dramatize the need for solutions, narrow the field, and in general provide the stimulus for active discussion.

The film should be chosen very carefully. What definite contributions will it make to the discussion? Does it assume too little or too much knowledge of the subject field or understanding of the problem? Do the acting and the technical aspects measure up to acceptable standards?

The film should be carefully reviewed by a committee familiar with group-discussion procedures. If it is about a professional or technical subject, it might be well to have an expert on the review panel. If the discussion is about a topic that is of official concern, such as civil defense, authorities should be consulted about the accuracy of the information presented.

While a film may be so provocative that the function of a discussion leader is limited to introducing the subject and recognizing those who wish to speak, most film forums require careful preparation. The leader should relate the subject matter to the individual and community interests of the group, and be ready with leading questions.

ARRANGING FOR FILM SHOWINGS. In many groups, needs might be adequately met through reliance on a local film council or other group especially interested in the field. In others, the program chairman might acquire an adequate knowledge of the sources of films, and of equipment available in the community. If the use of films is to be at all extensive, and especially if the group is to own its equipment, a special committee might be appointed.

COMMUNITY RESOURCES. Films appropriate for meetings, and the necessary projection equipment may often be obtained from individuals, organizations, and agencies in the community, such as the following:

1. Members. Some may have pictures of excellent quality.
2. The school audio-visual department. Such departments consider assistance to community groups an important part of their function, and

welcome requests for help. Some furnish projection equipment and a trained operator when the films selected contribute to public service ends.

3. Public libraries. Many, in addition to having directories, books, pamphlets, and periodicals, maintain collections of films for circulation. Some loan or rent projection equipment to responsible groups.

4. Government and private agencies in fields such as health and welfare; local business and industrial concerns, and the sales representatives of national corporations; the Red Cross and the Civil Defense organization; labor unions; and youth-service groups. Some local groups serve as outlets for free-loan films sponsored by national agencies and associations. Often they have staff workers skilled in projection techniques, with the necessary equipment at their disposal.

5. Local dealers in equipment, films, and photography supplies. Their libraries may include nominal rental and free-loan films. All dealers have lists and catalogues, and will assist in locating suitable titles.

UNIVERSITIES AND COLLEGES. Most universities and colleges are interested in encouraging the showing of nontheatrical films in communities. Many have extensive libraries. Some offer guidance in developing programs and welcome inquiries from organizations.

GUIDES, CATALOGUES, AND OTHER PUBLICATIONS. The organization with an active program may soon exhaust local resources. To meet particular interests, those in charge of the program should learn of the great variety of subjects available, and where and how to find them. The Sources of Aid sections at the close of other chapters of this book include sources of information about films for specific purposes. Appendix C describes standard guides and catalogues, selected listings, and some sources of free and low-rental films and film information of general interest. A collection of free catalogues, chosen from these sources, will provide the information necessary for a comprehensive program.

ORDERING FILMS. Orders should be placed as far in advance as possible. In many cases, alternate choices should be indicated to assure a showing on a scheduled date. If there is no possible substitute for a specific title, two or three additional dates should be listed in order of preference. Place such an order far enough in advance so that publicity for the showing can include the date for which the film actually has been booked. Film producers and major distributors often will refer your order to a branch office or local rental outlet.

Whenever possible, the picture should be previewed to verify its entertainment and educational quality, the condition of the film, its running time, and to determine what introduction should be prepared.

The possibility that a film may fail to arrive on time, may be in such poor condition as to make its showing undesirable, or that its subject matter or purpose has been misunderstood should be considered. Are appropriate substitutes available from local sources?

EFFECTIVE MEETING-PROMOTION MEASURES

The expression "nothing succeeds like success" applies to meetings as well as to other activities. One successful meeting well attended helps to develop good attendance at the next, so long as the needs and interests of members are met. Some measures, however, are usually necessary to tell the membership about programs.

Effective publicity is seldom a one-shot treatment. Your committee might see to it that not only is a calendar of meetings posted, but that each member receives a copy. Some groups issue calendar cards of a size convenient for carrying in a wallet or handbag.

Most organization newsletters or bulletins feature coming meeting attractions. Use the local papers as publicity media, even though the meeting is not open to the public. The story of a program to be presented not only is a reminder for the members, but makes the affair more important in the estimation of members and guests, and adds to the organization's prestige in the community.

Notices of meetings that draw good attendances usually are more than just announcements of the topic, time, and place. Use a provocative title. Instead of *Stamps as a Hobby*, perhaps *The Story of Nations Through Their Stamps*. If the feature of the meeting is to be a speaker, why is his topic especially important to the individual member at this particular time, and why is this speaker especially worth listening to on this subject?

A special effort might be made to have the form of the notice distinctive. Avoid plain postcards or mimeographed notices on white paper. Use colored ink, and eye-catching stenciled cartoons and decorations.

For meetings of special importance, at least one follow-up notice might be sent. Have each of ten members write two- or three-line personal notes to a few other members shortly before the meeting. Organize a telephone squad.

Even though attendance is open to all members, tickets of admission to special meetings are often issued. The ticket places a value upon the event, and is a source of reference for time and place. If there is to be a guest attendance, give each member three tickets with a statement that he is privileged to invite two guests. Everyone likes to give tickets to friends.

Organizations frequently invite other individuals and groups to special meetings. Music appreciation classes, for example, would welcome an opportunity to attend a good music program.

MEETING ARRANGEMENTS AND DIRECTION

The best of meeting and special-event programs may fall flat because of lack of foresight or carelessness. The following are some arrangement details that might be considered.

CHOOSING THE TIME AND PLACE. The time and place should be chosen carefully. Many programs are not well attended because committees fail to consider the competition of other meetings or community affairs. Confer with the program chairmen of major organizations. Newspapers, chambers of commerce, and libraries often keep calendars of coming events, which list social activities and public meetings of importance. Dates immediately before and after holidays are ordinarily unsatisfactory. Popular television programs may seriously affect attendance.

The meeting place should be chosen to fit the expected audience. A large auditorium is as unsatisfactory for a group of fifty as is a small room into which hundreds must be crowded.

If the meeting is scheduled for a public building, check the building's condition and facilities. At what time will it be open and custodial service available? Will it be adequately heated or ventilated at the time of the meeting? Is there an electric outlet conveniently placed for a projector, if one is to be used? Has the public address system been tested? Is the organization to be responsible for cleaning up? Is police assistance needed in handling traffic or parking cars? If the meeting is to be held at a private home, what assistance does the host require?

SCHEDULING THE PROGRAM FEATURE. At meetings that feature entertainment or a speaker, the time to be devoted to business often is limited. In some organizations, the chairman makes routine announcements, calls for committee reports, and takes care of other business matters in the course of a luncheon or dinner. Be sure speakers and others on the program know how much time they have. An inconspicuous signal system sometimes is arranged to help them keep within their time limits.

CONDUCTING THE PROGRAM. Good meetings move rapidly and smoothly from opening to close. Members have the feeling that everything is going according to schedule—without undue hurry, without drag. This effect usually is the result of careful arrangements. Here are some suggestions:

1. If there are many features, furnish the principals with a copy of the time schedule.

2. Make sure props, lights, lectern, projector, or other equipment is at hand, and properly placed.

3. Start on time, even though guests or program participants are delayed. Have activities with which to fill in.

4. Consider the possibility of postponing minutes or nonessential reports and announcements, or of issuing them in bulletin form.

5. Terminate promptly the meeting that has achieved its purpose.

ARRANGING FOR SPEAKERS AND ENTERTAINERS. Officials of federated organizations and others who do not charge a fee for speaking should be reimbursed for their traveling and hotel expenses. When entertainers are engaged, it is well to verify arrangements and terms, as in the case of speakers or lecturers. The type of entertainment usually determines the kind of reception. A noted violinist, for example, would be accorded the same kind of consideration given a distinguished lecturer on the arts. A troupe of tumblers or a drama group, however, because of their number, would probably make their own hotel and other arrangements. Special meeting-place provisions, though, are often the responsibility of the organization. Find out what props are to be furnished; what lighting, backdrops, or curtains are required. If a piano is to be used, make sure that it is in tune.

SPECIAL KINDS OF MEETINGS. Special kinds of meetings include the group discussion or conference, panel discussion, panel debate, symposium, regional conference, and banquet.

THE GROUP DISCUSSION. Group discussions are popular because they furnish opportunities for all to participate. Although many are more or less impromptu, advance preparation will help assure success. It is well to choose subjects in which the members have some experience or knowledge, and in which they have a vital, personal interest. Present a mimeographed list of topics from which they may indicate an order of preference among three to five.

All in a discussion group should have an opportunity to participate. The size, therefore, should be limited to not more than 25 persons. Have the group meet in a room that will encourage informality. Fix the length of the meeting at not more than two hours. Arrange the chairs in a circle or U, so that the participants can see one another.

Much of the success of a discussion depends on the skill of the leader. Choose him carefully. An effective leader should have a knowledge of the subject field superior to or equal to the others in the group. He should open the discussion with a short talk that reviews the background of the subject and defines the problem to be considered. His manner should suggest an interest in and a respect for the opinions of the group. He should assure everyone an opportunity to speak, encouraging those who are hesitant in expressing an opinion, and tactfully stopping talk that is irrelevant. He should recognize poorly phrased but important contributions and attempt to get clarification. He should withhold personal opinion, and at the end of the meeting summarize conclusions that seem acceptable to most of the group.

Discussion success may be measured in terms of how many members contributed to a clear understanding of the nature of the problem, the discovery of possible solutions, or a general acceptance of points of view or solutions. Such conclusive results, however, are the ideal. Usually a discussion is considered successful when all have had an opportunity to express their ideas, and major agreements and disagreements have been revealed.

PANEL DISCUSSIONS. Panels are of several types, each of which is distinguished chiefly by the fact that a small group, seated before an audience, carries the burden of the discussion. Such arrangements frequently are necessary because the group interested in a subject is too large to permit participation by everyone, or the subject is of such general interest that its discussion by well-known persons is a public service. Panel discussions are frequently broadcast and televised.

The panel discussion with a controversial subject is displacing the conventional debate, with its formalized structure and style. In determining the number on the debate panel the complexity of the question should be considered. If it is two-sided, a panel of four, two on each side, is usual. If three points of view or positions are to be taken, one speaker customarily presents each. Prior to the debate, the chairman should hold a meeting with the principals—to limit the field, determine what real differences in opinion or points of view exist, assign definite positions to the several speakers, fix the speaking and rebuttal time, and agree on the seating and speaking order.

DUTIES OF THE PANEL CHAIRMAN. The responsibilities of a panel chairman include the following:

1. Explaining the background for the discussion, and identifying the panel members.
2. Keeping each speaker on the subject and within the time limit, making sure that he can be heard.
3. Stimulating audience participation by direct appeal or by provocative questions.
4. Recognizing members of the audience, deciding on the relevancy of their questions or comments, and keeping order.
5. Closing the meeting by thanking the panel members, making appropriate references to the contributions of speakers and audience.

THE SYMPOSIUM. The panel debate is to be distinguished from the symposium—the presentation of a broad or complex subject, each major part of which is covered by an expert. The object of a symposium is completeness of treatment, not the presentation of opposing views.

AUDIENCE PARTICIPATION. Audience participation is a feature of many lecture and discussion-type meetings. Some committees arrange to have members ask questions from the audience to avoid the awkwardness that might result from no response to a suggestion that questions are in order. In situations in which there may be strong partisan feeling, it may be well to ask the audience to write out their questions. This permits tactful screening of questions by the chairman or moderator to avoid those that are personal, unfair, designed solely to embarrass, or are otherwise in poor taste.

REGIONAL MEETINGS AND CONVENTIONS. Prerequisite to a successful regional meeting or convention is the clear recognition of common purposes on the part of participating organizations. These purposes may include exchange of practical ideas about concerns such as attendance building, program planning, budget making and finance, and membership recruitment.

Responsibility for the organization and direction of such a meeting is usually divided between the host organization and the participating groups. Tasks to be assigned to either may include the following:

1. Arranging for an interorganization meeting to discuss purposes, formulate broad policy, and name a coordinating committee to organize, supervise, and relate the preparation and procedure activities of all other committees.

2. Making budget and other financial arrangements.

3. Securing an adequate assembly hall and other meeting places; providing and arranging necessary equipment, general decorations, music, and adequate parking space.

4. Drawing up an agenda for a general meeting, and scheduling conference and discussion sessions.

5. Naming resolutions, nominating, awards, and other business committees.

6. Providing material such as badges, programs, notices and signs, maps, dinner menus and favors, and bus and train schedules.

7. Making hotel reservations, and welcoming the delegates, their wives, and friends.

8. Arranging for the registration of delegates and guests, the collection of fees, the sale of tickets, and an information service.

9. Planning and directing special entertainment features such as a banquet, dance, boat ride, sightseeing trips, and sports events.

10. Arranging for supplemental or special bus or private-car transportation.

11. Providing for exhibits.

12. Promoting the meeting through a general publicity committee.

THE ORGANIZATION BANQUET. A firm deadline should be fixed for banquet reservations. Hotels will usually agree to serve additional, last-minute guests, but many times the original seating and serving arrangement cannot be changed, or the room becomes inadequate. The best of dinners can be ruined by overcrowding or poor service.

Important to the success of a banquet is the seating arrangement. Seat those who have active parts in the program at the head table, taking care to place speakers and distinguished guests near the center. Plan to have those who are to sit at the head table meet in an ante-room. Place them in their order of seating, and have them enter as a group, to avoid the awkwardness that results from each individual's search for his place.

The toastmaster has responsibilities in addition to that of introducing speakers in conventional fashion. He should present all at the head table, and other distinguished guests; avoid stealing the show from the speakers or entertainers; keep the program progressing; refrain from drafting guests not scheduled to speak; and take note of persistent distractions or discomforts such as drafts or too much smoke, and do something about them.

Formal speaking programs and entertainment should not be mixed. Group singing at the close of the dinner, however, is an effective way of filling in the time while dishes are being removed or while some few diners are finishing their meal. Dinner music should be in the background, so that it will not interfere with conversation.

THE BUSINESS MEETING. The term business meeting as here used denotes a meeting in which there is an attempt to act upon current organization matters, as distinguished from a meeting the purpose of which is to present a speaker, a demonstration, a film, an entertainer, or other attraction. In some meetings, business is only a part of the proceedings; in others, the order of business is, in effect, suspended after the call to order so that the special feature may be presented.

Every business meeting should follow a definite order. The following is typical:

1. Call to order
2. Reading and disposition of the minutes
3. Reports of officers and standing committees
4. Reports of special committees
5. Unfinished business
6. New business
7. Adjournment

Business meetings should be conducted in accordance with the rules of parliamentary procedure. Such a practice facilitates transaction of business, permits expression of the will of the majority, preserves the rights and privileges of all members, and assures full and free discussion. Although adherence to a formal procedure should never become an end in itself, membership knowledge of the essentials of parliamentary law is necessary for orderly meetings.

Appendix B includes a glossary of some terms commonly used in parliamentary procedure, an outline of kinds of motions, and an account of a meeting of the fictitious Greenville Citizens Association, which illustrates parliamentary procedure in typical situations.

SOURCES OF AID

Adult Education Association of the United States of America, 743 North Wabash Ave., Chicago 11, Ill. Publishes *Adult Leadership*, containing practical suggestions for program chairmen.

Air France, 683 Fifth Ave., New York 22, N. Y., and district offices in other major cities. Offers speakers for community-organization programs, and a series of free loan color travel films. Information available.

American Assembly, Graduate School of Business, Columbia University, New York 27, N. Y. A program of continuing conferences of representatives of business, labor, the professions, political parties, and government to study the major problems facing the United States. It encourages group study of these problems by furnishing study and promotion material for local "assemblies" and other community organizations.

American Association of Group Workers, 129 East 52nd St., New York 22, N. Y. Publishes *The Group*, a bimonthly magazine. Offers *A Selected Bibliography on Group Work*, a listing of 161 books, pamphlets, and mimeographed material.

American Bankers Association, Public Relations Council, 12 East 36th St., New York 16, N. Y. Has information about conducting forums on subjects such as personal financial planning, life insurance, wills, estates, taxes, trusts, and investments.

American Council on Public Affairs, 2153 Florida Ave., N. W., Washington 8, D. C. Publishes *Guide to Public Affairs Organizations*. Information about over 400 organizations includes names and addresses of chief personnel, the purpose of the organization, and types of books, pamphlets, discussion guides, audio-visual aids, periodicals, and consultation services available.

American Home Economics Association, 1600 20th St., N. W., Washington 9, D. C. Provides pamphlets useful in consumer-education programs.

American Jewish Committee, 386 Fourth Ave., New York 16, N. Y. Has available *Leader's Guide: A Manual on Better Human Relations for Leaders in Youth Agencies*. Includes a discussion of programming techniques, and the use of resources such as pamphlets, films, recordings, books, and games.

American Library Association, 50 East Huron St., Chicago 11, Ill. Pamphlets include *Suggestions for Discussion Leaders;* and *Library Film Forums*, describing the use of films as the basis for discussions of current issues.

American National Theatre and Academy, Department of Community and Industrial Showmanship, ANTA Playhouse, 245 West 52nd St., New York 19, N. Y. Maintains an advisory service for the planning and direction of conventions; furnishes theatrical and technical personnel.

American Standards Association, 70 East 45th St., New York 17, N. Y. Provides pamphlets useful in consumer-education programs.

Auer, J. Jeffery and Ewbank, Henry Lee, *Handbook for Discussion Leaders, A Practical Manual of Conference Techniques*, New York: Harper & Brothers, 1947. Contains concise explanations of how to organize the group, and a description of a leader's qualifications and his role in eight different types of discussions. Especially useful are the criteria for a good discussion, and bibliographies of discussion and leadership-training materials.

Brown, Ann Curphey and Geis, Sally Brown, *Handbook for Group Leaders*, New York: Woman's Press, 1952. Includes how to draw up a constitution, organize and direct committees, plan programs, use audiovisual aids, and control public relations.

Bureau of Educational Research, Ohio State University, Columbus 10, Ohio. Publishes booklet discussions of planning procedures, panel and discussion techniques, effective demonstrations, and other meeting concerns.

Bureau of Human Nutrition and Home Economics, United States Department of Agriculture, Washington 25, D. C. Conducts research on food, clothing, and other goods and services. Publishes bulletins, many of which are suitable for organization study and discussion programs. List of free materials available.

Community Services in Adult Education, 1804 East 10th St., Bloomington, Ind. Has available booklet suggestions for the planning and direction of 15 separate types of meetings.

Countrywomen's League, *The Country Gentleman*, Independence Square, Philadelphia 5, Pa. Offers a series of leaflets outlining programs adaptable to many women's groups. Material includes bibliographies and listings of pamphlets, films, filmstrips, and other materials, and suggestions for specific kinds of programs, such as an anniversary celebration.

Film Council of America, Evanston, Ill. Sponsors an Educational Film Discussion Project to correlate discussion materials with films for community groups. Materials offered on two subjects: "Great Men and Great Issues in Our American Heritage" and "World Affairs Are Your Affairs." Included are background literature, an organization manual, a leader's guide, and lists of recommended films. Detailed description of project is available.

General Federation of Women's Clubs, 1734 N St., N. W., Washington 6, D. C. Pamphlets include *Program Planning*. Representative section heads: "What Every Club Program Should Do," "Guideposts for Program Planners," "Discussion Techniques," and "Questionnaire to Determine Club Interest," a suggested form.

Junior Town Meeting League, 400 South Front St., Columbus 15, Ohio. Free booklets, useful in the sponsorship of any youth group, include *Youth Discussion Patterns and Techniques*, *Make Youth Discussion Conscious*, and *Developing Discussion in School and Community*.

League of Women Voters of the United States, 1026 17th St., N. W., Washington 6, D. C. Nominally priced publications include *Let's Have a Discussion*, a guide for community organizations.

Library Research Service, *Encyclopaedia Britannica*, 20 North Wacker Drive, Chicago 6, Ill. Offers outlines and reading references for full-year programs in each of the following fields: enhancing the home environment; gardens and gardening; costume, fashion, and design; home management; and family and social life.

National Planning Association, 1606 New Hampshire Ave., N. W., Washington 9, D. C. A nonprofit, nonpartisan membership association to work out solutions to current economic and related problems. Offers numerous pamphlet studies in low cost quantity lots to community groups. Listing available.

National Recreation Association, Correspondence and Consultation Bureau, 315 Fourth Ave., New York 10, N. Y. Publishes inexpensive pamphlets and leaflets about activities appropriate for meetings: music, drama, games, holiday celebrations, and others. Offers consultation service to community groups. Listing of publications available.

Newsweek, Club and Education Bureau, 152 West 42nd St., New York 36, N. Y. Each month, September through May, *Newsweek* publishes *Platforms*, an impartial review of current national and international problems. Useful material for a series of contemporary-affairs meetings. Single copy free to an officer of a civic, welfare, or education group.

New Tools for Learning, 280 Madison Ave., New York 16, N. Y. Has information about pamphlets, films, and recordings useful for the study and discussion of current issues. Catalogue available.

Ohio State University Discussion Service, 205 Derby Hall, Ohio State University, Columbus 10, Ohio. Issues *Let's Discuss It*, a free monthly guide useful in presenting controversial group-discussion programs.

Program Notes, 14 West 49th St., New York 20, N. Y. Published six times a year for women's groups by the National Association of Manufacturers.

Public Affairs Committee, Inc., 22 East 38th St., New York 16, N. Y. Has available a listing of over 60 public affairs pamphlets for discussions of current economic, political, and social questions; and leaflets describing packaged meeting programs, each of which includes suggestions for directing a discussion program, filmstrips, a script, and pamphlets furnishing background information.

Stigers, M. F., *Making Conference Programs Work*, New York: McGraw-Hill Book Company, Inc., 1950. Describes procedures used by business and industrial concerns in organizing and directing conferences. Identifies different types of conferences; tells how to phrase a problem, prepare an opening statement, guide a group in a solution to the problem, record data, and make reports.

Strauss, Bert and Frances, *New Ways to Better Meetings*, New York: The Viking Press, 1951. A nonacademic presentation of ideas about group action developed through research in group dynamics, and tested in management, labor, political, and educational organizations.

Superintendent of Documents, United States Government Printing Office, Washington 25, D. C. A great variety of pamphlet and other meeting program aids from several government agencies. Representative are the following: *Planning Recreation for Rural Home and Community*, including ideas for art, handicraft, music, dancing, drama, and other activities; *Conference Sense*, an amusingly illustrated booklet published for the Bureau of Naval Personnel as a guide for conference leaders and participants; *Putting Life into Meetings and Conferences; Ideas for Making Annual Meetings Effective*, practical ideas adaptable to your conference or convention; *Motion Pictures on Child Life*, a 60-page annotated catalogue; and catalogues of radio scripts and recordings.

Thompson, Nellie Zetta, *Vitalized Assemblies*, New York: E. P. Dutton & Co., Inc., 1952. Suggests 200 programs for schools, many of which may be adapted by adult organizations for meeting programs. Lists about 45 agencies and organizations that supply speeches and materials such as scripts and films for assembly programs.

Trecker, Audrey and Harleigh, *How to Work with Groups*, New York: Woman's Press, 1952. Representative sections: How the Democratic Leader Works, How to Conduct a Business Meeting, How to Lead a Discussion, How to Handle Group Finances, and a Primer of Parliamentary Law.

Twentieth Century Fund, 330 West 42nd St., New York 18, N. Y. Material valuable for meeting programs includes low rental films, and film discussion packets, made up of background pamphlets and procedure guides in fields such as housing, productivity, and world trade. Material is designed to be used with Twentieth Century Fund films. Information available.

United States Department of Agriculture, Extension Service, Washington 25, D. C. Sponsors home demonstrations at meetings. Has detailed program suggestions for 4-H Clubs and other groups interested chiefly in rural problems. Description of literature, exhibits, field services, and other aids is available.

Utterbach, William E., *Group Thinking and Conference Leadership*, New York: Rinehart & Company, Inc., 1950. A detailed treatment of small-group discussion meetings. Material is presented in three parts: principles that can be applied to all situations in which there is group thinking, suggestions for preparation and participation, and special problems in several discussion situations.

Wayne University Speakers Bureau, 5001 Second Ave., Detroit 2, Mich. Free pamphlets for program chairmen.

Woman's Home Companion, 640 Fifth Ave., New York 19, N. Y. Each month offers a free packaged program for women's groups. Service includes a guide and materials for an analysis of a problem of vital local and national interest, and suggested procedures for its solution.

Workers Education Bureau of America, affiliate of the American Federation of Labor, 1525 H St., N. W., Washington 5, D. C. Material available is of general community-organization interest. Representative is *How to Run a Union Meeting*, a simplified manual on parliamentary law.

SOME SOURCES OF FILMS AND FILM INFORMATION

The Sources of Aid section of each chapter includes an annotated listing of sources of films and film information useful in each specific field outlined in this book. Appendix C is an annotated listing of general and special catalogues and sources of films of general interest. Other representative sources of such aid in planning and conducting meetings are the following:

American Council on Education, 1785 Massachusetts Ave., N. W., Washington 6, D. C. *Projecting Motion Pictures in the Classroom* includes suggestions useful to an organization's projectionist.

American Film Forum, Inc., 516 Fifth Ave., New York 36, N. Y. Offers *Washington Spotlight*, a subscription film service for a monthly discussion program. Featured are outstanding national and international personalities in the field of public affairs. Service includes background material on speakers and discussion subjects. Description of service is available.

Audio-Visual Publications, 7064 Sheridan Road, Chicago 26, Ill. *Audio-Visual Projectionist's Handbook*, a pictorial manual for amateur operators.

Bell and Howell Company, Educational Division, 7100 McCormick Road, Chicago 45, Ill. Has available a series of booklets for organization film users. Offers help in solving special film-using problems.

Coronet Films, Coronet Building, Chicago 1, Ill. Has information about *Parliamentary Procedure, Fundamentals of Public Speaking,* and *Learn to Argue Effectively.* Useful for membership education program.

DeVry Corporation, 1111 Armitage Ave., Chicago 14, Ill. Free School Service Bulletins have ideas useful to adult citizen groups with motion picture programs. Representative bulletin titles: *Suggestions for Effective Techniques of Utilizing Motion Pictures in the Classroom, Suggestions for Organizing Student Operators' Club for the Projected Teaching Aids Department,* and *Re-Using Audio-Visual Materials.*

Division of Christian Education, The National Council of the Churches of Christ in the U.S.A., 79 West Adams St., Chicago 3, Ill. *Audio-Visual Resource Guide* includes descriptions of several free loan and rental films and filmstrips useful in leadership training.

Educational Film Library Association, 1600 Broadway, New York 19, N. Y. A major source of aid in planning and carrying out a film program. Publications include annotated film listings and descriptions of sources in special areas: *Public Affairs Film List, Film Guide for Economic Education, Audio-Visual Materials on Food Conservation, Motion Pictures for Art Education,* and others; *Index to Selected Film Lists,* compiled by Jessie B. Kitching and Emily S. Jones, describing over 170 lists; *Film Utilization*, by J. Roby Kidd and Carter B. Storr, a 47-page illustrated handbook; *A Guide for Film Evaluators*, by Edward T. Schofield, a 12-page handbook to be used with EFLA evaluation forms.

General Motors Corporation, Department of Public Relations, Film Section, 3044 West Grand Boulevard, Detroit 2, Mich. Free loan films include *How Not to Conduct a Meeting*. Colonel Stoopnagel in a comedy treatment of a typical meeting calls attention to the importance of such matters as adequate planning, acoustics, and ventilation. Description available.

Institute of Life Insurance, Education Division, 488 Madison Ave., New York 22, N. Y. Offers a free illustrated manual, *How to Insure a Successful Film Showing*.

Modern Talking Picture Service, 45 Rockefeller Plaza, New York 20, N. Y. Will help groups choose and book, free of charge, a program of weekly motion picture showings. Films available include subjects such as our economic system and the American way of life, consumer education, health and hygiene, homemaking, sports, and travel. General catalogue available.

National Film Board of Canada, 1270 Avenue of the Americas, New York 20, N. Y. Low rental films include several music subjects with animated drawings. Some have a bouncing ball with lyrics to encourage participation.

New York *Times*, 230 West 43rd St., New York 36, N. Y. Offers a free filmstrip each month for the use of groups interested in public affairs. Description of service available.

United World Films, Inc., Government Films Department, 1445 Park Ave., New York 29, N. Y. Information available about *How to Conduct a Meeting*.

Wayne University Audio-Visual Materials Consultation Bureau, 5272 Second Boulevard, Detroit 1, Mich. Nominal rental films about discussion participation techniques. Includes a demonstration of the feltboard, or visual board, techniques. Teaching guides available for most films. Descriptions available.

Young America Films, Inc., 18 East 41st St., New York 17, N. Y. Series of speech films includes *Conducting a Meeting*, an explanation of basic parliamentary procedures. Information available.

Some Sources of Films about Films

Educational Film Sales Department, University Extension, University of California, Los Angeles 24, Calif. Information about *Projecting Motion Pictures*, a 10-minute training film.

International Film Bureau, Suite 1500, 6 North Michigan Ave., Chicago 2, Ill. Rental films include *Facts about Projection*, an explanation of procedure; and *Facts about Film*, a demonstration of techniques such as film splicing and the maintenance of equipment.

Teaching Film Custodians, Inc., 25 West 43rd St., New York 36, N. Y. Information about a series of 12 one-reel titles explaining how motion pictures are made.

CHAPTER 3

Financial Administration and Fund Raising

INSEPARABLY BOUND to the other problems of administration are those having to do with maintaining your organization in a financially sound condition. This chapter discusses these problems.

THE BUDGET

An organization that fails to draw up and adhere to a hard and fast budget may be risking serious embarrassment or even financial disaster.

Budget preparation forces attention upon the need for long-range planning and guards against ill-considered projects. When budget items are carefully estimated, greater care usually is taken to collect dues and other revenues promptly, curb thoughtless and unnecessary spending, and standardize financial operations and records. By placing a specific money value on all activities, a definite goal is set for money-raising efforts. Moreover, budget figures provide a basis for comparison helpful in planning for other years.

Your budget, because it is an instrument and not something important in its own right to which a program must be tailored, should be drawn up at the opening of the fiscal year only after major activities have been decided upon, at least tentatively. The complexity of budget making will vary in direct ratio to the kind and number of your activities.

RESPONSIBILITY AND PROCEDURE IN BUDGETING. In many organizations, budgeting responsibility and procedure are prescribed in the bylaws. These typically call for planning by the finance committee, or a special budget committee; or, in small organizations, by the officers. The membership of a finance or budget committee usually includes the president and the treasurer, although it is general practice to appoint someone other than an officer as a committee head. In some organizations, the incoming president is charged with drawing up the budget in consultation with other officers and chairmen. In others a salaried executive officer prepares the budget and submits it to the governing board for approval.

The finance committee is the watchdog of the organization treasury, charged with keeping each committee's cost of operation within the budget. Too tight an adherence to a budget, however, may affect the smooth functioning of programs. A degree of flexibility, which would permit the transfer of some funds from one activity to another upon approval of the board or membership, is desirable.

The following budget procedure is suggested:

1. Have the board of directors, in cooperation with the officers and committee chairmen, decide on the scope and range of the year's activities.

2. Ask each standing committee to submit its budgeted program to be incorporated into a master budget.

3. Estimate ordinary income and operating expense. Such ordinary income includes initiation fees, dues, fines, and returns from the use of club facilities. Ordinary expenditures include the cost of maintaining the meeting place, presenting programs at regular meetings, national dues, the expenses of convention delegates, secretarial help, and the organization's bulletin or newsletter.

4. Plan to meet ordinary operating expenses from ordinary income whenever possible.

5. List all other proposed activities not essential to the existence of the organization as income producing and nonincome producing, and adjust the over-all program to balance the budget. Sacrifice first, when necessary, those activities that make the least contribution to the organization's purposes.

6. Submit the budget to the board of directors for study, possible revision, approval, and presentation to the members for action.

AUDITING ORGANIZATION BOOKS. Even if an organization's financial operations are very simple or do not involve the expenditure of much money, an audit of the books by a committee, or preferably, by a certified public accountant or other qualified, disinterested outsider is desirable. Most bylaws provide that an annual financial report or auditor's statement be submitted to the board of directors and the membership. Some large organizations require monthly reports. A report of the organization's financial condition is especially desirable when new officers are beginning their administration.

THE MEMBERSHIP AND FACILITIES AS SOURCES OF REVENUE

While a carefully planned and administered master budget is prerequisite to sound financing, for most organizations with varied meeting and service programs the perennial problem is where to get the money. Ordinary sources of revenue are the members themselves, through the payment of initiation fees, dues, fines, and fees for the use of club facilities; and the rental of club facilities such as meeting rooms, auditorium, sports and other installations.

THE MEMBERSHIP. Organizations with membership not limited by charter, constitution, or bylaws often meet revenue needs by membership procurement programs. Others adjust dues and admission or initiation fees to meet costs of operation. Some provide for honorary, supporting, sustaining, and contributing memberships.

Some organizations exact small donations for special entertainment funds on the occasion of a member's marriage or parenthood, or maintain a birthday box, into which members on their birthdays are expected to drop as many nickels or dimes as they are years old. By insisting that the celebrant drop the coins one at a time, the group may make the occasion one for good-natured fun making. The importance of such devices for raising money can be appreciated, a Rotary International *Bulletin* points out, when it is realized that a club of 100 members with an average age of 45 would receive approximately $450 annually if on his birthday each member contributed ten cents for each year he has lived.

The levying of assessments should be avoided, as it may have a serious effect on morale. In some groups members are protected from arbitrary assessment by bylaws that limit the practice or call for meeting action. Some groups, however, have systems of nominal fines as penalties for tardiness, absenteeism, and failure to observe some special convention of conduct at the meeting place.

CLUB FACILITIES. Club facilities for some groups are a major source of income. In some cases they make possible low dues and provide substantial amounts for charitable and other service projects. Some organizations depend on rentals to help finance building mortgages or maintain facilities. House and finance committee collaboration may be the answer to the money problem in your organization.

A club facility that has primarily to do with the maintenance of morale and good public relations, but which may also be a money-maker, is the organization bulletin or newsletter. Your members and their families may be an important consumer section of the community, making your publication a legitimate and worth-while advertising medium.

CONTRIBUTIONS

While most organizations meet ordinary expenses through membership dues and fees, or income from club facilities, extensive projects in community service or an unanticipated need may demand special measures. Frequently effective is a community-wide or limited campaign for contributions.

The fund-raising campaign should be launched only after careful consideration of its chances of success and its possible effects on the community and your organization. Have other recent money-raising drives seriously affected the community's ability to contribute? Would your drive, by adding one more appeal, have an adverse effect on the public's attitude toward giving? Would your campaign drain off reserves on which established community volunteer agencies almost wholly depend? Will dependence on this method of raising money tend to discourage ingenuity and resourcefulness on the part of your membership? And, finally, even though such an effort is a success, what possible changes might there be in the status of your group in the community?

EVALUATING THE MONEY-RAISING PURPOSE. If the money is to be used for an expansion of the organization's facilities or services, the drive should be justified in terms of benefits to the community. If the drive is to realize a sum to be donated to a charitable or welfare cause, steps should be taken to ascertain the complete worthiness of that cause. Consult the Better Business Bureau, the Chamber of Commerce, or the National Information Bureau.

Generally speaking, local charitable and welfare causes are well-intentioned and honestly administered. They vary, however, in degree of effectiveness and efficiency, and it is usually on these bases that they must be evaluated. Besides demonstrating a real need for help, the agency should be incorporated, be managed by a board that holds regular meetings, publishes regular reports that are generally available, has its accounts periodically certified by a public accountant, confines its fund raising to acceptable methods, and cooperates with other local groups engaged in charitable or welfare activities. The name of a charitable organization should never be used in connection with a fund-raising program without first obtaining its approval of the program.

PREPARING AND CARRYING OUT THE CAMPAIGN. It cannot be assumed that your community has an adequate background in the field of your organization interest. Important parts of the preparation for a money-raising drive are educational and promotional measures that will make effective solicitation possible. Most national charitable and welfare volunteer agencies furnish information, materials, and organization suggestions.

A program of community education should start, of course, with the workers themselves. They must be well grounded in the facts and able to use those facts in logical argument to support their appeals. Before the drive opens, every worker should know why he is asking for money, how much is needed, and how that money is to be spent. He must also be sold on the worthiness of the cause.

When the number of workers and the extent of the campaign warrant, organizations sometimes publish a handbook for workers that presents essential background information, a campaign procedure outline, and practical soliciting techniques. Other groups conduct training sessions at which interview techniques are demonstrated.

While the stereotyped sales talk is to be avoided, a planned procedure tried out in practice sessions enables the worker to adapt his approach and to develop his argument to meet individual situations. Something of the care with which house-to-house salesmen plan their talks and demonstrations should be given to this preparation. For example, a knowledge of the special interests of the prospect might be the key to a successful approach or furnish material for small talk that would lay the groundwork for a successful appeal.

An interview plan should be one easily kept in mind, adaptable to the conversation shifts that are bound to take place, but designed to keep the talk directed toward securing the contribution. An effective outline might consist of a series of questions which in their phrasing make an affirmative answer easy: "It's a shame that Centerville has no Boys' Club, isn't it?" "I'd give a week's pay check to feel that my son had a place to play and spend his time, wouldn't you?" A series of "yes" answers, of course, predisposes the prospect to a "yes" reply to a question asking for a contribution.

Although it is impossible to present a formula that can be used in all interview situations, some "do's and don't's" have been developed through organization experience. Do not overload your argument with a mass of data. Point up your appeal by dramatically emphasizing one or two facts. Be ready, however, to support or supplement those few facts with the full weight of all the facts when necessary. Even with the small home audience, charts and other graphic material are effective. Guard against the expenditure of more time than is necessary for getting the contribution and the good wishes of the donor.

Individuals tend to give relatively large amounts more readily when they can think of their contributions in terms of actual facilities or services. "Build and equip a cabin for the Scout camp," "Send one underprivileged boy to camp for 10 days," "Drill one foot of the school's artesian well," "Provide 100 bricks for the new hospital" are appeals that permit donors to appreciate fully the vital part they are playing in meeting community needs.

Because of differing and even conflicting interpretations of rulings relating to the deductibility of charitable donations, this argument in support of an appeal for funds should be used with discretion. In the absence of a ruling that applies specifically to your cause, it is better merely to state that many such donations are deductible and suggest that this one may be also.

Frequently, separate nonprofit organizations are formed to receive gifts in support of service programs. The names of thousands of organizations formed for "religious, charitable, scientific, literary, or educational purposes. . . ," contributions to which are deductible, are suggestive of the type that have met the requirements of the Treasury Department. A list may be obtained from the Superintendent of Documents.

Before soliciting gifts for a community center or other public facility, consideration should be given to a request for a ruling as to the applicability of the provisions of the Revenue Act permitting the deduction of gifts to municipalities.

MEETING SALES RESISTANCE. Sales resistance should be expected.

Anticipate objections; answer them confidently and directly. Ignore no legitimate inquiry. Do not permit yourself to be drawn into an argument.

"I can't possibly give that much now" need not be the final word. Accept pledges and arrange for their deferred or installment payment. In discussing such arrangements, stress the amount of each partial payment, rather than the total amount. It is in the ultimate interest of the cause and your organization, however, to keep the payments within the means of the donor.

In the event of failure to secure a contribution or a pledge, terminate the interview in such a fashion that a second approach is possible, or a cordial reception assured for another drive, or at least, the prospect is left with a feeling of good will toward the organization and its purposes.

A MOPPING-UP COMMITTEE. Campaigns for funds that fail to meet quotas should be extended only when it is absolutely necessary. Seldom does the additional money secured compensate for the loss of morale that often accompanies such further demands upon workers' time and energy. A better method is for the committee officially to close the drive on schedule, and constitute itself as a mopping-up squad to meet the deficit. It may comb unused, discarded, or temporarily not interested contributors' cards, or re-examine sources of contributors, and then make special approaches.

SPECIAL CONTRIBUTIONS. Organizations that resort to yearly or periodic appeals for funds sometimes develop a short list of prospects who may be depended on to give relatively large amounts. The mechanics of conducting such a limited campaign are the same as that suggested for the unlimited drive. The success of the recurring limited campaign depends, however, on sustaining the interest of these individuals by a special acknowledgment of their assistance and by keeping them informed of the accomplishments of the organization and its problems, through letters from the president and the bulletin.

The raising of money through the solicitation of large donations or gifts from a few individuals may be the function of a "special gifts" committee, or the responsibility of the membership committee when special membership status such as "sustaining" or "supporting" is conferred upon the donors.

OTHER SOLICITATION METHODS. Organizations have raised large

amounts through booths; street-corner solicitation; canisters in stores, restaurants, banks, theaters, and other public places; appeals to theater and other audiences; the sale of tags, a symbolic flower, or other item on special days; and various other attention-catching, ingenious methods.

The nominal amount suggested by such catchy titles as *Mile of Pennies* and *March of Dimes*, for example, makes it difficult for anyone to refuse a contribution. Once committed to giving, few make their gifts the minimum amount. Cards with slots for one foot of pennies are distributed by Kiwanians in a *Mile of Pennies* drive. Some organizations mail coin cards, and distribute them through school children. In hundreds of towns and cities Junior Chambers of Commerce are financing Christmas projects in campaigns advertised as the *Mile of Dimes*. Soliciting for dimes in Louisville, Kentucky, resulted in a $10,000 fund for the Mayor's Committee to provide Christmas gifts for the needy. Another effective solicitation method was used by a Lions Club in Chicago. Each member was given a dime bank. During a four-month period he asked friends and acquaintances to drop in donations for the care and rehabilitation of spastic children.

A sensational stunt-type event often draws large crowds that may be solicited through passing the hat. Hundreds of dollars were collected for a blue baby fund from a crowd that gathered to watch an ex-marine make a 4,000-foot parachute jump for a Kiwanis Club in Spokane, Washington.

Dickens' famous character is exploited in a Vineland, New Jersey, *Tiny Tim Fund* campaign, the proceeds of which go to children needing special measures to restore them to health. Groups of carolers, representing over 50 community organizations, tour the city in trucks and cars. After each caroling, donations are collected in tin cups. Many communites hold *Dollar Night* after the regular Community Chest Drive is over. Each participating organization covers an area. At a publicized night and hour, each family that can give "just one dollar more" switches on the porch light as a signal to a soliciting squad car.

MONEY-MAKING PROJECTS

Community organizations are realizing millions of dollars annually from entertainment ventures and other events for which an admission may be charged, and from the operation of businesses and services not covered by individual enterprise. Profit-making projects range from the sale of admissions to a meeting featuring a popular lecturer to the promotion of carnivals, bowl games, and rodeos attracting thousands of spectators; from business enterprises such as painting house and business numbers for a fee, to the yearly planting of marginal land with thousands of trees to be marketed at Christmas time.

Some organizations engage in a series of projects scheduled through the year or as financial need arises. Many depend on one entertainment event to attract attendances large enough to furnish revenue for the year's activities. Others offer a series of different events simultaneously or successively within a short period of time to make the most of community interest aroused in the promotion of a worthy cause.

CHOOSING THE PROJECT. The choice of a money-raising project should be given careful consideration. Many organizations fail to realize anticipated returns or suffer serious financial reverses because of ventures that lack adequate membership support. Many projects require greater resources than the membership and the community can provide, involve unfavorable contract agreements with the agents or managers of professional talent, or make demands on members' time and energy not justified by the profit realized. Some prove ill suited to the particular community, or offer educational, cultural, or entertainment programs of such a standard as to jeopardize the success of future organization money-raising projects.

Before committing the organization to a project, fully discuss the idea at a meeting. Secure pledges of help in doing specific tasks. Survey the membership and the community for talent possibilities. Be sure that your organization is adequately covered by insurance against losses through fire, theft, and accident. If the project is the sponsorship of a professional performance, consult organizations that have engaged the attraction, or ask your national headquarters for information. Secure the assistance of a lawyer in drawing up a contract. Be careful not to agree to too large a guarantee; many professional performances can be obtained on a percentage basis. Insist on a performance bond. Write into the contract specific agreements about the handling of money and every other important detail of arrangements.

COMMITTEE ORGANIZATION AND PROCEDURE. The more complex the money-raising project, the greater the number of committees required to bring about an efficient and equitable division of responsibility and work. Some projects, such as the operation of a booth at a bazaar, may be carried through the planning, organization, and operation stages by one relatively small group. Another, such as a fair or street party, may require committees such as those for executive direction, publicity, talent, personnel, special attractions, decorations, concessions, contests, management, and finance.

Typical responsibilities of an executive committee include drawing up a broad plan for board and membership approval; securing municipal cooperation or licensing; negotiating contracts; securing the cooperation and support of merchants, community organizations, and other groups; arranging for a ceremonious opening by the mayor or an official proclamation that the event is a community affair worthy of support; securing adequate police assistance in rerouting traffic, parking cars, and supervising a hall or grounds; choosing working committees, defining their duties, and supervising and correlating their planning and progress during the event.

PUBLICITY. The work of the publicity committee should get under way just as soon as the event has been planned in outline. Its efforts through the preparation, timing, and release of news and feature stories, posters, and stunts should be directed toward developing the attitude that the event is an important community occasion, the success or failure of which is of general concern. In many instances, as in the case of carnivals, an atmosphere of revelry should be developed; in others, such as sports contests, partisanship should be encouraged and exploited. Basic to any entertainment publicity program is the development of public anticipation through devices such as the announcement or suggestion of surprise features.

TALENT. The success of an entertainment or sports event may rest squarely upon the kind and quality of the talent secured. Your talent committee might consider the practicability of engaging individual professional entertainers to bolster local talent, or of sponsoring on a profit-sharing basis professional performances such as a sports event, play, concert, or rodeo. While financial returns from sponsored professional performances are sometimes limited, weeks and months of planning, rehearsing, and promoting amateur performances, with the possibility of artistic as well as financial failure, are avoided. In arrangements for most sponsored professional performances, organization responsibility includes only securing a suitable place, cooperation in promotion, and selling tickets. Organization profits usually include part of the admissions returns, and proceeds from the sale of advertising space in programs and the operation or sale of concessions.

Some amateur carnivals, fairs, and circuses feature a professional act of a spectacular nature as a climax to each evening's entertainment, with the sensational nature of the acts increased to something "colossal" on the closing evening. Celebrities in the entertainment and sports fields sometimes appear or perform in behalf of organization causes.

Most profitable events, however, depend solely on community amateur talent. A committee might start with a canvass of its own membership and their families for comedians, impersonators, and those with vaudeville, dramatic, or other entertainment experience. Schools and other agencies sometimes can furnish musical, dramatic, sports, and other talent. Recreation boards, college or high school physical education departments, Y.M.C.A.'s, and Y.W.C.A.'s may have information about amateur entertainers and athletes who have community or neighborhood followings. Use newspaper cut-out application forms to publicize the talent need and to facilitate its procurement.

In planning and organizing amateur plays, musicals, variety shows, minstrels, and the like, an audition committee holds a key position. Ask theater managers, actors, drama teachers, and coaches to assist you in screening applicants.

DECORATIONS. The problem of decorations will vary with the kind and complexity of the event. Decorations for such a seasonal occasion as a Thanksgiving holiday dance may consist of cornstalks and a few gourds and pumpkins donated by members and arranged in less than an hour by a committee of two or three. On the other hand, the decoration of fairgrounds and individual booths and other attractions, or the decoration of the main street of a community for an anniversary celebration may constitute a planning, organization, and installation job of considerable magnitude, requiring a large working committee.

While it is desirable that as much of the material and work as possible be supplied by members and the community, in some situations it may be necessary to engage the services of professional concerns that can furnish banners, floodlights, and other material and equipment not readily available or practicable to make.

Although in most projects such as carnivals, block parties, and fairs, freedom to create special effects, and most of the responsibility for the actual work of decorating must be left to those in charge of planning individual booths and other attractions, it is important that the various features be related to produce a unified effect. This, in addition to serving as a purchasing agent for decoration materials, is the chief function of most decorating committees.

PERSONNEL. The committee given the task of recruiting, instructing, and assigning workers to collect tickets, serve as stagehands, man booths, act as barkers, be in attendance at sideshows and concessions, take care of receipts, and do the many other jobs necessary for the functioning of an elaborate event has a difficult job to perform. It is important that every post be filled all the time, but that no one individual be given an unreasonably heavy share of the burden. In events that last a considerable time, such as dances and fairs, a shifts arrangement should be set up, with adequate emergency relief provided. Alternates should be named for key posts. Adequate supervision must be maintained.

TICKET SALES. The success of most sponsored performances and many other money-raising projects depends on the advance sale of tickets. Selling tickets often is the only responsibility an organization assumes in the presentation of sponsored performances. A ticket-selling drive may be undertaken in support of a worthy cause sponsored by the community or another organization, or it may be a project in which part of the ticket sale proceeds represents the organization's commission, as in the case of tickets for a school sports program or a music association's concert series. Special consideration should be given to the organization and training of the ticket committee as an effective sales force, and to the utilization of all available advertising media through cooperation with the organization's publicity committee.

Common methods of ticket selling include community-wide or selective distribution of tickets by mail; membership sales approaches to friends and acquaintances; a neighborhood canvass through school children; a house-to-house coverage of the community through news-carriers or members; setting up sales booths at street intersections, banks, department stores, and other public places; sale of blocks of tickets to gas stations, stores, and shops to be used as purchase premiums, or to other community organizations, schools, and business and industrial concerns at a discount, or to individuals or groups as special patrons.

For some organization affairs, such as carnivals, sports events, horse shows, and bazaars, at which it may be difficult to distinguish those who have paid for admission or for special events, badges or tags are distributed with tickets or used in place of tickets.

Important in fixing admission prices and in the accounting for funds raised through entertainment projects is a consideration of amusement taxes.

ATTENDANCE. In addition to publicity through ordinary channels, the following measures for improving attendance have proved effective:

1. Conducting a queen and court of honor contest, with an announcement of the community's choices and appropriate coronation ceremonies a feature of the event.

2. Presenting a preview of the coming event before school and other groups, and at street corners and other public places; organizing a traveling entertainment troupe to visit surrounding communities.

3. Offering door prizes, usually articles donated by local merchants.

4. Presenting gifts to the first 100 persons who present themselves.

5. Featuring free attractions, such as dancing, band concerts, and fireworks.

6. Arranging for the appearance of celebrities.

7. Conducting talent contests, with audience applause determining the winners.

8. Presenting easily solved riddles or puzzles with attendance at the event a condition of eligibility for participation in a drawing for prizes. Popular variations include finding among those present the "mystery woman," only part of whose features have become familiar to the community through poster and newspaper pictures; and riddles, the wording of which suggests the identity of well-known persons.

9. Securing the participation of other organizations that have large memberships.

10. Dedicating each day of an event to a different neighboring community.

11. Opening the event with a parade.

12. Using floodlights, music broadcast through loud speakers, and other attention-catching devices.

13. Offering special admission rates for two or more, or for repeat attendance at affairs lasting two or more days or evenings.

PATRONS. It often happens that members and others in the community who cannot participate as workers in a money-raising project such as a dance, concert, or art show, or feel that they cannot adequately contribute through attendance or a purchase of tickets, welcome the opportunity to make donations as patrons or sponsors. Such a source of revenue may be available to organizations undertaking most of the projects suggested in this chapter. Recognition may be given through the listing of patrons in news releases; and in programs, circulars, and other printed matter.

SUPERVISION. The general supervision of an affair such as a carnival, fair, rodeo, or sports event while it is in progress may be the responsibility of a member or of a salaried director and assistants, the event's executive committee, or a special management committee. In some projects, managerial duties may be assumed by the committee for grounds or hall arrangements.

Although many management problems arise in the course of the event and so cannot be anticipated, some are common to many situations and may be provided for in planning. For example, a serious loss of revenue is sometimes suffered because some features cannot be made the exclusve privilege of ticket holders; erection of canvas screens may remedy the situation. General dissatisfaction may be avoided and the safety, comfort, and convenience of patrons assured through provisions for such facilities as first-aid stations, a lost-and-found center, and rest rooms.

In planning for supervision, utilize the experience of members who have served on such a committee at similar affairs. Consult other organizations about arrangements at their events. The staffs of the municipal recreation department, the Y.M.C.A., Y.W.C.A., and the school sports department, for example, have had experience in presenting varied events and handling large crowds. Theater managers may have useful suggestions about checking services, selling and collecting tickets, and organizing and supervising ushers. The management committee of a county fair association would be of inestimable value as a source of aid in organizing the supervision of a fair, carnival, circus, or similar project. Professional caterers, restaurateurs, and concessionaires may outline methods of serving refreshments. The police department may organize the handling of traffic and parking and suggest measures to meet attempts to crash the gate, and to guard against pilfering.

One arrangement for the effective management of the complex activities of events such as carnivals, fairs, and expositions provides for division of the grounds or hall into sections, with a member of the management committee in charge of the supervision of events in each area, responsible for securing substitutes for members who fail to report for work, replenishing depleted stocks, supplying needed equipment, correcting inadequate lighting, supplying information, guarding against grifters and gamblers who follow such events, soothing the ruffled feelings of both workers and patrons, making collections, and helping to close booths for the night. A public address system is used in making announcements and giving instructions to personnel, as well as in promoting special events.

RECEIPTS. Important to the successful outcome of many fund-raising enterprises are the arrangements made for handling money received at the gate or box office, or as receipts from booths, side shows, concessions, or vendors. One member should be responsible for finances. He is assisted, in most cases, by a committee. If large sums of money are involved, and especially if part of the receipts is to be paid to other organizations or the management of professional performers, the individual who is to be responsible should be bonded.

While the operating and accounting system used will vary with the type and complexity of the affair, and with the particular situation, it is important that a uniform procedure be adopted and followed by members. Mimeographed requisition, receipt, inventory, and other forms might add to the smooth functioning of carnivals and fairs, which many times are scheduled to run for several days or evenings.

In the case of shows presented on more than one day or evening, collect money and check equipment and supplies at the close of each performance. Some organizations that present evening affairs ask police departments to take charge of receipts until the next day.

Many organizations set up a booth near the entrance to the carnival or festival grounds, or arrange for a table at a dance, at which money may be exchanged for scrip in denominations convenient for use in paying for games, admissions, and refreshments. Such a scrip system encourages spending, eliminates the risks involved in having many people handle money, keeps things moving at the booths by freeing attendants from change making, and simplifies an accounting system. Scrip and a list of leftover supplies should be collected from each feature at the close of each evening. In professional performance arrangements, members' participation with representatives of the agency or management in the handling of receipts protects the organization's interests.

CLEANUP. An important task involved in many money-raising projects such as dances, bazaars, and fairs is that of cleaning up after the event. Littered carnival grounds, for example, are unsightly during the day when there is no attendance, and may have serious effects on the organization's relations with the community. All the carnival personnel usually assist the cleanup committee.

IDEAS FOR MANY EVENTS. Some project ideas are widely used because they have been consistently profitable and because they are applicable to many organization and community events such as those intended primarily to contribute to the cultural life of the community, observe some special occasion, or encourage or provide recreation and sports opportunities.

Representative of such money-raising opportunities are the publishing of programs, the operation of booths and other concessions, exhibits and demonstrations, tent shows, children's attractions, and dancing.

PROGRAMS. The sale of advertising space and the listing of special patrons in programs for organization or other community plays, concerts, festivals, sports events, special celebrations, and other events may be an important source of revenue. In some organization projects, such revenue may be supplemental to admissions and other income. In others, where no admissions charge is possible or desirable, programs may, with the operation of concessions, be the only means of raising money.

Often, by providing an interesting printed program for other community functions in return for advertising rights, the organization may be performing a valuable service. Amateur drama groups, school sports departments, and the local motion picture theater, for example, frequently lack the experience, the business contacts, and the sales force necessary to publish an attractive program without a serious financial loss.

CONCESSIONS. At most entertainment events drawing large attendances there is a demand for refreshments and souvenir novelties, and such services as checking and parking. Rights to these opportunities for profit making at organization functions may be sold to established concessionaires, granted to other community groups, or reserved for the organization itself. In some such projects, proceeds from concessions constitute the major source of income for the organization. Concession rights sometimes are secured free of charge, or the organization may successfully bid for such rights at other affairs such as dances and sports events or special community celebrations. Parks, beaches, municipal golf courses, airports, main highways, and other public places not already served by regularly established businesses furnish organizations with opportunities for seasonal or all-year concessions as sources of regular income.

Booths. Chief among the features at events such as carnivals, fairs, festivals, bazaars, and block parties are booths offering games of skill, entertainment, and merchandise. Because they may be in continuous operation they usually represent the chief source of revenue. Their number and variety are limited only by the ingenuity of the money-raising group.

Vendors. Community affairs attended by large crowds offer opportunities for members to organize squads to sell programs, refreshments, and novelties, and in many instances to contribute color and a general impression of life and movement. Along the line of march at parades; at the approaches to stadia and among the spectators at sports contests; at carnivals, festivals, and street fairs have members hawk pennants, balloons, whistles and other noise makers, popcorn, ice cream, and candy. A peanut wagon, with a whistle simulating an old-fashioned peanut vendor's steam whistle, will attract patrons and add to the atmosphere at such an occasion as a street fair. At a dinner dance or a festival have attractively costumed girls sell cigarettes, flowers, and novelties.

Exhibits and Demonstrations. Exhibits and demonstrations of merchandise and equipment by local merchants and manufacturers not only add to the variety of the attractions at festivals, carnivals, and other events, and encourage the support of the business section of the community, but furnish income through the sale of space. Concerns often welcome such opportunities for promotion. A method of building community support and increasing attendance is to invite exhibits and demonstrations by groups such as garden clubs, Boy Scouts and Girl Scouts, and the fire and police departments.

TENT SHOWS. Many carnival-type entertainment features that can be presented but a few times in the course of the evening depend on suspense build-up, and require large audiences for profitable operation. Among such events practicable for community organization affairs of many types are amateur circuses, comedy and dancing acts, an amateur or professional hypnotist, boxing and wrestling bouts, and feats of strength. These attractions may be seriously presented or burlesqued.

CHILDREN'S ATTRACTIONS. Affairs that open in the afternoon sometimes provide special attractions for children, either as money-makers through admission charges or as a child-care service to permit mothers to participate. Some carnivals, circuses, and fairs have a special kids' day, which children may enjoy at reduced rates.

Rope or fence off an enclosure as a zoo, exhibiting readily available domestic animals and birds. Collect children's equipment such as jungle gyms, slides, seesaws, and swings. A popular feature might be a story-telling tent or a children's movie theater. Pony or donkey rides are always popular.

DANCING. Dancing is a feature appropriate for many entertainment events. At outdoor affairs such as carnivals, profits from this source sometimes justify the construction or rental of a dance floor on a raised platform, providing interest for spectators. Square dances have proved popular in some communities.

OTHER REPRESENTATIVE PROJECTS. Many organizations adopt a multiple approach to fund raising, to appeal to different community interests and to give many members an opportunity to participate. Your organization might find project ideas in the following additional activity suggestions:

Amateur and professional acrobatic circuses, air shows, water carnivals, ice carnivals, rodeos; talent contests and baby contests; old-fashioned, radio, "slave," and other auctions; sales of Christmas cards, white elephants, brooms, cakes, hobby products, and the personal services of members; renting cameras at parks; operating a business such as a thrift shop, circulating library, parking lot, trailer camp, chain of vending machines or juke boxes, a fix-it shop, or a mail-order service; conducting community tours of homes and gardens of distinction; publishing directories and guide books; presenting hobby, garden, and other shows; sponsoring sports and recreation events; selling advertising space and copies of special editions of the local paper;

collecting and selling scrap; and presenting novelty events and stunts such as turkey shoots, donkey basketball games, and turtle races.

SOME RELATED PROJECTS. Some projects in behalf of worthy causes, while not resulting in a revenue return for the sponsoring groups, involve collecting money or obtaining services and goods of money value. Typical of such projects are participation in the fund-raising efforts of youth groups, solicitation of materials and services, and the encouragement of self-help programs through the sale of articles made by the blind and others.

Community organization participation with youth groups in projects to raise money is usually to help them support their activities, to provide effective service training by giving young people an opportunity to engage in this type of project under adult supervision, or to encourage vocational training projects such as those of Junior Achievement. Adult participation may be limited to guidance and supervision, or it may include joint action.

While almost all the money-raising ideas suggested in this chapter may be adapted to youth groups or permit youth-group participation with adults, the following activities are particularly appropriate for young people: collecting and selling paper and scrap metal; door-to-door ticket canvassing; distributing throwaways; selling magazine subscriptions; manning information and sales booths; operating refreshment and other concessions; cooking and serving food, camp style; giving demonstrations and presenting exhibitions; presenting variety shows, fairs, circuses, and pet shows; operating special children's attractions; baby sitting at teas, bazaars, and other events; acting as messengers or errand boys; and performing odd jobs.

SOLICITATION OF PERSONAL AND OTHER SERVICES. Closely related to the fund-raising campaign, and governed by many of the same principles, are projects in which the contributions solicited take the form of the direct personal services of members and other citizens, merchandise and construction materials, and the loan of machinery and other equipment. In some situations, contributions of these types far exceed in value the money that could be expected from the more conventional drive for funds. An appeal for personal, physical help can be made very dramatic. Many who feel they cannot make substantial money contributions willingly give goods or services. Individuals receive the spiritual satisfactions that accompany such direct, personal giving, and the pleasures of close association with others in the community.

Typical projects include a union's contribution of labor in painting a Boys' Club with paint furnished by merchants and equipment supplied by contractors; an organization's enlistment of a pick-and-shovel gang to create a play area; mobilization of bulldozers, trucks, and other heavy equipment to provide a community airstrip; and solicitation and collection of articles and refreshments for use or resale at an organization's entertainment affair.

SOURCES OF AID

Important sources of aid are many of the business concerns that advertise in the publications of the large federated organizations, copies of which are available in most libraries. Among such concerns are those offering profit-sharing sales plans; scripts, costumes, props, and directions for minstrel shows and other presentations; and the services of lecturers, concert artists, vaudeville performers, and other entertainers. Other representative sources are the following:

American Kennel Club, Inc., 221 Fourth Ave., New York 3, N. Y. Literature includes a booklet describing procedures and rules for dog shows, which may be helpful in planning such an event as a money-raising project.

American Power Boat Association, 700 Canton Ave., Detroit 7, Mich. Will cooperate in planning features for regattas and other water events.

American National Theatre and Academy (ANTA), 245 West 52nd St., New York 19, N. Y. A nonprofit organization chartered by the Congress of the United States to encourage drama in communities. Its Department of Community and Industrial Showmanship offers theatrical and technical personnel and guidance for community celebrations.

Community Chests and Councils of America, Inc., 155 East 44th St., New York 17, N. Y. Pamphlets published primarily for local Chest agencies are suggestive of effective independent and other intergroup procedures. Subjects include how to plan and conduct appeals for financial aid, an employee group solicitation plan, and reports of new solicitation ideas and techniques. *Catalogue of Publications* is available.

Countrywomen's League, *The Country Gentleman,* Independence Square, Philadelphia 5, Pa. Offers low-cost pamphlets describing many money-raising projects for women's groups.

Curtis, Frieda S., *How to Give a Fashion Show*, New York: Fairchild Publications, Inc. Although written for retail merchants as a handbook for store presentation of a fashion show, its suggestions are also useful for the community organization's money-raising project.

Dennison Manufacturing Company, Framingham, Mass. *So You're Planning a Parade*, a pamphlet describing the construction of floats. Useful in organizing a floats competition.

Fellows, Margaret M. and Koenig, Stella A., *How to Raise Funds by Mail*, New York: McGraw-Hill Book Company, Inc. Covers subjects such as letter-writing techniques, duplicating, and the building of mailing lists. Discusses relation of giving to tax laws.

Girl Scouts of the United States of America, Program Department, 155 East 44th St., New York 17, N. Y. *Finance Manual for Girl Scout Councils*, a 97-page booklet, includes ideas useful for adult organizations. Subjects covered include organization and direction of a finance committee, building the budget, and raising and administering funds. Especially helpful are specimen forms for budget estimate and control, solicitation, acknowledgment of contributions, petty cash reports, treasurer's reports, requisition, and other finance operations.

League of Women Voters of the United States, 1026 17th St., N. W., Washington 6, D. C. Pamphlets useful to many community organizations include *How to Raise Money* and *The Public Relations Aspect of the Finance Drive*.

McDonald, Dora Mary, *Carnival Capers for Schools*. Northwestern Press, 2200 Park Ave., Minneapolis 4, Minn. Money-raising ideas may be adapted by many community organizations.

National Conference of Christians and Jews, 381 Fourth Ave., New York 16, N. Y. Has available without charge a pamphlet, *Fund-Raising Programs for Neighborhood Projects*, by Gertrude Hart Day.

National Information Bureau, Inc., 205 East 42nd St., New York 17, N. Y. Furnishes a subscribers' service that annually reports on over 600 fund-raising nonprofit organizations. Facts and advice guide groups in avoiding questionable causes. Publishes a pamphlet, *Giver's Guide to National Philanthropy*.

National Recreation Association, 315 Fourth Ave., New York 10, N. Y. Offers a variety of inexpensive pamphlets describing many money-raising recreation and entertainment projects.

National Theatre Conference, Western Reserve University, Cleveland, Ohio. Has available a booklet, *Organizing a Community Theatre*, which includes a chapter, "The Box Office," offering practical suggestions for promoting plays, arranging for the sale of reserve seats, box office accounting, and management.

Outboard Boating Club of America, 307 North Michigan Ave., Chicago 1, Ill. Offers community organizations aid in planning, organizing, and directing events such as races, regattas, and water carnivals.

Pan American Band Instrument Co., Elkhart, Ind. *Band and Orchestra Handbook.* Chapter on "Fund-Raising Ideas" for school music groups has ideas adaptable to community organization needs.

Ruml, Beardsley and Geiger, Theodore, eds., *The Manual of Corporate Giving.* The National Planning Association, 1606 New Hampshire Ave., N. W., Washington 9, D. C. Includes practical suggestions for evaluating the worthiness of many kinds of causes for which organizations frequently raise money, information about what contributions are deductible under the 5 per cent provision, a model certificate of incorporation of a foundation, and a form for setting up a charitable trust.

Sarachran, Harman A., *Campaigning for Members,* New York: The Association Press, 1949. Written for such organizations as the Y.M.C.A. and Y.M.H.A., which depend on large memberships as a substantial source of revenue. Some campaign organization suggestions may be used by any community group.

Superintendent of Documents, United States Government Printing Office, Washington 25, D. C. Pamphlet, *The Air Fair, Its Planning and Operation,* published by the Civil Aeronautics Administration, offers suggestions for organization and procedure applicable to such community events as a circus, a fair, or a water regatta. Subjects covered include the relations of the sponsors to private and official agencies, committee organization and functioning, publicity, program planning, policing, sanitary facilities, and exhibition and other booths. *Cumulative List of Organizations* is a Treasury Department booklet listing organizations, contributions to which are tax deductible.

Taylor, Eleanor K., *Public Accountability of Foundations and Charitable Trusts,* New York: Russell Sage Foundation, 1953. Reviews state and federal legislation relating to nonprofit organizations. Includes the Model Non-Profit Corporation Act prepared by a committee of the American Bar Association in 1952. Helpful to community groups considering the setting up of a tax-exempt foundation.

T. S. Denison and Company, 225 North Wabash Ave., Chicago 1, Ill. Pamphlets include *Everything for Your Minstrel Show* and *The High School Stunt Show and Carnival,* which include ideas that can be used in community organization fund raising.

Wennberg, S. G., Editor, *Chamber of Commerce Administration*, rev. ed., Chicago: National Institute for Commercial and Trade Organization Executives, 1951. Includes an excellent discussion of revenue-raising and financial administration problems of large organizations. Ideas helpful to all community groups.

SOME SOURCES OF FILMS AND FILM INFORMATION

American Humane Association, 135 Washington Ave., Albany 10, N. Y. Free loan films include *Let's Have a Pet Show* and *The Dog Show*, both of which present how-to-do-it ideas.

E. I. DuPont de Nemours and Company, Motion Picture Section, Advertising Department, Wilmington 98, Del. Free loan *This Is Nylon* includes a ten-minute fashion show.

Handmacher-Vogel, 533 Seventh Ave., New York 18, N. Y. Free loan sound and color, 23-minute *Tailored by Handmacher* includes shots of a fashion show suggestive of procedures for an organization-sponsored event.

International Harvester Company, 164 North Wacker Drive, Chicago 6, Ill. Free loan sound films include *County Fair* and *Illinois State Fair*, suggestive of money-raising ideas for your organization circus, fair, or carnival.

CHAPTER 4

Public Relations

COMMUNITY GROUPS are becoming increasingly aware that their effectiveness depends on something more than a competent personnel, sound administrative organization and policy, and a well-planned activities program energetically carried out. Despite the most careful attention to details of procedure such as those suggested in these chapters, all too frequently there is a perennial problem of attracting and holding members, or fund-raising campaigns consistently fail to meet quotas, or projects and programs in community service meet with public and official indifference.

Failure in many such cases can be attributed directly to the fact that the organization has not been fully accepted by individuals and other groups as one dedicated to the public interest, capable of leadership in the task of building a better community, identified with worth-while, interesting, successful undertakings.

Community acceptance or rejection of your organization and its purposes is a by-product of the innumerable and complex relations individual members and your officers and committee heads have with others in the community. These public relations exist whether or not your organization is aware of them or attempts to do anything about them. Every casual remark of a member about his group, every meeting, service project, telephone call, news story—literally everything that identifies or interprets the purposes and work of your group affects the impressions others have of it.

The development and maintenance of good public relations should not be left to chance, or to an occasional news release or publicity stunt. There should be a deliberate, continuing effort to use all official and unofficial contacts to demonstrate the worthiness of your group. Such an effort may be extensive, including measures such as educating members in their public relations responsibilities, choosing officers and committee heads for their public relations effectiveness, presenting meeting features and special events for their public relations value, giving careful attention to the public relations aspects of all community activities, and planning, correlating, and carrying out extensive publicity programs.

MEMBERS AND PUBLIC RELATIONS

Members on their jobs or in their businesses, as members of church and other community groups, and in their social activities can be most effective public relations agents. An important aspect of any effort to achieve wider organization acceptance therefore should be measures to give both old and new members a knowledge and appreciation of organization history, ideals, and purposes, a pride in its achievements, an enthusiasm for its programs, and an awareness of their responsibility to take every opportunity to present their organization in a favorable light.

Such an indoctrination effort may be an important part of a new-member assimilation program. Included might be a talk by the president or public relations chairman about the serious consequences to the organization's status of members' thoughtless actions and comments.

Affecting public relations in a very positive way is the active participation of members in other volunteer activities, such as those of the Red Cross, Community Chest, and Civil Defense Corps. Members might be urged to wear their membership buttons, and in other ways to identify themselves with the organization.

OFFICERS, COMMITTEE CHAIRMEN, AND PUBLIC RELATIONS

Your officers and committee heads are your representatives in the community. Not only in their official duties, but in every public affair in which they participate as individuals, and in many of their business and social activities, whether they wish it or not, they are identified with your organization. What they say, how they say it, and how they act tremendously influence the public's opinion of your group. Certainly, therefore, high among their leadership qualifications should be their status in the community, their sensitivity to public opinion, their ability to get along with others, and their effectiveness in interpreting your organization.

These few of the many official activities of officers and committee chairmen suggest the important public relations responsibilities they must assume: formulating and announcing matters of organization policy, serving as your representatives on community councils, corresponding with individuals and groups in the community, presiding at meetings at which other community leaders are present, directing campaigns for members or funds, and seeking the cooperation of municipal officials and the heads of agencies or other groups.

MEETING ACTIVITIES AND PUBLIC RELATIONS

Your meetings may make important direct and indirect contributions to better relations with the community. Invite community leaders and groups to meetings that have particularly worthwhile features, or to those that are devoted to a discussion of your service activities. These influential individuals will communicate to others their attitudes toward your group. Ask municipal officials and other key citizens to talk to the group, participate in panel discussions of local problems, and help in discovering ways by which your group can contribute to their solution.

The celebration of special occasions such as United Nations Day, Education Week, and patriotic holidays offers opportunities for making your group known to many other groups with common interests. Numbers of other citizens can learn of your organization and its role in the community through film showings, exhibits, and demonstrations to which the public may be invited.

A meeting, too, may be an excellent source of information about the community's opinion of your organization. Schedule a public relations clinic meeting, at which members tell of the attitudes of their friends and associates, and help officers and committeemen discover areas in which public relations are weak.

Committee meetings held as project post-mortems might reveal procedures that have undesirable public relations effects. The experience of canvassers, for example, in their face-to-face relations with many in the community, is invaluable in determining how the public is reacting.

COMMUNITY ACTIVITIES AND PUBLIC RELATIONS

Good public relations depend not only on solid achievement in meeting community needs, but also on the methods and the procedures by which these achievements are realized. It is in its community activities that an organization is in most direct relations with hundreds, perhaps thousands, of individuals.

Public relations conscious organization leaders should carefully appraise their programs. Before embarking upon a project do they consult public and private agencies or other volunteer groups with a traditional interest in the field? Do your committee heads publicize objectives that they frequently fail to attain? Are your projects of a one-shot, spectacular type with little or no follow-up? Are your committee chairmen and officers careful about according full recognition to individuals and other groups who contribute to your success? Are your sponsored events and promotion measures always in good taste?

A PUBLIC RELATIONS COMMITTEE

Most organizations can confidently expect good public relations as a by-product of an interesting, worth-while program of meetings and community activities, carried out by a public relations conscious membership.

Organizations with varied programs, large memberships, and complex relationships, or those experiencing limited success, however, may find a standing public relations committee very useful. Although such a committee might plan and carry out organization publicity, its duties should also include determining the status of the group in the community, identifying reasons for poor relations, creating positive measures to improve relations, and correlating all efforts to present the group as one worthy of community acceptance.

A public relations committee should include representatives of all points of view in the organization and community, as well as directors, officers, and the heads of other important committees. With such broad representation it can have an important advisory role, serving as a sounding board for policy changes or project and program ideas. Distinguished from official leadership, it might be able to find out more readily and accurately just what the community and the members themselves think of the organization.

Other important contributions of a public relations committee might include finding answers to questions such as these: Are members really sold on the activities in which they are engaged? Do the membership and fund-raising committees take full advantage of their opportunities to tell the public about their organization? Are the achievements of individuals and committees given effective publicity?

PUBLICITY

One of the most important factors in determining the kind of public relations your organization has is the publicity it receives. Certainly publicity is the most controllable of all the factors influencing public relations.

Publicity may be defined as a planned program to tell others about your organization, its ideals, its purposes, its activities—in order to secure their support. Many publicity programs are too narrowly conceived, often limited to uninspired, poorly written news releases about meetings or other activities.

Most organizations have a need for two general kinds of publicity: one with long-range objectives, designed to bring about wide understanding and appreciation; the other with a more immediate objective, designed to gain acceptance for, to promote, or to report the results of specific activities such as projects in the various fields of service outlined in the chapters of this book.

PUBLICITY WITH A LONG-RANGE GOAL. Publicity with a long-range goal permits careful planning. It may depend on the accumulative effect of repetition over a long period of time. Particularly useful in such programs are media such as the feature sections of local newspapers, especially those with Sunday editions; a speakers' bureau with a continuing program; interesting newsletters, annual reports, project scrapbooks, membership procurement and assimilation literature, made available to the public; and a series of radio or television panel discussions of subjects of community-wide interest.

PUBLICITY FOR SPECIFIC PROJECTS. Publicity for the purpose of promoting, or advertising the results of, a specific project—publicity with immediate objectives—is an inseparable part of any long-range effort. Measures often include all the attention-catching devices an ingenious committee can think up. In publicizing a project or program, or in building up a public readiness for its acceptance, all channels of communication should be considered: informal but planned and directed conversation with others in the community; small-group discussions with interested citizens; a schedule of talks before school, church, business, labor, and other important groups; rallies; radio and television talks, interviews, and skits; news releases, background articles, feature stories, and editorials; sound trucks; a letter campaign; letters to the press by the president, individual members, and other citizens; distribution of literature through members, youth groups, and newsboys; selected motion pictures and filmstrips; dramatic presentations; posters, exhibits, window displays, buttons, stickers, and blotters; attention-catching slogans; information booths; appearance of sponsoring celebrities at theaters and other entertainment centers; and spectacles such as parades and motorcades.

CHOICE OF PUBLICITY MEDIA. The publicity committee should realize that your organization has not one public but many publics. For example, the success of a project in the promotion of better industrial planning would demand that your organization contact the community's businessmen with an explanation of your objectives, information about how you hope to achieve them, and a plea for support. Publicity attempted through a radio broadcast at 10 A.M. might be almost a complete waste. Direct mail, talks before a businessmen's association, and a pamphlet presenting research findings might be effective ways of establishing good relations with this particular public. A youth-activities project would require that the young people themselves be informed, as well as their parents. Attempts to do this solely through the news columns of your community paper would probably result in indifferent success.

PUBLICITY TO LAUNCH A PROJECT. The publicity attending the launching of a project sometimes furnishes an impetus that carries through to the project's objective. How much fanfare, if any, should accompany a project's opening depends on the type of project and the character of the community. Cheesecake, the use of pretty young women to attract attention, might be considered poor taste in some situations. Publicity measures to start a campaign for the sale of tickets to a serious play would be very different from those used to advertise a carnival.

OTHER PROJECT PUBLICITY CONCERNS. An important phase of project promotion often neglected is that of keeping the public informed of progress. Continued pleas for public support without an acknowledgment of the responses that have been made imply that there has been no response. Use the press and radio, sound trucks, and thermometers to keep the public informed. Such measures not only give credit where credit is due, but help to develop the bandwagon atmosphere many times necessary for project success.

DEALING WITH THE PRESS. An organization that does not have the support of the local press is seriously handicapped in its efforts to let the public know what it is doing. The committee should establish good personal relations with members of the newspaper staff, develop an appreciation of news values, and release copy that a newspaper can use with a minimum of editing or rewriting.

The publicity chairman should become acquainted with the reporters, the desk men, and the editor who will cover your events and handle your news releases. Newspapers, too, know the value of good relations with community groups. An editor will be glad to talk with committeemen about what your organization is trying to do and about the kind of publicity that will help in doing it. Most newspapers welcome opportunities to describe the important role they play in community living and to explain how news is gathered and printed. Through such an interview, your committeemen and newspapermen can arrive at understandings upon which excellent organization-newspaper relations can be built.

An important function of your publicity committee is to help the newspaper give complete coverage to your activities. The paper should know well in advance what is to take place and when. Send tickets for luncheons, dinners, or entertainments to the press with a note of invitation several days ahead of the scheduled date. The day before the event, send another short announcement and invitation.

Your committee might call attention to opportunities for news pictures. If the paper cannot send a staff photographer, perhaps a member can take acceptable pictures, or your committee might engage a commercial photographer. Have glossy prints in the editor's hands well before the deadline for pictures.

Other provisions help assure newspaper coverage of your activities. Consider newsmen as special guests. A committeeman might be assigned to introduce a reporter to other organization leaders who might be good sources of news. Anticipate the needs of the reporter. For example, if the event is a speech or a lecture, provide pictures or mats, a brief biography of the speaker, reasons for the occasion, relevant facts about the organization, an estimate of the number present, a list of officers and important guests—complete with first names and middle initials, and copy paper and pencils. When possible provide advance copies of programs and speeches.

To maintain favorable relations with the press, do not use pressure to get a story into the paper. Reporters are good judges of news values. Avoid favoritism. Two or more newspapers in the community should be given equal opportunity to get all the news. If there are morning and evening newspapers, both should be considered in timing press releases.

An organization that receives unfavorable publicity should not rush into print with furious denials. Such an action may only add to the damage. When a denial or correction seems necessary, it should be good-humored and courteous. If a reporter misinterprets the facts, find out the cause of the misunderstanding and suggest a new angle for a second story in which the facts can be correctly presented.

Often it is the little things that count. If a reporter or a photographer does an outstanding job, let him know you are aware of it. A letter or telephone call to his editor may do much to show your organization's appreciation. Some organizations annually give a dinner for press, radio, and television leaders as a recognition of their contributions to community betterment.

PUBLICITY RELEASES. Staff and time limitations do not always permit newspapers to cover all activities, or to write feature articles about the organization. Many events, though newsworthy, are not important enough to warrant the presence of a reporter. A major job of a publicity committee, therefore, is to prepare reports of its organization's activities and to furnish interesting background and feature articles. Know your newspapers' deadlines for such news copy and pictures.

An editor must consider the number of readers who will find an interest in your release. Your stories should be timely, dramatic, factual, well written, easy to read, and be related to the interests of many in the community.

There are a few fundamental rules for writing publicity releases that anyone can follow. First, the name, address, and telephone number of the publicity chairman should be placed in the upper left corner of the first page. The release date should be placed in the upper right corner.

All copy must be typewritten on one side of the paper, and double spaced with wide margins. A half page of white space should be left at the top of the story for the editor's use. The original, not a carbon copy, should be sent.

It helps both the newspaper and your organization if stories are written so that they require a minimum of rewriting. Releases about activities should be written as objective news stories, free of opinion. Trying to tell too much is just as bad as not telling enough.

The lead is all-important in newspaper writing. It is the opening paragraph in which the essential facts are summarized. These essential facts usually are answers to the questions Who?, What?, Where?, When?, and sometimes How? and Why? Paragraphs following the lead give details or additional facts in the order of their importance and interest.

Absolute accuracy is essential. Names should be correctly spelled and complete. This point cannot be overstressed. But although names make news, particularly local names, they are not a substitute for subject matter.

Sometimes a good story cannot be written by your committee in time for the next edition. The facts of the story, in this case, should be telephoned to the newspapers. Once you know your newspapers well, you will know to whom the story should be called. Always ask for the reporter or editor on whom you can depend for accuracy and cooperation.

Some Newspaper Publicity Techniques. A number of legitimate devices may be used to develop more and better newspaper publicity. One of these is building up an event. If an organization is putting on a campaign, such as a get-out-the-vote or a fund-raising drive, or is promoting a large meeting with prominent speakers, all the facts need not be written into one story. It is better to build up the event by spacing a number of stories for repetitive effect. Each story should have a different feature and added information. However, the build-up should not start too far in advance of the event, or the readers and the news editors may lose interest. Promotion for most events should be concentrated in the two weeks before the opening. A year-round project, on the other hand, should be publicized throughout the year.

Human interest and other feature stories should not be overlooked. They are more difficult to write than straight accounts of happenings. It usually is best, therefore, to give the information to the newspaper and let a staff writer do the story. Organizations have found it a good idea to give exclusive feature stories to reporters who have done a particularly good job of regular coverage.

The interview is a valuable publicity feature. Ask a reporter to interview the chairman of your project committee or to talk with a prominent organization guest. Frequently such a feature, clearly identified with your organization, will be more widely read than some of the regular news releases on the same subject.

Editorials in support of your community projects are generally effective. If your group performs some noteworthy community service, undoubtedly its efforts will be recognized on the editorial page. However, the publicity chairman may suggest that the organization project is possible editorial material. Although editors will not usually publish an editorial written by a publicity chairman, they will sometimes use it as a guest editorial, when it is signed by a prominent citizen.

Letters-to-the-editor columns furnish opportunities for putting ideas before the public. Occasional letters keep an organization in the public eye and can be used to call attention to current projects. Columnists are always on the lookout for material. A one-sentence passing mention in a column is good publicity.

Advertising is the lifeblood of any newspaper. Without it, most newspapers cannot survive. Many publicity chairmen gain support for their projects and the good will of newspapers by sponsoring advertising dealing with the organization's project. Local businesses often cooperate by supporting a fund drive or other community activity in their advertisements. Such advertising has several beneficial effects: it gives the businessman an opportunity to contribute to community betterment, it provides additional income for newspapers, and it establishes your group as a strong community force.

The Advertising Council, representing national advertisers, advertising agencies, newspapers, and other mass media, offers advertising copy and mats promoting safety, health, better schools, religion, brotherhood, forest-fire prevention, Armed Forces prestige, and other organization interests suggested in this book.

RADIO PUBLICITY. The value of radio as a publicity medium for community organization activities and projects is often underestimated. In many instances it is completely overlooked.

Seventy-five per cent of all radio stations in the United States and Canada are local stations, particularly interested in helping to meet the needs of the communities in which they are located. Moreover, radio stations are required to schedule noncommercial public service broadcasts. They often allot radio time in the early morning and evening to community organizations. The manager of your local station will appreciate information about what you are doing, and how programs with listener interest can be built around your activities. Give him the facts—writing for radio and television is a job for the specialist.

Effective radio publicity material is available free of charge or at nominal cost from sources listed at the close of chapters of this book. Included are community service dramatic scripts, transcriptions of radio plays featuring well-known stars, transcribed interviews with nationally known personalities, recorded appeals for worthy causes, and scripts and transcriptions of spot announcements.

TELEVISION PUBLICITY. Television stations also schedule time for public service programs. Representatives of community groups discuss their activities on interview programs conducted by radio personalities, and present panel discussions of civic questions. Boy Scouts present "before and after" demonstrations in promoting their Christmas-toy repair shops. Frequently community groups prepare announcement placards for program breaks. Some groups have presented their own films of community projects, or have arranged for the local showing of free-loan and nominal-rental films in support of programs in fields such as health, safety, and religion. Before suggesting a film for televising, however, be sure that it has been approved for showing.

SOURCES OF AID

Many of the sources of aid listed at the close of other chapters offer aid in developing good public relations in the special areas of organization interest outlined. Other sources of such help are the following:

Advertising Council, Inc., 25 West 45th St., New York 19, N. Y. Source of slogans, posters, and timely advertising copy and mats for the promotion of community betterment programs. Description of services and materials is available.

American Bar Association, 1140 North Dearborn St., Chicago 10, Ill. *Public Relations for Bar Associations,* 1953, a 227-page book prepared by the Standing Committee on Public Relations, would serve as a handbook for any community organization. Contents include careful analysis of the problem, and discussion of the foundations for good relations. Of practical value are illustrated sections on the press; speakers' bureaus; radio; television; motion pictures; pamphlets, folders, and mailings; institutional advertising; complaints and protests about defamatory material; contests and awards; and reports of successful measures in various towns and cities.

American National Theatre and Academy, Department of Community and Industrial Showmanship, ANTA Playhouse, 245 West 52nd St., New York 19, N. Y. Offers help in staging community celebrations, industrial expositions, conventions, and other events in which publicity is important.

Association for the Study of Community Organization, Room 810, One Park Ave., New York 16, N. Y. Information about organizing and carrying out public relations programs for community organizations.

Association of Junior Leagues of America, Inc., Waldorf-Astoria Hotel, New York 22, N. Y. Publishes inexpensive pamphlet material on press, radio, and television relations.

Goetz, Rachel Marshall, *Visual Aids for the Public Service*, 1954. Public Administration Service, 1313 East 60th St., Chicago 37, Ill. Written primarily for citizens interested in local government affairs, book has ideas generally applicable to organization publicity problems. Covers broad problem of communication, and such practical matters as poster design, lettering, use of feltboard and other devices, making charts and graphs, deciding upon a method of reproduction, and choosing and presenting films.

Hodapp, William, *The Television Manual*, New York: Farrar, Straus and Young, 1953. A practical guide to production and programming.

Keith, John P., *Public Relations Program for a Citizens Committee*, Austin, Texas: The University of Texas, Bureau of Municipal Research, 1950.

League of Women Voters of the United States, 1026 17th St., N. W., Washington 6, D. C. Has pamphlet material on public relations, and on publicity through newspapers, radio, television, and other media.

Lundborg, Louis B., *Public Relations in the Local Community*, New York: Harper & Brothers, 1950.

National Association of Radio and Television Broadcasters, 1771 N St., N. W., Washington 6, D. C. Free material on radio programs in the public service.

National Broadcasting Company, Department of Information, RCA Building, Radio City, New York 20, N. Y. Has bibliographies of radio and television pamphlets and books.

National Publicity Council for Health and Welfare Services, 257 Fourth

Ave., New York 10, N. Y. Offers a series of "how-to-do-it" pamphlets on publicity and public relations techniques. Representative titles include *Bulletins—How to Make Them More Effective, Exhibits—How to Plan and Make Them, Guide to Illustrations, How to Make a Speech and Enjoy It, Working with Newspapers, Writing the Case Story.* Especially useful is *Publicity Directory,* which lists and describes about 200 selected pamphlets and books on publicity techniques, and sources of films and other materials and services—much of which is free. New titles are frequently added. Information available.

National School Public Relations Association, 1201 16th St., N. W., Washington 6, D. C. A department of the National Education Association. *Print It Right,* a 48-page illustrated manual about how to plan, write, and design school public relations materials, includes ideas and information useful to community organizations.

New York State School of Industrial and Labor Relations, Cornell University, Ithaca, N. Y. Materials available include pamphlets about how to evaluate news, use photographs, write speeches, prepare announcements, and perform other publicity jobs.

Office of Education, Department of Health, Education, and Welfare, Washington 25, D. C. Pamphlets on radio and television workshops and forums, and catalogues of free loan radio scripts and transcriptions, and television kinescopes.

Sterling Films, 205 East 43rd St., New York 17, N. Y. *Basic Motion Picture Technique.* How to shoot a film. A pamphlet useful for a group planning a publicity or public relations campaign using films of organization activities.

Superintendent of Documents, United States Government Printing Office, Washington 25, D. C. *Educational Exhibits—How to Prepare and Use Them,* a Department of Agriculture pamphlet.

United States Department of Agriculture, Office of Information, Washington 25, D. C. Free booklet *Television Report—Section III—Program Methods* is a step-by-step guide for the preparation of a television program.

Some Sources of Films and Film Information

British Information Services, 30 Rockefeller Plaza, New York 20, N. Y. Rental films include *Does It Matter What You Think?* Illustrates how public opinion is formed. Discusses mass media such as newspapers, and the importance of word-of-mouth communication. Description available.

Chamber of Commerce of the United States, 1615 H St., N. W., Washington 6, D. C. Sponsored low rental films include *Public Opinion*, an 11-minute analysis of what public opinion is, how it is formed, and what it can accomplish. Description available.

Coronet Films, Coronet Building, Chicago 1, Ill. Films include *Public Opinion in Our Democracy*, a demonstration of how public opinion about an important community issue is formed. Description available.

Curran, Charles W., *The Handbook of TV and Film Techniques*, New York: Farrar, Straus and Young, Inc., 1953. A manual for amateurs. Chapter headings include "What Kind of Film Do You Need?", "Color or Black-and-White," "Selecting the Film Producer," "Some Hazards of Film Production," "Some Do's and Don'ts of Film Making," and "What Should a Picture Cost?"

Encyclopaedia Britannica Films, Inc., 1150 Wilmette Ave., Wilmette, Ill. Rental films include *Newspaper Story*—how a paper gets, prints, and distributes its news. Description available.

Film Images, Inc., 18 East 60th St., New York 22, N. Y. Free loan films include *Telling the Story*, an explanation of how the Economic Cooperation Administration handles its public relations problems in Austria. Demonstrations of the use of newspapers, the radio, films, special displays, fairs, posters, and contests suggest many publicity ideas adaptable to American community situations. Description available.

General Mills, Inc., Film Library, 400 Second Avenue, South, Minneapolis 1, Minn. Free loan films for community-group use include *The Year's Work*, the story of a fiscal year in General Mills told through animated cartoons and straight photography. Suggests ways by which an organization can tell its story to its members or the public through a film. Description available.

Modern Talking Picture Service, 45 Rockefeller Plaza, New York 20, N. Y. Free loan films include *On the Air*, a 20-minute explanation of the planning and presentation of a radio show. Includes script writing, rehearsing, timing, and transmission. Description available.

National Film Board of Canada, 1270 Avenue of the Americas, New York 20, N. Y. Low rental films include *Home Town Paper*, the story of a Canadian small-town weekly and its service to the community. May give your public relations committee and members a better appreciation of your newspaper, and suggest how your organization may use it as a medium for improved community relations. Description available.

New York *Daily News*, 220 East 42nd St., New York 17, N. Y. Free-loan films describing the activities of the editorial staff of the New York *Daily News*, including editors, columnists, feature writers, and reporters. Descriptions available.

Ohio State University, Bureau of Public Relations, Columbus 10, Ohio. Free loan films include *Police Reporter*, an explanation of reporting techniques. Useful in giving a public relations or publicity committee some understanding of news-coverage procedures. Description available.

University of California, University Extension, Educational Films Sales Department, Los Angeles 24, Calif. Rental film *Four Ways to Drama* illustrates the special techniques of four media: stage, radio, television, and motion pictures. Helpful in determining the most effective medium for your organization's skits and other publicity projects. Description available.

PART II

The Service Program

CHAPTER 5

Organizing for Service

WHILE THERE is no formula for action applicable to all situations, volunteer group experience suggests some approaches to problems that are common to most service programs. This chapter offers answers to questions such as these: What kind of projects are usually successful? Who is to be responsible for initiating and planning them? Where can we find ideas? How can group acceptance of a project be secured? What committee organization and procedure have usually been effective?

CHARACTERISTICS OF SUCCESSFUL ACTIVITIES

Successful activities, while varying widely in kind and scope, have certain characteristics in common:

1. They are based on the needs of the community and the interests of members.
2. They contribute to the organization's basic purposes.
3. They are planned and operated with regard for other areas of community living.
4. They are properly integrated with the interests and activities of other organizations.
5. They are undertaken only after a careful consideration of personnel, financial, and other resources.
6. They have results commensurate with the cost to the membership and the community in money, time, and energy.

DETERMINING RESPONSIBILITY

Responsibility for service activities should be definitely fixed. In many organizations the board of directors is chiefly responsible for a program. In others, officers, working with committee heads, and guided in policy by the directors, perform this function. In some groups, the officers may represent the only effective leadership for such activities.

87

A PROJECTS COMMITTEE. Finding project ideas, and their correlation into an over-all program may be the tasks of a projects committee. Its work may be completed with the acceptance of the program by the membership, or, responsive to changing membership and community interests and needs, this committee may be a standing one to suggest additional activities or changes throughout the year. Its responsibilities may also include an appraisal of the year's program, and a report to the board and membership. The job of detailed planning, organizing, and implementing activities usually is left to special and standing committees.

Sometimes the standing committee charged with scheduling programs for meetings also initiates service activities. Working committees then develop and carry out the projects.

STANDING SERVICE COMMITTEES. Some organizations have a rather precise national and local departmentalizing of service activities, corresponding to the fields of community living in which their interests lie. In each department a standing committee plans and administers projects under the general direction of the officers and directors. In some cases, a vice-president in charge of external affairs coordinates the work of these committees. All, of course, are finally responsible to the membership for progress and results.

This arrangement has certain outstanding advantages. A continuing program in a particular field develops committee members who become specialists, equipped to recognize and evaluate needs and to meet them with timely, well-chosen, and carefully planned projects. The semipermanent nature of the committee personnel encourages good relations with private and official agencies in the field.

THE MEMBERSHIP. A project idea may be introduced as part of a meeting agenda, or it may be presented by a member as new business. The idea is evaluated, and procedure is discussed. It may then be referred to a standing or special committee for further investigation or for action.

When the whole group is included in choosing a service project, there is a general feeling of responsibility for its success, and the support of a majority of the members is assured.

PLANNING THE SERVICE PROGRAM

How desirable is a detailed activity plan for the year? What advantages are there in an opportunistic approach to community service?

Some projects may originate in almost spontaneous fashion, because of a generally recognized need. Assured of membership and public support, they are given an impetus that projects planned far in advance may not have. Time and energy may be utilized to bring immediate results. Greater freedom to meet changing community needs, membership interest, or emergency situations is possible. There is assurance that resources are being applied to real needs.

The advantages of the opportunistic approach, however, should be weighed against serious disadvantages. Project committees may act without adequate information or a full understanding of local situations. Unknowingly, they may be duplicating the efforts of other groups. Projects may be approved as the result of a passive or uncritical acceptance of ideas forcefully presented. The over-all program may lack balance or variety.

A long-term plan helps achieve a more complete coverage of needs; and balance, variety, proper emphases, and correlation not only of service activities but of meeting and community programs. Long-range service objectives also provide a challenge, with the major interests of members finding an outlet in service activity. Such a blueprint for service is of value in membership recruitment, and in public relations and publicity measures.

In adopting a long-term plan, guard against making it so inflexible that opportunities for timely or emergency service may be missed.

Experience suggests a middle course between the extremes of a rigid adherence to a detailed, tightly scheduled, year-round program and one that consists of several projects, each adopted only as a particular need becomes apparent or a special interest is shown.

FINDING PROJECT IDEAS

Those responsible for service activities might explore sources such as the following for project ideas:

1. The chapters of this book that suggest programs and projects to meet typical needs in each major area of community living, and list sources of activity ideas, materials, and program guides.

2. Regional, state, and national conferences, conventions, and institutes; and intergroup meetings about common community problems.

3. National organization publications.

4. A poll of membership interest and opinion.

5. The record of successful projects of other years.

6. Reports of committees that suggest action in related or other fields.

7. Newspaper stories, articles, and editorials revealing community needs.

8. Interviews with heads of municipal departments, editors, educators, clergymen, and other community leaders.

9. Reports of official and quasi-official municipal boards and commissions.

10. Studies of community needs made by official and private agencies.

11. An objective survey of community needs undertaken by the organization itself.

12. The returns from a Community Suggestion Box campaign conducted in cooperation with a newspaper, or a radio or television station.

13. An essay contest on better community living, arranged in cooperation with the schools.

THE FORMAL SURVEY. A survey may be an important project in community education—calling public and official attention to vital needs. The following suggestions may be helpful in planning and conducting such a project:

1. Study the methods and results of similar surveys.

2. Present a list of questions to community leaders to determine whether or not the survey is practical or desirable.

3. Test out the questionnaire form on a few of those for whom it is designed. Does everyone have the same understanding of each question? Does the wording avoid suggesting specific answers?

4. Adopt a standard interview procedure for workers, including a statement of purpose, the extent to which incidental remarks should be recorded, and the length of time to be devoted to each interview. Hold demonstration interviews.

5. Utilize the full membership as interviewers and consider the advisability of enlisting the aid of other groups in house-to-house canvassing.

When opinions, attitudes, or other intangibles are to be ascertained, the services of a research expert from a research bureau, a public or private social service agency, or a university may be invaluable in determining the most effective study methods and sampling procedures, and in helping with the statistical treatment of data and the interpretation of results.

USE OF SCORE SHEETS. Community needs in general or in a particular area may be measured through the use of a score sheet.

This method calls for the assumption of standards in education, recreation, health, or other fields. It then provides for a comparison of your community's facilities, services, and personnel with what is considered to be standard or desirable. Score sheets and suggestions for their use are available from government and private agencies and associations. Your group may want to make up its own score sheet, determining good practice or achievement through a study of neighboring communities.

SECURING ACCEPTANCE OF A PROJECT IDEA

A good project idea often fails to reach the action stage because its originators fail to gather and organize essential information, or to present it effectively to the board of directors or the membership.

Obtain the facts that establish the need, and details that dramatize the situation. Write out your idea in simple, direct language. Subject it to professional or expert criticism. For example, consult your health officer about project ideas in his field; the superintendent of schools about activities in education. Study the results of similar projects in your own or other communities. Explore alternate courses, anticipate the probable consequences of each, and compare their advantages and disadvantages. Anticipate also any obstacles to a clear understanding of the idea, as well as objections. Weaknesses in the idea, and possibly the source and kind of opposition that can be expected, may be discovered through informal discussion with officers and key members.

Members should be given an opportunity to modify or influence the development of project ideas as well as to participate in carrying them out. Include project discussion as part of the agenda of membership meetings.

Full discussion helps to reconcile important conflicts of interest and opinion that might jeopardize the success of a project. Members especially interested in community activities become known to officers and committee chairmen. Resources and talent, useful in carrying out special programs, are discovered. Other committees may receive valuable procedure suggestions. All committees may be given a better idea of the relation of their work to the proposed project. Members are more likely to volunteer as workers when the activity is fully explained.

IMPLEMENTING THE PROJECT IDEA

Usually a project is planned and carried out by one committee. Frequently, however, the activity is of such scope as to necessitate a division of work and responsibility, with a large committee organized into several subcommittees. A special executive, steering, or co-ordinating committee may choose and direct several working committees. In some situations, standing committees such as publicity and finance may contribute to the planning and operation of a special project.

In forming committees, care should be taken to distribute the work as evenly as possible, to utilize the special talents of members, and to cooperate with the membership committee in providing opportunity for new members to participate.

FACILITATING COMMITTEE ACTION. Drawing up a schedule of committee meetings, each with a definite purpose, divides the committee's project into manageable parts, offers a series of immediately attainable objectives, and furnishes a timetable by which progress can be measured.

Meetings are devoted to orienting members, identifying problems and agreeing upon solutions, making individual assignments, reporting progress, and evaluating results. To keep the number of meetings to a minimum, much routine business, such as giving information, checking individual performances, discussing procedure detail, or reporting progress may be handled through informal telephone or other conferences between the chairman and members.

Progress often depends on the thoroughness of preparation for meetings. The chairman should draw up an agenda in consultation with key committeemen, securing the approval of other members when possible. An agenda might include discussion of a series of possible solutions to a problem identified at a previous meeting, immediately bringing into focus chief differences of opinion.

Other measures to facilitate committee action include the following:

1. Giving members an adequate understanding of the reason for the project, and the general organization of personnel and other resources to carry it out; making clear the particular committee's role, with an emphasis on its limitations and its relations to other committees engaged in the project. Often desirable is a direct statement from the president defining the committee's duties.

2. Guarding against the substitution of lengthy discussion and deliberation for action.

3. Including all committeemen in assignments.

4. Maintaining an assignment sheet with the name of the person given the job, his telephone number, a precise statement of what is expected of him, and the dates for progress and completion reports.

5. Keeping the chairman free of responsibility for details, to permit time for adequate supervision.

6. Making an accurate record of committee meeting activities and members' progress reports, and securing approval of reports that are to be presented at organization meetings.

Carrying out most projects described in various chapters of this book involves the following important considerations: timing, gathering information, choosing specific goals, promotion, direction, and provision for change.

TIMING. Knowing when an objective can be realized and when action should be postponed is important. Is the community aware of the need? Is a preliminary program of education to develop this awareness practicable? Something of a dilemma confronts the group that, convinced of the need for action, is faced with an unreceptive public. Premature action means failure. A "wait it out" stand invites the criticism of members and community leaders who may have a knowledge and appreciation that the public has not acquired. Their support may be transferred to other groups. Do not abandon sound project ideas; include them in long-range public education plans. If it desires to retain its position of leadership, however, your organization may have to take a calculated risk to meet an important community need by initiating quick project action.

In planning projects such as entertainment or sports events, or a campaign for members or contributions, choose a date free of competing community activities. Ask the local newspaper editor about scheduled sports and social events, public meetings, and other occasions that might affect interest in the proposed project. Check with other active groups.

Consider seasonal interests. For example, a project in community beautification is usually more effective in the spring. Many projects may be timed to take advantage of the national promotion of holidays and other special days, weeks, and months.

Time allowances for preparation must be carefully estimated. The planning and organizing of many school projects, for example, are often completed in June so that action can be taken in September. Other projects require considerable time for collection of material, or training and organization of workers.

A calendar for the completion of various steps leading to the opening of the project on "D Day" will impress leaders and workers with the necessity for adhering to a careful schedule. "D-60," for example, might be the date for presenting the project idea to the membership; "D-50," the deadline for completion of a schedule of individual assignments; and "D-10," the date for launching a series of news releases and radio and television spot announcements.

GATHERING INFORMATION. Do not proceed with a project until all information has been gathered. Premature action may jeopardize the project's success.

Considerable information gathering should have taken place before the idea was proposed. In some cases much of the necessary information may have been secured. In others, it would not have been practical or desirable for the sponsors of the idea to have taken such measures without official sanction. Failure of a project idea to materialize after an intensive fact-finding operation would affect not only the morale of the members directly involved, but the organization's relations with those in the community who were needlessly imposed upon for information.

CHOOSING SPECIFIC GOALS. Your members should have a feeling of achievement within a reasonably short time. If the project has a long-range objective, perhaps it can be broken down into intermediate goals. A youth activities program, for example, may be a year-round effort, with a series of goals such as organization of a hobby group, introduction of a film program, and furnishing sports equipment. When a program or an elaborate project is divided into relatively simple and short-term steps, success in one develops the confidence that is needed for the next step, or for a more ambitious undertaking.

Objectives should be those that your members think important, even though they may not be given priority ratings by experts or others in the community. This is not to disparage other opinions, but rather to emphasize the importance of membership conviction and interest.

DIRECTING THE ACTIVITY. Successful project administration depends both on wise delegation of responsibility and concentration of over-all supervision in the hands of one or a few able individuals.

The project chairman should be free of routine duties in order to be able to anticipate or recognize trouble spots and take action to avoid or overcome them; fill key personnel positions if vacated through illness, the pressure of private business, or absence from the community; and evaluate progress and results. He must time the various moves, restrain the impulsive action of one individual or group, or spur another to greater activity.

Community and organization situations do not remain static. Project leaders should be sensitive to changes in needs and interests. They must be prepared to modify plans or change the direction of action. Unexpected obstacles may present themselves. Goals set may prove impractical. Frequently the actual working out of a project reveals new possibilities of achievement. Related projects that may be incorporated into a program may suggest themselves.

While changes in plans or even in objectives may be expected, it is important that all workers have a part in the consideration of as many of them as possible. Some changes may be forced on committee heads without an opportunity for consultation with members. They should be notified as soon as possible and be given an explanation of the situation.

USING THE SOURCES OF AID SECTIONS OF THIS BOOK. A tremendously important factor in the success of any group effort for better community living is the full use of the advisory and material help available from sources such as those described at the close of each chapter.

Government agencies, national associations, foundations, universities, corporations, labor unions, and others have a direct interest in community betterment. The volume of their aid is so great, its kind so varied, and its scope so wide, that only a study of the Sources of Aid sections themselves can give an adequate idea of its usefulness.

For example, over 50,000 federal government publications, most of which are nominally priced, are available from the Superintendent of Documents, United States Government Printing Office. Free material and advisory and field consultant services are offered directly by many federal agencies. Most state government departments and commissions in areas such as education, health, conservation, and the development of resources have free materials for local programs.

The great national associations in fields such as health, safety, and welfare depend upon groups in communities to implement their programs. They make available research conclusions, planning guides, background materials, and public education aids prepared by their professional staffs.

Corporations are directly concerned with community betterment in many fields, and place vast resources, usually without charge, at the disposal of local groups. Insurance companies, for example, in enlightened self-interest, have prepared excellent free program guides, study and discussion pamphlets, and public education materials for volunteer groups.

Preparation either for an occasional project or for a continuing or extensive program of community service should include an exploration of what these groups have to offer.

The following is intended to be only illustrative of help available: research conclusions in fields such as health, welfare, and safety; background information; study and discussion guides and materials; suggestions for discussion leaders and meeting chairmen; formal course outlines for leadership training; bibliographies; films, slides, charts, and demonstration materials; how-to-do-it manuals; descriptions of pilot programs; lecturers and discussion leaders; information and materials for public education programs; information about procedures for sponsoring youth groups; planning and directional help for community celebrations; and ideas for developing and maintaining good public relations.

MOTION PICTURES AND SERVICE PROGRAMS. The motion picture is of inestimable value in carrying out service programs. In almost all types of activity it is necessary to give members and the public a background of information if you are to have their interest and support. Often programs have as their sole objective the education of the public to an awareness of needs to be met or desirable standards of community living to be achieved.

Films, too, because of their dramatic appeal, may more effectively persuade individuals to take action than can speakers or the printed word. They may help assure attendance at organization sponsored public events. According to a Film Council of America bulletin, J. Roby Kidd, Canadian adult education leader, determined that 84 per cent of those in attendance at an important series of community meetings on public housing would have stayed home if films had not been announced as part of the program. Shown continuously during a convention, fair, exhibition, or other daylong affair, they are appropriate attractions and provide an opportunity for spectators to rest.

When used to help attain project goals, motion pictures should be chosen carefully. Not all good films in a particular field may be appropriate for your specific purpose. To present a motion picture about soil conservation to a farmer audience fully aware of its importance and techniques, but in need of information about marketing, would not only be a waste of time, but might seriously affect organization-farmer relations.

FOLLOWING UP THE PROJECT

A committee should continue to function after a project has been completed. Activities include newspaper and radio reports of the project's close; acknowledgments of special contributions by members, other individuals, and groups; the preparation of a report to the membership and board of directors; an evaluation of outcomes by committeemen, officers, and directors; and completion of a project scrapbook.

EVALUATING PROJECT OUTCOMES. In addition to tangible outcomes such as needs met or dollars raised for a worthy cause, there are intangible by-products that should be identified and evaluated. Among these are changes in the group's status in the community, an increase in public awareness of the value of cooperative action, heightened membership interest in service, and opportunities for leadership training.

REPORTS OF PROJECT OUTCOMES. As soon as possible after completing a project, your committee should submit a report both to the board and the membership. If the group meets infrequently, reports may be mailed to individual members. When complete information is not immediately available, a preliminary report might include attendance figures, profits if any, the number of members engaged in the project, and the number of man-hours expended.

In addition to evaluations of separate projects, the effectiveness of your group may be increased through frequent appraisals of the program as a whole. What evidence is there that persisting needs are being met through your activities? Are projects properly related? Are they contributing to other important organization purposes, such as fellowship or the leadership training of members? Are they satisfying the interests of members?

The board of directors or the projects planning committee, in finding answers to such questions, may consult informally with officers, committee chairmen, active members, and other individuals in the community, study written project reports, discuss projects at meetings, or have members fill out questionnaires.

MEMBERSHIP QUESTIONNAIRE. A poll of membership opinion, especially at the close of an administration, may have a dual purpose: to evaluate the program, and to secure information useful in planning the next year's activities.

Assuming that adequate project information has been made available, a questionnaire divided into as many sections as there are major areas of service is practical. Preface each section with a concise statement of your organization's aims in the field, followed by a brief description of specific activities carried out. Ask members to rate individual projects in terms of "excellent," "adequate," "poor," or "no opinion," and to appraise the program as a whole. Provide a space in which members may make more extended personal comment, such as suggestions for changes in policy or procedure, or for additional activities.

Keep the form short and simply organized. Experience has demonstrated that complex questionnaires, or those that require lengthy explanations, usually fail in their purposes.

RECOGNITION OF PROJECT ACHIEVEMENT. Recognition of the achievement of project groups is important. Such recognition may be given by featuring service committees in local news releases and in the organization's bulletin; by citing formally, through the board of directors, outstanding committees; by making scrapbooks available as evidence of achievement; by presenting awards to outstanding committees; and by encouraging the entering of projects in inter-organization projects competition.

THE PROJECT SCRAPBOOK. A scrapbook that traces the project's progress from the inception of the idea to the final report is of great value. It supplies information necessary for entering the project in regional, state, or national competition; is an effective form of membership recognition; assists those planning for the following year; suggests procedures for other projects; helps in evaluating the year's program as a whole; serves as documentary evidence of the organization's community role, useful in membership procurement and public relations; and becomes an important part of organization history.

Such a record usually includes data and other materials used in securing the approval of the project idea, accounts of official meeting action, names of those participating and descriptions of their contributions, newspaper clippings, testimonials, photographs of individuals and events, and souvenir programs.

Responsibility for a scrapbook may be placed upon the standing publicity committee, or upon a special committee. Its completeness and interest depend largely on the extent to which all workers supply information and ideas.

FILMING ORGANIZATION ACTIVITIES. Your organization might film its activities, using such motion pictures as project reports at local, regional, state, or national meetings, conferences or conventions; as an annual report; as a method of acquainting the community with the group's achievements; or as an aid in procuring new members. Recent developments have appreciably lowered the cost of amateur sound film production, making such an activity an inexpensive and practical project.

COOPERATION WITH OTHER COMMUNITY GROUPS

Cooperative action can hardly be avoided by groups with active programs. Many projects cannot be undertaken with the personnel and financial resources of one organization alone. Others require the cooperation of a municipal body such as a board of health, board of education, or a park commission. Some involve activities that overlap or touch on areas that lie within the interests of other organizations. Many projects become official or traditional community celebrations, in which it is appropriate to have the participation of representative groups.

Indiscriminate intergroup participation, however, may be harmful to the best interests of an organization. Before committing itself, a group should subject such projects or programs to the same evaluation procedure used in determining its own activities; and, most important, should stand ready to share the responsibility for the outcome of the activities it endorses.

Arrangements for planning, organizing, and directing a cooperative project, and the kind and degree of participation and responsibility by each organization vary as widely as the projects themselves. The formation of an intergroup committee, with an equal sharing of work and responsibility by all major community groups, represents the logical development of cooperation in broad service programs, or in particular fields such as health, education, and recreation. Extended to include representatives of official and private agencies, and citizens at large, such cooperation is often given a permanent council structure.

A council usually consists of representatives of all major interests organized on a permanent basis to work for a common purpose. Some councils are concerned only with determining needs to be met by appropriate agencies or organizations. Some serve as coordinating agencies. Others carry out programs with the help of cooperating groups. Important contributions to the solution of broad area problems are being made by such organizations.

Representation on such councils has definite advantages. A council provides a clearinghouse for service ideas, relates the needs of various service areas, and helps avoid wasteful overlapping and duplication. It makes possible volunteer planning and action for the whole community, assures community-wide support for projects assigned the organization, and provides a means of securing help in projects that are beyond the individual group's resources. It is an important medium through which good public relations may be developed and maintained.

SOURCES OF AID

The national headquarters of many federated community organizations have activity suggestions for local units. Valuable assistance in organizing for volunteer group action is available from many universities and colleges, which offer background material, project ideas, program guides, and correspondence and field consultation services. Each chapter of Part II of this book includes project and program development suggestions and sources of aid in its field. Other representative sources are the following:

American City Magazine Corporation, 470 Fourth Ave., New York 16, N. Y. Publishes *The American City*, a monthly. News reports and articles about community programs suggest activity ideas in fields such as government, civil defense, education, housing, recreation, public health, and safety.

American National Theatre and Academy, Department of Community and Industrial Showmanship, ANTA Playhouse, 245 West 52nd St.,

New York 19, N. Y. Offers theatrical and technical help, including personnel, for community events such as festivals, anniversaries, expositions, and conventions.

Association for the Study of Community Organization, Room 810, One Park Ave., New York 16, N. Y. A membership organization "to promote better understanding of the processes of community organization. . . ." Affiliated with the National Conference of Social Work. Helps organize and develop local discussion groups, and cooperates with individuals interested in community organization. Publishes a quarterly *Checklist of Current Publications on Community Organizations*, and a *Newsletter*. Full description of materials and services available.

Association of Community Councils, 519 Smithfield St., Pittsburgh, Pa. Has a pamphlet guide to the organization of urban community councils.

Bureau of Educational Research, Ohio State University, Columbus, Ohio. Information on how to draw up and administer a survey questionnaire.

Chamber of Commerce of the United States, 1615 H St., N. W., Washington 6, D. C. A major source of information, program ideas, and manuals. Local chambers cooperate with other community organizations, and are important sources of information about community needs and how they can be met through volunteer group action.

Community Adult Education, School of Education, University of Michigan, Ann Arbor, Mich. Offers information, advice, and pamphlet help to groups interested in community service activities.

Community Service, Inc., Yellow Springs, Ohio. A nonprofit membership organization to provide information and other services for small communities. Has available research reports on methods of developing a balanced economy in communities; and correspondence courses, speakers, and project reports and ideas. Publications of interest to project committees include *Directory of National Organizations of Service to Community Leaders*, a listing of over 200 groups classified under such titles as "Government" and "Health"; and *Community Service News*, a bimonthly bulletin. List of publications is available.

Community Services Committee of National C.I.O., 1776 Broadway, New York 23, N. Y. Has information about the union's responsibility in community affairs, and program outlines in fields such as disaster relief, civil defense, health, and foreign relief.

Coordinating Committee of Local Community Councils, Social Planning

Council, 505 North 7th St., St. Louis 1, Mo. Has available a guide to the establishment of local community councils. Pamphlet includes a description of types of community councils, what they are doing, and how they are started; a specimen organization chart, some basic principles for council action, and suggestions for meetings; a discussion of the development of local leaders; minimum standards for councils; and a model constitution and bylaws.

Countrywomen's League, *The Country Gentleman*, Independence Square, Philadelphia 5, Pa. Inexpensive pamphlets include many descriptive of project planning and direction procedures.

League of Women Voters of the United States, 1026 17th St., N. W., Washington 6, D. C. Pamphlets suggest procedures for determining community needs.

New York State Citizens Council, 613 East Genesee St., Syracuse, N. Y. Has information about organized volunteer action in many New York towns and cities.

Sanders, Irwin T., *Making Good Communities Better*, Lexington: University of Kentucky Press, 1950. Presents "guideposts" for community workers and group leaders by 17 authorities. Representative guideposts: "Scoring Your Community," "How to Size Up Changes Taking Place in a Community," and "Pointers in Developing a Community Recreation Program."

San Diego County Coordinating Councils, Board of Directors, 405 Civic Center, San Diego, Calif. Publishes *The Coordinator*, a magazine in the interest of the community council idea.

Stone, Walter L., *Community Welfare Planning and Organization*, Hanover, Ind.: Informal Education Service, 1949. Suggests principles and procedures in organizing for group cooperative action in fields such as health, family living, recreation, and welfare. Includes a selected bibliography.

Superintendent of Documents, United States Government Printing Office, Washington 25, D. C. Pamphlet *The Air Fair, Its Planning and Operation*, published by the Civil Aeronautics Administration, suggests procedures applicable to other community events. *Catalog of Radio Recordings* and *Radio Script Catalog* describe free loan Office of Education transcriptions and radio scripts in the fields of community activity suggested in this book. Possible uses for recordings include local radio station broadcasts and industrial and school public address system presentations in education or special observance programs; meeting features; and group discussion and study material and guides. The more than 1300 annotated radio scripts are suitable for adaptation by amateur groups for meeting, radio, or public address system presentation. Script subject classification includes American democracy at work, atomic energy, education, health and nutrition, the American heritage, holidays and special occasions, inter-American affairs, music and art, safety, and conservation. The scripts also provide valuable project background information and material, and are guides for study and discussion groups.

Some Sources of Films and Film Information

Valuable sources of aid in planning and implementing community activities in specific fields are the free loan and low rental films available through sources described at the close of other chapters. Further help is available from the following:

Educational Film Library Association, Inc., 1600 Broadway, New York 19, N. Y. Has available *The Projectionist's Manual, Making Films Work for Your Community*, and other booklets. Offers a motion picture evaluation service.

Sterling Films, 205 East 43rd St., New York 17, N. Y. *Basic Motion Picture Technique*. How to shoot a film. A pamphlet useful for a group planning a motion picture report of a project or an annual report.

Wilson, William H. and Haas, Kenneth B., *The Film Book for Education, Business, and Industry*, New York: Prentice-Hall, Inc., 1950. Includes a discussion of how to use films in the community.

CHAPTER 6

Community Arts

FREEDOM OF enterprise, with its resultant technological progress, permits Americans to enjoy a standard of living and a leisure unparalleled in the history of man. This development has released a tremendous creative force, which finds expression not only in continued material advance, but in the cultural growth of communities.

Organizations are contributing to this growth through activities in music, drama, motion picture appreciation, art, literature, folkways, and other fields.

MUSIC

The appeal of music is universal. Most people, as listeners or participants, can share in its enjoyment. Its recreation value is high. In thousands of communities there is a richer living because of organization programs to foster music appreciation and to encourage participation.

MEMBERSHIP ACTIVITIES. Meeting programs often reveal membership talent that can be used in programs for other groups or the general public. Some organizations have excellent glee clubs, quartets, bands, and orchestras that are scheduled for appearances at public gatherings and on radio and television programs. Events such as minstrels, variety shows, and musical reviews furnish opportunities for participation of local talent in the presentation of regional or American folk music, the best of popular music, and the lighter classics.

Groups that have a tradition of informal singing at meetings are particularly effective in the promotion of such activities at community gatherings. Your committee might plan for informal singing at sponsored public affairs, and influence its inclusion in events in which the organization has a cooperative role. Singing may be stimulated through distribution of copies of songs, introduction of new songs or medleys and other arrangements of old favorites, furnishing a public address system for more effective direction, or presentation of animated song films.

SPECIAL OBSERVANCES. Many special observances such as national patriotic holidays, United Nations Day, Pan American Day, Easter, and Christmas can be fittingly celebrated through song and music. The ancient custom of caroling, for example, is being preserved or revived in over 2000 towns and cities through organization-sponsored programs. In St. Louis, about 50,000 men, women, and children in approximately 3000 groups visit every block in the city and its suburbs to sing carols.

Provide caroling leadership, and support community-wide participation. Publicize the program through radio, television, and the press. Introduce the idea of a uniform carol costume, such as red hooded robes. Stimulate interest and make the event more colorful by staging a costume contest. Consider the advisability of using carolers to raise funds for Christmas charities. The St. Louis Christmas Carol Association each year collects about $25,000 for children's charities in this fashion.

SPONSORED MUSIC GROUPS AND PROFESSIONAL PERFORMANCES. Your organization can become an important patron of music in the community through its sponsorship of amateur music groups and professional performances. In New Haven, Connecticut, the Junior Chamber of Commerce sponsors the annual concert series of that city's symphony orchestra. During one season, over 72,000 attended six performances.

Amateur voice and instrument groups often become community institutions. They are in great demand, and, identified with their sponsoring organizations, have excellent public relations value. Some are self-supporting or a source of revenue through admissions or fees charged for their services.

Music festivals, in which groups such as bands, orchestras, glee clubs, and a cappella choirs participate, have become traditional events, often with community organization support.

Activities in behalf of established programs include urging members to attend, purchasing blocks of tickets for resale or for gifts to students, and aiding in promotion.

In sponsoring performances, try to determine community needs and interests. What programs have proved most successful? What listening opportunities has the community missed? School, church, and other music leaders may have valuable suggestions. A poll of the membership of groups with sponsored performance experience may be useful. National music organizations, such as those listed at the close of this chapter, offer aid in programming.

ACTIVITIES IN BEHALF OF YOUTH GROUPS. Music is recognized as an important influence in the development of character and personality. It provides a ready channel of self-expression and encourages desirable social relations. Participation in group activities helps to train youth in self-discipline and in the attitudes essential for co-operative living. The future of music as an activity in the community depends largely on the adequacy of the education and training young people receive.

Your organization may be especially effective in activities such as the following:

1. Stimulating an interest in music by having individuals and groups perform at meetings; by awarding certificates of achievement with appropriate ceremonies at a school assembly, organization meeting, or public gathering; by contributing a prize to be awarded each year to the graduating student who has made the greatest contribution to music in the school and the community; by establishing a loan or gift scholarship fund for advanced study, or for training at a summer music camp.

2. Introducing music activities as part of the program of youth groups: furnishing direction for informal singing, music games, and stunts; donating copies of songs suitable for meeting, hiking, and campfire use; and forming rhythm bands using homemade instruments.

3. Financing the purchase of instruments, to be paid for and maintained through nominal fees; or presenting instruments as gifts. Providing band uniforms, glee club or choir robes, sheet music, records, playbacks, insignia, and pins.

4. Providing support for public performances of youth groups through membership attendance and the block purchase of tickets. Helping to arrange and finance road tours of outstanding music groups or dramatic musical productions.

5. Arranging for the participation of youth music groups in parades, festivals, special celebrations, and at sports events.

6. Encouraging members of youth groups to attend concerts, recitals, and operatic performances by donating tickets, furnishing transportation, and providing supervision.

7. Contributing to establishment of a music department in the school library to provide music literature and sheet music, and to circulate recordings.

8. Enlisting the aid of amateur and professional musicians to supplement the work of teachers and youth-program directors.

9. Educating the public to an appreciation of the value of music education, and the necessity for well-trained teachers and directors.

OTHER MUSIC PROJECTS. Help establish and support a music department in the public library. Donate or solicit gifts of books, magazines, sheet music, and records to be circulated. Help the library staff secure playbacks equipped with headsets, soundproof listening booths, or a special auditioning room.

Your group can contribute to a better appreciation of music by opening a meeting or study-group appreciation program to others, or by sponsoring formal courses for the general public, in cooperation with the public school adult education department or the extension division of a university or college. Effective in introducing such a project is sponsorship of an outstanding recital or concert, followed by general or selected invitations to attend a discussion of the performance under the direction of a well-known music authority.

Assist local radio and television stations in determining cultural interests and needs, and in finding local talent. Such media make possible a widened listening public, and give individuals and groups a powerful incentive for greater participation.

DRAMA

The development of amateur dramatics has been phenomenal in recent years. Thousands of young and old are having the creative experience of writing, designing, and acting in their own plays. Hundreds of thousands are able to see the best that has been written for the stage.

MEMBERSHIP PRODUCTIONS. A play or a pageant may utilize many of the creative abilities of your members. A successful production uses not only acting and directing talent, but the skills required to plan and build scenery, arrange lighting, design and make costumes, contrive make-up effects, and write and publish an attractive program.

Much of the success of your play will depend on the leadership supplied by the director. Directing talent may be found in established theater groups, on the staffs of the recreation board and youth service agencies, or in the public school English and drama departments. Some groups utilize the services of concerns that furnish scripts, scenery, property, costumes, lighting, and other essentials for a production, as well as professional direction.

In choosing a play for public presentation, keep in mind the limitations of your membership and community actors, the available direction and staging talent, the playhouse, and the audience.

THE COMMUNITY THEATER. Stimulated by such programs as that of the American National Theatre and Academy (ANTA), the community theater has virtually supplanted stock and road-tour companies. Over 1500 well-established groups of amateurs are presenting regularly scheduled productions.

Your group can further this movement. A starting point may be your own drama projects, or the programs of schools, the municipal recreation department, drama clubs, youth service organizations, or churches. Support your community theater by membership participation, by fund-raising campaigns, and by the promotion of ticket sales.

INTERCOMMUNITY THEATRICALS. Intercommunity or regional theatricals have much to contribute to participating organizations and communities. Projects include arranging a road tour of a particularly successful performance, providing for the reciprocal promotion of drama events, exchanging talent, sponsoring neighboring community nights, sharing the expenses of a professional director, holding drama conferences, and promoting a regional theater.

DRAMA FESTIVALS. Public school and private school drama clubs and other groups participate in festivals, in which productions are given ratings for excellence in staging, acting, timing, and make-up. Participation often requires outside assistance. Your group might sponsor such an event, help finance a group's festival trip, or furnish automobile transportation and youth supervision.

A SUMMER THEATER. Summer theaters are important assets, attracting visitors from a wide area, offering an activity to balance other summer recreational and sports programs, and providing career opportunities for young people. Productions with dramatic merit are making important contributions to the cultural growth of communities.

Your organization might sponsor performances of amateur dramatic groups during the summer months, or arrange for a series by a professional company. Quarters may be found in converted barns, warehouses, mills, and obsolete schoolhouses. In some areas, barges and beached boats have become showboat theaters.

DRAMA WORKSHOPS AND FORMAL COURSES. An active community or summer theater presents an opportunity to sponsor a workshop or drama institute in appreciation, play writing, acting, directing, and other phases of play production. Urge that formal courses be made a part of the offerings of the adult education department. Arrange, if possible, for a university extension course in the community.

Conduct play-writing contests to publicize study programs, to stimulate an interest in play writing as a creative activity, to discover and recognize local talent, and to find plays that might be of special interest to community audiences.

DRAMATICS IN YOUTH GROUPS. Drama is an important part of a well-balanced youth activities program. Plan and supervise activities for your sponsored youth groups, and cooperate in popularizing such activities in other groups.

Youth programs typically include pantomimes, skits, stunts, charades, choral speaking, minstrels, musical reviews, and pageants, as well as one-act and full-length plays. When the youth group leadership avoids too great an emphasis on the finished performance, and arranges for a variety of activities, there is wide participation. The possibility for fun and for creative activity is limited only by the ingenuity of members engaged in the direction of the program.

CHILDREN'S THEATER. A children's theater may take many forms, from a series of after-school or Saturday morning dramatic readings to the presentation of plays by professional casts. Through a children's theater, groups seek to develop the child's understanding, taste and judgment, and equip him for active participation in high school and adult theatricals.

Any program of dramatic events for children should be planned and carried out with the cooperation of agencies having a special interest in child development. Consult local schools, youth service centers, churches, the library, and the P.T.A. about the creative needs of children, and methods by which your group may help meet them.

PUPPETRY. Young and old delight in watching puppet shows, in creating puppet plays, making puppets, building theaters, and presenting shows for other groups. Feature a professional or amateur puppet show at a meeting, to introduce the idea of puppetry as a community activity. Ask a local hobbyist to talk about puppets, demonstrating how they are made and manipulated.

A puppet show is effective as entertainment for those confined to hospitals, nursing homes, or similar institutions. It is an appropriate feature for an amateur circus, carnival, bazaar, or card party.

OTHER MEASURES. There are other measures of encouraging community drama. Invite the cast of school and other amateur theatricals to a meeting. Arrange for short previews of coming amateur dramatic productions to promote interest and attendance. Offer to schedule such previews for the meetings of other groups. Consider as a meeting feature the annual presentation of drama awards for outstanding individual and group performances, to be determined by a panel of judges chosen from amateur and professional drama circles and from the staffs of radio and television stations and local newspapers.

MOTION PICTURE APPRECIATION

Motion pictures may make important contributions to the cultural life of the community. They are an effective dramatic medium. They develop an appreciation of painting, literature, drama, music, and other arts. They encourage creative effort, and make clear special techniques.

Motion picture clubs, interested in showing the best of contemporary and classic films, not usually scheduled by local theaters, are active in hundreds of towns and cities. These groups range in size of membership and extent of activity from organizations such as Cinema 16 in New York City with over 4000 enrolled, to neighborhood families sharing the cost of film rentals. They frequently sponsor subscription programs, and serve as film information centers. Some are sponsored by universities and museums, and include the study and discussion of artistic, economic, political, and social problems as related activities.

AN INFORMATION CENTER. While some information about films is usually available from schools, libraries, and dealers, there is a need in many communities for a center where complete information about 16 mm films is readily available. Your organization, having acquired a background of experience in developing your own film program, may be effective in initiating such a service.

COUNCILS. Cooperative action to foster the use and appreciation of motion pictures may lead, as in other fields of public concern, to the

formation of a community council. Such councils are usually affiliated with either or both of the two major national associations: the
Film Council of America and the National Motion Picture Council.
Film councils usually confine their interest to 16 mm films, while
motion picture councils are interested primarily in pictures released
through commercial theater channels.

Represented on local councils are community organizations; commercial theaters, newspapers, radio and television stations; churches;
libraries; high schools, universities, and colleges; little theaters; music
clubs; film clubs; recreation boards, social service and welfare groups;
and photography equipment shops. Many of the major federated
organizations are affiliated with the Film Council of America.

Film Council activities include helping groups to plan meeting
programs; sponsoring youth and adult film clubs; providing a motion-
picture information service; presenting regional or state-wide film
festivals—showings and discussions of important entertainment,
educational, documentary, and experimental films; maintaining a subscription program; and promoting observances of National Audio-
Visual Education Week.

Motion Picture Council activities include choosing "best" pictures
of the year; preparing lists of recommended films with statements of
audience suitability, and securing publication of such lists as a regular
feature in the local newspapers; sponsoring discussion programs; cooperating with local theaters in programming special children's mati-
nees or Saturday morning showings; providing public motion picture
entertainment in communities without commercial theaters; awarding prizes for outstanding student reviews; and publishing a mimeographed *Film News*, a guide to motion pictures scheduled at commercial theaters.

ART

Your organization's promotion of fine arts and crafts might have
its beginnings in a public showing of members' creative efforts. The
showmanship experience gained through such a project might make
practical a community-wide exhibit.

Canvass the area for the oils, water colors, prints, and ceramics of
amateurs. Galleries, museums, art and antique dealers, and individual
collectors often loan art objects for community exhibits. Try to in-

clude the unusual, such as textile painting, glass etching, oils on wood and tin, print tinting, figurine painting, and stenciling.

Help preserve the crafts of your area, an important part of the cultural heritage. Sponsor an exhibit of the work of community craftsmen, or of craft articles from local shops and homes.

Your group might sponsor an American Art Week festival or arrange for a sidewalk show. Have each major business place feature a picture with a placard furnishing interpretative information. Museums and galleries cooperate with local volunteer groups by providing collections at this time.

In and about your community there may be individuals who own collections of rare paintings or other works of art. Your organization would be performing a valuable service in arranging for the public to view them. Sponsor a Community Arts at Home Day, featuring a conducted arts pilgrimage.

The current trend toward a greater utilization of community resources in the education of youth makes welcome such projects as circulating collections of inexpensive prints; presenting illustrated talks to classes and youth meetings; conducting essay contests in which young people defend their choices of "best" pictures; sponsoring art clubs with the help of local artists; furnishing supervision for trips to museum and art galleries, and for sketching picnics; offering graduation prizes to the boy or girl who has contributed most to the art of his school and community; and establishing an art scholarship fund. Many groups encourage the development of creative talent by displaying student-designed posters in connection with their service projects, offering awards for the most original or the most artistic.

LITERATURE

Literature can be said to be the chief instrument for preserving all our cultural heritage. Without the written record of what man has thought and felt, without the penetrating insights into modern living that the best of contemporary writers give us, much of life would lose its meaning.

Many groups see a grave threat to our cultural heritage in the increasing number of "comic" magazines and books of questionable content and literary quality, and in the popularity of motion pictures and radio and television plays that feature the merely sensational or shallow stereotypes.

Among activities to help raise the level of community appreciation are the following:

1. Sponsoring lectures by authors and critics.
2. Organizing a book club among members.
3. Sponsoring book-review and creative-writing classes in cooperation with the high school English and the adult education departments; encouraging the publication of a school literary magazine; and arranging for the school sale of pocket editions of good books.
4. Making collections of suitable books available in the meeting places of youth groups, and at churches, hospitals, and institutions.
5. Promoting the observance of Children's Book Week, through story-telling, book-jacket and book-review contests, and the distribution of posters.
6. Promoting the local showing of exceptionally good film adaptations of novels of literary merit.
7. Supporting the establishment of library branches or deposit stations, and bookmobile service; promoting a centralized library in an area of small communities.
8. Organizing a citizens advisory committee to support library activities.
9. Cooperating with other groups in helping newsdealers keep their shelves free of objectionable reading matter.

FOLKWAYS

A folk festival that tells the story of the region and its people strengthens a community's pride in its environment, and preserves its traditions and customs. Featured may be folk singing and dancing, an old-fashioned fiddlers' contest, a "singin' school" of grandmother's time, and an exhibition of handicrafts presented by citizens in the costume of the past or of the lands of their origin. A folk dance festival, staged in an outdoor theater, a park, or a stadium, is a colorful spectacle which provides participation for hundreds and brings many diverse groups together. It may establish your community as a cultural center.

A project which dramatically presents the wide range of community opportunities for cultural growth is an all-arts festival. In Plainfield, New Jersey, many citizen groups participated in an all-day Community Arts Festival, sponsored by the Recreation Commission and held in the public park.

Featured were exhibits of local arts and crafts, and performances of modern and folk dancing, music, and puppet shows. Community artists demonstrated fine arts techniques and craft skills in metal, leather, wood, and clay. Puppeteers showed how their characters were created and plays produced.

A printed program, with a map showing the location of booths, and a schedule of events, helped draw a large attendance.

MUSEUM ACTIVITIES

Museums have become more than mere repositories for objects of art or of historical interest. They are centers for music, drama, art, crafts, and other cultural activities. Your group might acquaint the community with the programs, facilities, and services of its museum; sponsor fund-raising drives for the establishment, maintenance, and expansion of museums and the carrying out of field trips; aid in collecting articles and materials for exhibits, especially those that can be related to the community; help develop a children's department featuring objects and programs on appropriate age levels; and restore and maintain monuments and buildings of cultural or historic interest.

SOURCES OF AID

GENERAL

Bureau of Educational Research, Ohio State University, Columbus, Ohio. Sponsors an annual Institute for Education by Radio-Television for representatives of radio stations and networks, television stations, schools, colleges, advertising agencies, and community organizations. Institute's purpose is to stimulate thinking and discussion about community radio and television, exchange ideas, and plan programs of service to the community. Offers awards to community organizations for outstanding service through radio and television.

Cooperative Recreation Service, Delaware, Ohio. A clearinghouse for ideas, information, and materials useful in cultural programs. Publishes inexpensive pamphlets on crafts, folk songs, dances, and plays.

Country Gentleman, Service Department, Independence Square, Philadelphia 5, Pa. Offers numerous leaflets useful in organizing and directing activities in the fields of art, crafts, drama, and music. Maintains a play loan library. Helps community organizations find plays appropriate for particular occasions or purposes. Supplies bibliography of other low-cost community-arts program materials.

Junior Programs, Inc., 45 West 57th St., New York 20, N. Y. A nonprofit organization. Arranges production of plays, operas, ballets, and concerts for young people at nominal admission rates. Has available recordings of several operas.

National Council of Teachers of English, 211 West 68th St., Chicago 21, Ill. A free catalogue of recordings of drama, poetry, and other subjects suggested in this chapter.

National Jewish Welfare Board, Program Section, 145 East 32nd St., New York 16, N. Y. *Jewish Center Program Aids*, a monthly publication, suggests project ideas adaptable to many organization and community situations.

National Recreation Association, Correspondence and Consultation Bureau, 315 Fourth Ave., New York 10, N. Y. Offers many inexpensive information and how-to-do-it pamphlets. Representative titles: *Arts and Crafts for the Recreation Leader; Craft Projects That Can Be Made with Inexpensive and Discarded Materials; Simple Puppetry; How to Produce a Play; Informal Dramatics; Inexpensive Costumes for Plays, Festivals, and Pageants; Planning and Producing a Pageant; Community and Assembly Singing;* and *Forty Approaches to Informal Singing.*

Recording Laboratory, Division of Music, Library of Congress, Washington 25, D. C. Offers a catalogue describing some of the 10,000 master recordings of over 40,000 songs and ballads, fiddle tunes, banjo and other American folk music, and readings by contemporary poets. Recordings available at nominal cost.

Superintendent of Documents, United States Government Printing Office, Washington 25, D. C. Pamphlet and booklet aid includes the following: *Planning Recreation for Rural Home and Community,* suggesting practical ideas for sponsored youth group activities in art, handicrafts, music, dancing, and drama; *Workshops of Wonder,* describing children's museum programs in various cities; *Catalog of Radio Recordings* and *Radio Script Catalog,* describing free loan Office of Education radio recordings and radio scripts.

Wells Publishing Company, Leonia, N. J. Has available *Television, A New Community Resource,* published by the Council of National Organizations of the Adult Education Association. Booklet is a report of a television workshop for community organization personnel.

MUSIC

American Music Conference, 332 South Michigan Ave., Chicago 4, Ill. A nonprofit organization to encourage music making and music appreciation in the community. Services available include (1) professional aid in surveying local music needs and facilities; (2) the assistance of field workers in establishing community music councils; (3) the operation of one- or two-day workshops for teachers, church workers, and community organization leaders; (4) furnishing films, pamphlets, posters, and other music promotion and education material. Literature describing services and materials is available. Representative Music Conference free literature: *How to Bring the Important Benefits of Music to Everyone*, a leaflet; *An Experiment in Music for Rural Communities*, a report of a project in Juneau County, Wisconsin; *Suggestions for Organizing a Community Music Workshop*, a manual; and *Manual for Developing a Music Council*.

American Society of Composers, Authors, and Publishers (ASCAP), 575 Madison Ave., New York 22, N. Y. Grants licenses for performances of members' work. Issues free licenses for nonprofit performances of the compositions of its members for charitable, religious, patriotic, and other public service purposes. Explanatory booklet available.

Associated Glee Clubs of America, Inc., East Rochester, N. Y. Promotes choral singing among men and boys through senior and junior clubs. Assists member groups with organization, programming, and publicity.

National Bureau for the Advancement of Music, Inc., 314 4th Ave., New York 10, N. Y. Fosters community interest in music programs. Publishes pamphlets. Offers consultation service.

National Christmas Carol Association, 418 Olive St., St. Louis, Mo. Has suggestions for the organization of carol singing in communities.

National Federation of Music Clubs, 445 West 23rd St., New York 11, N. Y. Sponsors music contests and festivals; assists with the organization and management of choruses, orchestras, bands, and study groups. Has available *Starting and Maintaining a Community Orchestra* and other pamphlets useful for an organization's meeting and service programs.

Office of Education, Department of Health, Education, and Welfare, Washington 25, D. C. Has available a collection of nominally priced recordings suitable for your organization's music education and appreciation program. Included are (1) a series of authentic American folk songs, such as those of cowboys, woodcutters, seamen, and Negroes, recorded on the spot; (2) songs that have come to America from other lands; and (3) many recordings by outstanding orchestras in America and other countries. Especially useful for the organization sponsoring a music festival with a regional theme is the 15-minute documentary *Mountain Festival*, describing the annual festival of music presented by mountain people near Asheville, North Carolina, under the supervision of the Asheville Chamber of Commerce.

University of Illinois, Library School, Urbana, Ill. Free materials include pamphlet suggestions for building and maintaining a music collection.

DRAMA

American Agriculturist, Savings Bank Building, Ithaca, N. Y. *Plays for Rural Groups,* a listing of inexpensive, royalty-free, easy-to-produce plays with a rural or small-town setting.

American Education Theatre Association, Drama Department, University of Texas, Austin, Tex. An association of teachers of speech, play writing, acting, directing, and design. Has available a catalogue of 16 mm free loan and rental films for use in the teaching of dramatics.

American Library Association, 520 North Michigan Ave., Chicago 11, Ill. *Index to Children's Plays;* and *Subject Index to Children's Plays,* 202 collections of plays, under about 800 subject headings.

American National Theatre and Academy (ANTA), 139 West 44th St., New York 18, N. Y. A nonprofit, public service membership organization chartered by the Congress of the United States for the purpose of stimulating interest in the drama and its development. Activities in support of community and regional theater groups include maintaining a clearinghouse of information and ideas; furnishing scripts; sponsoring play contests and play festivals; arranging for veterans counseling and on-the-job training; publicizing drama-group activities; supplying speakers and lecturers; and furnishing theatrical and technical aid for community celebrations, industrial expositions, and other events involving problems of showmanship. Publications include *Blueprint for Summer Theatre,* by Richard Beckhard and John Effrat; a digest of *Pre-Sales Ticket Plan,* by Burton James; *How to Build an Audience,* by A. Carl Messenger; *Children's Theatre Directory;* and a "Package Publicity Service."

Association of Junior Leagues of America, Inc., the Waldorf-Astoria, New York 22, N. Y. Has available *Children's Theatre Catalogue,* which includes an annotated, evaluated list of plays for the theater and puppetry, information about manuscript rental and royalty fees, and a bibliography of books about play writing, acting, costumes, lighting, make-up, and other problems of play producers; and *Arts and Our Town,* a plan for a community cultural survey.

Batchelder, Marjorie H., *Puppet Theater Handbook,* New York: Harper

& Brothers, 1947. Costumes, stages, scenery, lighting, properties, special effects, planning the show, and sources of plays.

Cornberg, Sol and Gebauer, Emanuel L., *A Stage Crew Handbook*, New York: Harper & Brothers, 1941. Information on scenery and lighting presented in question and answer arrangement. Illustrated.

Decca Records, Inc., 50 West 57th St., New York 20, N. Y. Has available an album of records presenting great theatrical moments, produced in cooperation with the American National Theatre and Academy (ANTA). Useful as membership and other group entertainment features, and for stimulating community interest in dramatic activities.

Enterline, Mildred Hahn, *Best Plays for the Church*, Philadelphia: The Christian Education Press, 1947. A 64-page annotated indexed bibliography of drama materials and manuals. Includes procedure suggestions that may be adapted to your program. Representative subject headings: Children's Plays, Patriotic Plays, Rural Life, Plays for Entertainment, Plays for All-Women Casts, Pageants, Costuming, Lighting, and Directing.

Lease, Ruth Gouser and Siks, Geraldine Brain, *Creative Dramatics in Home, School, and Community*, New York: Harper & Brothers, 1952.

National Theatre Conference, Central Office, Western Reserve University, Cleveland, Ohio. Information about the community theater movement. Offers free advisory help to veterans' groups interested in amateur dramatics. *Organizing a Community Theatre*, edited by Samuel Selden, is a series of articles on several aspects of the community theater by members of the Conference. Chapter titles: "The Idea of Community Theatre," "Organizing the Support," "Organizing the Working Groups," "Organizing the Audience," "Good Theatre and Good Business," "Typical Budgets," and "Typical Constitutions and Bylaws."

Players Magazine, P. O. Box 339, Gainesville, Fla. Publishes October through May. Presents ideas, how-to-do-it suggestions, and news reports in the fields of the children's theater, school dramatics, community theater, church theater, puppet theater, and radio and television.

Puppeteers of America, 4846 Tulane Drive, Baton Rouge, La. A membership association interested in encouraging puppetry in the community. Arranges exhibits and demonstrations; conducts workshops in the techniques of puppetry; and offers technical advice. Materials available to member organizations include a bibliography of books on puppetry, information about materials and equipment with the names and addresses of firms supplying them, and a list of free puppet films and their sources.

Other Sources of Catalogues of Drama Materials

D. Appleton-Century Company, 35 West 32nd St., New York 1, N. Y.
A. S. Barnes and Company, 67 West 44th St., New York 18, N. Y.
Walter H. Baker Company, 178 Tremont St., Boston, Mass.
Cooperative Recreation Service, Delaware, Ohio.
T. S. Denison and Company, 225 North Wabash Ave., Chicago 1, Ill.
Dramatic Publishing Company, 59 East Van Buren St., Chicago 5, Ill.
Eldridge Entertainment House, Franklin, Ohio.
Samuel French, 25 West 45th St., New York 19, N. Y.
Penn Play Company, 1617 Latimore St., Philadelphia, Pa.
Dramatists Play Service, 6 East 39th St., New York 16, N. Y.

MOTION PICTURE APPRECIATION

Film Council of America, 600 Davis St., Evanston, Ill. A nonprofit educational organization. Has available a series of low-cost pamphlets useful in initiating and participating in group cooperative film programs. Representative titles: *How to Form a Film Council, How to Obtain and Screen Films for Community Use, How to Conduct a Survey of Community Film Needs and Resources, How to Organize a Community Film Information Center, How to Organize and Conduct Community Film Workshops, How to Conduct a Community Film Forum, How to Evaluate Films for Community Use,* and *How to Organize a Film Festival.* Publishes *The Film Counselor* monthly except July and August. Maintains preview centers in over 50 communities. Information about preview centers and how such a project may serve your community is obtainable from the Film Preview Project Division at the above address.

Motion Picture Association of America, Inc., 28 West 44th St., New York 36, N. Y. Offers *Joint Estimates of Current Motion Pictures.* Helpful in preparing lists of recommended motion pictures.

Motion Picture Research Council, Stanford University, Stanford, Calif. Promotes the use and appreciation of motion pictures as a community influence. Publishes research studies and bulletins.

National Board of Review of Motion Pictures, Inc., 31 Union Square West, New York 3, N. Y. A citizens' nonprofit organization interested in improving the quality of commercial motion pictures through selecting and appraising films, and disseminating information about them. Policy is implemented by local motion picture councils, composed of representatives of community groups, affiliated through the National

Motion Picture Council. Offers advisory service and various pamphlets and periodicals for local organization use.

ART

American Association of University Women, 1634 Eye St., N. W., Washington 6, D. C. Education program includes the encouragement of American contemporary art in a community setting.

American Federation of Arts, 1083 Fifth Ave., New York 28, N. Y. A nonprofit association of art organizations and individuals to foster appreciation among the American people. Its activities include maintaining a traveling exhibition; arranging illustrated lectures; functioning as a clearinghouse for ideas and information about art activities in the United States; furnishing outlines for program planning, and study material; and advising groups on organization and project planning and personnel. Has available *Films on Art*, edited by William McK. Chapman, describing about 500 titles. Periodicals include *The Magazine of Art*, a monthly October through May; the *American Art Annual* and *Who's Who in American Art*, issued in alternate years.

General Federation of Women's Clubs, 1734 N St., N. W., Washington 6, D. C. Has available *Penny Wise—Art Conscious*, a leaflet describing the General Federation's Penny Art Fund to encourage community appreciation.

Museum of Modern Art, 11 West 53rd St., New York 19, N. Y. Promotes creative-art education. Has information and materials for planning and carrying out organization-school projects. Maintains traveling art exhibits. Film library has about 600 rental films. Catalogue available.

National Art Education Association, Kutztown, Pa. Circulates children's art gathered through the Junior Red Cross. Information available.

National Gallery of Art, Washington 25, D. C. Maintains circulating exhibitions. Information available.

LITERATURE

Great Books Foundation, 246 Fifth Ave., New York 1, N. Y., or 37 South Wabash Ave., Chicago 3, Ill. A nonprofit educational corporation to promote adult liberal education through community group reading and discussion. Offers plans and text materials for five one-year courses. Supplies a manual for discussion leaders. Conducts Great Books Leader Training Courses in communities. Prepares and distributes promotional materials. Detailed information available.

FOLKWAYS

Folk Arts Center, Inc., 271 Hicks St., Brooklyn 1, N. Y. Promotes folk arts, such as music and dancing, through loan exhibitions, an information bureau, and a reference library on folk arts in America and other countries. Conducts folk art research. Maintains training courses for leaders.

Folkways Music Publishers, Inc., 666 Fifth Ave., New York 20, N. Y. A series of record albums of authentic songs, dance music, and chants from many parts of the world.

MUSEUM ACTIVITIES

American Association of Museums, Inc., Smithsonian Institute, Washington 25, D. C. Maintains a correspondence and conference consultation service on questions of museum organization, management, finance, technique, and building. Books of use to community organizations in establishing or expanding museums include *Manual for Small Museums* and *Historic House Museums*.

Some Sources of Films and Film Information

GENERAL

Association Films, Inc., 347 Madison Ave., New York 17, N. Y. Large collection of films related to community group interests in art, crafts, literature, drama, and music. Sound and silent, black and white, and color. Sale, rental, and free loan. A 64-page general catalogue is available.

Athena Films, Inc., 165 West 46th St., New York 19, N. Y. Chinese paintings, bronze, costumes, literature, dancing, and other cultural subjects. Sound, color. Sale, rental. Catalogue available.

Bailey Films, Inc., 6505 De Longpre Ave., Hollywood 28, Calif. Films include *ABC of Puppets* and *ABC of Pottery Making*. Sound, and black and white. Sale, rental. Descriptions available.

British Information Services, Film Division, 30 Rockefeller Plaza, New York 20, N. Y. Art activities in British communities; regions made famous through literature or associated with British authors; a series depicting single instruments, orchestras, and other group performances. Sound, black and white, and color. Free loan. Catalogue available.

Coronet Instructional Films, Coronet Building, Chicago 1, Ill. Film subjects include music, art, and literature. Sound, black and white, and color. Sale, rental. Catalogue available.

D. D. Livingston Film Library, 353 West 45th St., New York 19, N. Y. A source of films about the dance as an art form.

Educational Film Library Association, 1600 Broadway, New York 19, N. Y. Pamphlets include *Motion Pictures for Art Education*, an annotated listing. Has information about the film *Books and People: The Wealth Within*, which dramatizes the numerous services of public libraries.

Encyclopaedia Britannica Films, Inc., 1150 Wilmette Ave., Wilmette, Ill. General cultural offerings: entertainment-cultural films for children; music films, including instruction in basic techniques and demonstration of rhythm activities for young people; the casting, rehearsing, and direction of a community play; literature, biography, and appreciation. Sound and silent, black and white, and color. Sale, rental. General catalogue and special listings available.

Film Images, Inc., 18 East 60th St., New York 22, N. Y. Films about French culture, adapted for use in America: French painters, musicians, famous symphony recitals, authors and regions associated with French culture, scenes from classic plays, architecture, and Moroccan rugs and tapestry. Most in sound. Many in color. Nominal rental or free loan. Catalogue available.

Franco-American Audio-Visual Distribution Center, Inc., 972 Fifth Ave., New York 21, N. Y. Official distributor of free loan French government sponsored films. Literature, music, art, travel, and other subjects. Catalogue available.

Government of India Information Services, 2107 Massachusetts Ave., N. W., Washington 8, D. C. Films include many about Indian fine art, crafts, dancing, and music. Sound and silent, black and white, and color. Sale, rental. Catalogue available.

Harmon Foundation, 140 Nassau St., New York 38, N. Y. Films on water color techniques, clay modeling, dancing, and other art subjects.

Life Filmstrips, 9 Rockefeller Plaza, New York 20, N. Y. Filmstrips in color and in black and white. Based on *Life* magazine's pictorial essays on art, literature, and other cultural subjects. Single filmstrips or subscription series for sale. Descriptive brochure available.

National Film Board of Canada, 1270 Avenue of the Americas, New York 20, N. Y. Popular French and English folk music in appropriate settings. Many how-to-do-it features in several art media. Black and white, and color. Sale, rental, free loan. Listing available.

Princeton Film Center, Carter Road, Princeton, N. J. Offers a great variety of rental films on cultural subjects: interpretations of modern painting, sculpture, architecture, and allied subjects; screen versions of classics such as *Macbeth*, *Othello*, *Cyrano de Bergerac*; literary background subjects such as Tennyson's *Land of the Lyonese*; and folk dances and ballet.

Teaching Film Custodians, Inc., 25 West 43rd St., New York 36, N. Y. A great variety of music and other cultural subjects. Representative are films about Scottish folklore; a series about the music of other lands; adaptations of popular feature films such as *Naughty Marietta* and *Night of Love*, prepared in collaboration with the National Music Conference; community singing; familiar patriotic songs; a series of films presenting episodes from famous English and American novels and background for other national literature. Black and white, and color. Lease and rental from local film libraries. Information available.

Thomas J. Bouchard, 80 West 40th St., New York 18, N. Y. Modern dance, music, and other cultural subjects. Sound and silent. Black and white, and color. Sale, rental. Catalogue available.

MUSIC

Brandon Films, Inc., 200 West 57th St., New York 19, N. Y. Films include many featuring popular patriotic songs and music, and American folk songs. Black and white, and color. Sale, rental. Catalogue includes suggestions for organizing and directing a film club.

Castle Films, Department of United World Films, Inc., 1445 Park Ave., New York 29, N. Y. Cultural films in all areas. Several films of great symphonic performances. Sale, rental. Catalogue available.

Cathedral Films, 140 North Hollywood Way, Burbank, Calif. Films presenting performances of church music. Representative offerings include many hymns, the St. Luke Choristers, scenes from the Cathedral of Notre Dame against a background of sacred music, and the Doxology accompanied by an organ. Black and white, and color. Sale, rental. Catalogue available.

Eastin Pictures Company, Putnam Building, Davenport, Iowa. Films include a series presenting dance music, and solo and group instrument features. Black and white. Sale, rental. Listing available.

Educational Film Department, United World Films, Inc., 1445 Park Ave., New York 29, N. Y. Films on history of music, the development of music instruments, and techniques in instrument music. Black and white, and color. Sale, rental. Listing available.

Hoffberg Productions, Inc., 362 West 44th St., New York 18, N. Y. Sale and rental films featuring the Vienna Philharmonic, and the

Viennese State Ballet and Opera Company. Titles include "Ballet of the Dolls," from *Coppelia;* "Castle in Sevile," *Don Giovanni;* "Like a Dream," *Martha;* "Pilgrims' Chorus," *Tannhauser;* "Seven Magic Ballets," *Freischuetz;* "Steersman's Song" and "Senta's Ballad," *Flying Dutchman.* Descriptions available.

Music Educators National Conference, 64 East Jackson Boulevard, Chicago 4, Ill. Offers *Handbook on 16 mm. Films for Music Education.*

National Music Camp, Ann Arbor, Mich. Films about the talent-finding program of the National Music Camp, how interest in the arts is created, the application of scientific devices to the learning of music; sound pictures of music groups rehearsing and performing; and pictures of the performance of famous musicians and orchestras. Black and white, and color. Free loan. Listing available.

Official Films, Inc., 25 West 45th St., New York 36, N. Y. Cultural films include performances by various vocal groups, a community song-fest, orchestral music, and illustrations of piano and other music techniques. Black and white. Sale, rental. Catalogue available.

University of Southern California, Audio-Visual Services, 3518 University Ave., Los Angeles 7, Calif. Free loan color films include *Ballad of Idyllwild,* a presentation of the summer program of the Idyllwild School of Music and the Arts, featuring the singing of ballads and folk songs; *Trojan Band,* the planning and practice that go into a finished performance; and *Music Education Workshop,* a demonstration of voice-teaching techniques.

DRAMA

International Film Bureau, Suite 308–316, 57 East Jackson Boulevard, Chicago 4, Ill. Rental sound films in black and white and color include such how-to-do-it titles as the following: *Acting Problems, Directing a Play, Designing a Set, Building a Set, Make-up for Boys, Make-up for Girls,* and *Managing a Play.*

Library Films, Inc., 25 West 45th St., New York 19, N. Y. Information about *Let's Make Puppets,* a step by step demonstration of how to make puppets from newspapers, flour paste, and crayons.

MOTION PICTURE APPRECIATION

Community Cinema Corporation, 148 West 57th St., New York 19, N. Y. Offers information about how to obtain and show foreign films.

Film News, 444 Central Park West, New York 25, N. Y. Publishes *Film News,* nine times a year. Includes background articles and news about films, filmstrips, television, and recordings. Suggests film programs for special purposes; previews and reviews films and filmstrips; and reviews books, pamphlets, periodicals, and catalogues. Offers consultation service.

ART

Carl Schurz Memorial Foundation, Inc., 420 Chestnut St., Philadelphia 5, Pa. German art subjects. Free loan.

Contemporary Films, Inc., 13 East 37th St., New York 16, N. Y. A source of rental color films. Catalogue available.

Educational Film Library Association, Suite 1000, 1600 Broadway, New York 19, N. Y. *Motion Pictures for Art Education*, a mimeographed annotated listing.

Metropolitan Museum of Art, Fifth Ave. and 82nd St., New York 28, N. Y. Filmslides available for loan and purchase. Information available.

National Gallery of Art, Washington 25, D. C. "The Christmas Story in Paintings from the National Gallery of Art." Flemish and Italian masterpieces, with a critical discussion of each. Thirty-four slides, 2 by 2 inches, and 3¼ by 4 inches. Color. Free loan. Description available.

Pictura Films Corporation, 487 Park Ave., New York 22, N. Y. Offers a series of rental films about the lives of great artists, with reproductions and interpretations of their works. Illustrated catalogue available.

Princeton Film Center, Inc., Carter Road, Princeton, N. J. Rental films include *What Is Modern Art?*, in two 10-minute parts. Filmed in full color at the Museum of Modern Art in New York City. Questions and answers about a controversial subject. Description available.

United World Films, Inc., 1445 Park Ave., New York 29, N. Y. Free loan subjects include the one-reel *Sculpture Is Fun*, a how-to-do-it film. Information available.

Zeus Art College, 650 Ocean Ave., Brooklyn 26, N. Y. Rental films on arts and crafts, graphic arts, artists, and art appreciation. Catalogue available.

LITERATURE

E. L. Morthole, 8855 Lincolnwood Drive, Evanston, Ill. Cultural subjects include a New England authors series: scenes associated with the work and lives of authors such as Hawthorne, Whittier, Holmes, Emerson and Thoreau. Sound and color. Sale, rental. Catalogue available.

CHAPTER 7

Sports and Recreation

THE SOCIAL and economic changes that have brought to communities planned programs such as those outlined in Chapter 6 have also stimulated the steady, closely related growth of sports and other recreation activities.

Important influences on this growth are organization projects to determine sports and recreation needs and promote official action; to furnish space, facilities, equipment, and personnel for official and volunteer programs; to provide supplemental opportunities for all age groups; and to meet the needs of their own members.

So numerous and varied are these activities that no inclusive review is possible within the limits of this chapter. The following is intended to be only illustrative of what can be done through volunteer action.

AN ADEQUATE MUNICIPAL PROGRAM

Community organizations have been in the forefront of efforts for adequate tax-supported programs. Through speakers, films, and other media, they have successfully promoted the idea that recreation is essential for physical and mental health, and for development of good citizens and able leaders. They have demonstrated that an adequate program can successfully combat juvenile delinquency, and effectively reduce the number of play and sports accidents.

EVALUATING NEEDS, FACILITIES, SERVICES. Prerequisite to any volunteer group action is a study of existing community needs, and facilities and services. Consult recreation officials, the heads of neighborhood associations, directors of school activities, and private agency leaders. Invite representatives of the youth council and youth groups to discuss their interests. Arrange for the members of your committee to see recreation programs in action. Study programs in comparable communities.

Limited municipal recreation budgets often do not permit an adequate community-wide survey. Organizations sometimes furnish the man power for official evaluations, join with municipal departments and other groups in such projects, or carry out independent surveys.

A survey typically seeks answers to questions such as these: What recreation facilities are currently provided by the recreation department, schools, youth service agencies, churches, industries, community organizations, and commercial agencies? Do they accommodate all ages? Are they broad in scope? Are proper leadership and supervision provided? Is equipment adequate and properly maintained? Are recreational opportunities available the year round? Are municipally owned parks, playgrounds, vacant lots, and water areas utilized to the fullest extent? Are school buildings available for community recreation purposes?

PROMOTING AN ADEQUATE PROGRAM. An organization may perform an important community service by publicizing the findings of such a survey. Measures that have led to widespread support, not only for an expanded municipal program but for volunteer-group activities as well, include furnishing newspapers with the facts uncovered in the study; dramatizing needs on radio and television; distributing fliers, posters, and other graphic material; giving talks before other groups; and showing motion pictures that present standards to be aimed at in the community.

Having aroused a general interest in recreation, promote adequate budget provisions. Sponsor public meetings, and have members attend budget and other hearings. Urge the introduction of necessary enabling acts. Enlist the aid of other groups in organizing and carrying out an effective referendum campaign.

SPACE, FACILITIES, AND EQUIPMENT

Organizations are directly providing necessary space and adequate facilities and equipment. They are purchasing recreation areas and building recreation centers. They are mobilizing volunteer work squads and equipment to clear and grade vacant lots. They are building camps and beaches. They are equipping areas to meet special needs such as those of preschool children and the elderly.

Dearborn, Michigan, has what *The American City* for July, 1953, described as a "country club for all residents." Camp Dearborn, started in 1946 by a camp commission composed of representatives of community organizations, now offers residents, without charge,

552 acres of fields, woods, lakes, and streams, beaches, bathhouses, beach umbrellas, over 100 unsinkable rowboats and pedal boats, camp sites, playground equipment, and picnic conveniences.

Projects to provide play and sports facilities need not, however, be on an elaborate scale. The Lions of Sallisaw, Oklahoma, secured donations of pipe, paint, and lumber, and contributions of labor to provide needed play equipment. Milan, Missouri, has an eight-acre park because of the labor of Lions volunteers, who pulled stumps, cleared brush, built a circular driveway, and provided picnic tables and other conveniences at a small cost. Lions gave Clarkesville, Georgia, a football field largely through donations of labor and material. The Kiwanis Club of Monmouth, Illinois, organized volunteer action to establish a community camp. It secured an inexpensive lease on 33 acres surrounding a conservation lake, remodeled an old barn as a main lodge, obtained the loan of equipment, and mobilized volunteer labor squads to build an all-weather road. Rotarians raised the money to dredge and grade a beach.

Often lack of individual equipment limits sports and recreation participation. Urge your organization to undertake fund-raising projects to meet such needs. Canvass your membership and other groups for equipment no longer in use, such as balls, gloves, skates, rackets, and skis.

MEETING PERSONNEL NEEDS

Municipal budgets and the resources of private agencies usually are not adequate to supply the trained personnel necessary to meet all sports and recreation needs. Many of your organization members may have special skills to contribute to an expanded program.

Activities to provide such help include the following:

1. Urging members to serve on recreation advisory boards; organizing and supporting community and neighborhood recreation associations; sponsoring the formation of playground Mothers' Clubs and Dads' Clubs to help plan and supervise activities.

2. Training leaders in junior auxiliaries and sponsored youth groups to guard children at wading pools, maintain safety patrols, provide first-aid facilities, prepare and distribute recreation news bulletins, and take care of supplies and equipment.

3. Officiating at games and meets, serving as contest judges, and ushering at sports and recreation events.

4. Supervising hobby clubs; teaching crafts, sports, and games; providing transportation and supervision for field trips.

Some organizations are helping to meet personnel needs through their support of leadership training workshops, institutes, and formal courses. Such programs emphasize the nature and importance of community recreation; provide an orientation course in local programs and problems; arrange for practice in various popular sports and recreation activities; develop teaching and demonstration skills; and show volunteer trainees how to plan and direct leagues, tournaments, and social events such as parties for large groups.

ACTIVITIES FOR CHILDREN AND YOUNG PEOPLE

Volunteer groups are making important contributions to the health, character, and personality development of children and youth through their sports and recreation programs. These programs support and supplement those of municipal departments, schools, youth service agencies, and churches. They are planned and carried out after a careful consideration not only of needs but of the facilities, equipment, and personnel available. Often the young people themselves are consulted about their interests through interviews and questionnaire surveys among school, youth council, and other groups.

Organization contributions include projects to provide indoor and outdoor sports, games, nature study, hiking, camping, and social activities for junior auxiliaries and sponsored youth groups; play opportunities for preschool children; competitive sports for younger children, often not included in school or other established programs; support for high school and other teams; water sports; winter sports; leagues and tournaments; sports training schools and clinics; hobby clubs; and social activities to meet many needs and interests.

The special resources of some organizations permit them to bring unusual opportunities to communities. Soap box derbies, in which children design, build, and race homemade cars, attract hundreds of participants and thousands of spectators. In Ogden, Utah, 20,000 attended a soap box meet.

Some activities not ordinarily a part of a formally organized recreation program are successfully carried out through volunteer group effort. More than 3 million boys and girls, for example, have participated in supervised fishing sponsored by these groups. In many areas, streams and ponds are stocked with fish for the exclusive sport of children and young people.

In some communities relatively few children, teenagers, and young adults have opportunities for competitive team sports because of lack of facilities, equipment, and personnel to organize and supervise games and matches. Organizations are sponsoring basketball, baseball, bowling, and other team leagues. In some communities, each major group has sponsored a team for participation in a league or tournament. In 1953, organization sponsored baseball leagues for boys under 12 included about 12,000 teams in almost 3000 leagues. About 20,000 boys 13 and 14 competed in 286 leagues in 36 states.

The Junior Chamber's Annual Amateur Golf Championships for boys under 19 has attracted thousands of participants. About 300 local units sponsor tennis programs, providing facilities, equipment, coaching, and planning and supervising aid for community-wide matches.

Junior Rifle Clubs offer boys under 19 an opportunity to learn to shoot, and to compete as individuals and team members in supervised programs. Many such locally sponsored groups are affiliated with the National Rifle Association, which provides awards and instruction manuals, and helps groups qualify for enrollment with the Army's Office of the Director of Civilian Marksmanship, which supplies equipment and materials without cost.

HIGH SCHOOL SPORTS. Activities in support of high school sports include raising funds for stadia; furnishing uniforms and equipment; supplementing the coaching staff; helping to supervise groups of teenage rooters on out-of-town trips; arranging for victory celebrations; recognizing achievement through awarding emblems such as gold footballs; promoting the community as a site for the play-offs of county, state, and regional contests; helping with publicity; and promoting the sale of season tickets.

WATER SPORTS. Water sports may be encouraged through providing swimming instruction, sponsoring community-wide swimming and diving meets, and sponsoring regattas and water carnivals. Regattas feature rowing, outboard, inboard, and sailing races. Water carnivals often include parades, beauty contests, and spectacular beach and water exhibitions.

WINTER SPORTS. The outdoor play season may be lengthened by providing opportunities for ice hockey, skiing, tobogganing, coasting, and other winter sports. Activities include securing temporary use of private property for coasting and skiing, flooding level areas such as tennis courts to make skating rinks, providing lights for evening skating and coasting, furnishing loudspeakers for music, constructing ski jumps, and erecting warming houses.

Special events such as an ice carnival increase interest and participation in winter sports. These affairs usually are colorful, featuring, in addition to competitive events, ice sculpture, an ice palace, and the choosing and coronation of an ice queen.

SPORTS AND RECREATION INSTRUCTION. Arranging for instruction for members and others is an important contribution to community sports and recreation. The Southwest Chicago Kiwanis Club provides bowling instruction for eighth-grade pupils. The Kids Baseball School in Muskegon, Michigan, with organization support, annually enrolls over 500 young people for five days of instruction by prominent major-league players. One of the largest ski schools in the world is operated by the Portland, Oregon, Junior Chamber of Commerce.

Such projects help make communities sports conscious, encourage participation, provide material for local amateur and semiprofessional teams, and promote safer sports.

Organizations frequently cooperate with schools and colleges, recreation departments, coaches' associations, and other groups in bringing instructional services to communities through arranging for publicity, providing meeting places, helping to raise funds for instructors' expenses, furnishing equipment, sponsoring exhibition games and demonstrations, providing prizes for teams and individuals, and holding an awards dinner.

HOBBY CLUBS. The organization of hobby clubs among children and teenagers is especially important in those communities where opportunities for handicraft and hobby activities are not provided by school or municipal recreation agencies. Typical interests include stamps, photography, radio, nature study, sewing, art, handicraft, and cookery. Volunteer group help includes arranging for meeting places, providing equipment, furnishing leadership and supervision, sponsoring trips, and presenting exhibitions.

The growing number of model airplane clubs illustrates the importance of hobbies. It is estimated that over 5 million young people are affiliated with such groups. Meets, scale-model exhibits, and power-model shows provide aeronautical education as well as recreation for the hobbyists and the thousands of fans who attend. Model airplane clubs arouse interest in occupational and professional careers, and are proving grounds for aviation talent, making important contributions to the nation's defense.

In furthering this worthwhile hobby, your organization will find the following activities practical: scheduling model-plane making as part of your junior auxiliary and sponsored youth group program; cooperating with recreation centers and other youth service agencies in furnishing leadership for model plane clubs; providing a place to meet and to work; supplying instruction manuals and materials; securing a regulation power-model airport and helping to supervise and maintain it; sponsoring shows, exhibitions, and competitions; and arranging club visits to aircraft factories, airfields, and air shows.

SOCIAL ACTIVITIES. Social activities play an important role in the lives of children and adolescents, and should be an integral part of a recreation program. Adult organizations with junior memberships and sponsored youth groups consider the encouragement and direction of such activities part of their responsibility to the young people. Volunteer groups frequently contribute to playground programs by arranging for wiener roasts, watermelon feasts, square dancing, talent shows, and other events. Social activities are made a part of the programs of sponsored affairs such as harvest celebrations and carnivals. Weekly block dances have been very successful.

In many communities organizations actively support teen centers through financial aid and the volunteer services of their members. Organizations, too, have established teen centers that offer year-round programs. In Kingsport, Tennessee, for example, the Junior Chamber of Commerce and the Kiwanis Club gave the community a $50,000 building with a reading room, dance floor, game and hobby rooms, a soda fountain, and other facilities for meeting the varied interests of young people.

ACTIVITIES FOR ADULTS

Organizations have a traditional interest in adult sports and recreation. Their successful promotion of recreation opportunities in fields such as music, drama, literature, fine arts, and crafts is reviewed in Chapter 6.

Sports activities include sponsoring community amateur and semi-pro teams, presenting elaborate sports events such as rodeos, showing sports films, sponsoring the appearance of professional teams, presenting exhibition games, sponsoring novelty contests such as donkey basketball, furnishing opening day prizes, inviting players as meeting guests, arranging for group excursions to out-of-town games, presenting awards to outstanding teams and players, organizing community celebrations of sports victories, and sponsoring sportscasts.

Illustrative of the very many widely diversified sports programs was that of the El Paso, Texas, Junior Chamber of Commerce. The featured exhibitions included a semiprofessional baseball tournament, drawing entries from Texas, New Mexico, and Mexico; a softball tournament in which 27 amateur teams participated; and a three-day Golden Gloves tournament.

Sports programs have become community-wide celebrations. Thirty-four organizations cooperated in the production of Greater Muskegon Aquacades, a ten-day water festival in Muskegon, Michigan. Thirty-six varied events and contests provided sports opportunities for hundreds, as well as spectator interest for many thousands.

These community sports programs frequently become of regional and even national importance. The annual Football Festival of the Berkeley, California, Junior Chamber, for example, usually attracts over 250,000 to a parade, the prelude to a program of team competition drawing over 65,000 fans.

National associations, agencies, and sports equipment and other concerns offer valuable planning and material help in fields such as bowling, golf, tennis, boxing, professional football and baseball, hunting and fishing, speedboat racing, water festivals, air events, and sports fishing. The Office of the Director of Civilian Marksmanship in Washington will supply M-1 .30 and .22 caliber rifles, ammunition, and other equipment and supplies without cost to groups interested in forming a rifle club. Consultation service for groups interested in boating, camping, fishing, and hunting is available from the Outdoor Boating Club of America. The Civil Aeronautics Administration offers field consultation services and pamphlet help in providing facilities and planning events for the air minded. These and other sources are described at the close of this chapter.

SOCIAL ACTIVITIES FOR ADULTS. Picnics, clambakes, and community dinners are traditional parts of summer recreation programs. Games and contests feature such organization sponsored affairs. Softball, horseshoe pitching, foot races, swimming events, and stunts and novelty contests are popular. Group singing adds to good fellowship. Family nights, card parties, seasonal celebrations, suppers, dances, and many other events provide recreation throughout the year.

ACTIVITIES FOR SPECIAL GROUPS

Recreation gaps often occur in municipal programs because of personnel or other inadequacies. Among such gaps frequently filled through organization action are the needs of special groups such as underprivileged and handicapped children, migratory and defense-industry workers, newcomers to the community, those in sparsely settled and rural areas, and the elderly. Activities for meeting some of these needs are suggested in Chapters 10, 17, 18, and 20.

Older people in the community constitute an increasingly important special group, the welfare of which is a major concern of many organizations.

All the problems of the aged—health, financial security, and social adjustment—are interrelated and are the responsibility of the whole community. By providing recreational outlets, your group will add immeasurably to their confidence, self-esteem, and enjoyment of life.

Churches, women's clubs, P.T.A.'s, and other volunteer groups have organized Golden Age, Sunset, Happy Hours, Three Quarters Century, and Old Timers clubs. In such groups, members enjoy common interests, which may include games, crafts, dancing, movies, community singing, and sightseeing tours.

In Philadelphia, some 40 old-age clubs have been sponsored by various groups under the guidance of the recreation department, and new clubs are organized whenever there is a demonstrated need. Volunteers serve as club leaders. In Milwaukee, 10 clubs regularly meet for games, movies, and social activities. Golden Age Clubs in New Orleans meet for weekly sings, folk dances, and parties. A Retired Men's Club and a Kaffee Klatsch for women are active in Teaneck, New Jersey.

In Newark, New Jersey, the Soroptimist Club, the Council of Social Agencies, and the Welfare Federation have for several years sponsored a five-day hobby show for old folks. The interest aroused by the show was reflected in the increasing number of entries, which rose from 400 to over 1000. Hobbies vary from knitting to demonstrations of glass blowing.

Providing recreation space for older people may be a project for your organization. A section of a park or play area may be set aside especially for their use, and equipment furnished for such games as horseshoes and croquet. A meeting room in a community recreation center, a library, or a church, and kitchen and dining-room privileges will further promote the success of an older people's recreation program.

A well-planned program for older people makes use of their experience and knowledge, and allows them to feel the sense of accomplishment that comes from using their energies toward socially useful ends. Your organization may help older people achieve a sense of usefulness by offering them opportunities to serve the community. These activities may include making toys for needy children, sewing for the Red Cross, and supervising younger recreation groups.

ACTIVITIES FOR MEMBERS

Sports and recreation programs for members pay important dividends in terms of membership interest and development. They provide bonds of common interest, develop the enthusiasm necessary for effective action to achieve other organization purposes, and directly contribute to the fellowship aims common to many such groups.

Through sponsoring intergroup leagues and tournaments, organizations are appreciably adding to the recreation opportunities of the community.

The following membership activities may be appropriate for your group:

1. Showing films on subjects such as golf, bowling, softball, and tennis. These films arouse interest in sports generally, demonstrate the practicability of membership participation, teach sports skills, and aid recreation committees in organizing teams and scheduling games and matches.

2. Featuring talks and demonstrations in fields such as golf, tennis, fly casting, and bridge.

3. Arranging for group instruction in popular sports and games, and dancing; or for private instruction at special rates.

4. Enlisting the aid of school coaches, drama teachers, civic-minded professional actors, and others with special talents for planning and directing activities.

5. Maintaining a broad and varied program to meet the needs of sponsored youth groups; urging the fullest possible membership participation in such activities.

6. Enlisting the aid of wives, husbands, and friends of members in

organizing social events such as dances, card parties, picnics, and beach parties.

7. Entering organization bowling, softball, and other teams in intergroup leagues and tournaments; taking the initiative in arranging for such leagues and tournaments.

8. Offering individual and team awards for achievement at an annual sports recognition dinner or other special meeting.

SOURCES OF AID

Academy of Model Aeronautics, 1025 Connecticut Ave., Washington 6, D. C., a division of the National Aeronautics Association. Sponsors and regulates scale- and power-model meets, including the Annual National Championship contest. Sponsors Academy Chapters and chartered clubs, "licenses" model airplane flyers, and publishes model records established in the United States. Offers *Club and Chapter Manual*, containing information on how to organize a chapter, and a sample constitution and suggestions for projects; *Official Model Aircraft Regulations*; and several magazines: *Air Travel*, *Model Airplane News*, *Model Aviation*, and *Flying Models*. Source of literature and materials such as contest kits and books on model glider and airplane design.

Amateur Athletic Union of the United States, 233 Broadway, New York 7, N. Y. Publishes official rule books in all sports, physical fitness tests, and a monthly magazine, *The Amateur Athlete*. Maintains a uniform test for amateur standing. Awards amateur championships. Source of free loan and rental recreation films. Listing available.

American Association for Health, Physical Education, and Recreation, 1201 16th St., N. W., Washington 6, D. C. Publishes recreation pamphlets and books. Furnishes free bibliography of recreation literature.

American Bowling Congress, 1572 East Capitol Drive, Milwaukee 11, Wis. Sponsors a league plan for bowling, stressing uniformity in equipment, rules, and regulations. Publishes the monthly magazine *Bowling*, a history of bowling, a book of rules, a bowler's manual, a model constitution and rules for sanctioned bowling leagues, and promotional pamphlets. Source of bowling films.

American Junior Bowling Congress, 10417 South Campbell Ave., Chicago, Ill. Sanctions bowling leagues for teams of boys and girls sponsored by local individuals or organizations. Publishes *How to Organize and Sanction an American Junior Bowling Congress League*; *Program of the American Junior Bowling Congress*, a booklet containing rules and regulations for AJBC bowlers, and information on the supervision and financial setup of a league; and *Prep Pin Patter*, a monthly magazine. Furnishes official forms, including sanction certificates, membership cards, handicap forms, league schedules, a secretary's handbook, and literature on banquet plans. Provides trophies and awards for local and national winners.

American Legion, 777 North Meridian St., Indianapolis 6, Ind. Has information about its sponsored Junior Baseball program.

American Motorcycle Association, Inc., P. O. Box 1049, Columbus 8, Ohio. Publishes pamphlets on organizing motorcycle clubs and girls' auxiliaries, a *Manual of Instruction and Rules for Competition*, and a booklet of suggested activities. Furnishes safety banners, official arm bands, and trophies. Source of free loan films.

American Power Boat Association, 700 Canton Ave., Detroit 7, Mich. Publishes *Stock Utility Outboard Racing Rules*, and *Propeller*, a monthly magazine.

A. S. Barnes and Co., Inc., 232 Madison Ave., New York 16, N. Y. Source of literature on table games, card games, social games, and arts and crafts.

Athletic Institute, Inc., 209 South State St., Chicago 4, Ill. Source of recreation films, film guides, and books and pamphlets dealing with facilities, equipment, and instruction in all types of sports and recreation. Listing of materials available.

Audubon Junior Clubs, 1130 Fifth Ave., New York 28, N. Y. Sponsored by the National Audubon Society. Clubs may be formed for any group of ten or more boys and girls. Provides nature leaflets, colored pictures of birds, and membership buttons and certificates for each club member. Furnishes each club with a subscription to *Outdoors Illustrated*, published four times a year; and a *Nature Program Guide*, written especially for club leaders, containing suggestions for a complete activities program.

Babe Ruth League, Inc., 524½ Hamilton Ave., Trenton 9, N. J. Sponsors "little-bigger leagues" for boys 13, 14, and 15 years of age. Arranges local, state, and "world series" competition. Information available.

Better Fishing, Inc., 509 South Wabash Ave., Chicago 5, Ill. Promotes fishing for boys and girls through Better Fishing Rodeos held annually throughout the nation. Helps local groups organize rodeo programs. Provides prizes, including complete fishing outfits, to local boy and girl champions.

Brunswick-Balke-Collender Company, 623 South Wabash Ave., Chicago 5, Ill. Source of materials useful in organizing and conducting bowling leagues and tournaments. Publishes pamphlets about how to bowl, provide facilities, and organize bowling clubs.

Chevrolet Division, General Motors Corporation. Local dealers provide information and other help in sponsoring soap box derbies.

Civil Aeronautics Administration, Department of Commerce, Washington 25, D. C. Major source of information, materials, and guidance for aviation programs. Regional offices offer field consultant services. Publications available from the Superintendent of Documents, United States Government Printing Office, Washington 25, D. C., include *The Air Fair, Its Planning and Operation*, giving detailed information about the staging of all-day, airport-centered events. Covers relations of community groups to cooperating agencies, committee organization and functioning, financing, publicity, program planning, policing, concessions, sanitary facilities, and exhibition booths. Other literature includes *The Flying Club*, a detailed outline for the organization and operation of a flying club; and *Sources of Information on Model Airplanes, Gliders, and Kites*.

Department of the Army, Office of Director of Civilian Marksmanship, Washington 25, D. C. Furnishes senior and junior rifle clubs, chartered by the National Rifle Association and complying with OCDM enrollment rules, with the following free aid: a limited number of M-1 .30 and .22 caliber rifles; ammunition; targets; cleaning rods; magazine assemblies; and lubricating oil and grease.

Fisher Body Craftsman's Guild, General Motors Building, Detroit 2, Mich. Furnishes complete model car designing instructions from clay modeling to final wood, plaster, or plastic product. Publishes *Guild News*, official bulletin of Fisher Body Craftsman's Guild, and various hobby pamphlets. Conducts yearly model car competition for boys 12 through 19 years of age. Enrollees are supplied free of charge with booklets of instructions. Awards university scholarships, cash, and trips to the Guild convention for winners of state, regional, and national contests.

General Electric Company, 1 River Road, Schenectady 5, N. Y. Furnishes a free community recreation kit, which includes 10 copies of *Recreation Is Everybody's Business*, a manual for community leaders; 10 copies of *Recreation Is Good Business*, a booklet for industrial leaders; and 200 copies of a recreation check list. Source of free loan recreation film, *A Chance to Play*.

Glass Bottle Blowers Association of the United States and Canada, 12 South 12th St., Philadelphia 7, Pa. An affiliate of the American Federation of Labor. Promotes "pony league" baseball for boys 13 and 14. Has available the official rule book.

Hillerich and Bradsby Company, Inc., 434–436 Finzer St., Louisville 2, Ky. Offers *Official Softball Rule Book*, illustrated, without charge.

Hobby Guild of America, 550 Fifth Ave., New York 19, N. Y. Sponsors National Hobby Month, usually in April. Offers information about how local arts and crafts, sporting goods, hobby, garden supplies, and other shops can cooperate with hobby groups in presenting exhibits and sponsoring contests.

International Ladies' Garment Workers' Union, 1710 Broadway, New York 19, N. Y. Offers, without charge, *And the Pursuit of Happiness*, an illustrated 38-page booklet describing the union's recreation program.

Mossberg and Sons, Inc., New Haven, Conn. Publishes *The Guide Book to Rifle Marksmanship*, a free illustrated manual of six lessons.

National Golf Foundation, 407 South Dearborn St., Chicago 5, Ill. Offers aid to community groups interested in stimulating greater interest in golf. Includes financing plans and consultation on the design and operation of municipal golf courses. Source of pamphlets about how to play golf, and how to organize and direct tournaments. Has free loan instructional slide films. Description of aids available.

National Recreation Association, 315 Fourth Ave., New York 10, N. Y. A primary source of books, pamphlets, and brochures on all phases of recreation and recreation problems. Literature deals with subjects such as the need for playgrounds; opportunities for churches and other agencies to provide recreation; recreation in industry and in rural areas; and the community's responsibility for solving recreation problems. Suggestions are given for conducting social activities and for providing year-round programs of youth and adult recreation. Maintains bureau of correspondence and consultation. Offers field services in all areas of recreation. Conducts training institutes for supervisors and volunteer workers. Functions as a clearinghouse for community recreation news and ideas. Cooperates extensively with local, state, and national agencies. Publishes *Recreation*, a monthly magazine, and special bibliographies; and maintains a biweekly bulletin service. Lists of publications are available.

National Rifle Association of America, 1600 Rhode Island Ave., N. W., Washington 6, D. C. Furnishes information about how to organize both senior and junior rifle clubs. Provides comprehensive shooting programs for both senior and junior groups. Awards medals, pins, emblems, and diplomas for excellence. Provides member clubs with complete instruction materials, manuals, wall charts, and training films for the operation of schools at the club range. Supplies official referees for shooting matches, and consultation services on technical questions. Member clubs eligible to receive issues of rifles and ammunition from the Department of the Army, Office of the Director of Civilian Marksmanship, Washington 25, D. C. Publishes *The American Rifleman*, a magazine.

Outboard Boating Club of America, 307 North Michigan Ave., Chicago 1, Ill. Publishes booklet information about how to stage water carnivals, boat regattas, and outboard motor boat races. Information covers matters such as financing, selecting dates, planning the program, securing sanctions, publicizing the event, determining awards, and assuring the safety of participants and spectators. Offers consultation service to groups interested in boating, fishing, swimming, camping, and hunting.

Richardson Rod and Reel Company, 3150 North Sawyer Ave., Chicago 18, Ill. Publishes free, illustrated pamphlets on fresh water fishing.

Royal Crown Cola, Teen Age Headquarters, Columbus, Ga. Free publications include pamphlets on how to provide a teen club headquarters, furnishings and equipment; raise funds for operational expenses; plan parties, dances, and other activities; and attract new members.

Science Research Associates, Inc., 57 West Grand Ave., Chicago 10, Ill. *Life Adjustment* booklets include several about youth group organization and recreation activities. Descriptive listing available.

Sporting Arms and Ammunition Manufacturers' Institute, 343 Lexington Ave., New York 16, N. Y. Free instructional and program planning pamphlets.

Superintendent of Documents, United States Government Printing Office, Washington 25, D. C. Publishes sports and other recreation literature for federal agencies such as the Extension Service of the Department of Agriculture, the Office of Education, and the Civil Aeronautics Administration. Pamphlets include ideas for group activities that may be adapted to both urban and rural settings, and bibliographies in fields such as sports, art, handicrafts, music, dancing, and drama.

United States Lawn Tennis Association, 120 Broadway, New York 5, N. Y. Promotes tennis as an amateur sport. Offers pamphlet material on tennis court construction and maintenance.

United States Table Tennis Association, 22 West Monroe St., Chicago

3, Ill. Publishes instructional pamphlets, and *Table Tennis Topics,* a newspaper issued eight times a year.

Williams, Arthur, *Recreation for the Aging,* New York: The Association Press, 1953. Published for the National Recreation Association.

SOME SOURCES OF FILMS AND FILM INFORMATION

Aetna Life Affiliated Companies, Public Education Department, 151 Farmington Ave., Hartford, 15, Conn. Free loan films such as *Aim for Safety, Ski Tips,* and *Hook, Line, and Safety.* Descriptions available.

A. G. Spalding and Brothers, Inc., 180 Wabash Ave., Chicago 1, Ill., and other major cities. Free loan films include *Famous Fairways,* scenes of play on six of the nation's most famous golf courses; and *Inside Football,* a demonstration of several skills by famous football stars. Both are in full color. Information available.

American and National Leagues of Professional Baseball Clubs, 64 East Jackson Boulevard, Chicago 4, Ill. Free loan films include World Series contests; batting and pitching techniques, featuring famous stars; the history of baseball; teaching films for coaches; and the role of the umpire. Descriptions available.

Arbogast and Company, Inc., 313 West North St., Akron, Ohio. Source of free loan films about bait casting and fly fishing in Quebec Province, Maine, Michigan, Wisconsin, Florida, Louisiana, and other areas. Descriptive brochure available.

Association Films, Inc., 347 Madison Ave., New York 17, N. Y. Rental and free loan films on subjects such as baseball, boxing, basketball, tennis, track and field sports, hunting and fishing, water sports, winter sports, rifle marksmanship, and model railroads. *Selected Motion Pictures* is available.

Boy Scouts of America, Visual Education Service, 2 Park Ave., New York 16, N. Y. Low rental films about camping and other Scout activities. Descriptions of films and filmstrips available.

Business Screen Magazines, Inc., 7064 North Sheridan St., Chicago 10, Ill. Publishes *Sports, Physical Education, and Recreation Film Guide,* an annotated listing of 800 titles.

Canadian National Railways, Motion Picture Library, 630 Fifth Ave., New York 20, N. Y. Free loan travel and resort films include fishing, boating, and other sports scenes. Catalogue available.

Canadian Travel Film Libraries, 1270 Avenue of the Americas, New York 20, N. Y. Free loan films about travel and resort life include fishing, boating, skiing, tobogganing, skating, and other recreation activities. Catalogue available.

Chicago *Tribune*, Film Bureau, 33 West Madison St., Chicago 11, Ill. Offers free loan films of professional football teams in action. Descriptions available.

Eastern Air Lines, Inc., Film Division, 10 Rockefeller Plaza, New York 20, N. Y. Free loan films include *Flying Fisherman* and *Flying Hunter*, which present dramatic scenes of battles with tarpon and sailfish, and hunting. Descriptions available.

Evinrude Motors, 4143 North 27th St., Milwaukee 9, Wis. Free loan films about recreation and sports in Wisconsin, Mississippi, Ohio, and other areas, and the Albany to New York Outboard Marathon. Catalogue available.

Ford Motor Company, Film Library, 3000 Schaefer Road, Dearborn, Mich. Free loan films include the 500-mile Indianapolis Speedway classic, several demonstrating techniques in baseball and other sports, and an explanation of the organization of a junior baseball program. Descriptions available.

Gaines Dog Research Center, 250 Park Ave., New York 17, N. Y. Has several free loan films on raising and training dogs. Descriptions available.

General Mills, Inc., Film Library, 400 Second Ave., South, Minneapolis 1, Minn. Free loan films on baseball, basketball, and football. Descriptions available.

Girl Scouts of the U.S.A., Visual Aids Service, 155 East 44th St., New York 17, N. Y. Rental films include *Adventures at Day Camp*. Shows planning for shelters, equipment, leadership, and transportation, and typical camping activities. Descriptions available.

Goodyear Tire and Rubber Company, Motion Picture Department, Akron 16, Ohio. Free loan films include subjects such as balloon racing and motorcycle stunt riding. Descriptions available.

Herkimer Tool and Model Works, Inc., 137 Hartner St., Herkimer, N. Y. Free loan color film *Model Plane Wings over the World* shows the manufacture of planes and engines, boys and fathers building and flying planes, and activities at the International Model Plane Contest at Detroit. Description available.

Ideal Pictures Corporation, 65 East South Water St., Chicago 15, Ill. Free loan films include subjects such as carp spearing, fishing and hunting in the Lake Superior area, and deep sea fishing. Catalogue available.

Modern Talking Picture Service, Inc., 45 Rockefeller Plaza, New York 20, N. Y. Free loan and rental how-to-do-it sports and other recreation films in fields such as hunting, golf, and baseball. Catalogue available.

P. and K. Incorporated, 122 North Dixie Highway, Monence, Ill. Free loan films about fresh- and salt-water fishing in various sections of the country. Descriptions available.

Phillips-Ramsey Company, 604 First National Bank Building, San Diego 1, Calif. Offers free loan films about deep-sea fishing, and the production and use of various types of rods and reels. Descriptions available.

Physical Fitness Division, Department of National Health and Welfare, 700 Jackson Building, Ottawa, Canada. Offers *Here's How to Do It*, a free catalogue of free loan and rental films on sports, games, hobbies, and handicraft.

Remington Arms Company, Inc., 939 Barnum Ave., Bridgeport, Conn. Free loan film, *Gunning the Flyways*, about duck and goose shooting in North America. Description available.

South Bend Bait Company, 1108 High St., South Bend 23, Ind. Free loan films include subjects such as trout, bass, tarpon, and other game fishing; canoeing; boat trips; pack trips; and the production and use of rods, reels, and lures. Descriptions available.

Sportsmen's Service Bureau, 250 East 43rd St., New York 17, N. Y. Offers two free films: *Making of a Shooter*, the story of a youngster who, under proper supervision, developed qualities of sportsmanship and habits of safety; and *Shooting Safety*, the story of a parent who assured shooting safety for his son through helping to organize and operate a basic shooting school for youngsters. Both are in color. Information available.

Teaching Film Custodians, Inc., 25 West 43rd St., New York 18, N. Y. Information about *Lambertville Story*. How citizens organized to establish a Saturday night teenage recreation center in Lambertville, New York.

Union Pacific Railroad Company, 1416 Dodge St., Omaha 2, Neb. Free loan films include activities at the Sun Valley (Idaho) Ski School, and a film record of Olympic tryouts and Harriman Cup competitions. Descriptions available.

United States Department of Agriculture, Office of Information, Washington 25, D. C. Offers a series of free loan swimming instruction films. Listing available.

United States Rubber Company, Advertising Department, 1230 Avenue of the Americas, New York 20, N. Y. Free loan films include *Soap Box Derby*, presenting complete details, including entry requirements, how boys prepare, local elimination contests, and the finals in Akron, Ohio. Other free loan films include organizing and directing a "little baseball league," the little league in action, and shots of college football teams. Descriptions available.

CHAPTER 8

Safety and Fire Prevention

MOST FAMILIES in America are directly or indirectly affected by accidents and fires. According to the National Safety Council, in one year 91,000 persons met accidental death and 9.5 million were injured. In that one year the cost to the nation in wages lost, in medical fees and hospital expenses, and in insurance payments and property loss was over $7.5 billion. Property damage from fire, according to the National Board of Fire Underwriters, amounts to about $700 million annually. This waste is important at any time, but today it represents a serious drain on resources needed for national security.

Statistics tell only part of the story. No figures can describe the terrible toll of human suffering—the maimed, families broken up and children left homeless, the talented who can never make their promised contributions to society, the heavy burdens assumed by individuals and families. This tremendous cost is all the more tragic because to a great extent it might have been prevented.

Suffering and loss undoubtedly would be much greater were it not for the safety activities of organizations in our communities. With the help of the great national volunteer associations, the insurance companies, industry, and government, these groups are making steady progress toward safer communities.

The following pages suggest practical activities in the areas of home, school, recreation, traffic, and farm safety.

HOME SAFETY

Since home accidents and fires cause the greatest toll in death and injuries, organizations, particularly women's groups, should find the home front a special challenge. The National Board of Fire Underwriters estimates that every minute of the day and night two fires break out in this country—one of them in somebody's home.

The first step is to find out the facts. Fire and accident statistics may be obtained from police, fire, and health departments, hospitals, the Red Cross, and through a community survey.

A survey seeks answers to questions such as these: How many home fires occur in your community each year? What is the principal cause? Misuse of matches? Cooking or heating stoves? Inflammable liquids? Electricity? How many lives are lost? What is the estimated property damage? Are the water supply, the water pressure, and the number and location of hydrants up to standard? Are fire alarm and fire communications systems adequate? Is fire prevention information regularly publicized? Are the special events on the fire prevention calendar, such as Fire Prevention Week in October, properly advertised and promoted?

HOME SAFETY EDUCATION MEASURES. Homes in many towns and cities are safer places in which to live because of the education measures of organizations. These groups are distributing fire and accident prevention literature supplied by national agencies and associations, often reaching every home in the community with the aid of Boy Scouts and other youth groups. They are presenting dramatic free loan films illustrating the causes of home fires and accidents, and methods by which fires may be fought and the consequences of accidents minimized. First-aid courses and clinics, workshops, and institutes on safe housekeeping methods are sponsored and supported. Home safety forums feature talks by fire and police officials, physicians, public utilities personnel, Red Cross instructors, and other experts.

Effective publicity is given case studies of home fires and accidents. Seasonal hazards, such as turning on the heat for the winter season, burning leaves, using poison sprays, canning, and decorating the home with Christmas lights, are called to public attention. In cooperation with public utilities and merchants, exhibits and demonstrations are presented to identify important causes of home accidents such as faulty wiring, misuse of kitchen and other appliances, and carelessness with tools.

OTHER HOME SAFETY ACTIVITIES. Members sometimes assist in making house-to-house inspections to point out hazards to householders. Where this has been done, the number of dwelling fires has dropped sharply, and in some communities has been halved. Another successful activity is the distribution of home inspection blanks through school children, whose interest is often stimulated by interclass or interschool contests, with awards for groups that secure the greatest number of completed forms.

Organizations have made important contributions through well-organized and publicized clean-up campaigns. In Providence, Rhode Island, for example, volunteer groups helped to collect and dispose of about 1680 tons of rubbish. In a single year, home fires dropped from 550 to 201.

SCHOOL SAFETY

Recognizing the fact that public schools and their programs are the responsibility of the whole community, volunteer groups, in cooperation with administrators, are concerned with safety in three major areas: safe buildings and equipment; safety instruction and training; and student activities that develop safety-conscious habits and attitudes.

SCHOOL BUILDINGS AND FACILITIES. Arrange for a survey of school buildings and equipment, playgrounds, parking areas, and grounds approaches. Background information, minimum standards, survey guides, checklists, and other aids are available from the federal Office of Education, state boards of education, the National Education Association and other professional groups.

Help school staffs determine whether machines in woodworking and other shops have adequate accident prevention devices, exits are clear of obstructions, storage areas are free of debris, passageways are well lighted, floor finishes furnish good traction, and traffic is regulated to avoid congestion in corridors. Do school bus contracts stipulate the type and condition of buses? Are bus drivers carefully screened? Are teachers periodically briefed concerning classroom and other hazards and their personal responsibilities for the safety of those in their charge?

SAFETY EDUCATION AND TRAINING. Modern schools assume responsibility for much more than the traditional 3 R's. Objectives include development of individuals competent to live safely not only in the school and home environment, but in our complex industrial society.

Organizations cooperate in planning and conducting formal courses in general accident and fire prevention, or contribute to the development of such a unit as part of a course in health. In cities where such courses are given, fire alarms have been cut 50 per cent. Comprehensive outlines, study materials, and audio-visual aids for various age levels are available without cost or for a nominal fee from national agencies and associations.

Informal organization-school approaches to the safety education and training of children and youth also have been effective. Groups are supplying many excellent free-loan films for classroom showing. Members talk to classes, lead group discussions, and organize assembly programs.

Quantity lots of safety pamphlets are given schools for distribution to pupils. Mass education media such as posters and slogans are made available. Every phase of the local safety problem frequently is given concentrated attention in a series of school special safety months. Essay and art contests educate not only the participants but the hundreds of young people who see the exhibits and attend assemblies or other awards ceremonies.

PUPIL PLANNED AND DIRECTED ACTIVITIES. Children and youth become safety-conscious, acquire safety knowledge, and develop desirable attitudes and habits most readily through doing. Organizations help school administrators encourage young people to identify unsafe school areas and fire hazards, and to plan and put into effect preventive measures.

Student councils discuss school safety and make recommendations to the principal. They keep records of accident-free days for each grade, and at monthly or other intervals present awards with suitable assembly ceremonies. Key Clubs and similar school service groups have adopted greater school safety as a major objective.

Organizations frequently help form and train safety patrols. They supply arm bands or other insignia, and in the case of traffic patrols, raincoats and rainhats. Inside-the-building patrols render valuable service in helping teachers keep pupils moving safely in corridors and down stairways. Members of fire patrols inspect buildings daily and perform other duties, such as directing auditorium traffic, seeing that fire exits are open, and helping to supervise fire drills.

RECREATION SAFETY

Your organization is, of course, responsible for the safety of its own recreation facilities. In addition, many groups are helping to eliminate the hazards of street and other unsupervised recreation through projects to secure suitable and safe municipal facilities such as playgrounds and equipment, swimming pools, beaches, camps, tennis courts, parks, and community centers. They are also promoting safe practices in sports such as diving, swimming, boating, hunting, and fishing through instruction, distribution of literature, showing films containing safety hints, and direct supervision by members.

Many organizations cooperate with the Red Cross in conducting courses in first aid, and in distributing posters that dramatize the importance of avoiding sunburn, poisonous plants and snakes, and insects.

A further field for action is prevention of forest fires, caused in large part by careless campers and thoughtless motorists. According to the American Forest Products Industries, forest fires, in an average year, burn 25 million acres of land, destroying millions of trees.

Organizations in areas where forest fires are a potential menace cooperate with state and federal agencies in education programs and other activities. Groups often conduct forest fire prevention projects during the vacation season. These include issuing warnings to motorists and tourists, posting highway warning signs, and working with youth groups to teach safe camping practices. Displays, sidewalk signs, radio and television programs, distribution of literature, lectures, and showings of forest fire films at meetings of adult and youth organizations have been found to be effective.

TRAFFIC SAFETY

Throughout the country, organizations are carrying out thousands of independent, supplementary, and group-cooperative projects that are materially reducing accidents on our streets and highways.

In Milwaukee, for example, a volunteer group study of the city's traffic accidents, which showed that 37 per cent of traffic fatalities were children, provided the impetus for an outstanding program conducted by the Milwaukee Safety Commission.

Community organizations played an important part in the campaign. Parent-teacher associations sponsored safety education in the schools. Labor unions distributed over 9000 copies of a commercial drivers' bulletin. Recreation centers were established to keep children off the streets, and newspapers featured a proclamation by the chief of police entitled *Children Are Playing, Look Out!* on their front pages. As a result of the campaign, child traffic accidents were reduced almost immediately. The following year only 8 per cent of the total traffic fatalities were children.

An unusual approach to the problem of keeping children safe from traffic accidents was worked out by the Safety Council and the Parent-Teacher Association of Oklahoma City. These two groups prepared and distributed through school children a map of streets near several of the city's schools. The map gave parents information about preferred routes. It urged them to guide their children at least once over these selected routes in order to teach them safe pedestrian habits.

In Topeka, the need for drastic action was indicated when the city was judged fifty-seventh in a national traffic safety contest among 64 cities in its population class. Volunteer groups organized a safety council, raised a $16,000 fund, and appointed a director to head an all-out safety campaign.

In the next few months, members of organizations distributed safety literature and digests of traffic regulations, sponsored films and talks, and presented public demonstrations dramatizing the need for safety. In the business districts, Girl Scouts roped off crosswalks at main intersections as the lights changed; Boy Scouts handed jay-walkers cards reading *You Were Lucky* or *You Made it This Time*; and bandaged members of organizations rode in wheel chairs carrying signs reading, *I Crossed on a Red Light*. Placards and spot announcements were used on television and radio programs, and the subject was stressed at organization meetings.

At the end of 185 days, not a single traffic fatality had occurred in Topeka. In one year the city reduced its traffic death toll 55 per cent and stood in fourth place in traffic safety instead of fifty-seventh.

Comprehensive or year-round traffic safety programs sponsored or supported by organizations have had a similar success in other communities. In Abilene, Texas, a program spearheaded by the Junior Chamber of Commerce was launched with a publicity attack on drunken and careless driving. Traffic safety films were shown in leading theaters, wrecked automobiles were exhibited, Jaycee safety stickers were affixed to windshields, and displays were featured in department store windows.

In a brake-survey campaign, 2000 cars were checked by the Jaycees working with city police and the highway patrol. Letters were sent to the leading merchants and truck fleet operators urging their cooperation in the promotion of safety. With the assistance of the Rotary, Lions, Optimist, Exchange, Kiwanis, and women's clubs, the Jaycees formed a Citizens Traffic Committee and launched a

"T-men" drive. This group made a concerted effort to inform careless drivers of traffic violations. Letters from the chief of police warned such drivers and requested their future cooperation.

As a result of these measures, the goal of Abilene's traffic safety program—to equal the record among cities of its class, 702 deathless traffic days—was not only reached but exceeded.

The Salt Lake City Kiwanis Club furnished an automobile, and organized a safe-driving program with the cooperation of the city police. An instructor provided by the police department trained 250 persons during one summer, awarding certificates to drivers who completed the course. The enterprise was considered so successful that the Kiwanis Club sponsored a safety education car for the use of the school safety patrol officer. Painted white, the car bears the names of the club and police department, and displays numerous safety slogans.

Citizen groups in Stillwater, Oklahoma, have made important contributions to an enviable safety record of 3782 consecutive days— over 10 years—without a traffic fatality.

The Chamber of Commerce sponsors safety exhibits. The Junior Chamber provides free car inspections. The Lions Club equips school patrols. Girl Scouts carry out fund-raising projects to provide reflector tape for bicycles. Boy Scouts patrol streets to warn jay walkers. Church groups feature safety at meetings.

Under the direction of the Stillwater Safety Council, the program is a continuing one. Winner of safety awards for several years, Stillwater has been proclaimed "America's Safest City" by the National Safety Council.

Such achievements as these may suggest activities to meet needs in your community. Other practical activities are the following:

1. Cooperating with the traffic safety programs of youth groups by registering bicycles and providing luminous tape markers for fenders; and conducting safe-driving contests.

2. Studying high-accident locations and recommending measures to eliminate hazards.

3. Promoting improvements in parking arrangements, pavement marking, a signal system and other controls, and street and highway illumination.

4. Sponsoring a special "traffic safety" edition of a local newspaper.

5. Staging spectacular publicity events such as a horror parade of wrecked cars.

6. Promoting the enforcement of traffic regulations, and establishment of a traffic law violators' school.

7. Publicizing seasonal and holiday traffic hazards through the press, radio and television, and other outlets.

8. Initiating and supporting a safety council.

FARM SAFETY

Accidents and fires reduce farm man power, perennially in short supply, and seriously affect farm income, many times directly dependent upon current crops and livestock stored or housed in highly inflammable structures.

In farm areas, safety activities are major projects not only of adult organizations but of many sponsored and supported youth groups such as Future Farmers, 4-H Clubs, Future Homemakers, Boy Scouts, and Girl Scouts.

No stock program will prove practicable for every area. Farming in different parts of the country is characterized by particular hazards. In the California fruitgrowing region, for example, 11 per cent of the agricultural injuries in one year involved ladders, according to the National Safety Council. On the other hand, in Kansas, 32 per cent of agricultural accidents occurred in the operation of tractors.

In seeking information about local farm accidents and fires, consult the county agent, home demonstration agent, and officials of the Grange, the local chapter of the Red Cross, and the local farmer cooperative or other agricultural association.

The use of a checklist for common hazards on the farm is an effective fact-finding device. Is machinery kept in good repair? Are guards kept in place on power shafts, belts, and chains? Is machinery blocked and power turned off before adjustments are made? Are children kept away from machinery? Are farmyards clear of garden tools, forks, and waste? Are wells and cisterns adequately protected? Is a water supply available in case of fire? Are stairs and ladders sound? Are electric appliances in proper condition? Are dangerous animals, such as bulls and boars, securely penned? Is the burning of rubbish on a windy day, or near buildings or hay stacks avoided? Is gasoline properly stored?

Some activities that are having good results include utilizing the publicity resources of an organization to bring preventive measures to the attention of farm managers and farm families; initiating and supporting safe livestock handling and equipment use demonstrations; cooperating with rural youth groups in organizing safety checks on their own and other farms, and in conducting essay, poster, and other contests; presenting safety films; cooperating in the organization of regional or interfarm fire-fighting units, and helping to provide trucks and needed equipment; making surveys of water supplies that can be used to fight fires; locating portable pumps; and numbering farm entrances for the guidance of the fire departments of neighboring communities.

A year-round campaign, with emphasis on seasonal farm hazards, may be highlighted by special activities during Farm Safety Week. National publicity given farm safety during this time will spur interest in local projects. Rural adult and youth organizations should take advantage of the occasion to obtain suggestions and materials from the county agent and from the national organizations listed at the end of this chapter.

Farm Safety Week is usually planned so that some special phase of accident prevention may be stressed each day of the week. The following is a typical schedule: Sunday, sermons and Sunday school talks on farm safety; Monday, accident hazards in the home; Tuesday, methods of handling livestock; Wednesday, safe farm housekeeping; Thursday, rules of safe driving and walking; Friday, safe operation of farm machinery; and Saturday, review of all phases of farm accident prevention.

SOURCES OF AID

Advertising Council, 25 West 45th St., New York 19, N. Y. Furnishes kits of posters, newspaper mats, and other materials useful for organization-sponsored safety programs.

American Automobile Association, 17th St. at Pennsylvania Ave., N. W., Washington 6, D. C., and local clubs. Provides information about how to organize a school safety patrol; conducts National Traffic Safety Poster Contest; sponsors National Pedestrian Protection Contest for cities and states; conducts an extensive program to aid high schools develop driver education courses; helps schools obtain dual control cars; produces text materials and numerous driver testing devices; publishes community traffic safety brochures; furnishes bicycle and automobile safety films and film bibliographies; and provides the services of education consultants for one-week teacher preparation courses.

American Forest Products Industries, 1816 N St., N. W., Washington 6, D. C. Furnishes posters, pamphlets, and study aids for schools, and publishes books on the protection of forests. Conducts "Keep America Green" campaigns in cooperation with official and volunteer state agencies.

American National Red Cross, 17th & D Sts., N. W., Washington 13, D. C. Organizes courses in first aid. Furnishes safety checklists for schools. Offers consultant and cooperative services in first aid, accident prevention, home safety, and water safety to any community organization. Publishes instruction manuals.

American Standards Association, 70 East 45th St., New York 17, N. Y. Establishes and disseminates free information about safety standards in industry, on the highway, and in the home. Description of services available.

Association of Casualty and Surety Companies, 60 John St., New York 7, N. Y. Promotes driver education in schools through High School Driver Award programs. Provides manuals and testing devices for use of administrators and teachers of driver training programs. Offers industrial safety suggestions and materials.

Automotive Safety Foundation, 700 Hill Building, Washington 6, D. C. Coordinates the traffic safety work of many national organizations; provides grants-in-aid for national programs. Is a source of information on community traffic problems.

Center for Safety Education, New York University, New York 3, N. Y. Offers advisory services in safety education. Publishes *Guidebook for Automobile Driving Schools* and pamphlets in safe driving practices. List of materials available.

Chamber of Commerce of the United States, 1615 H St., N. W., Washington 6, D. C. Has available pamphlet literature for community accident and fire prevention programs.

Eno Foundation for Highway Traffic Control, Inc., Saugatuck, Conn. Has available *A Manual on Uses of Traffic Accident Records*.

Forest Service, United States Department of Agriculture, Washington 25, D. C. Issues kit of materials on forest fire prevention: posters, stamps, bookmarks, radio scripts, blotters, car cards, and advertising mats. Sponsors Forest Fire Prevention campaigns.

Inter-Industry Highway Safety Committee, 1200 18th St., N. W., Washington 6, D. C. Offers a free kit of materials to meet varied citizen-group highway and safety interests. Kit includes suggestions about how to encourage and directly support a high school driver education program; information about the availability of other aids for such an education program, such as textbooks, instructional and promotional films, psychophysical testing equipment, dual-control equipment, and training courses for instructors; detailed plans for the sponsorship of community and inter-community teenage traffic safety conferences; Man-to-Man and Dad-to-Daughter agreement forms which present fundamental rules for safe driving—available in quantity; samples of available posters and illustrated booklets to promote safe driver and pedestrian habits; and leaflets suggesting step-by-step procedures to secure more adequate streets and highways for your community.

Liberty Mutual Insurance Company, 175 Berkeley St., Boston 17, Mass. Offers pamphlets on safe driving habits; instructions for beginners; quizzes for drivers; and booklets, posters, and other material on all phases of home and industrial safety. Cooperates with community organizations in conducting traffic surveys.

National Association of Automotive Mutual Insurance Companies, 20 North Wacker Drive, Chicago 6, Ill. Distributes *Here's How,* an illustrated 64-page report of traffic safety projects successfully carried out by community organizations.

National Board of Fire Underwriters, 85 John St., New York 7, N. Y. Makes surveys and analyzes community fire control measures. Provides inspection checklists for homes, schools, farms, hotels, hospitals, industrial plants, mercantile establishments, night clubs, restaurants, and other places of assembly. Furnishes posters, leaflets, stickers, and booklets for use in fire prevention programs. Provides free loan films on forest fire protection, the role of the fireman in American life, what to do in case of fire, and how to prevent fire. Provides fire-safety material for the use of youth groups.

National Commission on Safety Education, National Education Association, 1201 16th St., N. W., Washington 6, D. C. Makes available a comprehensive bibliography on accident and fire prevention, and study outlines and other education material.

National Fire Protection Association, 60 Batterymarch St., Boston 10, Mass. Publishes national fire codes, educational pamphlets, and fire records, reports, and bulletins. Furnishes signs, posters, and motion picture lists. Provides field services to assist local fire prevention committees.

National Fire Waste Council, 1615 H St., N. W., Washington 6, D. C.

Supplies technical and specialized advice for fire prevention programs. Conducts contests, and publishes fire casualty statistics and educational material.

National Safety Council, 425 North Michigan Ave., Chicago 11, Ill. Helps establish local councils and sets up standard procedures for organization and action. Provides consulting services in all phases of safety. Furnishes posters, bulletins, leaflets, brochures, and other materials for accident prevention campaigns. Provides kits of safety education materials for schools. Offers specialized industrial safety programs. Publishes *National Directory of Safety Films*, which lists about 1000 motion pictures, sound slidefilms, and silent filmstrips dealing with safety education in special industries, transportation, traffic, school, home and farm. Other National Safety Council publications: *National Safety News, Public Safety, Safety Education, Farm Safety,* and *Home Safety.*

National Society for the Prevention of Blindness, 1790 Broadway, New York 19, N. Y. Offers free consultation, pamphlet, poster, and other aids to groups interested in industrial safety.

Readers Digest Association, Inc., Pleasantville, New York. *Public Service Guide to Fire Protection,* a nominally priced pamphlet.

Superintendent of Documents, United States Government Printing Office, Washington 25, D. C. Source of material on building construction, fire fighting services, fire and accident prevention education, and model traffic ordinances. Of special interest are the recommendations of the committees organized at the President's Highway Safety Conference. Pamphlet reports include *Action Program,* a summary of findings; and *Public Information, Organized Public Support, Laws and Ordinances, Education, Accident Records, and Enforcement.*

Travelers Insurance Companies, Public Information Department, Hartford, Conn. Offers an annual booklet of street and highway accident data. Interestingly written and illustrated, booklet is free in single copy or quantity lots.

United States Department of Labor, Washington 25, D. C. Provides safety information such as national accident reports. Publishes technical bulletins about industrial safety. Descriptive listing of publications available.

Some Sources of Films and Film Information

Most of the national associations and other agencies described above are major sources of free loan and low rental films and film information. Other important sources are the following:

Aetna Life Affiliated Companies, Public Education Department, Hartford 15, Conn. A major source of free loan films, most of which are in sound and color. Wide range of subjects include safety procedures in hunting, boating, and other sports; safe sports equipment and clothing; how to reduce accidents on construction and other jobs; how members of a family can cooperate in preventing home accidents; safety on the highway; artificial respiration and other first-aid procedures. Catalogue available.

American Legion, 777 North Meridian St., Indianapolis 6, Ind. Free loan films include *Teach Them to Drive*, the story of how two parents waged a successful campaign for the adoption of driver education and training in their community's schools. Description available.

American Petroleum Institute, 135 South LaSalle St., Chicago 3, Ill. Offers the free loan color film *Farm Tractor Safety*, covering every phase of safe tractor operation and maintenance. Description available.

American Society of Bakery Engineers, Department of Visual Education, 208 Third Ave., S. E., Minneapolis 14, Minn. Free loan films illustrate how fires start in the home, common-sense precautions to prevent fires, fire fighting techniques, and industry measures to prevent accidents and fires. Descriptive listing available.

Bicycle Institute of America, Inc., 122 East 42nd St., New York 17, N. Y. Primary source of free loan films demonstrating safety for bicycle riders. Descriptive listing available.

Bureau of Communication Research, Inc., 13 East 37th St., New York 16, N. Y. A major source of free loan sound films about fire prevention and fire fighting. Many in color. Subjects include the story of the development of fire fighting methods and equipment, the training of firemen, how a fire department safeguards lives and property, how citizens cooperate with fire prevention officials, how fires start in the home, how to combat small home fires, how a family may conduct a home fire inspection and fire drill, how a well-administered school cooperates with fire officials, how to recognize common fire hazards in industry, and shots of spectacular fires. Catalogue available.

Employers Mutual Liability Insurance Company, Engineering Department, Wausau, Wis. Free loan films, some in color, about safety in the home, at school, in industry, on the highway, crossing streets, and riding bicycles. Descriptions available.

Farm Bureau Insurance Companies, Public Relations Department, 246 North High St., Columbus 16, Ohio. A series of free loan films about farm safety. Descriptive listing available.

Ford Motor Company, Film Library, 3000 Schaefer Drive, Dearborn, Mich. Offers a free loan series of six driver education films: *Driving Under Adverse Conditions, Driving at Night, Driving on the Highway, Driving in the City, Parking the Car,* and *The Care of the Car.* Descriptive listing available.

General Motors Corporation, Department of Public Relations, Film Section, General Motors Building, Detroit 2, Mich. Free loan films inclue *Safe as You Think,* stressing the importance of safety consciousness at home, in school, on the job, and on the street. Description available.

Illinois Central Railroad, Library of Audio-Visual Aids, Room 600A, 135 East 11th Place, Chicago 5, Ill. Free loan films depict causes of highway crossing accidents and suggest methods of avoiding them. Descriptive listing available.

Modern Talking Picture Service, 45 Rockefeller Plaza, New York 20, N. Y. Free loan sponsored films include several dramatizations of problems of careless driving, and demonstrations of what can be done about them through education and other community-wide measures. Descriptions in general catalogue.

Pyrene Manufacturing Company, 444 North Lake Shore Drive, Chicago, Ill. Offers the free loan *Fight That Fire,* a description of the fundamentals of fighting fires of several types. Description available.

Venard Organization, 702 South Adams St., Peoria 2, Ill. Free loan sponsored films on farm and home accident prevention. Descriptions in general catalogue.

Young America Films, Inc., 18 East 41st St., New York 17, N. Y. Information about 10-minute *Bicycle Safety.* Demonstrates proper bike inspection, the need for essential equipment, and the importance of rules of the road.

CHAPTER 9

Health

AN ESSENTIAL for better community living, the common goal of all the service programs suggested in this book, is a healthy citizenry—free from the ravages of disease, capable of material, cultural, and spiritual growth, with the vitality to act vigorously to solve its political, economic, and other pressing problems.

While the strategy of the ceaseless war upon disease and the causes of disease is planned, and new materials and techniques developed by medical and other scientists in their laboratories, the battlefront itself is in the community. Volunteer organizations are playing important roles through programs to provide a more healthful community environment, to establish and maintain essential facilities and services, and to combat specific diseases.

A HEALTHFUL COMMUNITY ENVIRONMENT

The health level of a community is the result of many factors, some of which are imperfectly understood even by medical science itself; some of which are not readily controllable through either official or volunteer action. Other factors, however, are understood, are controllable, and may be influenced by practical volunteer group programs.

Among these controllable factors are the varied aspects of the physical environment. Through organization action, water and air pollution is being eliminated; rats and other pests destroyed; harmful weeds eradicated; and food contamination reduced.

CONTROL OF WATER AND AIR POLLUTION. Wastes emptied into rivers and streams may affect not only the health of those near the sources of such pollution, but the health of thousands along the water courses, many miles away. In addition, stream pollution lowers land values, destroys the livelihood of fishermen on both inland and coastal waters, and greatly restricts recreational opportunites.

In a campaign for elimination of such pollution, your group will find enthusiastic and effective help from the United States Fish and Wildlife Service, state conservation authorities, and national and local conservation associations. Sportsmen's clubs are especially interested in pollution-free lakes and streams, and may be a valuable source of information and support.

The problem posed by the smoke nuisance is also serious in many industrial cities, and offers a similar challenge to community organizations. Such agencies as the United States Public Health Service and the American Public Health Association have information about the prevalence and seriousness of the problem, and may suggest procedures adaptable to your situation. Organizations in cities that have had antismoke campaigns may be able to supply information of great value.

Representative organization activities include sponsoring a survey of public waters, identifying sources of water and air pollution, publicizing the dangers of such pollution, conducting educational campaigns, prevailing on industry to control industrial waste and smoke, promoting establishment or expansion of sewage facilities, and supporting local ordinances and state and national legislation.

PEST CONTROL. Hundreds of communities are more healthful, more prosperous, and pleasanter places in which to live because organizations have initiated and supported campaigns to destroy rats, flies, mosquitoes, and other pests.

Many groups enlisting the aid of county agriculture agents, local health officials, farm association leaders, and others with a special interest in pest control are waging continual war on rats. Through posters, advertisements, news reports, pamphlets, films, and broadcasts they are publicizing the tremendous cost in terms of disease, food spoilage, and property damage. They organize clean-up squads, and spread poison at public dumps and other areas of infestation. They encourage householders and farmers to remove all possible sources of rat food and to ratproof their homes and buildings.

In a systematic program to destroy rats, the Lebanon, Kentucky, Chamber of Commerce, for example, divided the city into four sections. A squad of 20 men was assigned to each. Rat bait was provided and distributed under the direction of a district agent and an observer sent by the United States Fish and Wildlife Service. Each worker was supplied with a block map so that no building in the area would be neglected. In Akron, Ohio, community groups joined in a rodent-control program that reduced the infestation of buildings from 50 per cent to less than 5 per cent.

Like rats, flies and mosquitoes can become health hazards as well as serious public annoyances if they are not controlled. To be most effective, antifly and antimosquito projects should begin in the spring. Early spraying of breeding places will make later control measures easier. The Greenwich, Connecticut, Junior Chamber of Commerce carried out a project in which members purchased insect-fogging equipment, borrowed a half-ton pickup truck, and manned it in a series of nighttime spraying operations.

FOOD SANITATION. Organizations have found that food sanitation is another area of public health in which service activities are practical. This is particularly true in communities where health regulations are inadequate or where markets, dairies, restaurants, and other places are not properly inspected and supervised.

Your group can be effective in arousing public interest in and support for local ordinances and state legislation, and in persuading food producers, processors, and handlers to adopt measures to assure the wholesomeness of their products.

Illustrative of successful action in this field was the sponsorship of a two-day Institute for Restaurant Operators and Food Handlers in South St. Paul, Minnesota, by the Civic and Commerce Association, in cooperation with the health department. Among the subjects considered were the cleanliness of personnel such as waiters; the handling of dishes and silverware; dishwashing methods; preservation, storage, and display of foodstuffs; control of insects and rodents; and care of toilet facilities, kitchens, and dining rooms.

ESSENTIAL FACILITIES AND SERVICES

Forty million Americans lack the services of a public health department. Establishment of a local health unit, if one is lacking in your community, should have top priority in the health activities of your organization. Employment of a full-time public health officer is essential to the progress and extension of services, both because of his value as an administrator and because financial aid from the federal government for some health purposes is limited to local health agencies administered by a full-time officer.

In cooperation with health departments and other official and volunteer agencies, organizations are making possible more adequate facilities and services, such as well-baby clinics, dental clinics, blood banks, modern hospitals and equipment, and enough doctors, nurses, and other health personnel to protect their communities.

WELL-BABY CARE. Volunteer group supported well-baby clinics, such as those sponsored by the Fraternal Order of Eagles in a national program, are maintained in many towns and cities. Such clinics discover and correct early physical defects in children, instruct mothers in infant care, stress the importance of regular physical examinations, and generally promote the physical and mental health of the preschool child.

DENTAL PROGRAMS. Dental health is one of the country's most serious problems. The present number of dentists is far from adequate, and dental health is beyond the means of a large part of the population. To remedy this situation, organizations have initiated school surveys and dental programs; set up community clinics with the aid of local and state health agencies, dentists, and dental supplies manufacturers; sponsored mobile clinics; furnished equipment, funds, and other aid to clinics; and promoted use of fluorine in city drinking water.

BLOOD BANKS. Disaster in its many forms can strike any community. In the present state of world tension, the possibility of an atomic or other devastating attack cannot be ignored. Establishment of a blood bank, therefore, is a most important community concern. Organizations can render invaluable service by cooperating with the American Red Cross in meeting this need.

The Junior Chamber of Commerce of Minneapolis studied blood-bank projects in other cities, obtained approval for their program from the local hospital association and the city medical society, and raised over $70,000 for a War Memorial Blood Bank Building. In Lansing, Michigan, an outstanding blood-donor program conducted by the Fraternal Order of Eagles resulted in creation of a Red Cross regional blood-donor center that has saved many lives. In another community, the Parent-Teacher Association sponsored diabetes tests, lung and heart x-rays, and secured blood samples from over 1000 people. All who passed through the clinic were asked to pledge a pint of blood. In another community, which could not afford facilities to keep stocks of whole blood in storage, an organization established a Walking Blood Bank, a registry of citizens willing to donate blood in emergencies.

may be had in the community; presenting radio and television dramatizations, panel discussions and spot announcements; and sponsoring short seminars of civic leaders to encourage a concerted, community-wide education effort.

CASE-FINDING PROGRAMS. In the community struggle against many afflictions such as mental disorder, cancer, tuberculosis, and venereal disease, early discovery of individuals who need medical and other attention is especially important. For example, it is estimated that about 9 million Americans are today suffering from mental and emotional disorders. About 650,000 are in mental hospitals. Many of these cases would not have developed or reached the hospitalization stage had their symptoms been recognized early enough, and preventive and curative measures taken. At least one-third of the victims of cancer each year, authorities state, could have been saved by early diagnosis and treatment.

Within 50 years, tuberculosis has dropped from first to sixth place as a leading cause of death in America. This progress has been accomplished not only through new techniques of treatment, but through successful procedures for its detection in communities. Similar success has followed volunteer group support of venereal disease case-finding and the contact tracing services of public health agencies.

Of tremendous importance to the successful drive
diseases, therefore, is your group's support of pro
Specific activities that have had marked suc
and supporting information and diag
formational literature and sho
low-cost mass x-ray, Wass
citizens to ch
Junior

HOSPITALS. Hospital facilities are a
public health. Federal financial assistance is
of hospital projects approved under a state hospita
Applicants must furnish to their state survey and plan
usually the state health department—proof of their ability t
their share of the construction costs and to operate and maintain th
project for a two-year period. Your organization might initiate studies
to determine local requirements and to consider the advisability of
federal aid.

In some communities, including a number in rural areas, hospitals have been constructed largely through the fund-raising efforts of farsighted organizations. In other areas, new hospital wings or rooms have been financed. The Arlington, Virginia, Junior Chamber of Commerce, in one such project, sponsored the building of a 40-bed hospital for the care, treatment, and rehabilitation of polio and other orthopedic patients. Jaycee committees solicited materials and man power from business firms and individuals. Plans and specifications for a fireproof two-story building were contributed by an architect. The site was cleared by Jaycees, who provided continuous assistance during the construction of the building. Church groups, the Chamber of Commerce, business firms, and individuals also contributed material, man power, and other help to complete the project.

Hospital services may be substantially expanded by gifts of equipment. Community groups have donated items such as portable oxygen units, iron lungs, crutches, wheel chairs, infant incubators, ceiling projectors, orthopedic equipment, hospital beds, and ambulances. Equipment of this type will help your community to cope with everyday health needs and vastly increase its effectiveness in dealing with accidents, epidemics, and disasters.

COMBATING SPECIFIC DISEASES

Community groups are playing indispensable roles in the fight being waged by great national associations such as the National Foundation for Infantile Paralysis, the American Cancer Society, and the American Heart Association. These roles include contributing the financial support and the personal services of members, implementing education and publicity programs, supporting case-finding efforts, establishing and supporting facilities such as clinics, and giving effective, understanding aid to those who are convalescing.

SUPPORT. Chapter 3 suggests criteria ... can appraise the worthiness of groups ... and other local support to combat specific ... practical ideas for planning, organizing, and directing campaigns in their behalf.

Other direct support that your members can offer includes distributing handbills and pamphlets; participating in surveys to discover individuals who need help; serving on a speakers' bureau; serving at information and case-finding centers; assisting in the clerical and supervisory detail of mass x-ray and similar programs; helping plan and carry out recreation and other therapeutic activities; and providing transportation for those who are impaired.

EDUCATION AND PROMOTION ACTIVITIES. Public education is an important objective in the fight against diseases such as tuberculosis, cancer, and heart trouble. It is necessary that desirable attitudes toward the diseases and their victims be developed, that the symptoms be known, that the public be impressed with the necessity for early detection, that individuals be familiar with community facilities for prevention and cure, and that all-out financial and other support be mobilized.

Your organization might offer to plan and direct a local education campaign, in cooperation with the health department and other groups. National associations such as those listed at the close of this chapter welcome such aid. They often have carefully planned campaign guides and interesting pamphlet literature, free-loan films, and other audio-visual aids designed for local volunteer group use.

Such an education campaign is especially effective when it is ... up with special observances such as National Mental Hea... National Heart Week, Cancer Control Month ... Dimes campaign. Almost 8000 towns and citi... programs during Mental Health Week ... where to find help in local obser... Your educational ... offered in Appendix A. ... meeting featur... ming a ... chu...

---

tures by members of the local medical society, health classes and discussions, and spectacular, mechanical question-and-answer arrangements using buzzers and flashing lights.

FACILITIES FOR THE TREATMENT OF SPECIFIC DISEASES. Most dramatic are organization activities that directly contribute to successful treatment of persons afflicted by these major diseases.

In addition to carrying out projects such as those suggested in this chapter under other headings, your group might survey existing facilities and consider the adequacy of personnel; visit hospitals and sanatoria; sponsor legislation in behalf of institutions; urge the establishment of municipal mental health, heart, tuberculosis, cancer, polio, and other clinics; help establish special recreation and health camps; and provide beds and equipment such as iron lungs and hot-pack machines.

AID FOR CONVALESCENT VICTIMS. Convalescence is the stage of the health struggle in which the personal interest and friendship of your members can play an important part. Activities may include arranging for and participating in social and other recreation programs at hospitals and convalescent centers, presenting entertainment, organizing vocational and other rehabilitation programs, establishing job placement bureaus for those impaired, helping convalescents to improve their living conditions and habits to prevent recurrence of diseases such as tuberculosis, and providing convalescents with transportation to church services and community events.

RECRUITMENT OF NURSES AND DOCTORS. The American Hospital Association has estimated that 50,000 recruits must be enrolled yearly to meet the need for nurses. Community organizations are active in this field. The General Federation of Women's Clubs promotes the vocation of nursing through guidance and promotional programs, and the Junior Chamber of Commerce, Rotary, and other organizations carry on recruitment activities.

In one community, Rotarians organized a Committee for Nurse Recruitment. High school girls were told the story of nursing, an... visited hospitals to observe, and to interview staffs. The Rot... also organized a Junior Nurses Club to interest sixth-grade... week this group receives simple instruction, learning h... as how to make beds, fold bandages, and serve meal... munity, a volunteer group raised $21,000 to ... ships.

To attract resident doctors and dentists to the community, organizations frequently join in providing living quarters, guaranteeing annual fees, and furnishing medical equipment, office space, and hospital facilities. The state health department and the state medical society are good sources of assistance in finding doctors. The Council on Medical Service of the American Medical Association maintains a list of those who have not decided on communities in which to practice.

COMPREHENSIVE HEALTH PROGRAMS

Many organizations conduct a variety of public health activities in one campaign. Such programs are usually featured during Health Week, or complement fund-raising drives. An outstanding week-long program conducted in one community included a rat-control project, a tuberculosis x-ray survey, a heart fund drive, an Easter Seal sale for crippled children, and the community observance of National Mental Health Week. Measures used to arouse interest included the distribution of 40,000 pieces of literature and a tour of state mental institutions by over 1000 citizens.

In another community, the Kiwanis Club conducted a health slogan contest; showed films on communicable and other diseases; sponsored lectures on nutrition, hearing, vision, and blood banks; presented polio-care demonstrations; and arranged for blood typing.

Health councils often foster understanding of a wide variety of health problems by devoting each day of a Health Week to a separate phase of public health. These may include Child Health Day, Student Nurse Enrollment Day, Food Sanitation Day, Mental Health Day, Know-Your-Hospital Day, and Industrial Health Day.

SCHOOL HEALTH EDUCATION. In many states, community organizations have been instrumental in securing legislation to make health and physical education compulsory in all schools. Local health and physical education programs have been strengthened through sponsored contests and other projects, and support for facilities, services, and courses of study.

SOURCES OF AID

Advertising Council, 25 West 45th St., New York 19, N. Y. Supplies newspaper mats and other promotion materials for a program to recruit student nurses.

American Association for Health, Physical Education, and Recreation, the National Education Association, 1201 16th St., N. W., Washington 6, D. C. Many low cost pamphlets useful in organization-school health programs. Listing available.

American Association of Social Workers, One Park Ave., New York 16, N. Y. Publishes *Social Work Year Book*. Includes authoritative articles in many health fields, bibliographies, and agency listings.

American Association of University Women, Publications Clerk, 1634 Eye St., N. W., Washington 6, D. C. Pamphlets include *Study-Bibliography in Mental Health* and *Health Insurance Plans—a Bibliography*.

American Cancer Society, Inc., 47 Beaver St., New York 4, N. Y. Provides free pamphlets, films, exhibits, transcriptions, complete program kits, and furnishes speakers for community organizations. Has available *Film List*, describing films for lay audiences. Publishes *Cancer News*, a monthly journal for lay readers.

American Dental Association, 222 East Superior St., Chicago 11, Ill. Materials include program plans for youth and adult groups; and films, transcriptions, pamphlets, and radio scripts and spot announcements. Sponsors Children's Dental Health Day. Offers a listing of dental health education materials, including descriptions of free loan films.

American Heart Association, Inc., 44 East 23rd St., New York 10, N. Y. Source of pamphlets, films, slides, and exhibits. Furnishes posters, plastic hearts, and other materials for National Heart Campaigns. Provides field assistance in organizing local heart treatment facilities.

American Hospital Association, 18 East Division St., Chicago 10, Ill. Has transcribed radio programs and films to help you in telling your hospital's story. Pamphlets include *Establishing a New Hospital* and *Fund Raising Manual for Hospitals*.

American Medical Association, 535 North Dearborn St., Chicago 10, Ill. Provides free loan films, transcriptions, radio scripts, exhibits, pamphlets, and catalogues. Is a source of books and pamphlets on health education. Publishes *Today's Health*, a magazine for lay readers.

American National Red Cross, 17th and D Sts., N. W., Washington 13, D. C. Furnishes opportunity for personal service. Provides films, radio scripts, exhibits, posters, pamphlets, lists, and catalogues on subjects such as health, nursing, nutrition, and first aid. Conducts the National Blood Program.

American Public Health Association, Inc., 1790 Broadway, New York 19, N. Y. A major source of information. Provides field personnel for surveys of community health problems and facilities, and consultation services. Publishes books on public health practices, and the *American Journal of Public Health*. Especially useful is *Guide to the Sanitation Evaluation Schedule*.

American Social Hygiene Association, Inc., 1790 Broadway, New York 19, N. Y. Furnishes free loan films and filmslides, window display material, educational pamphlets, social hygiene program guides for industrial management, material suitable for distribution to industrial employees, and suggestions for organizing a community social hygiene program. Provides material for Social Hygiene Day speeches. Description of materials is available.

Children's Bureau, Department of Health, Education, and Welfare, Washington 25, D. C. Source of reprints of special articles on child health. Publishes *The Child*, a monthly magazine containing news about child health and child welfare laws, standards, and programs. Offers a film guide for community organizations.

Committee for the Nation's Health, 2212 M St., N. W., Washington 7, D. C. Has available a 16-page nominally priced pamphlet, *Health Needs and What to Do about Them*, a summary of the President's Commission on the Health Needs of the Nation.

Division of Rodent Control, Fish and Wildlife Service, United States Department of Interior, Washington 25, D. C. Provides services of trained technicians to assist community rodent control programs. Will furnish a complete kit of materials useful in planning an antirat program.

Health Information Foundation, Inc., 420 Lexington Ave., New York 17, N. Y. Provides a free series of recordings of documentary radio programs, each illustrating a community solution of a health problem. For 16-inch, 33⅓ rpm playback machines. Publishes a bulletin, *Progress in Health Services*.

Manufacturing Chemists Association, Inc., 246 Woodward Building, 15th and H Sts., N. W., Washington 5, D. C. Offers *Air Pollution Abatement Manual*, at nominal cost.

Metropolitan Life Insurance Company, 1 Madison Ave., New York 10, N. Y. Provides free loan films, and pamphlets, posters, and exhibits.

National Association for Mental Health, Inc., 1790 Broadway, New York 19, N. Y. Furnishes posters, booklets, educational pamphlets, dramatic transcriptions attacking mental health misconceptions, radio scripts, and audio-visual materials. Provides advisory services. Maintains film library at 13 East 37th St., New York 16, N. Y. Publishes *The Psychiatric Aid*.

National Foot Health Council, P. O. Box 57, Rockland, Mass. Sponsors National Foot Health Week in May, and Child Foot Health Month in September. Has available leaflets, reprints, radio talks, and posters.

National Foundation for Infantile Paralysis, 120 Broadway, New York 5, N. Y. Maintains a four-point program of action: medical care, epidemic emergency aid, research, and education. Provides pamphlets, posters, free loan films, and exhibits. Descriptive listing of publications, films, and exhibits is available.

National Health Council, Inc., 1790 Broadway, New York 19, N. Y. Offers full information about the organization of local councils. Provides kit that includes pamphlets, leaflets, and reprints for use in improving community health programs.

National Institutes of Health, Public Health Service, Department of Health, Education, and Welfare, Washington 25, D. C. Provides funds to states for health purposes. Furnishes advisory services, exhibits, pamphlets, study kits, and free loan films. Film catalogue available.

National Organization for Public Health Nursing, 2 Park Ave., New York 16, N. Y. Source of films, radio scripts, pamphlets, publicity kits, and posters. Evaluates community nursing services. Catalogue of materials available.

National Publicity Council for Health and Welfare Services, Inc., 257 Fourth Ave., New York 10, N. Y. Furnishes information on public relations and public education for health and welfare. Publishes list of selected publications.

National Tuberculosis Association, Inc., 1790 Broadway, New York 19, N. Y. Publishes a series of pamphlets on home care of tuberculosis victims. Provides leaflets, brochures, free loan films, and other educational materials. Assists community organizations in case finding, health education, rehabilitation programs, and all other phases of local campaigns against the disease.

Office of Education, Department of Health, Education, and Welfare, Washington 25, D. C. Offers a series of 15-minute radio recordings and scripts dramatizing problems in fields such as cancer, tuberculosis, venereal disease, and mental illness. Materials are suitable for public education programs over local radio stations, for industry and school health projects, and for study and discussion meetings. Recordings are for 16-inch, 33⅓ rpm playback machines. Has catalogues with suggestions for the use of recordings and scripts.

Public Affairs Press, 2153 Florida Ave., N. W., Washington 8, D. C.

Publishes *American Health Directory*, listing organizations in all fields of health and health facilities and services.

Social Protection Division, United States Public Health Service, Department of Health, Education, and Welfare, Washington 25, D. C. Publishes pamphlets for the use of community leaders in setting up a social hygiene program. Source of outstanding films.

Superintendent of Documents, United States Government Printing Office, Washington 25, D. C. Has available a listing of low cost government publications in health and related fields. Publishes *Mental Health Motion Pictures*, a selected annotated listing.

United States Public Health Service, Department of Health, Education, and Welfare, Washington 25, D. C. A major source of information about public health problems. Has background information, planning guides, promotional materials, and free loan films and film information.

Some Sources of Films and Film Information

The major source of free loan and low rental health films and filmstrips, and information about such aids, is the United States Public Health Service, described above. Many of the health associations and agencies listed above are primary sources of such help in their specialized fields. Most of the films and filmstrips available are dramatizations of health problems, of preventive and curative procedures and techniques, and of methods by which volunteer action can support or supplement official action.

The following incomplete listing of subjects is suggestive of the great range of interests that may be served by such material: dental health in the community, the feeling of hostility in children and how to combat it, the services of a child guidance center, field procedures in eliminating the mosquito nuisance, the problems of venereal disease, breast self-examination and other procedures for the control of cancer, descriptions of research programs, the story of the use of sodium fluoride in community water supplies, the organization and operation of a communicable disease center, nurse and doctor recruitment, the search for individuals with tuberculosis, sources of contamination in communities, rabies control, and utilizing community facilities to combat polio and its effects.

Other Representative Sources:

Association Films, Inc., 79 East Adams St., Chicago 3, Ill. Free loan films include subjects such as the role of the health department as the guardian of community welfare, common-sense precautions against the common cold, the story of the progress made in public health, and the importance of planned nutrition. Catalogue available.

Caterpillar Tractor Company, Advertising Department, Peoria 8, Ill. Free loan film *A Community Problem* illustrates various common methods of garbage disposal; explains the advantages of the landfill method. Description available.

Committee on Careers in Nursing, 2 Park Ave., New York 16, N. Y. Free loan films useful in an organization's recruitment program. Descriptions available.

Committee on Medical Motion Pictures, American Medical Association, 535 North Dearborn Ave., Chicago 10, Ill. Offers *Sources of Motion Pictures in Health.*

Communicable Disease Center, Audio-Visual Production Services, P. O. Box 185, Chamblee, Ga. Free loan films on the training of professional and lay personnel in the fields of sanitation and public health. Descriptions available.

Educational Film Library Association, 1600 Broadway, New York 19, N. Y. *Health Films Catalogue* is a descriptive listing of about 350 titles available on a free loan or rental basis.

Encyclopaedia Britannica Films, Inc., 1150 Wilmette Ave., Wilmette, Ill. Offers a low rental *Health and Hygiene Series* describing the factors affecting the health of a city, and the role of a model city health department. Catalogue available.

Film Library of the National Association for Mental Health, 13 East 37th St., New York 16, N. Y. Has free 16-page catalogue of selected rental films, with a listing of those cleared for television.

General Electric Company, Visual Education Division, 1 River Rd., Schenectady 5, N. Y. Free loan films include *Clean Waters*, a forceful portrayal of the serious consequences of water pollution.

Health Publications Institute, Inc., 216 North Dawson, Raleigh, N. C. Publishes *Motion Pictures for Mental Health Programs*, an annotated list with suggestions for effective presentations.

Institute of Inter-American Affairs, 499 Pennsylvania Ave., N. W., Washington 25, D. C. Free loan and low rental films present the varied services of a community health center; introduce the problem of the control of pests, and suggest control measures; discuss sanitary facilities and practices necessary to protect communities, such as provisions for safe water, the disposal of sewage and garbage, and the protection of food supplies. Descriptions available.

International Film Bureau, Suite 308–316, 57 East Jackson Boulevard, Chicago 4, Ill. Information about *Another Light,* the story of how a community came to appreciate its new hospital, and how citizens mobilized their resources for its support. Available on a free loan basis from most state health departments and film libraries.

Modern Talking Picture Service, Inc., 45 Rockefeller Plaza, New York 20, N. Y. Rental films include the 25-minute film *A Citizen Participates*—a story of how citizen effort secured a doctor for a community. Shows Kiwanis Club committees in action. Description available. Television rights are held by the American Medical Association.

National Film Board of Canada, 1270 Avenue of the Americas, New York 20, N. Y. Low rental films include a series about the need for a mental health program in the community, and *Behind the Menu*, a demonstration of how sanitary restaurants may be assured through better food storage, more effective dishwashing methods, and other measures. Catalogue available.

Purdue University, Film Library, Lafayette, Ind. Has available the rental film *Kill 'Em with Gas*. Dramatizes the economic importance of the damage done by rats. Shows sanitation and ratproofing measures, and the use of cyanide gas and poisons. Description available.

Samuel P. Orleans and Associate, Inc., 211 West Cumberland Ave., Knoxville 15, Tenn. Offers *Your Health Department in Action*, a presentation of the varied services of a well-rounded community public health program. Description available.

See and Hear Magazine, 7064 North Sheridan Ave., Chicago 10, Ill. Publishes *Audio-Visual Resources for Health and Welfare*, which describes about 650 films and filmstrips.

United World Films, Inc., Government Films Department, 1445 Park Ave., New York 29, N. Y. Information about a community fly control series: types of domestic flies, how flies transmit disease, and methods of control.

CHAPTER 10

Welfare

THROUGH THEIR support of public and volunteer welfare agencies, and through their own cooperative and supplemental welfare programs, various organizations are helping to bring physical comfort, peace of mind, and happiness to individuals who cannot help themselves through their own resources alone. These efforts are making important contributions to community self-sufficiency, and are making it possible for millions of organization members to experience the spiritual satisfactions of giving.

Chapters 3, 7, and 9 offer suggestions that may be helpful to your committee in planning and carrying out its welfare program. This chapter suggests further activities in behalf of children and youth, the physically handicapped and chronically ill, the institutionalized, the aged, the socially maladjusted, and victims of disaster.

CHILDREN AND YOUTH

The record of organization financial, personal service, and other contributions to official and volunteer agencies in the field of child and youth welfare, and the gains made through their cooperative and supplemental projects are impressive. Representative of the kinds of such aid are programs for maternal and child health, community and regional foster-home arrangements, shelter and welfare homes, summer camps for needy and neglected children, Christmas and other holiday cheer for needy children and their families, nurseries for the children of working mothers, and programs in behalf of the handicapped.

FAMILY-LIFE EDUCATION. The family is the greatest single influence on the lives of children and youth. To provide opportunities for education for family living, therefore, is an important welfare objective. Any activity designed to assist parents in maintaining a secure and protective home environment, and to assist youngsters in constructive family-life participation will be of immeasurable value to children and youth and to the general welfare of the community.

Local chapters of the General Federation of Women's Clubs contribute to stable family living through a National Youth Conservation Program. Included are family councils, to promote youth participation in family planning; a Build Freedom with Youth Contest, to provide youth with habits of good citizenship; a youth employment program, to encourage and assist youth in becoming a productive part of the community; and a Family Night at Home Program, to help establish family solidarity and emotional security for youth.

In Texas, an annual state conference of Junior Women's Clubs is held to promote a youth conservation program in every community in the state. Local units implement state programs through demonstration projects; parent-teacher education on child development; and family gardens, community centers, and other cooperative projects.

In California, the State Federation of Women's Clubs, with the State Adult Education Department, conducts conferences on family life and sponsors local study programs that include counseling on child training and the problems of adolescents.

MATERNAL AND CHILD CARE. Organizations are offering vigorous support to programs to educate mothers and prospective mothers in child care, and to assure children a healthful environment and proper medical attention.

Activities successfully carried out in this field include distributing child-welfare pamphlets; presenting lectures, study-discussion meetings, and films about child development; sponsoring marriage and family counseling services; supplying prenatal guidance and child-care material assistance; collecting and reconditioning children's clothing; donating food, clothing, and other necessities for distribution through child-care agencies; establishing well-baby clinics; and encouraging members to volunteer for service with child-care agencies.

HOMES FOR NEEDY CHILDREN. Youngsters in homes broken by death and divorce, and those neglected by their parents often need help in becoming well-adjusted, happy, and productive individuals. While state and local agencies, assisted by federal funds, are providing essential institutional and foster-home care for most of these children and youth, welfare gaps remain to be filled by volunteer group action.

Many child-care institutions are obsolete or poorly equipped; some are understaffed, or staffed with untrained workers and administrators. There is a high rate of personnel replacement because of low salaries. Your organization can do much to improve such a situation by its financial support of both public and volunteer agencies, and by its advocacy of legislation for better child-care provisions.

Important contributions to the enrichment of the life of children and youth in institutions include sponsoring fund-raising drives; donating books, sports, and other equipment; providing special parties, film showings, and other entertainment; and sponsoring and aiding in the supervision of educational and other field trips.

In many areas community organizations are active in helping to place young people in foster homes, and in promoting legislation for better adoption practices.

SUMMER CAMPS. Many needy children are attending summer camps through organization aid. Volunteer groups arrange for the attendance of individuals. They finance, equip, and sometimes operate camps. Your group might consult child welfare agencies, youth service groups, churches, and schools about opportunities for such service. Your newspaper might cosponsor a community-wide program to give camp experience to children whose family resources are inadequate.

THE HANDICAPPED AND CHRONICALLY ILL

In supporting and supplementing the work of great national associations such as the American Red Cross, the National Society for Crippled Children and Adults, and the American Epilepsy League, organizations have helped thousands of afflicted individuals develop satisfying and useful lives.

In Rochester, New York, the Eagles provided school quarters, facilities, and trained personnel for the cerebral-palsied children of the city. The Junior League of Toronto, Canada, established the first clinic and school for the cerebral palsied in that country. The Pueblo, Colorado, Rotary Club built, equipped, and staffed a curative workshop for children afflicted with spastic paralysis. In Seattle, Kiwanians initiated a successful state campaign for a $1 million spastic hospital and a continuing program of state-wide aid.

In one year, Lions Clubs throughout the country carried out over 8000 individual projects in behalf of the blind and partially blind. They provided clothing, food, household goods, and funds; supported sight clinics; conducted sight surveys; bought sight-testing equipment; improved school lighting; held Christmas parties and provided gifts and baskets; supplied Braille books, Braille writers, typewriters, talking books, and radios; arranged for Braille instruction; sponsored sight-saving classes; initiated sports and recreation programs; financed purchases of glasses, artificial eyes, and white canes; provided for medical examinations and supplies; and helped with the sale of merchandise made by the blind.

Other organizations have outstanding records. The Optimist Club of St. Petersburg, Florida, sponsors a child hearing clinic that has helped thousands of children. In Tuscaloosa, Alabama, the Kiwanis Club cooperates with the University of Alabama in a program that provides testing and remedial and other help for the school children of that city.

Other practical organization activities in behalf of handicapped and chronically ill children and adults are:

1. Supporting the March of Dimes, the Easter Seal Sale, and other national fund-raising drives.

2. Assisting national associations in their programs to give the public an appreciation of the problems and needs of handicapped persons.

3. Establishing free hospital clinics and rehabilitation centers.

4. Sponsoring the training of counselors, teachers, and therapists.

5. Providing braces, wheel chairs, iron lungs, and other orthopedic and mechanical appliances.

6. Securing state and county aid for the establishment of special classes in public schools, and initiating local programs of special help.

7. Providing swimming pools, camps, and special recreation areas under the direction of trained workers.

8. Carrying out education programs to help define parental responsibilities in carrying out directives and providing a home atmosphere conducive to good child and youth morale.

9. Scheduling visits to shut-ins—providing magazines and books, radio and television sets, and ceiling motion picture projectors for the bedridden.

10. Sponsoring vocational rehabilitation programs such as those outlined in Chapter 16.

11. Maintaining scholarships for handicapped students.

12. Sponsoring general education, recreation, cultural, and other programs.

13. Financing needed operations.

THE INSTITUTIONALIZED

The plight of those in orphanages, hospitals, sanatoriums, prisons, reformatories, and other institutions is serious. Most such individuals lack, either temporarily or permanently, the financial, physical, mental, or social resources with which to build satisfying lives. Many need more help than institutions can give if they are to be rehabilitated.

Community organizations, nationally and locally, are providing these resources through important contributions of money, time, and member interest and friendship. Some groups have established and are supporting institutions to meet various community and regional welfare needs. Many programs include members' clerical, supervisory, and other personal services.

Suggestions for activities in behalf of institutionalized young people and adults are offered in Chapters 6, 12, and 16. Typical activities include sponsoring youth groups such as Boy Scouts, Girl Scouts, and 4-H Clubs for those in institutions; providing films, books, pictures, and craft supplies; organizing projectionist squads to show films; sponsoring holiday celebrations; presenting dramatic skits, musical programs, and other entertainment; and arranging for individual and group attendance at community events.

Representative of the types of organization welfare programs in this field is the year-round Sunshine Program of the Optimists of Milwaukee, carried out in behalf of more than 1500 boys and girls in institutions in the city area. Activities usually include about 17 different projects, such as an indoor circus, a costume roller-skating party, ice frolic, hobby shows, and several one-night trips.

THE AGED

The increasing number of aged in our population is presenting many communities with a very real problem, some aspects of which are discussed in other chapters. Chapter 7, for example, suggests programs to meet their need for wholesome diversion and companionship; Chapter 16 points to the practicability of their retraining and utilization in business and industry.

Many aged are not, however, fully employable. They must be given financial security, as well as opportunities to use their time in a worthy fashion and to continue to lead satisfying lives. Many of these individuals are chronically ill, in need of medical and nursing attention.

Your organization might study the welfare provisions for the aged in your community. Do family agencies have the resources and facilities to cope with the problem? Are institutions still dominated by the almshouse tradition? Do nursing homes meet minimum standards?

Some specific activities, carried out successfully by volunteer groups working in cooperation with official agencies, are conducting surveys to determine needs, promoting boarding plans, canvassing the community for homes, arranging for paid and volunteer housekeeping services, promoting measures to provide supervision for private homes, arranging for training of practical nurses, organizing and supporting ladies' aid units, making arrangements to provide cheer through such measures as the regular donations of flowers and personal gifts, and providing transportation to church services and community events.

THE SOCIALLY MALADJUSTED

Volunteer groups today are assuming more and more of a responsibility for control and rehabilitation of individuals who have failed to make an adequate adjustment to life. They are showing an increasing concern for the tremendous social cost, for example, of juvenile delinquency, adult crime, and alcoholism.

JUVENILE DELINQUENCY. Youths between the ages of 16 and 21 commit serious crimes far out of proportion to the number of this age group in the population. Just as there is no one cause of antisocial behavior, so there is no one cure. Delinquency is a social problem that must be attacked on all fronts to achieve lasting effects. While providing some delinquents with satisfactory alternative interests, recreation programs and teen centers will fall short of solving the problems of others. Your organization should back basic community services, or aid in establishing new ones if they are found to be required, so that the needs of every child may be met.

Rehabilitation of youngsters who have offended against society presents opportunities for practical welfare activities such as helping local agencies to secure needed case workers, psychologists, and psychiatrists; promoting the establishment of a temporary detention home in the community; promoting progressive youth welfare legislation; organizing councils of adults and teen-agers; aiding in establishing counseling services for youngsters with mental health problems; promoting the establishment of a Youth Correction Authority; initiating a Big Brother movement in your community; helping to organize a Junior Police unit; and sponsoring narcotics and temperance education programs.

THE ADULT OFFENDER. As in the case of prevention and control of juvenile offenses against society, law enforcement and adult rehabilitation agencies are utilizing the resources of all other community groups, including those of volunteer organizations.

Chapter 16 suggests what can be done by your organization through offering vocational training opportunities for those in houses of correction, and occupational information and job placement services to parolees and released convicts. Members of your group might also serve as unofficial counselors for offenders, helping them budget their time and money wisely, and find opportunities for diversion and personal advancement. In many communities, citizens have organized prisoners' aid societies that have been singularly successful in helping many achieve useful and satisfying lives. Your group might offer aid to the National Probation and Parole Association in its efforts to take rehabilitation of adult offenders out of politics by fixing standards of professional training.

In many communities, there is a great need for public understanding of the nature of alcoholism. Your organization might conduct an education campaign or promote the establishment of a rehabilitation center.

VICTIMS OF DISASTER

Victims of disaster—individuals and family groups with resources strained by serious and prolonged illness or the death or unemployability of the chief wage earner, or made destitute through fire, flood, or other catastrophe frequently receive organization aid.

Representative of many thousands of projects are the following: In Biloxi, Mississippi, the Kiwanis Club financed a "blue baby" operation for a needy youngster. The El Monte, California, Lions contributed funds to finance an eye operation for a local child. Liverpool, Nova Scotia, Kiwanians paid for 23 operations to restore to normal living a girl badly disfigured as a result of a fire. In Ephrata, Pennsylvania, a family lost its home and all its possessions in a fire. A relief committee, organized by community organizations, collected money, furniture, food, and clothing, and mobilized and directed volunteer workers in converting a barn into living quarters. In areas ravaged by floods, paralyzed by heavy snow falls, or threatened with financial disaster by prolonged drought, community organizations have joined with other groups in measures to save lives and property.

Christmas, Thanksgiving, and other celebrations that emphasize ideals of charity, good will, and brotherliness are particularly appropriate occasions for welfare projects. Organizations collect, repair, and distribute toys; sponsor telephone, radio, and television appeals for aid to needy families; establish collection depots for food, clothing, toys, and other gifts; give parties for needy children, the blind, the crippled, the aged who have no family ties or are in homes, patients in hospitals, and those in reformatories and prisons; and "adopt" families and provide them with guidance and material help.

SOURCES OF AID

So numerous are government agencies and volunteer national associations and other groups offering welfare program aid, or worthy of organization support, that only a relatively few can be listed here. Additional sources are described at the close of Chapters 3, 7, 9, and 16. An organization with an extensive welfare program will find the *Social Work Year Book, 1954,* published by the American Association of Social Workers, useful as a guide to other sources of aid. It is available at most libraries.

The following are representative of agencies, associations, and other groups interested in the welfare fields suggested in this chapter, and of books of practical help:

Alcoholic Foundation, Inc., 141 East 44th St., New York 17, N. Y. Headquarters of Alcoholics Anonymous. Pamphlet descriptions of program are available.

American Association of Social Workers, Inc., One Park Ave., New York 16, N. Y. Publishes *Social Work Year Book, 1954,* a description of organized activities in social work and related fields. Useful in determining the scope of your organization welfare program, and in finding out what official and volunteer agencies offer aid to community groups or are worthy of your support. Includes descriptive listings of national official and volunteer welfare agencies in fields such as the aged, the blind, disaster relief, family social work, juvenile delinquency, and youth services.

American Foundation for the Blind, Inc., 15 West 16th St., New York

11, N. Y. Offers assistance in planning local programs in behalf of the blind. Furnishes research and other education materials. Maintains scholarship funds. Its publication *Directory of Activities for the Blind in the United States and Canada* is an important source of aid in finding help for programs to meet specific needs.

American Friends Service Committee, 20 South 12th St., Philadelphia 7, Pa. Represents the Religious Society of Friends and other organizations and individuals with welfare programs. Activities include relief and rehabilitation work, and self-help housing projects.

American National Red Cross, 17th and D Sts., N. W., Washington 13, D. C. Local units offer organizations and their members opportunities for service in various welfare fields. Organizes community resources in preparation for effective action in time of emergency.

American Public Welfare Association, 1313 East 50th St., Chicago 37, Ill. Acts as a clearinghouse for information in the public welfare field, and publicizes and interprets welfare programs. Makes surveys, provides consultant services, and publishes pamphlets, bulletins, and a monthly magazine, *Public Welfare*.

American Women's Voluntary Services, Inc., 500 Park Ave., New York 22, N. Y. Units in over 80 towns and cities. Recruits, mobilizes, and trains women as volunteer social workers. Typical activities: transporting disabled veterans and civilians, working in veterans and civilian hospitals, staffing and maintaining child-care and information centers, reconditioning clothes for the needy, and sponsoring and directing youth welfare programs.

Andrews, F. Emerson, *Philanthropic Giving*, New York: Russell Sage Foundation, 1950. Describes the major fields of philanthropy, suggests safeguards against charity rackets, discusses Community Chest and independent money-raising drives, and offers information and advice about income-tax deductions and gifts.

Big Brothers of America, Inc., 1347 Broad Street Station Building, Philadelphia 3, Pa. An association of Big Brother agencies, made up of volunteers who with professional supervision offer guidance to delinquent and predelinquent boys.

Braille Institute of America, Inc., 741 North Vermont Ave., Los Angeles 29, Calif. Provides consultation services and home instruction in the use of Braille. Prints and publishes books in Braille, available to the blind at cost. Donates appliances, games, and materials. Maintains a free Braille lending library.

Buell, Bradley and Associates, *Community Planning for Human Services*,

New York: Columbia University Press, 1952. Discusses both official and volunteer health and welfare procedures.

Child Study Association of America, Inc., 132 East 74th St., New York 21, N. Y. Organizes parent study groups, and provides lecturers, training for professional workers, and individual counseling service. Publishes pamphlets and *Child Study*, a quarterly.

Child Welfare League of America, Inc., 24 West 40th St., New York 18, N. Y. An association of about 225 child welfare agencies. Promotes cooperative group action in behalf of children. Furnishes field services to community groups. Source of pamphlets, booklets, bulletins, and books on child welfare subjects. Publishes *Child Welfare*, monthly except August and September.

Children's Bureau, Social Security Administration, United States Department of Health, Education, and Welfare, Washington 25, D. C. A primary source of information, and consultant and field service in child welfare programs. Publishes *The Child*, a monthly. *What's Happening in Your Town?*, prepared especially for community organizations, is a guide to an appraisal of official and private agencies; the services of the police department, juvenile court, and probation officers; and detention and rehabilitation institutions. Pamphlet is available from the Superintendent of Documents, United States Government Printing Office, Washington 25, D. C.

Community Chests and Councils of America, 115 East 44th St., New York 17, N. Y. "To develop and preserve community unity and solidarity in providing funds to be directed toward promotion of private health and human welfare." Organizes and directs fund-raising campaigns; disseminates information; promotes an appreciation of social needs; maintains speakers' bureaus, and radio and television programs; distributes pamphlets and releases news stories; sponsors "come and see" tours of community agencies and institutions.

Council of Jewish Federations and Welfare Funds, Inc., 165 West 46th St., New York 36, N. Y. Assists in organizing community resources to meet Jewish welfare needs.

Family Service Association of America, Inc., 192 Lexington Ave., New York 16, N. Y. A voluntary membership federation of about 250 organizations providing direct services for families in difficulties. Provides personnel and consultation services. Publishes books and pamphlets about family social work.

National Braille Press, Inc., 88 St. Stephen St., Boston 15, Mass. Publishes Braille periodicals for free distribution to the blind.

National Child Labor Committee, 419 Fourth Ave., New York 16, N. Y. Assists community agencies and volunteer groups in improving conditions of training and employment for youth. Publishes *American Child*, eight times annually.

National C.I.O. Community Services Committee, 1776 Broadway, New York 19, N. Y. Has pamphlet discussions of labor's role in volunteer welfare programs.

National Conference of Social Work, Inc., 22 West Gay St., Columbus 15, Ohio. Represents 1200 organizations interested in promoting discussions of social welfare problems. Fields include child care, delinquency, the aged, and community planning for welfare.

National Planning Association, Inc., 1606 New Hampshire Ave., N. W., Washington 9, D. C. Publications include *The Manual of Corporate Giving*, edited by Beardsley Ruml with the collaboration of Theodore Geiger. A series of articles by specialists in fields of philanthropy such as community arts, health, welfare, and education. Includes background information and advice adaptable to volunteer group programs in support of organized charities.

National Probation and Parole Association, Inc., 1790 Broadway, New York 19, N. Y. Interested in the prevention of delinquency, and the establishment of juvenile and domestic relations courts. Sponsors conferences, conducts surveys, provides training courses, and offers consultation services. Available is a 32-page *Selected Reading List*. Offers low rental films about probation work.

National Publicity Council for Health and Welfare Services, Inc., 257 Fourth Ave., New York 10, N. Y. A nonprofit clearinghouse of information on public relations and public education for health and welfare. Offers selected publications for community leaders. Listing available.

National Recreation Association, 315 Fourth Ave., New York 10, N. Y. Nominally priced pamphlets include *Recreation Standards for Children's Institutions* and *Starting a Recreation Program in a Civilian Hospital*. Annotated pamphlet listing is available.

National Social Welfare Assembly, Inc., 345 East 46th St., New York 17, N. Y. A federation of about 56 national volunteer organizations and federal agencies. Conducts research, and serves as a clearinghouse for ideas about effective welfare organization and programs. Representative publications include *A New Look at Governmental and Voluntary Services*; *Shall We Make a Survey?*, questions to be considered before a survey is undertaken; *Young People and Citizenship*; and *Mustering National and State Resources*.

Office of Education, Department of Health, Education, and Welfare, Washington 25, D. C. Offers a series of free loan transcribed dramatizations of community welfare problems and suggested solutions. Subjects include the work of the Red Cross, state hospitals, the care of mental patients, occupational rehabilitation, the rehabilitation of convicts, and the care of the aged.

Osborne Association, Inc., 114 East 30th St., New York 16, N. Y. Conducts national surveys and studies, and offers advisory services in behalf of both juvenile and adult social offenders. Supplies recreation guidance, job placement, and temporary financial aid to ex-offenders.

Society for the Prevention of Crime, 114 East 30th St., New York 16, N. Y. Source of literature on the causes and prevention of juvenile delinquency.

Sowers Printing Company, Lebanon, Pa. Publishes a booklet, *A Guide to the Operation of Group Day-Care Programs.*

State Charities Aid Association, 105 East 22nd St., New York 10, N. Y. Has available a guide for a program to help foster parents in your community.

Superintendent of Documents, United States Government Printing Office, Washington 25, D. C. Has listings of pamphlets published by various government agencies interested in the welfare of children and youth, the aged, the disabled, and others. Of special interest are the 18 reports of the National Conference on Prevention and Control of Juvenile Delinquency. Titles include *Recreation for Youth, Youth Participation, Citizen Participation, Church Responsibilities,* and *Rural Aspects of Juvenile Delinquency.* Complete listing available.

Some Sources of Films and Film Information

Many of the agencies and other groups listed above have free loan or low rental films and film information available. Other sources of films related to welfare problems are described in other chapters, particularly 9 and 16. The following are additional representative sources:

Association Films, 347 Madison Ave., New York 17, N. Y. Rental films include a discussion of the relation of slums and juvenile delinquency, methods of combating juvenile delinquency, programs at camps for underprivileged children, the influence of Scouting and other youth programs, and dramatizations of typical family problems. Descriptions included in a general catalogue.

Jack F. Morgan, 3500 West Howe St., Seattle 99, Wash. Information about *Upstream,* a 25-minute color film of a state-wide program for the cerebral palsied in Washington, initiated by a Kiwanis Club in Seattle.

Loyal Order of Moose, Moosehart, Ill. Offers free loan films about facilities provided for the care and education of orphaned children at Moosehart, and the program for the aged at Moosehaven in Florida.

McGraw-Hill Book Company, Inc., 330 West 42nd St., New York 18, N. Y. Has a "Child Development Series" of five films describing the normal development patterns of infancy and childhood. Useful in developing a background for a child welfare program. Catalogue available.

New York State Department of Commerce, Film Library, 112 State St., Albany 7, N. Y. Low rental (free loan in New York State) films depict the extent and cost of juvenile delinquency, and suggest methods of prevention. Descriptions available.

New York University Film Library, 26 Washington Place, New York 3, N. Y. Rental films include subjects such as the effect of home and community upon child development, the effect of divorce upon children, a well-rounded nursery-camp program, juvenile delinquency and its prevention, and the organization of a community youth council. General catalogue available.

United World Films, Inc., 1445 Park Ave., New York 29, N. Y. Free loan films include newsreel type presentations of the peacetime activities of the American Red Cross. Films suggest the innumerable ways by which an organization and its individual members can support the Red Cross. Catalogue available.

CHAPTER 11

Brotherhood

THE DEMOCRATIC ideal of the brotherhood of men of all races, religions, and national origins has found strong support in the practical, volunteer action of community groups. In continuing face-to-face relations on the community level, individuals are losing their prejudices, suspicions, and hostilities, and are finding a mutual understanding and increasing respect for the dignity and worth of one another, demonstrating that brotherhood need not be a vague, remote ideal, but a concrete reality to be attained in appreciable measure now.

In few other fields of service can you find such ready assistance. Many national organizations and federal and state agencies and commissions offer their experience and resources to community groups. They furnish professional personnel to help identify, analyze, and find solutions to special problems; offer program guides; maintain consultation services; and provide without charge or at very nominal cost a great wealth of education and promotion materials such as descriptions of successful projects, research reports, how-to-do-it manuals, books, pamphlets, study and discussion outlines and information, films and filmstrips, and posters.

This chapter calls attention to some general principles that have characterized successful brotherhood programs, describes some representative community organization activities, and suggests practical procedures for your group.

SOME GENERAL PRINCIPLES FOR PROGRAMMING

The experience of community groups points to the following as sound principles for action:

1. There should be general membership agreement on what is meant by brotherhood.

2. In its official acts and in the social attitudes and actions of its

187

members, an organization should reflect the ideals that its program proposes to foster in the community.

3. Action should be realistic, undertaken with a full appreciation of community patterns of living, and based on a careful appraisal of community intergroup relations.

4. Projects and programs should be correlated with efforts being made by other local and national organizations and agencies.

5. Projects and programs should be planned to take advantage of the religious, racial, and national-origin group affiliations of members.

6. Action in behalf of better intergroup relations should enlist the co-operation of minority groups involved.

7. An important objective of all projects should be education of individuals to an acceptance and appreciation of differences in cultural and other values.

8. Education activities should be carried on among those who are indifferent or hostile, not among those already sold on the idea of brotherhood.

9. A brotherhood program should never attempt to reconcile theological differences, or to suppress or minimize the cultural values of minority groups.

REPRESENTATIVE ORGANIZATION ACTIVITIES

The following activities are representative of what is being done by groups such as yours:

Service, fraternal, civic, veterans', and other community organizations, through the Montclair Forum and the Montclair Intergroup Council, conducted the Montclair, New Jersey, Community Audit, a project that has become a pattern for self-surveys throughout the nation. With the help of field workers from the National Association for the Advancement of Colored People and consultants from New Jersey State Teachers College, volunteers determined how much discrimination, if any, existed in areas such as employment, housing, recreation, education, public health, and public facilities. Publication of the survey findings was a major intergroup education project, advancing the cause of brotherhood not only in Montclair but in numerous other cities that adapted the Montclair approach to an analysis of their intergroup problems.

In "Northtown," a small Eastern city, 16 community organizations, representing a cross section of the population, participated in a survey of group relations with the help of the Commission on Community Interrelations of the American Jewish Congress. Over 75 volunteer members investigated the extent of discrimination in housing, education, employment, and public facilities and services. Their findings were given wide publicity, and used in public meetings and in group discussion programs. A marked decline in discriminatory practices in several areas was attributed to the educational effects of the survey. The planning, organization, and procedure experience of Northtown's citizens has been made available to organizations in other communities through a how-to-do-it manual published by the American Jewish Congress.

Community organizations in New Haven, Connecticut, contributed effective support to the dramatically successful New Haven Neighborhood Project to overcome prejudice and intolerance. The project's development is an illustration of what can be achieved from small beginnings. A few individuals of different cultural backgrounds from a Parent-Teacher Association and representatives of neighborhood churches met informally in one another's homes for the purpose of getting acquainted. They discovered a common willingness to work together to find solutions to mutual problems.

With the assistance of the National Conference of Christians and Jews and other groups interested in fostering human relations programs in communities, a more formal organization and program have been adopted. Activities include projects such as book clubs, festivals, study and discussion groups, and an interracial play school. The neighborhood project idea spread to other sections of New Haven and to hundreds of other communities. In one New York City neighborhood, children representing about 67 national-origin groups are engaged in get-together activities sponsored by volunteer groups.

Through their Adult Education Council, community organizations in Springfield, Massachusetts, play an active part in implementing the famous Springfield Plan for racial and religious tolerance through education programs and intergroup activity.

Another well-known interracial program, that of Philadelphia Fellowship House, was established and is maintained with the help of community organizations. Fellowship House projects include sponsorship and support of an 80-voice choir of individuals of all creeds and races; speaking trios of individuals of different cultural backgrounds for group meetings in Philadelphia and other cities; round-table discussions; fellowship clubs for interfaith understanding;

and sports, recreation, and cultural activities. Many of the projects developed by Fellowship House have been adopted in other cities.

Organization sponsored youth groups in many towns and cities have taken the lead in combating intolerance. In Madison, Wisconsin, for example, a youth council organized under National Social Welfare Assembly auspices, supported by local groups, produced and is making available a 20-minute documentary film *Make Way for Youth*.

Church groups have long been in the forefront of the fight to eliminate prejudice and discrimination. In Tonawanda, New York, a Presbyterian youth group attended churches of other faiths, scheduled sports events, and exchanged visits with other racial groups. In Kansas City, a youth group sponsored a church service in which five languages were used. In the Greenwich Village section of New York City, the Village Presbyterian Church and the Village Jewish Temple have shared the facilities of the Presbyterian Church and have jointly sponsored neighborhood events such as bazaars and recreation activities.

Labor unions are maintaining intergroup education and other programs in many communities. In Buffalo, New York, several unions established a Labor Committee to Combat Intolerance. Its activities include furnishing films, slidefilms, posters, speakers, and discussion materials to all interested groups in the area.

The San Francisco Junior Chamber of Commerce sponsored the organization of an Institute on the Employment of Members of Minority Groups to create a better understanding of minority employment problems, and to encourage employers to utilize sources of man power often denied employment opportunity. Another effort in this direction is that of the Hoopeston, Illinois, Migrant Council, composed of volunteer organizations, whose activities have resulted in virtual disappearance of segregation in public accommodations, recreation, and other areas of community living.

Twenty-four organizations in San Francisco, through a Regional Council for Civic Unity, are helping to solve intergroup problems brought about by migrations of Negro workers from the South, an influx of Mexicans, and the presence of Japanese minority groups.

Community organizations in those areas with Indian populations are helping to develop an appreciation and respect for Indian culture. Typical is the Missoula, Montana, Kiwanis Club sponsorship of an

Indian pageant, during which an Indian Village was set up, and the public entertained with Indian dancing and story telling.

SOME PRACTICAL PROCEDURES

These and hundreds of other activities suggest the practicability of procedures such as the following:

1. Develop in your own organization and sponsored youth group membership a better social, religious, and national origin balance.

2. Correlate your brotherhood program with the activities of other organization committees such as those for the cultural growth of the community, international understanding, religion, and Americanism.

3. Include minority group representation in your intergroup projects and programs.

4. Celebrate special occasions such as Brotherhood Week, Freedom Day, Race Relations Sunday, United Nations Day, and national holidays with brotherhood significance, such as Lincoln's Birthday, with appropriate meeting features. Introduce such observances, as well as minority group folk celebrations, as community events.

5. Offer the resources of your organization in support of the programs of other local groups with a special interest in fostering intergroup harmony, such as church groups, fellowship clubs, labor unions, and welfare agencies.

6. Urge adequate minority group representation on volunteer and official boards, committees, and commissions for housing, recreation, education, and other concerns which affect intergroup relations.

7. Publicize the contributions to your community and to America of individuals of minority racial, religious, and national origin groups. Effective media are special book collections, exhibits of works of art, and other evidences of achievement displayed in school and public libraries; the presentation of skits and plays at youth group and other meetings; recordings; newspaper feature articles, and radio and television programs.

8. Help develop leaders for intergroup cooperation through sponsorship and support of institutes, workshops, summer study camps, and formal courses of study. Encourage specialized training for public school teachers and other youth leaders.

9. Initiate and support a citizens unity committee to encourage intergroup planning. Ask the mayor to appoint a mayor's committee to improve intergroup relations. Urge the formation of a fair play committee in situations in which minorities are threatened with loss of civil rights or other injustices.

10. Sponsor establishment of neighborhood councils that feature in-

tergroup activities in fields such as music, art, literature, homemaking, sports, and recreation.

11. Initiate and support youth action, such as surveys of community intergroup attitudes and practices; conferences on minority and intergroup relations problems; reciprocal visits by students from schools serving populations of different races, religions, or national origins; Brotherhood Week talks by high school students; and the formation of interfaith, interracial, and international clubs.

12. Cooperate with school heads in conducting essay and other contests; planning brotherhood assemblies; showing films; supplying classes with study guides and materials; and giving other areas of the school program, such as dramatics, art, literature, and music, an intercultural emphasis.

13. Organize trips for members, school children, youth groups, and others to areas in which people of similar racial or national origin have concentrated. Arrange for groups of young people from areas with different racial, religious, or national origin backgrounds to visit your community as guests of your members.

14. Organize "trialogues," panels of three people with different beliefs or cultural backgrounds, to demonstrate how to talk things over, come to different conclusions, and find areas for common action—in an atmosphere of mutual respect.

15. Sponsor round-table programs at public meetings or on radio or television to counter popular misconceptions about race.

16. Stimulate public interest in the problem of intergroup relations by staging demonstrations of how prejudice develops. Successfully used by many organizations is the Anti-Defamation League's Rumor Clinic, in which an audience can see how the truth is distorted as an account of a film action is passed orally from person to person.

17. Ask churches to cooperate through featuring in sermons and at meetings practical measures individuals can take to further the brotherhood ideal.

18. Initiate a program to assimilate migratory workers into the social and recreational life of the community.

19. Maintain a guidance and placement service for minorities with special employment problems.

20. Sponsor interfaith projects such as recitals featuring ritual and other music of Christian and Jewish origin; common use of church facilities; cooperative sponsorship of worthy causes; and joint celebration of such religious occasions as Christmas and Chanuka, Easter and Passover.

21. Cooperate with local commercial motion picture theaters in pre-

senting feature length films such as those sponsored by the Broadcasting and Film Commission of the National Council of the Churches of Christ, the Anti-Defamation League of B'nai B'rith, and the National Conference of Christians and Jews.

SOURCES OF AID

Advertising Council, Inc., 25 West 45th St., New York 36, N. Y. Public service projects include cooperation with national and local groups engaged in brotherhood programs. Supplies advertising material such as posters and newspaper mats, and a series of free loan one-minute animated films for local television use.

American Association of University Women, 1634 Eye St., N. W., Washington 6, D. C. Has available pamphlets describing the nature of the problem of intergroup tension and the effects of discriminatory practices; study outlines; and suggestions for investigative procedure in specific community living areas such as housing, health and medical care, and employment.

American Federation of International Institutes, 11 West 42nd St., New York 36, N. Y. Cooperates with local groups in establishing "International" houses to promote better understanding among peoples of differing ethnic and national backgrounds.

American Friends Service Committee, 20 South 12th St., Philadelphia 7, Pa. Furnishes consultation service and professional personnel to community groups interested in overcoming prejudice and discrimination. Literature describing program and specific projects is suggestive of action appropriate in many community situations.

American Jewish Committee, Community Relations Service, 386 Fourth Ave., New York 16, N. Y. Program includes assistance to community organizations interested in bettering intergroup relations in general, as well as in countering anti-Semitism. Furnishes booklet descriptions of the organization and direction of community self-surveys, materials for youth leaders, free loan films, filmstrips, exhibit materials, bibliographies of radio scripts and recordings, stories, news releases, plays, cartoons, comics, and suggestions for the organization and direction of a youth council for the elimination of intergroup friction. Many pamphlets and booklets, free or nominally priced, are available in quantity.

American Jewish Congress, Commission on Community Interrelations, 15 East 84th St., New York 28, N. Y. Works in cooperation with community groups carrying out programs for interfaith and interracial understanding. Community Consultation Division has field workers to help organizations utilize new techniques. Furnishes speakers for community organization programs. Offers pamphlet material in quantity, free or nominally priced. Films available on a free loan basis include a series of one-minute animated television spot announcements.

Anti-Defamation League of B'nai B'rith, 212 Fifth Ave., New York 10, N. Y., or 327 South LaSalle St., Chicago 4, Ill. Maintains 25 regional offices in principal cities. Seeks to promote better human relations among all Americans by education, by force of public opinion, and, where practicable, by the power of legislation. Offers a consultation service for the organization of community programs. Has available a 42-page booklet, *Materials in Intergroup Relations*, describing books for youth and adults, songs, cartoons, posters, matchbooks, schoolbook covers, blotters, free loan and rental films, filmstrips, and other audiovisual aids.

Bureau for Intercultural Education, 157 West 13th St., New York 11, N. Y. Cooperates with schools and community agencies and organizations in promoting harmony among Americans of different beliefs, races, and national origins. Program includes consultant services for organizations with brotherhood programs. Helps communities study and find solutions for specific problems. Publishes books and pamphlets for intercultural education. Makes available the results of human relations research projects.

Bureau of Indian Affairs, United States Department of the Interior, 608 South Dearborn St., Chicago 4, Ill. Facilitates cooperative cultural assimilation programs. Publishes *Indian Education*, a fortnightly, and *Indians at Work*, a bimonthly, both available without charge.

Catholic Interracial Council, 20 Vesey St., New York 7, N. Y. An organization of white and Negro Catholics to further interracial cooperation. Offers to collaborate with organizations in brotherhood projects. Pamphlets available. Publishes *Interracial Review*, which includes reports of progress, background articles, and reviews of books, plays, and motion pictures about the problem of intolerance.

Children's Book Council, 50 West 53rd St., New York 20, N. Y. Will aid in scheduling and organizing book activities in observance of special occasions that may be given an intergroup and intercultural emphasis.

Committee on Education, Training, and Research in Race Relations of the University of Chicago, 5750 Ellis Ave., Chicago 37, Ill. Publishes monthly *Inventory of Research in Racial and Cultural Relations*, a systematic coverage of the literature in the field.

Common Council for American Unity, Inc., 20 West 40th St., New York 18, N. Y. Supplies community organizations and agencies with information about special problems affecting national origin and racial groups. Maintains a press and radio release service in 19 languages. Works for an appreciation of the contributions of minority groups to American life. Publishes *Interpreter Releases,* a subscription service.

Council Against Intolerance in America, 17 East 42nd St., New York 17, N. Y. Created to study the causes of prejudice in America and to develop techniques to combat it. Will help arrange rallies and other public meetings to promote unity among racial and religious groups. Furnishes background material and manuals for youth leaders. Publishes *American Unity,* a monthly available without charge. Other material includes posters, films and filmstrips, maps, charts, cartoons, traveling exhibits, and collections of photographs which illustrate intergroup problems.

DuBois, Rachel Davis, *Neighbors in Action,* New York: Harper & Brothers, 1950. Describes procedures used in bettering group relations in a New York City area populated by groups of different national origins. Programs described are adaptable to many community situations.

Fellowship House, 1431 Brown St., Philadelphia 30, Pa. Has available an account of the development of Fellowship House, and descriptions of programs adaptable to other community situations.

Institute for American Democracy, Inc., 212 Fifth Ave., New York 10, N. Y. An educational, nonsectarian, nonprofit organization to encourage unity among Americans of every race, creed, and national origin. Furnishes guidance and materials for community organization programs. Offers consultative service through field representatives. Materials available at cost include outdoor billboard posters, indoor posters, car cards, transcribed radio programs, spot announcements, blotters, matchbooks, schoolbook covers, postage meterplates, newspaper advertising mats, and cartoons. Has available guides for teachers and other youth leaders.

Interracial Fellowship of Greater New York, 316 West 122nd St., New York 27, N. Y. Descriptions of Fellowship organization and operation may suggest approaches to problems in your community.

Marrow, Alfred J., *Living without Hate,* New York: Harper & Brothers, 1951. A discussion of ways of overcoming prejudices, based on the findings of research organizations interested in better human relations.

National Association for the Advancement of Colored People, 20 West

40th St., New York 18, N. Y. An organization to safeguard the civil rights of Negroes. Furnishes legal aid. Has available a number of books and pamphlets about general and individual Negro problems in fields such as housing, public accommodation, and education. Publications: *Crisis*, a monthly magazine, and the *NAACP Bulletin*, a quarterly.

National C.I.O. Committee to Abolish Racial Discrimination, 718 Jackson Place, N. W., Washington 6, D. C. A source of information about labor community-education programs for tolerance.

National Conference of Christians and Jews, National Headquarters, 381 Fourth Ave., New York 16, N. Y. and offices in major cities in over 50 areas throughout the country. Sponsors nation-wide observance of American Brotherhood Week, during the week of Washington's birthday. Aids to community groups include program suggestions and materials for Brotherhood Week celebrations; cooperation in establishing human relations courses, workshops, and institutes; handbooks for teachers and other youth leaders; guides and background material for forums and discussion groups; radio scripts, transcriptions, spot announcements, and other material for local radio use; books, pamphlets, comics, and stories for children of all ages; free loan films, filmstrips, and other audio-visual aids. Helps in establishing intercultural centers for children and adults. A bibliography of material is available.

National Council of the Churches of Christ in the U.S.A., Department of Racial and Cultural Relations, 297 Fourth Ave., New York 10, N. Y. Has available a folder of program suggestions for groups of different types.

National Education Association, Commission for the Defense of Democracy through Education, 1201 16th St., N. W., Washington 6, D. C. Information about programs in the public schools. Suggestions for organization-school cooperation. Materials useful for organization public-education programs include many of the Personal Growth leaflets, available in quantity at very nominal cost.

National Labor Service, 386 Fourth Ave., New York 16, N. Y. Founded to promote good will among American workers of all races and religions. Supported by C.I.O., A.F. of L., and their affiliates. Maintains a workers' education program in the labor press, in union halls, and at conferences, conventions, institutes, and schools. Aid to local unions and other community groups include consultant service in setting up antidiscrimination committees; trained personnel to help organize formal courses, schools, and institutes; speakers; radio scripts and recordings, free loan films and filmstrips; and books, pamphlets, cartoons, and advertising mats. *Labor Education Materials on Minority*

Problems, an annotated listing, and a manual of instructions about the use of Labor Service intergroup materials are available.

National Social Welfare Assembly, Inc., 345 East 46th St., New York 17, N. Y. A welfare planning body for government and voluntary agencies. Functions include disseminating data, encouraging citizen participation, and coordinating programs. Has numerous publications of interest to local groups. Descriptions of programs, listings of materials, and bibliographies available.

National Urban League, Inc., 1133 Broadway, New York 10, N. Y. A national interracial social agency to improve the economic life and well-being of Negroes in America. Has local units in about 56 major cities throughout the United States. Aid to community organizations includes expert consultant services for programs to eliminate friction; cooperation in industrial relations programs to widen Negro opportunity in business and industry; assistance in providing vocational guidance and training for Negroes; and reports, pamphlets, articles, and other literature providing information about intergroup relations.

New York School of Industrial and Labor Relations, Cornell University, Ithaca, N. Y. Publishes research reports in pamphlet form.

Public Affairs Committee, Inc., 22 East 38th St., New York 16, N. Y. An organization to make available in inexpensive form the results of research on economic and social problems. Many pamphlets are of interest to organizations with brotherhood programs. Listing available.

Superintendent of Documents, United States Government Printing Office, Washington 25, D. C. A wide variety of materials about intergroup relations. Especially useful as project background material is the *Report of the President's Committee on Civil Rights.* Useful also are catalogues describing Office of Education radio transcriptions and scripts available to community organizations on a free loan or purchase basis.

Woman's Home Companion, 640 Fifth Ave., New York 20, N. Y. Offers reprint of *Your Town Could Do It Too,* by Helena Huntington Smith, describing how Springfield, Massachusetts, combats racial and religious bigotry. Also a pamphlet prepared by Dr. Clyde Miller of Teachers College, Columbia University, as a guide for community organizations planning a program in intergroup relations.

Wormser, Margot Haas and Selltiz, Claire, *How to Conduct a Community Self-Survey of Civil Rights,* New York: Association Press, 1951. A tested method of gauging discriminatory practices against minority groups as a basis for remedial action.

SOME SOURCES OF FILMS AND FILM INFORMATION

Many of the sources of general aid described above are also major sources of films and film information. Other representative sources of such aid are the following:

Association Films, Inc., 347 Madison Ave., New York 17, N. Y. A major source of low rental films on intergroup relations. Catalogue available.

Broadcasting and Film Commission, The National Council of the Churches of Christ in the U.S.A., 200 Fifth Ave., New York 10, N. Y. Has information about films and filmstrips with brotherhood themes. Sponsors feature length film showings at commercial theaters.

Current History Films, 226 East 22nd St., New York 10, N. Y. Rental films about the achievements, contributions, and place of the Negro in American history.

Encyclopaedia Britannica Films, Inc., 1150 Wilmette Ave., Wilmette, Ill. Rental films to furnish background for a program in intergroup relations. Listing available.

Film Images, Inc., 18 East 60th St., New York 22, N. Y. Rental offerings include films presenting the culture of racial and national origin groups. Catalogue available.

Film Publishers, Inc., 25 Broad St., New York 4, N. Y. Intergroup relations series includes *How to Be Happy and Free*, a discussion of relations in neighborhoods; *To Secure These Rights*, based on the report of the President's Committee on Civil Rights; *Free to Be Different*, how Americans differ in national and cultural origins, and how all benefit by these differences; and *One Nation*, the story of America's minority groups.

International Film Foundation, Inc., 345 East 46th St., New York 17, N. Y. Free loan films include *Boundary Lines*, a plea for the elimination of the invisible barriers of color, origin, and religion.

CHAPTER 12

Religion

NO DESIGN for democracy is complete that does not include the religious forces that gave democracy its birth and continue to provide the idealism and faith essential to its character. This idealism and this faith inspire our people to devote time and energy and talent to the service of their fellow men.

Service, fraternal, business, labor, and other community organizations, as well as church-affiliated groups, are giving increasing emphasis to the moral, ethical, and spiritual values inherent in democratic living. They are strengthening the churches of the community as institutions essential to the American way of life, and are applying the basic principles of religion to solutions of social, political, and economic problems.

For the convenience of those charged with program planning, suggested activities are here presented as those customarily sponsored by civic organizations and those sponsored by groups with church affiliation.

ACTIVITY SUGGESTIONS FOR CIVIC ORGANIZATIONS

In introducing religion as a meeting activity or as an area of service, organization leaders will find that the church is a major concern of members. One federated organization estimates that nine in ten of its members are regular churchgoers; another reports that 80 per cent of its several hundred thousand members are active in church affairs, and that more than 20,000 are Sunday school teachers.

It is all too common, though, for civic organizations to refrain from religious activities on the grounds that religion is a personal matter and that the differences in faiths make such activities inadvisable. To overcome such objections, your leaders might undertake a series of lectures and discussions, to make clear the great common purpose of all faiths. In introducing the idea of organized action in behalf of religion, care should be taken to stress the fact that it cannot be the purpose of your organization to bring about a synthesis of doctrines; that your organization's support of any church and its program is in the interest of the community as a whole.

RELIGION AS AN ACTIVITY IDEA. Those who are active in church groups can be of considerable influence in promoting religion as an activity idea through their informal relations with other members and through their influence on organization policy, meeting procedure, and meeting program planning. Suggest that ministers from different churches be asked to give the invocation at meetings. Provide opportunities for members to say grace at luncheons and dinners. Use appropriate prayers on the occasion of the death of a member, a time of community or national emergency, or of thanksgiving.

Are clergymen invited to become members? Do your organization prospectus, membership procurement letters, and other literature emphasize the moral, ethical, and spiritual ideals and purposes of your group? Is orientation in such matters provided for in new-member programs?

Does your meeting calendar include programs with a religious theme? Popular features are talks or panel discussions by clergymen of the major faiths, recordings of sacred music, religious films, plays, pageants, tableaux, and other events in observance of special occasions such as Christmas, Easter, and the Jewish New Year.

A survey of your own membership to reveal church affiliations and activities will uncover experiences and skills with which a program in support of religion can be built. Suggest the formation of a committee to report on the religious needs of your community, and to recommend a program of activities to meet them. Ask clergymen and lay leaders to consult with the committee and to attend the meeting discussion of its report.

TYPICAL ACTIVITIES. Among the many successful programs in which nonchurch groups have played important roles are the go-to-church campaigns sponsored nationally by church councils and federations, organizations such as the Laymen's National Committee, and associations of businessmen and other responsible leaders, such as the Advertising Council.

If your community has a ministerial association, church council, or a federation of church groups, urge it to utilize the help of organizations. Offer the specific, concrete support of your group in arranging essay and poster contests; organizing youth groups for door-to-door canvassing; forming a motorcade to transport the aged and otherwise handicapped to services; and sponsoring intergroup membership church attendance contests.

Nonchurch groups have made contributions of personal services in repairing and renovating churches of all faiths. Unions have contributed skills, using donated materials and equipment. In some communities church worship services have been made more effective through organization-inspired help to provide chimes, an organ, choir robes, or other aids.

Other successful activities suggest measures such as these:

1. Urge membership support for the programs of church groups.

2. Ask clergymen and church lay leaders to contribute to a program for the moral, ethical, and spiritual development of members of your sponsored youth group.

3. Secure church representation on councils in fields such as education, health, recreation, and labor-management relations.

4. Contribute the special personnel, business organization, transportation, public relations, and other resources of your membership to interdenominational church surveys.

5. Include among your sponsored events the observance of special national occasions closely related to the religious life of communities. According to the National Council of the Churches of Christ, over 10,000 communities, for example, observed Youth Week in one year.

6. Help bring worship services to those unable to attend church. In Cleveland the Junior Chamber of Commerce arranged for 500 crippled and ill persons to attend Protestant, Catholic, and Jewish Wayside Worship services at the city's drive-in theaters.

7. Encourage attendance at services on Sunday and weekday religious schools by helping to provide bus or private-car transportation. Consult the company furnishing school transportation about arrangements.

8. Join with church organizations, schools, youth service agencies, and other groups in publicizing the materialistic and mechanistic bases of communism and other godless ideologies. Contribute to efforts to counter secularism whenever it is advanced as public policy.

9. Make church directories, worship service schedules and programs, and other information available at railroad stations, bus terminals, hotels, and tourist centers.

10. Join with other groups in presenting a Clergymen's Day. Ask your local newspaper to feature personality sketches and photographs.

11. Sponsor contests with spiritual themes. What My Church Means to Me, for example, would be an appropriate student essay topic.

12. Include support for rural churches as part of your program for better urban-rural relations.

ACTIVITY SUGGESTIONS FOR CHURCH ORGANIZATIONS

Paralleling the development of a renewed emphasis on the function of religion in everyday life and a renewed appreciation of the privileges and responsibilities of laymen, has been a tremendous growth of church organizations.

In varied and extensive programs these groups are contributing to the fullest possible development of their members as spiritually motivated individuals; to the realization of the great social aims common to all churches; and to the achievement of the fundamental, universal purposes of religion through their support of their churches as institutions, and their participation in efforts to make worship services more effective.

Church organizations are utilizing the talents of their members in initiating and carrying out activities that furnish a multiplicity of church contacts for all age groups. Preschool children learn the story of the Bible before they can read, through story telling, films, plays, pageants, and tableaux. They grow creatively as they participate in dramatic play. Sunday, weekday, and vacation schools have greater vitality because of lay participation. Gymnasiums, recreation rooms, and snack bars are providing a wholesome social-religious atmosphere for young people. All ages are developing new capacities through discussion and study groups, handicraft and hobby classes, and social clubs. Those seeking jobs, preparing for marriage, striving to meet their religious obligations as parents, or struggling with other perplexing problems receive counseling help through church organization services.

Both adult and young people's groups are participating in areas formerly reserved for the clergy. They survey church and community needs and resources; actively participate in community evangelism campaigns; schedule visitations; and plan and direct noonday and other special devotion.

No set of project ideas applicable to all church organizations can be offered here. Current church and community needs must determine goals. Many factors influence the choice of a project or program: church policy, traditional relations between the clergy and laity, group resources, the existence of a council of local churches, for example. The following are representative areas of action.

SECURING TOTAL PARTICIPATION. A vital church is one in which there is total membership participation in planning and carrying out its activities. Your group can be of inestimable service by popularizing this idea, and by taking definite action to make it a reality.

Ask your pastor to call together the leaders of all groups to consider what responsibilities, traditionally or by default assumed by the pastor or a few officers, can appropriately be assigned to individuals or groups, permitting the pastor to be more effective in those areas of primary church concern.

ADMINISTRATIVE DETAILS. Many details of administration, which in some churches tax the time and energy of clergymen and church officers, may be effectively performed by laymen. Your organization might adopt some of the following activity ideas:

1. Contributing to church efficiency by applying modern business methods to office organization and procedure.

2. Furnishing part-time secretarial and clerical personnel.

3. Organizing members to supplement calls upon the sick or otherwise afflicted.

4. Welcoming newcomers to the community.

5. Furnishing leadership for sponsored youth groups.

6. Arranging for counseling services.

7. Providing volunteer personnel for Sunday, weekday, vacation, and other religious education programs.

8. Planning and directing measures to facilitate transfer of youth to adult participation in church activities.

CHURCH FACILITIES. Often church programs are seriously handicapped by inadequate space, and by lack of proper furnishings, equipment, and facilities. Your organization might undertake a survey of the physical facilities of your church. Do meeting rooms include a place where young people will not disturb other groups? Does the pastor have a room appropriate for conferences? Is there a library or reading room? Can several study or discussion groups meet at the same time?

Sponsor the formation of a planning committee to consider expansion needs and how to meet them. Mobilize members to help improve and maintain facilities and equipment. Particular groups have special contributions to make. Members of the men's association may have had home experience in painting, wallpapering, and making minor repairs. A boys' group might build partitions, make tables, chairs, book shelves, display boards, or a tract rack as part of its weekday activities program. Women's groups might provide such decorative details as draperies and pictures, and such essentials as china and silverware.

CHURCH-COMMUNITY SURVEYS. The solution to many pressing church problems frequently requires the gathering of concrete and objective data about the church membership, a neighborhood, or the community at large. If your group is to have a part in planning and carrying out church programs, it is important that its members help discover and appraise the facts on which such programs are based.

Does the church program meet the real needs of children, youth, and adults? In what areas of community living can your church be of greatest service? Is the traditional allocation of funds in the best interest of church members and the community? What are the causes of declining church or Sunday school attendance?

Finding answers to questions such as these frequently provides opportunities for membership participation in activities such as door-to-door interviewing; analyzing other community surveys; observing school, library, and municipal recreation programs; determining the geographical, occupational, national origin, and other distribution of church members; and studying transportation facilities.

CHURCH MEMBERSHIP. Organizations are assuming greater responsibility for maintaining church membership and attendance at services, and for assimilating new and reactivated members. Leaders of men's and women's groups, with the pastor and church officers, may serve as an executive or coordinating committee for a consideration of the relation between membership and attendance and the over-all church program, and for planning and directing membership and assimilation campaigns.

New members and those persuaded to resume active status should be assimilated without delay. The following organization sponsored procedures have been successful:

1. Plan and direct a social hour to follow classes and services.
2. Prepare and distribute a church handbook, to include data about the various organizations newcomers may join, as well as essential matters of faith and a description of the church program.
3. Invite new members to a dinner to meet the clergyman and lay

leaders, and to hear about the church program and plans. Sponsor social events for newcomers.

4. Assign a member of your group to pay special attention to each newcomer. Suggest that a record of his assimilation progress be kept. At the end of a few months, is this person attending services regularly? Is he affiliated with a church organization? What skills and group activity experiences has the newcomer that may be more fully utilized in service to the church and community?

5. Ask newcomers to evaluate their experience as members of your group and the church. In what ways, in their opinion, could your organization or general church program be improved?

Church organizations are effectively supporting programs of religious education. If your resources permit you may adopt one or more of the following activities:

1. Sponsor the formation of a religious education committee to procure personnel, provide lay training, organize curricula, and plan and carry out projects for special groups such as parents and those about to marry. Such a committee should be a cross section of the congregation, including representatives of the board, men's and women's associations, and youth groups.

2. Present a dedication service at the opening of the church school year and an annual recognition day.

3. Help supervise children's groups at Sunday, weekday, and vacation schools.

4. Arrange to have professional and business men talk to groups about religion in their everyday activities.

5. Organize a visual aids department to be used in both formal and informal education programs. Contribute equipment and funds to maintain the department.

6. Schedule religious films as meeting features.

7. Sponsor special teacher training for promising laymen.

8. Install and service a tract rack, book shelf, or magazine table in youth group and other meeting places.

9. Arrange for teacher-parent conferences and other measures to strengthen the work of teachers of religion.

CHURCH LEADERSHIP. It is generally accepted that a pastor is not engaged to administer the church on behalf of members, but to direct members in self-administration. A primary concern, therefore, is that there be a continuing replenishment of lay leadership for expanding programs. This leadership must be developed—the need cannot wait upon its discovery.

Your organization can provide leadership training opportunities through measures such as these:

1. Find and encourage individuals with the capacity for leadership. Facilitate the transfer of leaders from youth to adult activities.

2. Finance the attendance of representatives of your youth groups at conferences such as those sponsored by the United Christian Youth Movement of the National Council of Churches.

3. Sponsor periodic conferences of group leaders for an exchange of ideas about procedures and techniques, and initiate and support community and regional leadership conferences, summer camps, and formal study courses.

4. Recognize leadership achievement through citations and awards.

5. Organize a church or interdenominational retreat.

WORSHIP SERVICES. The life of a church is centered in its worship services. Church organizations can contribute to their effectiveness, and on special occasions can furnish leadership. Here are some suggestions:

1. Form an intergroup committee to consider ways by which the sanctuary and church can be made more beautiful. Arrange for the services of a professional decorator in renovation projects.

2. Have members visit other churches to observe worship arrangements and procedures, and make recommendations.

3. Aid in organization and training of choirs from different age groups. Help furnish robes, sheet music, and other aids.

4. Sponsor formation of a committee to choose and arrange flowers for main services and other devotions.

5. Plan a series of instruction and discussion meetings to improve ushering.

6. Sponsor a children's service at the time of the main service. Such a "children's church" or "junior worship" project not only gives children a genuine worship experience, but permits parents to attend church without distraction. Schedule organization members to conduct a short service. Enlist the aid of other groups in planning and directing creative activities. Children should take part in reading the Scriptures, ushering, taking up the offering, and singing.

7. Provide a nursery, during the main service, for children under six. Some churches have a room equipped with cribs and playpens. Girls' and women's groups often share in the supervision of such a project.

8. Sponsor the formation of luncheon clubs among church members, with brief devotions and short talks by laymen as meeting features.

BUDGETING AND FUND RAISING. The participation of members in budget making and fund raising provides an education in church responsibilities and the ways and means by which the church proposes to meet them.

In many churches, children and young people draw up their own budget, raise funds, and control their budget operation. Such a program of intelligent, elective, and self-governed giving is an important sharing experience for young people, and an excellent training in stewardship and leadership. Supervisors might be limited to an adult general advisor and an adult treasurer to work with a youth treasurer. It is important, however, that the children and young people see their relation to the total church program and its financial problems. Arrangement for placing the youth budget within the master budget should be carefully made.

UNITED CHURCH CANVASS. In hundreds of communities, churches have been aided in finding solutions to their financial problems through affiliation with the United Church Canvass, organized and directed by local church councils. Participating churches have improved membership and public relations generally by restricting pleas for funds to an annual period, have emphasized the importance of churches to the community through concerted education and promotion campaigns, and have developed close interfaith and interdenomination relations as a basis for community service. Your group might urge consideration of such an interchurch approach to the problem of financing activities.

RELIGION IN THE COMMUNITY. Programs to stimulate the religious thinking, feeling, and action of citizens, to offer all citizens solace and opportunities for worship, and to give material and moral support to all churches should, of course, receive first consideration in community activities planning.

Important for the success of these activities are the support and participation of other community volunteer groups. Take advantage of the group affiliations of your members to enlist cooperation in projects such as these:

1. Emphasizing the spiritual significance of Easter, Thanksgiving, Christmas, and other traditional celebrations, through events such as a

passion play; pageants; tableaux; caroling; and candlelight, sunrise, hill-top, and other special worship services and devotions.

2. Bringing church services to centers with transient or temporary populations, such as auto courts, trailer camps, migratory workers camps, and vacation resorts.

3. Helping your radio or television station maintain an interdenominational program, or secure sponsorship for such a program. Features might include special worship services for the sick, the aged, and other shut-ins; Sunday school lessons during the summer months; organ concerts; religious drama; tri-faith panel discussions; interviews; and news about the achievements of all churches and churchmen.

4. Cooperating with your local newspaper in publishing a church column or page featuring a worship service schedule, a weekly calendar of church events, and reports of the activities of church organizations; and supplying devotional material for Lenten, Easter, Christmas, and other religious seasons.

5. Joining with other community groups in providing chapels, and worship, counseling, and other services for correctional institutions, orphanages, homes for the aged, and hospitals.

6. Distributing prayer cards to members and other groups on occasions such as United Nations Day. Prayers for special occasions are available from sources such as your denominational headquarters and those listed at the close of this chapter.

7. Scheduling a series of noonday meetings for prayer and meditation in business and industrial centers.

8. Organizing meetings of occupational and professional groups to discuss opportunities for implementing their religion in various fields. Some church and other community organizations sponsor area-wide guilds, such as a Guild of Christian Salesmen or a Guild of Christian Craftsmen.

9. Sponsoring a prayer-writing project among the community's youth. Ask the schools to relate the project to their language program. Publicize outstanding prayers, chosen on the basis of sincerity, directness, simplicity, and application to some current problem.

10. Sponsoring public lectures, forums, and 16 mm films with religious themes.

11. Presenting full-length 35 mm religious films at local theaters.

12. Sponsoring a week-end retreat for lay leaders.

13. Forming lay organizations with religious programs, such as those sponsored by the National Laymen's Movement.

14. Establishing and maintaining a public-library collection of books with religion as a theme.

THE GENERAL WELFARE. Lay leaders recognize that efforts in behalf of man's spiritual well-being are intimately tied up with efforts to secure his material well-being. Programs to reduce the social cost of discrimination and intolerance, or to promote the United Nations, for example, are also programs to support the religious ideal of the brotherhood of man under one God. Volunteer group efforts through vocational guidance to utilize fully the productive capacities of all individuals sometimes involve considerations of personal spiritual problems. Labor-management issues are often moral and ethical issues, to be solved only in the full appreciation of the dignity and worth of individuals. To reduce the cost of disease and accidents, and to provide wholesome recreation and sports for youth and adults are purposes in close harmony with the purposes of religion.

The inclusive community program suggested in this book may be properly considered a pattern for extensive church community service activities. Measures such as the following are particularly appropriate:

1. Offer the services of your organization to other groups carrying on programs of service.

2. Arrange for full community use of all church facilities and services, standardizing, so far as is practicable, arrangements for meeting maintenance costs and other expenses.

3. Popularize the idea of week-end work projects such as those sponsored by the Friends Service Committee. Possible activities include clearing land for a recreation center, building a Boy Scout cabin, and painting a church.

4. Sponsor organization of a citizens group to combat legislation that is not in harmony with generally accepted moral, ethical, and spiritual beliefs.

5. Distribute register-and-vote pledge cards to church members. Keep the church open for prayers for guidance on election day. Arrange to have all the church bells of the community ring simultaneously at intervals during voting hours.

6. Establish an "overseas friendship center" for collecting, processing, and shipping gifts to needy areas.

7. Help rally all pulpits to call to the attention of congregations matters of common social concern, such as laxity in law enforcement, juvenile delinquency, and inadequate housing.

8. Cooperate with other groups in influencing a more liberal interpretation of the principles governing the relations of churches and public schools.

9. Initiate and cooperate in rehabilitation programs for juvenile delinquents.

10. Participate in vocational guidance, family welfare, and other community-service centers.

SOURCES OF AID

Denominational headquarters are primary sources of aid for church groups. Other important sources of guidance and material help to both church and civic organizations are the following:

Agricultural Extension Service, Ohio State University, Columbus, Ohio. Program helps for rural church groups.

American Bible Society, 450 Park Ave., New York 22, N. Y. Asks the cooperation of local groups in making copies of the Bible available to all people at home and abroad. Has suggestions for special projects such as bringing the spiritual consolation of the Bible to those in war-devastated areas, providing the Armed Forces with copies of the Scriptures, furnishing the blind with Braille editions, and providing students of religion with inexpensive essential texts and other material.

Boy Scouts of America, 2 Park Ave., New York 16, N. Y. Information about sponsorship procedures available from local councils or national headquarters.

Boys' Club of America, 381 Fourth Ave., New York 16, N. Y. Offers suggestions for church programs in observance of National Boys' Club Week.

Broadcasting and Film Commission, The National Council of the Churches of Christ in the U.S.A., 220 Fifth Ave., New York 10, N. Y. Sponsors radio and television programs channeled through local stations; carries out national observances of events such as the Religion in American Life campaign and National Family Week; provides radio transcriptions for local use, a series of color Bible films cleared for television, and information about films, recordings, and other audio-visual aids for church programs. Provides a list of religious films and the name of your nearest dealer. Offers consultation services to local churches, ministerial associations, and councils of churches in organizing and directing radio and television programs, institutes, and workshops.

Bureau of Church Building and Architecture, The National Council of the Churches of Christ in the U.S.A., 300 Fourth Ave., New York 10, N. Y. Offers aid to churches in the study of building, improvement, remodeling, and equipment needs. Reviews plans and makes recommendations. List of over 100 books, brochures, and leaflets is available.

Camp Fire Girls, Inc., 16 East 48th St., New York 17, N. Y. Has available booklets describing how the Camp Fire program may develop a deeper appreciation of spiritual values and support the religious programs of Catholic, Jewish, and Protestant faiths. Offers information about procedure in sponsoring a Camp Fire group.

Catholic Association for International Peace, 1312 Massachusetts Ave., N. W., Washington 5, D. C. A membership organization to foster the application of Christian principles to international affairs. Provides local groups with assistance in programming, speakers for meetings, special bibliographies, a monthly newsletter, and periodic pamphlets and reports. Full description of program and materials available.

Catholic Library Association, Maryknoll Seminary, Glen Ellyn, Ill. Sponsors Catholic Book Week, February 21–27. Materials include ideas for observance of Catholic Book Week, lists of books suggested for children and adults, posters and other promotion materials. Listing of materials available.

Chicago Federation of Christian Family Action, Room 1808, 100 West Monroe St., Chicago, Ill. A Roman Catholic movement to strengthen Christianity in the home. Literature descriptive of the organization and program in the Chicago archdiocese is suggestive of action in other communities.

Christian Century, 407 South Dearborn St., Chicago 5, Ill. Publishes *Christian Century*, a weekly magazine. Has available reprints of the *Great Churches of America* series, a discussion of factors that have made 12 churches outstanding successes.

Christophers, 18 East 48th St., New York 17, N. Y. An informal organization to encourage individuals with Christian ideals to participate in public life and to enter occupations and professions in which they may influence large numbers of people. Literature includes leaflets reporting the accomplishments of individuals, and suggestions for group and individual action. Has information about films which support the ideal of individual responsibility for action in behalf of a better world.

Commission on Youth Service Projects, The National Council of the Churches of Christ in the U.S.A., 79 East Adams St., Chicago 3, Ill. Publishes *Invest Your Summer*, an annual 32-page catalogue of youth summer service opportunities.

Department of Leadership Education, The National Council of the Churches of Christ in the U.S.A., 79 East Adams St., Chicago 3, Ill.

Offers consulting and field service for development and promotion of leadership training programs. Certifies instructors of leadership classes. Available material includes textbooks, instructors' guides, course outlines, and evaluations of current audio-visual materials in the field. Publishes *Leadership Education Newsletter* three times annually.

Division of Christian Education, The National Council of the Churches of Christ in the U.S.A., 79 East Adams St., Chicago 3, Ill. Maintains an extensive program of service to local church groups. Supplies guides and materials for children's church work, organization and administration of church schools, weekday religious education programs, camps and day camps; holds conferences and an annual workshop for supervisors of children's education and other programs; supplies audio-visual materials for the Christian education of children, youth, and adults; maintains a Learning for Life study program for adults; and suggests programs for the institutionalized.

Division of Christian Life and Work, The National Council of the Churches of Christ in the U.S.A., 297 Fourth Ave., New York 10, N. Y. Services include making available pamphlets and study guides on the ethical aspects of current economic problems and issues, and program material for such special observances as Labor Sunday and Church and Economic Life Week.

Division of Home Missions, The National Council of the Churches of Christ in the U.S.A., 257 Fourth Ave., New York 10, N. Y. Aid includes information about church programs for migratory workers and other transient groups, and pamphlet discussions of problems faced by urban fringe area churches.

General Department of United Church Women, The National Council of the Churches of Christ in the U.S.A., 156 Fifth Ave., New York 10, N. Y. Sponsors local observances of World Community Day, May Fellowship Day, and World Day of Prayer; supplies informational and promotional materials for programs to study community needs and develop plans for action in areas such as child and youth welfare, labor-management relations, and race relations; offers plans for enlisting the aid of church women, and organizing and directing councils of church women; has suggestions for publicizing church programs through newspapers, radio and television stations, and films and other visual aids.

Girl Scouts of the U.S.A., 155 East 44th St., New York 17, N. Y. Materials include the pamphlet *Girl Scouting and Religious Groups*.

International Society of Christian Endeavor, 1201 East Broad St., Columbus 5, Ohio. An organization "to reach, hold, train, and inspire young people in Christian living and Christian service." Sponsors awards for distinguished youth citizenship. Conducts essay contests on the subject of the application of Christian ideals to citizenship. Suggests program procedures for church groups, and furnishes inspirational and informational pamphlet material. Publishes *The Christian Endeavor World*, a monthly report of activities.

Jewish Publications Society of America, 222 North 15th St., Philadelphia 2, Pa. Addresses of leading rabbis, Jewish organizations, and publications.

Joint Department of Evangelism, The National Council of the Churches of Christ in the U.S.A., 297 Fourth Ave., New York 10, N. Y. Prepares and distributes plans and materials for special occasions such as Universal Week of Prayer, World-Wide Communion Sunday, Church Attendance Crusade Month, Reformation Sunday, and Watch Night Services. A booklet descriptive of a 15-month program of evangelism, including noonday theater meetings and other activities appropriate for church groups, is available.

Joint Department of Family Life, The National Council of the Churches of Christ in the U.S.A., 79 East Adams St., Chicago 3, Ill. Sponsors local and regional family-life conferences in cooperation with church and other community groups. Supplies leadership for a family-life institute. Offers family-life program consultation services by mail, interview, or field personnel. Materials include a family-life program packet, a family counselor's kit, a community institute manual, detailed program plans for one- and two-day institutes, promotional material for National Family Week, and literature about how to achieve church and home cooperation.

Joint Department of Stewardship and Benevolence, The National Council of the Churches of Christ in the U.S.A., 257 Fourth Ave., New York 10, N. Y. Serves as a clearing house for ideas about stewardship promotion and benevolence. Has available materials such as suggested budget plans, guides for a church canvass, and promotional films and filmstrips. Publishes a bibliography of selected stewardship material, and a packet for an annual United Church Canvass.

Landis, Benson Y., *The Yearbook of American Churches*, Lebanon, Pa.: Sowers Printing Company. Lists over 200 Protestant denominations, their national headquarters, schools, and publications.

Laymen's Missionary Movement, 19 South LaSalle St., Chicago 3, Ill. An organization to develop support for missions. Sponsors conventions, conferences, and dinners. Promotes the observance of Men and Missions Sunday. Publishes a speaker's manual.

Laymen's Movement for a Christian World, 347 Madison Ave., New York 17, N. Y. A nonsectarian membership organization. Maintains a research and training center to develop techniques for putting religious ideals into practice. Distributes copies of prayers, and literature about the organization and programs of prayer groups and retreats. Publishes *Christian Laymen*, a monthly bulletin.

Laymen's National Committee, Vanderbilt Hotel, New York 16, N. Y. Materials for the observance of Bible Week include adult programs, youth programs, newspaper releases, radio and television talks, and posters.

National Catholic Welfare Conference, 1312 Massachusetts Ave., N. W., Washington 5, D. C. Coordinates Roman Catholic church programs in education, social welfare, immigrant aid, and other areas. Has a comprehensive list of publications. Publishes *Catholic Action*, a monthly.

National Council of Catholic Men, and The National Council of Catholic Women, 1312 Massachusetts Ave., N. W., Washington 5, D. C. Federated local organizations to develop among Catholics a better understanding of problems of the church, and a more active participation in their solution.

National Council of the Churches of Christ in the U.S.A., 297 Fourth Ave., New York 10, N. Y. An interdenominational body representing most of the major Protestant church groups, and about 1000 city, county, and state councils. The most inclusive single source of aid, covering every church-group concern. The Central Department of Publications and Distribution publishes two valuable aids for groups with extensive programs: *Handbook* describing the programs, plans, services, and materials available from the departments, divisions, commissions, and committees of the National Council; and *A Catalogue of Basic Publications*, a 32-page annotated listing of books and pamphlets prepared by its divisions and other units. Representative of the catalogue's subject matter classification are the following: adult work, audio-visual aids, Christian education, church attendance, every-member canvass, your building program, leadership training, and radio and television. Other, more specific kinds of help are described in this section under various divisions, departments, commissions, and committees of The National Council of the Churches of Christ in the U.S.A. Some of the pamphlets particularly useful in carrying out programs suggested in this chapter are *Improving the Total Program of Your Church*, *Home and Church Work Together*, *The How of Vacation Church School*, *Using Audio-Visuals in the Church*, *The Church*

School and Parish House Building, Your Church Library, and *Public Relations Manual for Churches.*

National Education Association of the United States, 1201 16th St., N. W., Washington 6, D. C. *Personal Growth* leaflet series include many particularly appropriate for church group study and discussion. Available in quantity at a nominal price. List of titles available.

National Jewish Welfare Board, 145 East 32nd St., New York 16, N. Y. *Catalog of Publications* includes manuals and other pamphlets about Jewish group programs for community service, leadership training, and religious and other special observances.

National Recreation Association, 315 Fourth Ave., New York 10, N. Y. Suggestions for music, drama, crafts, sports, and other recreation programs for all age groups, and for celebration of special occasions such as Easter and Christmas. Publishes a manual, *Recreation and the Church.*

P. J. Kennedy and Sons, 12 Barclay St., New York 7, N. Y. Addresses of Roman Catholic clergy, organizations, and publications.

Religion in American Life, 300 Fourth Ave., New York 10, N. Y. A movement to bring increased attendance and support for all religious groups. Sponsored by a National Laymen's Committee of representatives of the three major faiths. Offers program guides and promotional material for particular types of community organizations, as well as for a community-wide campaign. Description of materials available.

Synagogue Council of America, Committee on Jewish Family Life, 110 West 42nd St., New York 18, N. Y. Literature includes program suggestions and materials for an observance of National Family Week.

SOME SOURCES OF FILMS AND FILM INFORMATION

American Association for Jewish Education, 1776 Broadway, New York 19, N. Y. *The Jewish Audio-Visual Review,* a monthly, includes descriptions and evaluations of films and filmstrips on the Bible, Jewish history and religion, and intercultural relations.

American Optical Company, Scientific Instrument Division, Buffalo 15, N. Y. Offers *The Church Uses Visual Aids,* a handbook for the use of the opaque projector in church programs.

Association Films, Inc., 347 Madison Ave., New York 17, N. Y. Catalogues of motion pictures selected for church and community use. *Selected Religious Films* lists over 130 films dealing with religious subjects.

Bell & Howell, Educational Division, 7100 McCormick Road, Chicago

45, Ill. Has available *Teaching Eternal Truths*, a handbook for the use of audio-visual aids in church programs.

Catechetical Guild Educational Society, 147 East 5th St., St. Paul 1, Minn. Roman Catholic teaching films, Kodachrome slides, and filmstrips. Catalogue available.

Cathedral Films, Inc., 140 North Hollywood Way, Burbank, Calif. A main source of religious films. Catalogue available.

Chicago Theological Seminary, Extension Service Office, 5757 University Ave., Chicago 37, Ill. Offers an eight-page *Selected List of 16 mm Sound Films for Church Use*.

Christian Herald Association, Audio-Visual Aids Editor, 27 East 39th St., New York 16, N. Y. Information about films and other audio-visual aids.

Church-Craft Pictures, Inc., 3312 Lindell Boulevard, St. Louis 3, Mo. Teaching films, slides, and filmstrips for religious education. Catalogue available.

Concordia Films, 3558 South Jefferson Ave., St. Louis 18, Mo. Rental films illustrating the application of Christian principles to everyday living. Subjects include marriage, the influence of Sunday school, faith in God and happiness, and the celebration of Christmas in a Christian family.

Cornell Film Company, 1501 Broadway, New York 36, N. Y. Rental films include a series of Biblical films filmed in Israel.

Division of Christian Education, The National Council of the Churches of Christ in the U.S.A., 79 East Adams St., Chicago 3, Ill. Publishes *Audio-Visual Resource Guide for Use in Religious Education*. Maintains a Visual Education Fellowship. Members receive the *Audio-Visual Resource Guide*; *Visual Education Newsletter*, a quarterly; and *Evaluation Bulletin*, a monthly.

Encyclopaedia Britannica Films, Inc., 1150 Wilmette Ave., Wilmette, Ill. Rental films include several that dramatize the inspiration and guidance that Christianity has to offer for everyday living. Representative subjects: the power of faith to bring encouragement in ill health, the happiness to be gained through service to others, and the better human relations that can be established through the application of Christian principles of conduct.

Family Films, Inc., 8840 West Olympic Boulevard, Beverly Hills, Calif.

Interdenominational films for teaching moral precepts. Listing available.

Film News, 444 Central Park West, New York 25, N. Y. Offers film program consultant service to church and other community organizations.

Foundation Film Corporation, 303 Citizens Savings Bank Building, Pasadena 1, Calif. Films for Sunday school and other church programs. Catalogue available.

Harmon Foundation, 140 Nassau St., New York 38, N. Y. Literature in the field of audio-visual aids for church programs.

Jewish Education Film Library, 13 East 37th St., New York 16, N. Y. Catalogue available.

Loyola Films, Eightieth and Loyola Boulevard, Los Angeles 45, Calif. Maintains a Catholic Teaching Film Library of rental films under the supervision of the Jesuit Fathers of Loyola University.

Moody Bible Institute, Film Section, 820 North LaSalle St., Chicago 10, Ill. Offers a rental teacher training package consisting of a 16-minute color film, *No Vacant Chairs,* and a series of filmstrips in color, each demonstrating one of the seven basic laws of learning. Films include *Sermons from Science,* documentary and fictional treatments of missionary work, youth welfare activities, and preparation for the ministry. Catalogue available.

National Gallery of Art, 6th and Constitution Ave., Washington 25, D. C. "The Christmas Story in Paintings from the National Gallery of Art," a series of free loan color slides of Flemish and Italian masterpieces, with a critical discussion of each. Description available.

Selected Films Release Service, Whittier, Calif. Publishes a *Master Guide* to religious films and other films suitable for church use.

Simpex Religious Classics, 1564 Broadway, New York 19, N. Y. Illustrated catalogue available.

United World Films, Inc., Religious Films Division, 1445 Park Ave., New York 22, N. Y. Free loan and rental films include stories from the Old and New Testaments, productions of the Broadcasting and Film Commission of the National Council of the Churches of Christ in the U.S.A., presentations of Roman Catholic history and ritual, and secular films of particular interest to church and community organizations. Catalogue available.

Victor Animatograph Corporation, Davenport, Iowa. Maintains a visual-aid consultation service for churches.

Visual Text Publications, 812 North Dearborn St., Chicago, Ill. Publishes *Church Screen*, a quarterly.

Youth Films, Inc., 7904 Santa Monica Boulevard, Hollywood 46, Calif. Series of eight *Scenic Psalms* and other worship-service films in color. Catalogue available.

CHAPTER 13

International Relations

SCIENCE, IN helping to remove the barrier of distance between nations, has created international problems so grave that the good will and understanding of peoples everywhere, reaching out from community to community across national boundaries, are required for their solution.

That the peoples of the world, voluntarily organized, have a recognized place in international affairs is evidenced by the United Nations Charter itself, which gives consultative status to 83 volunteer groups, representing millions of persons. Among them are the major federated organizations, church groups, labor unions, farm groups, and education associations.

These groups, with their units in the community, are working for increasing good will and understanding among nations. Their achievements suggest practical activities for your organization.

EDUCATION IN INTERNATIONAL AFFAIRS

In many communities, organizations are sponsoring lectures, discussions, forum meetings, institutes, and workshops to develop a better understanding of international affairs. Rotary Clubs, for example, have conducted Institutes of International Understanding, closely coordinated with school and other study programs, for over 16 years. Literally millions of women throughout the world are receiving an education in international affairs through the study clubs and other programs of the General Federation of Women's Clubs.

Permanent community organizations, such as those affiliated with the Foreign Policy Association, are especially effective. In Cleveland, the Council of World Affairs has attracted world-wide attention with its annual World Affairs Institute. In Des Moines, the Chamber of Commerce, schools, and other agencies have cooperated with the Western Policy Committee in maintaining institutes and forums which relate regional, national, and international problems.

Such groups often provide valuable supplementary services. The following may be adapted to the special needs in your community:

1. Making available a wealth of free and inexpensive materials through a pamphlet shop organized in cooperation with the library.
2. Compiling special bibliographies with the help of library staffs.
3. Listing local experts in foreign affairs, and helping other groups secure them as speakers, panel members, and discussion leaders.
4. Providing meeting places for citizen groups interested in discussing international relations.
5. Maintaining local radio and television programs.
6. Aiding schools in planning study units on various world problems.

THE UNITED NATIONS. If the hope of attaining a free and peaceful association of peoples is to be realized, citizens on the community level must support wholeheartedly the threefold effort of the United Nations: to eliminate armed conflict through peaceful settlement of disputes, and through agreements leading toward disarmament and atomic energy control; to establish a just, lawful, and orderly society of nations; and to bring about the well-being of all the peoples of the world through increasing the production of the necessities of life and assuring their wider and more equitable distribution.

You can enlist support for these great objectives at the community level. Promote a United Nations Week or United Nations Day, October 24, either as a prelude to a program in international relations, or as a climax to the year's activities. Experience has developed many practical activities for year-round programs, most of which are designed primarily as education projects:

1. Exhibiting flags, maps, photographs, books, costumes, dolls, and the handicrafts of other countries; distributing United Nations pamphlets; and making available promotional material such as posters and stamps.
2. Cooperating with merchants in special window displays and newspaper advertisements.
3. Arranging for public film showings, and speakers.
4. Cooperating with local radio and television stations.
5. Sponsoring a United Nations ball, or a festival featuring the music, costumes, and pageantry of other lands.
6. Arranging for groups to attend sessions of United Nations commissions, committees, or the General Assembly.
7. Supplying sets of United Nations flags to local institutions.

8. Promoting church programs that stress United Nations ideals.

9. Establishing a United Nations Center in the public library and, during United Nations Week, information booths in theaters, banks, and public buildings.

THE UNITED NATIONS AND THE SCHOOLS. The role of the public schools in developing a better understanding of America's relations with other nations, and a deeper appreciation of the need for good will is recognized by all major federated groups. National organizations urge state education departments to require that the United Nations and its activities be made a part of school programs. State groups cooperate in planning formal courses, supply curriculum materials, and stimulate interest through contests and other measures. Local groups contribute through activities such as:

1. Donating United Nations Week Kits. Each kit is a collection of posters, articles, and teaching aids.

2. Contributing a United Nations flag or a set of flags of all nations.

3. Furnishing speakers and films for assemblies.

4. Recruiting citizens of the community with varied backgrounds to aid in preparing a music national origin festival, a program of folk dances, or a pageant.

5. Presenting a radio or television school-community forum on United Nations problems.

6. Cooperating with local papers in reporting school United Nations observances; publishing essays, stories, and poems with United Nations themes; and sponsoring essay and art contests.

7. Sponsoring and supporting an International Relations Club in the high school; and arranging intercity or interregional meetings of such groups.

8. Helping students to organize a United Nations dance, featuring the costumes, music, and dancing of other peoples; or a fair, in which each booth features the art, crafts, products, scenic attractions, and history of a nation.

9. Cooperating in a Little United Nations model assembly, to be presented to the public.

INTERNATIONAL THEATER MONTH. Other special occasions in celebration of international cooperation give local groups opportunities to take advantage of nation-wide publicity, and to utilize the special materials made available at such times. For example, hundreds of community theaters, schools, churches, and organizations observe

International Theater Month in March with plays, pageants, dances, and music that present the UNESCO ideals of understanding and tolerance. High schools use UNESCO themes as drama material. In the language departments of schools and colleges, foreign-language plays are produced. Your support for such activities would be a worthwhile education project in the field of international affairs.

INTERCHANGE OF PERSONS

The road to peace is being constructed by people talking to people, getting to understand one another, and removing their differences. Community organizations are among the many groups in the United States that are furthering this movement through arranging for the interchange of tens of thousands of students, teachers, trainees, professional men, and technicians.

STUDENT EXCHANGE. Of tremendous importance for increasingly better international understanding and good will are the thousands of students throughout the world who have been able to study and work in other lands through community group support for the scholarship funds of the great federated organizations, and their cooperation in support of other exchange arrangements. Gifts, large and small, from thousands of communities, for example, have made it possible for the Rotary Foundation to give over 500 young people of varying national backgrounds the opportunity to exchange points of view and find common ground for agreement. These young people have attended over 7000 Rotary Club meetings in 83 countries, visited members' homes and businesses, and traveled widely with Rotarians' help.

In a two-year period alone, the General Federation of Women's Clubs awarded international scholarships to students from 20 nations. The American Association of University Women has established an endowment fund of over $1 million for an extensive fellowship program. Over 100 students from 22 nations were in the United States in one year through scholarships made available by the American Field Service.

The National Grange sponsors "young farmer" and "teenager" interchange projects through which thousands live for a period on the farms of other lands, study different agricultural methods, and participate in the cultural and social life of host communities.

Church leadership is of great importance in the strengthening of world democracy. Outstanding contributions in this field are the exchange of theological students through scholarship grants, and the supervision of hundreds of vacation work-study groups throughout the world. In more than 200 countries, over 40,000 young men and women, under the auspices of church and other volunteer groups, each year study and work in mutual trust and understanding.

There are a number of things your organization can do to further student interchange. As the local unit of a national organization, you can encourage adoption of an international program, or contribute funds for current projects. You can provide the supplementary funds needed to enable a foreign student to accept a scholarship. Many times, students must decline scholarships and fellowships because of the cost of living in the United States.

EXCHANGE OF TEACHERS. The exchange teacher in a foreign community is in a particularly favorable position to promote international cooperation and good will. He teaches not only his own subject, but the ideals, attitudes, and values of his country. On his return from abroad he is able to contribute more effectively to his school program, and through talks to community groups, interviews, and articles, to publicize information about the country in which he has lived and worked.

Community organization interest has encouraged teacher exchanges, and in many cases has made them financially possible. Your group might suggest such a project to your school board. Since your teacher and the visiting teacher both receive their regular salaries, the extra cost to the community is slight. Grants are available under the Fulbright Act to American teachers going to certain foreign countries. A foreign teacher may apply to the United States Educational Foundation for help in meeting the cost of round-trip travel to the United States. However, supplementary funds are sometimes needed. The United States Office of Education has detailed information about how your organization can help.

FOREIGN LECTURERS. Active clubs are usually familiar with lecture bureaus. Few, however, take advantage of the presence of noted authorities from abroad. There may be foreigners visiting, studying, or training in your area who are well qualified to talk about some aspect of international relations. The Institute of International Education has the names and addresses of all such visitors.

EXCHANGE OF EXPERTS. A good example of cooperative action by government agencies and volunteer groups is the exchange of experts sponsored by the American Military Government.

German political leaders have studied American election procedures. German women have come to the United States to observe the active part American women take in civic affairs. Japanese police heads and other officials have visited United States cities for suggestions about organizing the internal security of their country.

Although the Military Government bears the costs of these projects, it relies directly on the services of local volunteer groups for details of programs, effective use of the visitors' time, and the kind of reception that will permit the foreign experts to take home a lasting impression of American good will.

EXCHANGE OF SKILLED WORKERS AND TRAINEES. Foreign workers and trainees learn American industrial know-how in on-the-job training programs and return to their homelands to work toward greater and more efficient production. In some American industries, workers and technicians need the skills and knowledge of processes used in plants abroad. Their presence in European and other communities leads to better understanding and good will. Through the industrial and business affiliations of your members, urge adoption of such an exchange program by concerns in your area.

A COMMUNITY-WIDE EXCHANGE PROGRAM. Your organization may make its exchange of persons program a community-wide affair. Organizations in Glens Falls, Jamestown, Ithaca, Schenectady, and other New York cities, for example, have taken prominent parts in the Ambassadors of Good Will program of the Community Service Council of Young Adults, through which individuals are chosen to represent their cities in visits to comparable communities in Sweden, Denmark, and The Netherlands.

The program, a continuing one, involves five steps, each effective in a pattern of community education in international relations:

1. The sponsoring organization explains the project to the community, and secures the cooperation of other groups. As a result, members of many organizations are impressed with the need for international understanding.

2. A committee of civic leaders selects the young men who will serve as "ambassadors of good will." The publicity given the project focuses attention upon the importance of the development of community leadership for international understanding.

3. Those chosen make a special study of the historical, social, political, and economic backgrounds of their own communities so that they may talk intelligently about them abroad.

4. The "ambassadors" travel overseas, live in representative communities with representative families, and report their experiences through news articles and letters.

5. On their return, the emissaries provide leadership for international affairs programs in their communities.

HOSPITALITY PROGRAMS. Organizations in many towns and cities are acting as community hosts to thousands of students and other visitors from abroad. They are arranging for their reception, scheduling special luncheon and other meetings in their honor, finding suitable living quarters, and planning visits to schools, churches, recreation and cultural centers, and business and industrial establishments. As a result, visitors from abroad receive an extensive over-all view of what the American way of life means.

FOREIGN RELIEF AND REHABILITATION

Your organization can find inspiration and practical procedure ideas in the successful relief projects carried out by great national federations and local groups.

Limitations of space permit only a suggestion of their tremendous scope and variety. Over 600 clubs have donated tons of handknit sweaters, blankets, and layette units, under the auspices of the Save the Children Federation; 600,000 German boys and girls in one month alone were clothed through the help of the General Federation of Women's Clubs; $330,000 worth of milk was sent to the children of Europe by San Diego area Junior Chambers of Commerce; the C.I.O. sent relief to Europe of a total value of $11 million over a four-year period; the American Legion shipped over 4 million toys—friendship gifts from the children of America—in one year. Throughout the nation, organizations have initiated "adoption procedures" through which their communities have provided relief for entire towns and cities abroad.

"The war cut us off from periodicals in English," one European recently wrote in a national organization publication. "We have been victims of barriers to the free exchange of ideas by the printed word, and in many cases we have lost our ability to pay the cost of even the meager supply of newspapers and periodicals, and technical and cultural magazines. You must understand that we who read your language are hungry for magazines in English."

By supplying cultural and educational materials, your organization can help establish another channel through which better understanding and good will may come to the nations of the world. Organize a book collection depot at your meeting place, a public school or library, or other centrally located place. Cooperate with the school affiliation department of the American Friends Service Committee in encouraging student correspondence, and the exchange of gifts and classroom work. Utilize the Gift Coupon Plan of UNESCO in making education, scientific, and cultural donations.

Detailed descriptions of programs such as these, and specific, practical procedures for supporting and independent relief projects are available through the sources of aid listed at the close of this chapter.

INTERNATIONAL TRADE RELATIONS

Since World War I, volunteer organizations like the International Chamber of Commerce have been working unceasingly for the understanding and good will that follow mutually beneficial commercial relations. Today there is a general recognition of the fact that trade must be a two-way street.

Support for trade cooperation, as in other international fields, must come from the people themselves. Every American has a personal stake in making his country strong commercially, and in encouraging its leadership in expanding world trade. The following suggestions may provide ideas for your group:

1. Sponsor lectures, forums, and discussions about international economic organizations such as the International Monetary Fund, the World Bank, and the Economic and Social Council of the United Nations.

2. Arrange visits of teachers and students to industries engaged in manufacture for export.

3. Show world-trade films to school and other audiences.

4. Participate with The Propeller Club "port" in your area in an observance of National Maritime Day, May 22, to direct attention to the contribution of world trade to domestic employment, and to the general welfare of people both here and abroad.

5. Arrange library and school exhibits of ship models, prints, and pictures, with brief accounts of the history and importance of foreign trade.

6. Cooperate with merchants in presenting window displays that dramatize our dependence on foreign sources of materials and markets.

INTER-AMERICAN RELATIONS

An impressive demonstration of the fact that nations differing sharply in ethnic and cultural makeups can live together in harmony is the Organization of American States, commonly known as the Pan American Union. This association represents over 275 million people in the 21 independent countries of the Western Hemisphere. Community organizations are logical and effective media through which to further the development of this inter-American solidarity.

Many of the project suggestions in this chapter may be helpful in planning your inter-American program. Additional activities might include arranging "across the border" visits, and intergroup meetings and projects; observing the presence in your community of other American nationals by appropriate meeting and public events; encouraging the schools to organize Pan American clubs, to correspond with students of other American nations, and to include in their programs a study of the history and culture of the other nations of the Americas; and sponsoring a community-wide celebration of Pan American Day, April 14.

SOURCES OF AID

American Aid to France, Inc., 159 East 63rd St., New York 21, N. Y. Arranges aid for French children. Details available.

American Association for the United Nations, 345 East 46th St., New York 17, N. Y. Helps local groups plan year-round and special United Nations programs. Provides a great wealth of discussion and promotion material, and a leader's guide with bibliography. Offers pre-tour information to individuals and groups visiting United Nations headquarters in New York City.

American Association of University Women, 1634 Eye St., N. W., Washington 6, D. C. Issues a brochure especially for chairmen of committees on international affairs. Covers considerations such as program planning, choice of speakers, preparation for the speaker, and types of discussion groups. Encourages projects involving the exchange of professional personnel.

American Council of Voluntary Agencies for Foreign Service, Inc., 20 West 40th St., New York 18, N. Y. Represents major national organizations in facilitating resettlement of displaced persons. Its Emergency Council for Displaced European Professionals cooperates with industrial, business, and civic groups in placing professional and technical personnel. Forty-one member agencies are willing to cooperate in collecting clothing, bulk food, and individual food packages; and arranging for individual child support, and personal contact with needy individuals.

American Farm Bureau Federation, 261 Constitution Ave., N. W., Washington 1, D. C. Offers services to local groups interested in the exchange of persons in the agricultural field. Active in encouraging international affairs projects in 4-H Clubs. Low cost educational pamphlets available.

American Field Service, 113 East 30th St., New York 16, N. Y. Cooperates with many local groups in projects to make European youth acquainted with our way of life through their visits to America. Literature available.

American Friends Service Committee, 20 South 12th St., Philadelphia 7, Pa. Promotes understanding through international work-study groups. Maintains relief programs. Literature and free loan films available.

American Institute of France, 19 East 64th St., New York 21, N. Y. Encourages and arranges the exchange of students between French and American universities.

American Jewish Joint Distribution Committee, 270 Madison Ave., New York 16, N. Y. Supports United Israel Appeal. Has information about Jewish relief needs abroad.

American Junior Red Cross, 17th and D Sts., N. W., Washington 13, D. C. Has information about its International School Art Program to send paintings by American youth to European countries to help develop mutual understanding and respect.

American Labor Education Service, Inc., 1776 Broadway, New York 19, N. Y. A national membership organization. Activities include arranging study programs and travel itineraries for visiting worker-students, and screening and sending books to labor schools in Germany and Austria. Has information about other sources of aid in planning programs for workers from abroad.

American Merchant Marine Institute, Inc., 1701 K St., N. W., Washington 6, D. C. Publicity materials for celebration of National Maritime Day. Gives addresses of Navy, Coast Guard, and Maritime units that cooperate in community observances.

American National Red Cross, 17th and D Sts., N. W., Washington 13, D. C. Grants scholarships and fellowships, sponsors foreign study visits, and arranges teacher exchanges.

Brookings Institution, 722 Jackson Place, N. W., Washington 6, D. C. Authoritative background material for major problems of United States foreign policy. Publishes *Major Problems of United States Foreign Policy* annually.

CARE-UNESCO Book Fund, 20 Broad St., New York 5, N. Y. Established to supply important new technical books to universities, libraries, and medical and scientific centers overseas. Cooperates with UNESCO, the Library of Congress, the American Library Association, and medical and scientific groups. Solicits aid of community organizations.

Carrie Chapman Catt Memorial Fund, Inc., 461 Fourth Ave., New York 16, N. Y. Established by the League of Women Voters to encourage foreign visitors to study community affairs in the United States.

Catholic Association for International Peace, 1312 Massachusetts Ave., N. W., Washington 5, D. C. Publishes a series of pamphlets about application of Christian teaching to international affairs.

Chamber of Commerce of the United States, 1615 H St., N. W., Washington 6, D. C. Publications include *International Issues*, a monthly news sheet which presents authoritative background material for international relations discussions; and studies of the interdependence of the trade of the United States and other countries.

Church Peace Union and World Alliance for International Friendship through Religion, 170 East 64th St., New York 21, N. Y. Furnishes United Nations program suggestions for churches, synagogues, and religious organizations.

Church World Service, Inc., 120 East 23rd St., New York 10, N. Y. Official reconstruction and relief agency of many Protestant and Orthodox churches. Has pamphlets useful in relief programs. Provides films, display material, and radio scripts. Arranges for American training for European theological students.

Columbia University Press, 2960 Broadway, New York 27, N. Y. Agent for the *UNESCO Courier*, an international periodical devoted to the work of UNESCO and to activities and developments throughout the world in education, science, and culture. Offers a list of UNESCO publications.

Committee for Economic Development, 444 Madison Ave., New York 22, N. Y. Has background material for a membership program in international trade relations, and for a community panel discussion on world trade affairs.

Committee on Educational Reconstruction, United States National Commission for UNESCO, Department of State, Washington 25, D. C. Information about the UNESCO Gift Coupon plan. Kits containing stamp booklets, stamp consignment forms, and remittance forms for mailing the proceeds of sales to UNESCO. Additional UNESCO materials available.

Committee on Nongovernmental Organizations of the Economic and Social Council of the United Nations, United Nations, New York 17, N. Y. Information on the role voluntary groups are taking in the functioning of the United Nations.

Cooperative for American Remittances to Europe, Inc. (CARE), 20 Broad St., New York 5, N. Y. Arranges for the sending of relief packages to Europe. Information available.

Council for Inter-American Cooperation, Inc., 111 Broadway, New York 5, N. Y. Has list of speakers on inter-American commerce. Offers suggestions for study groups.

Council on Foreign Relations, 58 East 68th St., New York 21, N. Y. A nonprofit organization to study American foreign affairs. Publications include *Foreign Affairs*, a quarterly; *The United States in World Affairs*, an annual survey; and various research reports. Publishes *Let's Talk About* . . . , a monthly magazine distributed in quantity lots to discussion groups without charge. Each issue includes an article reprinted from *Foreign Affairs*, an introduction, and a discussion outline.

Council on World Affairs, 922 Society for Savings Building, Cleveland 14, Ohio. Pamphlet material describes Council's community education program. Assists local groups interested in international affairs. Its program for the International Students Group of the Council on World Affairs may suggest projects in your community.

Countrywomen's League, *The Country Gentleman*, Independence Square, Philadelphia 5, Pa. Inexpensive pamphlets on international relations include suggestions for presenting a pageant.

Division of Exchange of Persons, United States Department of State, Washington 25, D. C. Administers the exchange of professors and specialists with other American republics. Cooperates with other agencies and volunteer groups in administering the Fulbright Law. These groups include the Institute of International Education (for graduate study); the United States Office of Education (for teaching in elementary and secondary schools); and the Conference Board of Associated Research (for college affiliation). Cooperates with American missions abroad. Acts as a clearinghouse for ideas and information.

Experiment in International Living, Inc., Putney, Vt. An educational student travel organization to develop groups to help build mutual understanding and good will. Arranges for young Americans to live in communities abroad, and for foreign young people to live in American towns and cities.

Foreign Policy Association, 345 East 46th St., New York 17, N. Y. Interested in organizing community programs for extensive study of American foreign policy. Local organizations eligible for affiliation. Publishes authoritative, simply worded booklets about important world issues. Gives foreign policy reports by experts, and publishes a four-page weekly, *Foreign Policy Bulletin.* Offers Discussion Packets, and operates a loan service for maps, films, recordings, and charts.

Institute of Adult Education, Teachers College, Columbia University, New York 27, N. Y. Publications include *Education for International Understanding,* a book by Thomas R. Adam. Describes methods and materials used in programs for international understanding throughout the country.

Institute of Inter-American Affairs, 333 3rd St., N. W., Washington 25, D. C. A free packet of materials telling the story of the Point Four Program in Latin America.

Institute of International Education, 1 East 67th St., New York 21, N. Y. Chief source of information about student exchange. Provides guidance service. Assists local groups in placing students both here and abroad. Administers scholarship funds for private groups. Arranges lecture tours for visiting experts. Has a list of addresses of foreign visitors available as speakers.

Interdenominational Commission on Youth Service Projects, 79 East Adams St., Chicago 3, Ill. Publishes *Invest Your Summer,* a pamphlet describing opportunities for participation in summer service projects abroad.

International Documents Service, Columbia University Press, 2960 Broadway, New York 27, N. Y. United Nations Study Kit includes an introduction to the United Nations, and selected United Nations films, recordings, booklets, bulletins, and pamphlets that present a clear account of how the specialized agencies came into being, how they work, and what they have accomplished.

International Federation of Agricultural Producers, 712 Jackson Place, N. W., Washington 6, D. C. Represents several major farm groups in arranging for exchange of farm workers.

International House, Bancroft at Piedmont, Berkeley 4, Calif. Has detailed information about an American Way of Life program for foreign visitors which can be adapted by any community group.

James Gray, Inc., 216 East 45th St., New York 17, N. Y. Publishes *United Nations Reporter*, a monthly digest of United Nations happenings.

League of Women Voters of the United States, 1026 17th St., N. W., Washington 6, D. C. Low cost pamphlets include discussions of citizen responsibility to support the United Nations, efforts being made to strengthen the United Nations through reform, the effect of foreign trade upon the average citizen, and studies of the technical assistance program for under-developed countries. A free listing of pamphlets is available.

Manhattan Publishing Co., 225 Lafayette St., New York 12, N. Y. *The Story of Interdependence*, a documentary program about the United Nations. Includes filmslides, stills, narration, and short dramatic skits. Pamphlet material includes *The United Nations, Its Record and Prospects*, prepared for the Carnegie Endowment for International Peace by A. M. Rosenthal.

National Broadcasting Company, 30 Rockefeller Plaza, New York 20, N. Y. Provides community groups with advance notices of United Nations Week radio programs.

National Education Association, Committee on International Relations, 1201 16th St., N. W., Washington 6, D. C. Furnishes a variety of pamphlet and other material useful to committees on international relations. Has available the addresses of information offices of foreign governments, and the information directors of specialized international organizations.

National Federation of Music Clubs, Department of International Music Relations, 445 West 23rd St., New York 11, N. Y. Has available *Suggested Programs and Supplementary Lists of Music of Many Countries for International Music-Relations Programs*, a pamphlet.

National Foundation for Education in American Citizenship, 36th St. and Sunset Ave., Indianapolis 7, Ind. *American Foreign Policy* presents basic principles involved in problems of international relations.

National Recreation Association, Correspondence and Consultation Bureau, 315 Fourth Ave., New York 10, N. Y. Has suggestions for using the music and dances of the United Nations; a bibliography of plays, pageants, dances, and music of Central and South America; ideas for giving a festival a South American atmosphere; and complete inter-American party plans, including decorations, invitations, refreshments, games and other entertainment.

New Tools for Learning, 280 Madison Ave., New York 16, N. Y. Has available international economic relations kits that include group discussion materials and guides, and visual materials such as maps, charts, pictures, filmstrips, lantern slides, and commentaries. Descriptions available.

New York State Education Department, Bureau of Adult Education, Albany, N. Y. Has information about how young adults in New York communities choose and send their representatives to live in comparable communities in Europe. Gives detailed information about procedures.

Office of Educational Exchange, United States Department of State, Washington 25, D. C. Literature describes in detail how an organization can take an active part in the United Nations exchange program: how to make a choice of type of person, where to find help in making arrangements, and costs involved.

Pan American Union, Connecticut Ave. at 17th St., N. W., Washington 6, D. C. Permanent Secretariat of the Organization of American States. Two publications: *Americas*, a monthly illustrated magazine dealing with current developments in inter-American relations; *Annals*, a quarterly record of all documents and official acts of O.A.S. Also offers descriptive booklets on individual countries, bibliographies, and miscellaneous materials on cultural and economic subjects. Special publications are furnished free to groups observing Pan American Day. Especially valuable is a 10-meeting program for the use of clubs, including background information, Kodachrome slides, exhibits of books loaned by Pan American Union, bibliographies, and other aids. Also has suggestions for programs for special groups, such as schools, colleges, and universities, and church, service, fraternal, women's, and other organizations.

Pan American World Airways, 135 East 42nd St., New York 7, N. Y. Will supply ideas and materials for exhibits illustrating the contribution of foreign lands to the American economy. Has travel films of interest.

Propeller Club of the United States, 17 Battery Place, New York 4, N. Y. "To promote, further, and support an American Merchant

Marine." Its over 100 "ports" throughout the country promote community observances of National Maritime Day, May 22.

Save the Children Federation, Inc., 345 East 45th St., New York 17, N. Y. Sponsors local foreign relief programs. Offers free loan films presenting factual reports of conditions in European areas and suggesting what can be done to help.

Spicer, Dorothy Gladys, *Window Open to the World*, New York: The Woman's Press, 1946. Offers handbook of projects based on nationality and racial customs. Includes sections about how to dramatize folk material, organize a festival, and arrange a foreign handicraft exhibit.

Superintendent of Documents, United Staes Government Printing Offive, Washington 25, D. C. The booklet *Where to Go for U. N. Information* includes an annotated listing of official sources, brief descriptions of volunteer associations, information centers, publications, radio and television materials and facilities, visual aids and where to find help in using them. Pamphlet and other material includes copies of official documents concerning international relations; *UNESCO News;* information about educational exchange groups; background material for a study of United States world trade; reports of the Interdepartmental Committee on Scientific and Cultural Cooperation among American States; and *Catalog of Radio Recordings* and *Radio Script Catalog*, describing free loan and purchase transcriptions and scripts.

Tribune Productions, 40 East 49th St., New York 17, N. Y. Offers a series of recordings of United Nations procedures suitable for an observance of United Nations Day.

United Christian Youth Movement, 79 East Adams St., Chicago 3, Ill. Publishes a catalogue of service opportunities for church-affiliated groups.

United Nations Department of Public Information, New York 17, N. Y. Has booklet describing all available United Nations materials.

United Nations Volunteer Educational Centers. In over 50 education institutions in all 48 states. Address of nearest one is available through the United Nations, Department of Public Information, New York 17, N. Y. Each center has one set of materials about the United Nations for reference, and others for loan. Centers answer questions and furnish help in planning meeting and community programs.

United Nations Volunteer Services, sponsored by the Carnegie Endowment for International Peace, 700 Jackson Place, N. W., Washington 6, D. C. Acts as a clearinghouse for individuals and organizations wishing to extend hospitality to United Nations personnel and their families.

United Nations World, 319 East 44th St., New York 17, N. Y. Publishes monthly magazine, *United Nations World*, featuring foreign affairs articles by leaders in government, business, and the professions. Each month there is a 30-page survey of a particular nation: its history, people, trade, customs, and relations with other nations.

United States Book Exchange, Library of Congress, Washington 25, D. C. Has information about overseas needs for books and magazines, and school supplies. Offers information about how to organize and implement a local program.

United States Commission for the Care of European Children, Inc., 215 Fourth Ave., New York 10, N. Y. The official source of information about orphan children to be resettled in America. Works through local agencies.

United States Committee for United Nations Day, 816 21st St., N. W., Washington 6, D. C. Offers *Leader's Guide for Individual and Community Action*. Other free material in quantity includes pamphlet information and posters. List of materials available.

United States Department of Agriculture, Office of Foreign Agriculture Relations, Washington 25, D. C. Can give up-to-the-minute information about how world trade is related to agricultural production in any area. Will provide local groups with publicity materials.

United States Department of State, Division of Publications, Washington 25, D. C. *An Appraisal of the United Nations Educational, Scientific, and Cultural Organization* (UNESCO) summarizes as well as evaluates major programs and activities.

United States National Commission for UNESCO, UNESCO Relations Staff, United States Department of State, Washington 25, D. C. Offers the 112-page *UNESCO Story*, a resource and action booklet for organizations and communities. Includes specific, practical suggestions for projects.

Voluntary International Assistance Division, Room 2201, United Nations, New York 17, N. Y. Offers a free copy of the script of *To Live in Faith*, play which explains the UNESCO Gift Coupon system.

Women United for the United Nations, 22 East 46th St., New York 17, N. Y. An organization of women observers at the United Nations. Maintains an information center.

Woodrow Wilson Foundation, 45 East 65th St., New York 21, N. Y. Publishes *United Nations News*, monthly except August and September, when it is bimonthly.

SOME SOURCES OF FILMS AND FILM INFORMATION

Association Films, Inc., 347 Madison Ave., New York 17, N. Y. Many free loan and low rental films suitable for developing an understanding of other lands and the need for good will. Catalogue available.

CARE Film Unit, 20 Broad St., New York 5, N. Y. Many free loan films about the need for foreign relief, and how your organization and community can help meet that need.

Coronet Films, Coronet Building, Chicago 1, Ill. Information about *Introduction to Foreign Trade*, presenting the mechanics of international commerce, the role of monetary standards and control, and the distribution of raw materials and markets.

Educational Film Library Association, Inc., Suite 1000, 1600 Broadway, New York 19, N. Y. Has catalogues of evaluated rental and purchase films suitable for programs in international affairs. *Films and People*, 31 pages, edited by Emily S. Jones, has full descriptions and appraisals of selected films on United Nations and UNESCO topics, with purchase and rental sources. *Films for International Understanding*, 134 pages, edited by Elizabeth H. Flory, is a symposium of articles by film and international relations authorities. Includes a selected list of about 250 films.

Encyclopaedia Britannica Films, Inc., 1150 Wilmette Ave., Wilmette, Ill. Rental films include *World Affairs Are Your Affairs*, a presentation of the work and objectives of the Cleveland Council on World Affairs. Shows how your organization can benefit from the formation of such a community council; suggests procedures for establishing a council.

Film Images, Inc., 18 East 60th St., New York 22, N. Y. Lists about 45 rental films demonstrating America's interest in a strong and stable Europe. Catalogue available.

Film Publishers, Inc., 25 Broad St., New York 4, N. Y. Offers filmstrip subjects such as atomic energy, the Marshall Plan, and the importance of two-way trade. Catalogue available.

Films of the Nations, Inc., 62 West 45th St., New York 36, N. Y. Over 100 films about foreign nations, each emphasizing the importance of international understanding. Sound and silent. Black and white, and color. Sale, rental. Catalogue available.

Foreign Policy Association, 345 East 46th St., New York 17, N. Y. Operates a film loan service for local units. Helps local units organize, equip, and train staffs for Mobile Film Units. Detailed information available.

Instructional Materials Center, University of Washington, Seattle, Wash. *Films on International Understanding*, a five-page mimeographed listing.

League of Women Voters, 1026 17th St., N. W., Washington 6, D. C. Free loan films on the subject of international understanding include *The Challenge of World Trade*, a presentation of the necessity of two-way commercial relations with other nations of the world. Description available.

National Education Association, Committee on International Relations, 1201 16th St., N. W., Washington 6, D. C. Offers an annotated list of films and film sources on the United Nations, its member states, and related subjects.

New York *Times*, 230 West 43rd St., New York 36, N. Y. Offers a filmstrip presenting a record of many United Nations projects in health, agriculture, and other areas. Useful for study and discussion groups. Description available.

Princeton Film Center, Inc., Carter Road, Princeton, N. J. Rental films include the 20-minute *Now the Peace*, showing incidents leading to the failure of the League of Nations, and World War II. Contrasts the two peace organizations. Valuable for information and discussion purposes. Description available.

Superintendent of Documents, United States Government Printing Office, Washington 25, D. C. Film catalogues and listings include *Motion Pictures on the Other American Republics*, issued by the Office of Education.

Twentieth Century Fund, 330 West 42nd St., New York 18, N. Y. Rental films include several about the importance of international cooperation in trade, and how America's trade contributes to higher standards of living and increases good will among nations. Descriptions available.

United Nations Film Division, Department of Public Information, New York 17, N. Y. Offers a comprehensive and illustrated catalogue of official productions of the United Nations and its specialized agencies, and independently produced films which contribute to an understanding of the United Nations.

United States Rubber Company, Public Relations Department, 1230 Avenue of the Americas, New York 20, N. Y. Free loan films include the 15-minute *Two Way Street*, explaining the importance of international trade to American economy. Description available.

CHAPTER 14

Americanism

ORGANIZATIONS ARE taking an important part in a great resurgence of interest in Americanism. Through programs in thousands of communities, they are giving citizens a more complete understanding of fundamental American concepts, a heightened appreciation of the advantages of being an American, and a deeper devotion to their country.

Although this chapter emphasizes organization action to foster a knowledge of our history and an appreciation of our traditional ideals of social, political, and economic freedom, it is not the author's intent to narrow the concept of Americanism. Other aspects of Americanism, such as equality of opportunity in all phases of community living, universal brotherhood, and the spiritual bases of our way of life are considered in other chapters.

PROMOTING AMERICANISM

Organizations are active in programs to promote the American way of life. The Chicago Junior Association of Commerce and Industry reached over 200,000 persons in 600 meetings with a graphic demonstration of the importance of the preservation of our heritage of individual freedom. The Industrial and Personnel Club of Chattanooga organized a Volunteer Corps that presented a similar program before meetings totaling about 20,000 people. Kiwanis Clubs distributed more than 29.5 million educational folders in a two-year "It's Fun to Live in America" campaign. Millions listened to a follow-up series of radio dramatizations of the lives of prominent business and professional men whose careers illustrate the promise of the American way.

THROUGH MEETINGS. Meeting programs furnish opportunities for effective promotion. Ask other organizations to cooperate in activities such as:

1. Scheduling inspirational speakers and Americanism films.

2. Making available pamphlets and other literature describing the stake every individual has in the preservation of American ideals and principles.

3. Providing copies of documents on which the American way of life has been founded, such as the Declaration of Independence and the Constitution.

4. Arranging a quiz program to stimulate an interest in the factual background for Americanism.

5. Scheduling group visits to points of historic interest.

6. Presenting local music groups in programs with patriotic themes.

THROUGH LOCAL NEWSPAPERS. The active support of local newspapers is necessary if the purposes of any community-wide Americanism promotion program are to be realized.

Newspapers in small communities are often limited in staff. An Americanism committee may help provide copy and other materials, such as stories having to do with a community's beginnings, emphasizing traditional American attributes; accounts of the role taken by the community in national events; old photographs or engravings of citizens, places, or events that have local historic importance; mats and other material from such sources as the American Heritage Foundation and the Advertising Council.

Your Americanism committee will find helpful the general discussion of organization newspaper publicity in Chapter 4. Specific measures to secure newspaper cooperation and support for many successful Americanism programs include:

1. Ask the local newspaper to carry syndicated articles and cartoon strips on Americanism subjects.

2. Work to get full coverage of events that have significance for Americanism.

3. Suggest joint sponsorship of contests to further the knowledge of American history, ideals, and principles.

THROUGH RADIO AND TELEVISION PROGRAMS. Local radio and television stations welcome opportunities to use their facilities for significant community projects. Develop and maintain a weekly Americanism program; present the idea of sponsoring such a program to local business firms. Provide newscasters with information to enable them to give complete coverage to your Americanism activities. Arouse a general interest in American ideals and principles through dramatizations, speeches, and round-table discussions. Sponsor community arts with an Americanism background. Present events such as American history quiz programs.

THROUGH THE LOCAL PUBLIC LIBRARY OR MUSEUM. Various services can be rendered by your public library or historical museum, such as assembling special collections of books and materials, preparing reading lists, and posting announcements. Your organization can help by supplying display items, and pamphlets available from sources such as those listed at the close of this chapter.

YOUTH GROUP ACTIVITIES

Especially important in the development of citizens with a knowledge and appreciation of our American heritage are those activities carried out in behalf of youth groups. Organizations help plan and direct patriotic programs for junior auxiliaries, Boy Scout and Girl Scout troops, Boys' Clubs, 4-H Clubs, and others.

Community groups take an active interest in courses in history, civics, and other social studies which directly contribute information and develop attitudes important to Americanism. They supply valuable supplemental materials such as copies of important American documents, American creeds, citizenship pledges, the flag history and code, and visual aids. The Daughters of the American Revolution sponsor Junior American Citizens Clubs in schools in 25 states. Legionnaires, school administrators, and teachers maintain Legion-Schoolmasters Clubs to stimulate interest in youth Americanism activities.

Organization members volunteer as guest lecturers on the American economic system. They provide transportation and supplemental supervision for trips to museums and points of national and local historic interest.

Many groups assist in school observances of patriotic occasions by planning programs, furnishing speakers and films for assemblies, presenting flags, awarding prizes to winners of contests with patriotic themes, and contributing special study materials. Among the patriotic observances celebrated by schools in most communities are, in school-year order, Citizenship Day, September 17; Columbus Day, October 12; Armistice Day, November 11; Bill of Rights Day, December 15; Lincoln's Birthday, February 12; Washington's Birthday, February 22; Memorial Day, May 30; and Flag Day, June 14.

Notably successful in stimulating student interest in Americanism are essay and speech contests sponsored by federated community groups such as the United States Junior Chamber of Commerce, the American Legion, and both the Sons and the Daughters of the American Revolution. Such programs stimulate thoughtful consideration of the meaning of democracy by those who participate, and bring the message of Americanism into millions of homes through short transcribed "pilot" speeches by prominent national personalities, broadcast over hundreds of local stations to help young people with their entries. In some communities entire high school populations participate. Over 25,000 entered one year's event in Philadelphia.

AMERICANIZATION

Traditionally, community organizations have taken the lead in citizenship education of the foreign born through Americanization classes. In cooperation with federal judges and the Immigration and Naturalization Service of the United States Department of Justice, they have made the granting of citizenship an occasion of great significance through appropriate ceremonies.

These efforts to Americanize the foreign born, more important now than in many years because of America's acceptance of large numbers of displaced persons, go far beyond encouragement of formal courses to meet literacy requirements, or participation in the ceremonial observances of induction into citizenship. Organization leaders recognize that an individual is not wholly Americanized unless he is adequately meeting his everyday problems, has the feeling of belonging to the community, and is motivated by a love for the principles and ideals that have given Americans their unique freedoms.

Organizations of all types support groups which traditionally have an interest in naturalization and assimilation. Some aid in compiling accurate lists of those who are prospective citizens. Others invite them to meetings which feature Americanism programs. Organization-sponsored commencement exercises at the close of Americanization courses make such occasions important community affairs. Volunteer groups join with the local judiciary and the bar association in creating appropriately impressive induction ceremonies.

The following induction procedure is typical of those used in many communities: a flag ceremony, invocation by a clergyman, singing of the national anthem, speeches by community leaders, administration of the oath of citizenship, call for new voters to accept responsibility for the welfare of the nation and community, response by a representative of the new voters, awarding of certificates of recognition, and a mass pledge of allegiance to the flag.

Other practical projects that give newcomers the idea that they belong, and which contribute to their assimilation include the following:

1. Providing information about essential matters such as housing, job opportunities, and compulsory education.

2. Sponsoring group study and discussion of everyday concerns such as currency, taxes, postage, traffic regulations, the role of American police departments, and supermarkets and other consumer facilities.

3. Providing "Meet Your Neighbor" opportunities.

4. Arranging group tours to historic shrines and other places of interest.

5. Distributing copies of biographies of great Americans, available without cost.

6. Entertaining groups at meetings and luncheons.

7. Providing opportunities for group affiliation and participation in community affairs.

CELEBRATION OF PATRIOTIC HOLIDAYS

Our great holidays, such as the birthdays of Washington and Lincoln, Memorial Day, Labor Day, and Independence Day, must not be allowed to become merely days off, or days for special fun making. Their original purpose—commemoration of those who have made great contributions to our national life, or of events important in our development—must be preserved.

ORGANIZATION ACTIVITIES. Service, civic, fraternal, and veterans' groups plan preholiday membership meetings or help arrange interorganization meetings and luncheons, featuring inspirational speakers or films; join in sponsoring radio and television programs dramatizing the holiday; arrange for posters and exhibits illustrating the theme of the occasion; and march in parades and attend other patriotic events, as units.

Veterans' organizations have a special interest in sponsoring parades, conducting memorial services, and providing special holiday entertainment at veterans' hospitals.

Women's groups create exhibits; arrange costume dances to stimulate interest in historic backgrounds; organize teas to popularize women's participation in celebrations; act as hostesses at museums, historic centers, and restorations; hold literary or other cultural meetings with Americanism themes; and recreate the atmosphere of the American past through pageants, tableaux, and other features.

Such organizations as the Future Farmers of America, 4-H Clubs, Boy Scouts, Girl Scouts, youth service agencies, and school clubs sponsor or participate in activities such as a preholiday rally in school, neighborhood, or community. Young people's speakers' bureaus supply talent for youth meetings and organization luncheons and dinners. Boys and girls go on Americanism pilgrimages to places of historic interest. Youth groups present plays and tableaux before parent audiences, and promote Americanism at sports events through flag-raising ceremonies at which Americanism awards are presented.

Church organizations include appropriate patriotic activities in their programs, with clergymen pointing out the spiritual and ethical aspects of American ideals and principles.

COORDINATION OF COMMUNITY EVENTS. Your group may take the lead in coordinating events in celebration of patriotic holidays. Well-planned community-wide observance permits the widest possible participation, with each group assuming that part of the program for which its interests and resources best fit it. The American Heritage Foundation suggests its *Nine Promises of a Good Citizen* as a pattern for coordination in which each organization or group of organizations plans its activities with one of the promises as a theme:

1. The League of Women Voters, the Good Government Association, and other groups with a special interest in government might choose to emphasize the first promise: "I will vote at all elections. I will inform myself on candidates and issues and will use my greatest influence to see that honest and capable officials are elected. I will accept public office when I can serve my community or my country thereby."

2. The local bar association has a special interest in popularizing the second promise: "I will serve on a jury when asked."

3. Big Brother organizations, Police Athletic Leagues, and others concerned with law enforcement are especially equipped to carry out educational programs and projects related to the third: "I will respect and obey the laws. I will assist public officials in preventing crime, and the courts in giving evidence."

4. Any organization with an interest in community financing has an

incentive for promoting the fourth: "I will pay my taxes understandingly."

5. Veterans' organizations, groups particularly interested in civil defense, teachers' associations, and church groups could sponsor the fifth: "I will work for peace, but will dutifully accept my responsibilities in time of war, and respect the flag."

6. Church groups, teachers' associations, and other groups concerned with the removal of bigotry have a natural theme in the sixth promise: "In thought, expression, and action, at home and in all my contacts, I will avoid any group prejudice based on class, race, or religion."

7. P.T.A. groups, teachers' associations, and others are interested in the seventh: "I will support our system of free public education by doing everything I can to improve the schools in my own community."

8. All groups interested in community betterment, such as the Chamber of Commerce, and civic and professional organizations have policies that support number eight: "I will try to make my community a better place in which to live."

9. Women's clubs, youth service organizations, church groups, and P.T.A. units have close relations with the home. To them the ninth promise appeals: "I will practice and teach the principles of good citizenship right in my own home."

Planning the celebration of a national holiday to utilize the interests of special groups and to achieve a climactic effect by scheduling events for the week prior to the holiday was the purpose of the Junior Chamber's Independence Week in Bristol, Virginia-Tennessee. Friday was designated Labor-Management Day, with talks by local leaders in labor and industry; Saturday, Youth Day, with stadium, field, and track events for all ages; Sunday, Freedom of Religion Day, marked by Americanism sermons in churches; Monday, Women's Day, with talks by prominent women over local radio stations, and an Americanism luncheon discussion meeting; Tuesday, July 4, traditional Independence Day events—a parade led by the Third Army Band, an elaborate fireworks display, and the crowning of a Miss Liberty Belle.

Another suggestion for a week-long celebration, made by the United States Junior Chamber of Commerce, is that each of the five days prior to and including Independence Day be dedicated to an important freedom: June 30, Freedom of Religion; July 1, Freedom of Speech; July 2, Freedom of the Press; July 3, Freedom of Opportunity; and July 4, Freedom to Assemble.

MEASURES TO COUNTER SUBVERSION

A positive, community-wide, year-round Americanism program, such as that suggested in this chapter, is the most effective defense against un-Americanism. Organizations must, however, be aware of the ever-present threat of subversion. Seldom is that threat an open one. The method of subversion is a "gnawing from within." It has been estimated that communists have organized, used, and then abandoned over 1000 front organizations in the United States alone.

Measures to combat this danger are difficult, both because our laws against treason, sedition, and espionage are difficult to apply, and because of the ever-present need for a scrupulous regard for basic American rights of free expression.

What counter measures can community groups take without encroaching upon areas that belong to government, and without infringing on individual rights? These suggestions are based upon successful programs carried on by hundreds of community groups:

1. Invite representatives of organizations with a special interest in anticommunist measures to talk to your group.

2. Arrange for an intergroup or public series of lectures by experts available through the F.B.I. and Army and Navy Intelligence.

3. Publicize the need for a careful analysis of written or spoken attacks against American institutions, with special attention to the sponsorship of speakers, and the sources of materials.

4. Make available information about international communism and its tactics here and abroad.

SOURCES OF AID

Advertising Council, Inc., 25 West 45th St., New York 19, N. Y. Furnishes newspaper, poster, and other promotion aids for local Americanism programs. Helps correlate organization projects with nationwide efforts.

American Association of School Administrators, a department of the National Education Association of the United States, 1201 16th St., N. W., Washington 6, D. C. Thirty-second Yearbook, 1954, is titled *Educating for American Citizenship.* Useful for citizen-group appreciation of school programs to foster Americanism.

American Bar Association, 1140 North Dearborn St., Chicago 10, Ill. Has available the reports and recommendations of a special committee on communist objectives, strategy, and tactics.

American Heritage Foundation, Inc., 345 East 46th St., New York 17, N. Y. Has program outlines, procedure suggestions, a kit of materials for presentation of a "good citizenship" radio campaign, and other aids for an extensive Americanism program.

American Legion, National Americanism Committee, 777 North Meridian St., Indianapolis 6, Ind. Literature for local Post membership and community programs may suggest cooperative activities for your group. Includes an outline for an extensive course of study; course materials such as the flag code and flag etiquette; and projects for sponsored youth groups. The Committee compiles and keeps up to date a list of officially cited "front" organizations, publishes background information for considerations of current un-American problems, and suggests practical measures to combat subversion in your community.

American Library Association, 50 East Huron St., Chicago 11, Ill. Maintains a continuing program of adult community discussions of the American heritage and its contemporary application. Local libraries provide groups with meeting places, discussion leaders, background materials and films. Association has a pamphlet description of its American Heritage project, and a listing of films with Americanism themes.

America's Future, Inc., 210 East 43rd St., New York 17, N. Y. Offers a series of transcriptions of short Americanism interviews with national leaders, suitable for local broadcasts.

Carrie Chapman Catt Memorial Fund, Inc., 461 Fourth Ave., New York 16, N. Y. Created by the League of Women Voters of the United States. Study pamphlets include a discussion of individual liberty in the United States, and threats posed by communist and other un-American ideologies.

Chamber of Commerce of the United States, 1615 H St., N. W., Washington 6, D. C. National headquarters has program suggestions, study and discussion aids, background pamphlets and other publications, and recordings. Offers detailed suggestions for community volunteer anticommunist action. Furnishes bibliographies of books and periodicals from both communist and anticommunist sources. Has film suggestions and low rental films about our economic and other freedoms, and the communist threat.

Christophers, 18 East 48th St., New York 17, N. Y. Has suggestions for procedures in establishing community career guidance schools to counter the efforts subversive groups are making to infiltrate the professions and occupations.

Citizens Foundation, Inc., 332 South Warren St., Syracuse 2, N. Y. An organization of civic leaders active in Americanism education in New York State. Annual reports include descriptions of successful antisubversive measures taken by Foundation-sponsored Free Enterprise Clubs.

Civic Education Foundation, 5 Chauncy St., Cambridge, Mass. Offers *The Living Democracy Series*, which includes several pamphlets useful for youth-group programs to strengthen American ideals. Information available.

Countrywomen's League, *The Country Gentleman*, Independence Square, Philadelphia 5, Pa. Nominally priced leaflets include copies of short talks on Washington, Lincoln, and other famous Americans, written for meeting presentation; and other program ideas for patriotic occasions.

Daughters of the American Revolution, 1776 D St., N. W., Washington 6, D. C. A source of information about youth and adult Americanism education and citizenship programs effective in many communities. Offers copies of the *Declaration of Independence*, the *Constitution of the United States*, *Lincoln's Gettysburg Address*, the *American Creed*, a flag history and etiquette, and other materials. Publishes a course of study for prospective citizens.

Department of Immigration and Naturalization Service, United States Department of Justice, Washington 25, D. C. Aid includes information about qualifications for citizenship, how to plan and stage induction ceremonies, and lessons on the Constitution and government of the United States.

DoALL Company, 254 North Laurel Ave., Des Plaines, Ill. Has available a catalogue of pamphlets, films, and other material from a number of sources. Sales and service centers in 32 cities furnish economic education material and trained personnel to help in presenting them to civic groups in their sales areas.

Forbes Magazine, 80 Fifth Ave., New York 11, N. Y. Offers a listing of booklets, pamphlets, films, charts, and other materials.

Freedoms Foundation, Inc., Valley Forge, Pa. A nonprofit, nonsectarian, nonpolitical foundation to promote an appreciation of our American ideals. Offers medals, certificates, and cash awards annually for the best expression of Americanism by an individual or group. Entries may be contributions to Americanism through news or magazine articles, sermons, speeches, photographs, or community organization service programs.

General Federation of Women's Clubs, 1734 N St., N. W., Washington 6, D. C. Has a list of speakers auditioned by General Federation representatives, and agencies through which they may be scheduled.

Harding College, Searcy, Ark. Maintains an adult program for education in the American way of life, operating in close relation with community organizations throughout the country. Its program includes quarterly five-day Freedom Forums for business and other civic leaders at Searcy, the resources of which are available to civic groups; a weekly editorial column syndicated in about 3600 publications; *The Harding College Letter*, a publication presenting articles about significant current problems in American affairs; a staff of lecturers available to civic groups; special helps for Americanism speakers, such as guides for the inexperienced; kits of unique visual aids; the *Speakers Handbook*, a looseleaf volume of suggestions and documented materials; and free loan radio transcriptions and films.

Institute for Democratic Education, 212 Fifth Ave., New York 11, N. Y. *Lest We Forget These Great Americans,* a series of recordings for children.

John Hancock Mutual Life Insurance Company, 200 Berkeley St., Boston 17, Mass., and local offices. Offers biographies of famous Americans without cost.

National Association of Manufacturers, 14 West 49th St., New York 20, N. Y. A catalogue of booklets, research reports, posters, motion pictures and other visual aids, recordings, and periodicals about our system of free enterprise.

National Association of Radio and Television Broadcasters, 1771 N St., N. W., Washington 6, D. C. Has a series of transcriptions of Jaycee sponsored "I Speak for Democracy" contest-winning speeches.

National Education Association, 1201 16th St., Washington 6, D. C. Material includes background information, suggestions for attaining Americanism objectives through school activities such as assemblies, and study materials such as *The American Citizens Handbook*. Reports of the annual National Conference on Citizenship, sponsored jointly with the Department of Justice, suggest activities in observance of National Citizenship Day. Cosponsors Legion-Schoolmasters Clubs. Listing of pamphlet and other Americanism material is available.

National Recreation Association, Correspondence and Consultation Bureau, 315 Fourth Ave., New York 10, N. Y. Inexpensive pamphlets include plays and pageants based on incidents in American history, citizenship, and other patriotic subjects, and program materials for national observances such as Lincoln's and Washington's birthdays, Memorial Day, Flag Day, Fourth of July, and Armistice Day.

Public Affairs Committee, Inc., 22 East 38th St., New York 16, N. Y. A nonprofit educational organization for the study of American social, political, and economic problems. Study results in pamphlet form include *Loyalty in a Democracy*, suggesting community action to safeguard essential American values.

Sons of the American Revolution, Hotel Plaza, New York 19, N. Y. Sponsors Americanism education measures and patriotic observances. Description of program available.

Superintendent of Documents, United States Government Printing Office, Washington 25, D. C. Has descriptive listings of many government pamphlets and booklets on Americanism. Available is *Guide to Subversive Organizations and Publications*, prepared by the House Un-American Activities Committee. *Catalog of Radio Recordings* describes Office of Education transcriptions that may be borrowed without cost. Representative titles include *Molly Pitcher*, *The Man without a Country*, *Citizen Tom Paine*, *We Hold These Truths*, and *Platform for Democracy*.

Twentieth Century Fund, 330 West 42nd St., New York 18, N. Y. Makes available research literature useful for organization study and discussion, and public education measures.

United States Marine Corps, Division of Public Information, Washington 25, D. C. Has 31-page illustrated free booklet, *How to Respect and Display Our Flag*.

United States Office of Education, Department of Health, Education, and Welfare, Washington 25, D. C. Monthly magazine *School Life*, pamphlets, bibliographies, and lists of films include citizenship-education program suggestions useful in organization-school projects. Description of material is available.

Veterans of Foreign Wars, Americanism Department, Broadway at 34th St., Kansas City 2, Mo. Free materials include *The Flag*, a question-and-answer presentation of information; *Ten Short Stories about the Stars and Stripes*; and a 10½ by 12½ inch facsimile of Lincoln's "Gettysburg Address" on parchment paper.

SOME SOURCES OF FILMS AND FILM INFORMATION

Association Films, 347 Madison Ave., New York 17, N. Y. Low rental films in sound and color present American community life and its advantages. Catalogue available.

Allegheny Ludlum Steel Corporation, 2020 Oliver Building, Pittsburgh 22, Pa. Free loan sound films include *The Fifth Freedom*, a three-reel documentation of what freedom of opportunity means to all Americans. Illustrated folder available.

Farm Film Foundation, 1731 Eye St., N. W., Washington 6, D. C. Free loan films that help develop an understanding and appreciation through dramatization of actual community accomplishments. Descriptive listing available.

Film Council of America, 600 Davis St., Evanston, Ill. Offers descriptions and evaluations of many films with Americanism themes. Furnishes program guides and discussion materials to be used with Council-recommended films about great Americans and great American issues.

General Motors Corporation, Department of Public Relations, Film Section, 3044 West Grand Boulevard, Detroit 2, Mich. Offers a series of four free loan sound films demonstrating the stake the average citizen has in the maintenance of the competitive character of our enterprise. Description available.

Ideal Picture Corporation, 65 East South Water St., Chicago 15, Ill., and branch offices in 25 other major cities. Free loan films include Our America, a dramatic summing up of the factors that distinguish our way of life from that of other social, political, and economic systems. Description available.

Kelvinator Division, Nash-Kelvinator Corporation, 14250 Plymouth Road, Detroit 32, Mich. Free loan films include Of This We Are Proud, presenting people, places, and events in American culture. Description available.

Midland Cooperative Wholesale, 739 Johnson St., N. E., Minneapolis 13, Minn. Free loan films include some produced especially for children's understanding of our economic system. Descriptions available.

Minneapolis-Moline Company, Box 1050, Minneapolis 1, Minn. Free loan films include the 45-minute sound and color This Heritage of Ours, telling the story of how freedom-loving Americans carved from the wilderness the greatest nation on earth. Description available.

Modern Talking Picture Service, 45 Rockefeller Plaza, New York 20, N. Y., and offices in 27 other major cities. Free loan sound films include several which dramatize the place of competitive enterprise in the American way of life. Catalogue available.

Princeton Film Center, Inc., Carter Road, Princeton, N. J. Rental films include the 15-minute Backfire!, a dramatic explanation of the American way of life. Produced in cooperation with the American Economic Foundation. Film received the 1952 Award, Free Enterprise, Economic

Division, Cleveland Film Festival; and a medal of honor from Freedoms Foundation.

Research Institute of America, 292 Madison Ave., New York 17, N. Y. Has information about low rental films demonstrating the communist approach to factory workers and suggesting effective counter measures.

RKO Radio Pictures, Inc., Educational Division, 1270 Avenue of the Americas, New York 20, N. Y. Offers a series of 16 mm rental films, *This Is America*. Description available.

Superintendent of Documents, United States Government Printing Office, Washington 25, D. C. Publishes a catalogue of motion pictures with democracy as a theme, compiled and evaluated by the Office of Education, Department of Health, Education, and Welfare. Includes films about our democratic heritage, the meaning of democracy, the democratic processes, and films for patriotic occasions.

United Service for New Americans, Inc., 15 Park Row, New York 7, N. Y. Has free loan sound films about resettlement of European refugees in the United States and the problems of immigration adjustment. Catalogue available.

United States Treasury, Savings Bond Director, your state capital. Free loan films include the inspirational *America the Beautiful* and its sequel *Power behind the Nation*, which tell the story of the development of America from the days of the pioneers.

Venard Organization, 702 South Adams St., Peoria 2, Ill. Films produced especially for community organization use include several on Americanism subjects, available on a free loan basis. Representative titles: *The Story of Our Flag, Our Declaration of Independence,* and *Our Constitution.* Illustrated folder available.

CHAPTER 15

Education

COMMUNITY ORGANIZATIONS traditionally have an interest in public schools. Today they are important influences in a great nation-wide citizen movement to meet needs that suddenly have become acute.

Other chapters in this book suggest ideas and procedures for organization-school projects in fields such as community arts, safety, and Americanism. Many organizations, however, maintain an education committee to correlate such activities, and to furnish more direct support through programs to better the community's understanding of school problems; to provide necessary buildings and equipment; to secure and maintain a competent, stable teaching staff; to bring about a greater utilization of all community education resources; and to initiate and support community-wide study and planning groups.

COMMUNITY UNDERSTANDING OF SCHOOL PROBLEMS

In sponsoring a program to bring about a more general citizen understanding of school problems, an organization should start with its own members.

MEMBERSHIP ACTIVITIES. Schedule background films, speakers, and discussion sessions. Invite the superintendent of schools to talk about education objectives and how citizens can help meet them. Have supervisors and heads of departments present a panel discussion of current local problems.

Often a talk falls flat, fails to have a point, or is spread too thin to be of real value, because the speaker has not been told what the audience would like him to talk about. "Please talk about the schools" is a large order. The chances are the speaker will try to cover every phase of school business and leave the group with little solid substance. Your committee might suggest timely and important topics. Questions prepared in advance may result in a more interesting and worth-while discussion. In what ways are parents encouraged to have frequent consultation with teachers? What is the extent of teacher turnover? What studies have been made of the reasons for pupils leaving school before graduation? Answers to such questions may suggest needs that your group can help meet.

There are other practical approaches to your group's understanding of school problems. Members might attend a typical faculty meeting. Your group might invite key members of a school staff to a luncheon or dinner discussion of community-school concerns. Perhaps one of the departments, English, mathematics, or social studies, for example, might stage a demonstration department meeting.

In many communities, P.T.A.'s and other groups have arranged "back to school" days. Accompanying a student through his school day, the interested adult soon discovers things "aren't what they used to be"—that the needs of modern youth call for different subject matters and procedures. Pooling of observations by several members might be used as the basis for an interesting meeting report.

Visits, except for the purpose of inspecting the plant and observing morale generally, should be by arrangement with the principal. Because of last-minute changes in schedule, the giving of tests, or assemblies, an observer's visit might be a waste of time.

COMMUNITY ACTIVITIES. The quality of public education in any community, education leaders maintain, is largely determined by the public's appreciation of its schools' objectives, and its understanding of school problems. Administrators often are too burdened with details, or discouraged by public indifference or outright hostility, or limited because of lack of skill or opportunity, to present effectively their story to parents and citizens. Your organization can help bring about public appreciation and understanding by including in its program activities such as the following:

1. Sponsoring a series of "know your school" discussion meetings, preferably in cooperation with other groups. The annual all-day Borough of the Bronx, New York City, School-Community Conference, for example, is sponsored by over 22 community organizations.

2. Encouraging public attendance at drama, music, debate, sports, and other school events.

3. Making the literature and promotional material offered by the Advertising Council available in the community.

4. Arranging for a series of newspaper articles, and sponsoring radio and television dramatizations of local school needs.

5. Aiding the school system in the publication of a pictorial report to the community, or helping to finance and produce a documentary film.

6. Promoting a Business-Industry-Education Day, with the schools in the role of host.

7. Cooperating with the P.T.A. and the American Legion in sponsoring American Education Week, observed annually from Sunday through Saturday of the week of Armistice Day.

8. Sponsoring a layman-teacher conference or workshop on Better Schools Through Improved Lay-Professional Relationships.

9. Arranging for a wider community use of school facilities and the talents of faculty members.

10. Helping to plan and conduct a community-wide survey of attitudes toward your schools, to be used as the basis for a long-range school-organization know-your-school campaign.

11. Cooperating with a staff community coordinator in devising ways of bringing school and neighborhood closer together.

ADEQUATE SCHOOL BUILDINGS AND FACILITIES

Because of the suspension of building programs during the war, the materials shortages after the war, and the failure of municipalities to adjust fiscal policies to the spiraling costs of materials and labor, necessary school plant expansion in thousands of communities is now long overdue.

The situation has become critical in many towns and cities, as schools strain their facilities to accommodate the unusually large numbers of children born during the war years. Health and safety are threatened by overcrowding; obsolete buildings with serious fire hazards; inadequate sanitary facilities; poor lighting; and cafeteria, recreation, and other facilities that fall far short of meeting generally accepted standards.

Such situations are being met through projects that range from directing a drive for the approval of a school-building bond issue, to providing hot lunches. They include:

1. Surveying school buildings and grounds, and mobilizing volunteers to make necessary repairs and renovations.

2. Sponsoring a money-raising drive for facilities not provided for in the budget, such as a library, a cafeteria, or a locker room.

3. Organizing a house-to-house canvass, a speakers' bureau, poster distribution, and other measures to acquaint the public with building needs.

4. Planning a special appeal to the community's businessmen, pointing out the dollars-and-cents value of a good school system.

5. Presenting models, photographs, or 16 mm films to make graphic the need for adequate buildings.

6. Compiling and publicizing comparative cost figures demonstrating the reasonableness of school expansion requests.

7. Offering planning assistance, utilizing the services of members with professional and technical backgrounds, such as realtors, construction executives, and architects.

8. Cooperating with your government affairs committee in supporting legislative and budgetary provisions for an adequate school system.

9. Helping to determine population trends as a guide for a long-range building program.

10. Urging the correlation of school and recreation, highway, land use, and other planning.

A COMPETENT TEACHING STAFF

Schools throughout the nation have failed to regain most of the 350,000 teachers lost to the military services or to business and industry during the war. Many communities have had to engage men and women who do not meet minimum training standards set by state boards of education and professional teachers' associations. The number of boys and girls who choose teaching as a career falls far short of meeting current needs or of building a reservoir of teaching talent for the expected enrollment peak to be reached in a few years.

TEACHERS' SALARIES. Your organization can help place your school system in a good competitive position for obtaining personnel by securing necessary salary schedule revisions. Through a speakers' bureau, and newspaper, radio, and television campaigns, call attention to the individual teacher as the preponderant influence in the education process. Publicize data showing that teachers' salaries have not kept pace with rising living costs, and with salaries in other occupations and professions in your community. Make available explanations of salary schedules in effect in comparable towns or cities noted for the excellence of their school systems.

TEACHER ASSIMILATION. A competent teaching staff is not wholly a matter of an adequate salary schedule. A recent United States Junior Chamber of Commerce bulletin to local education committees declared that a survey of teachers indicated that 39 per cent feel that the community is not interested in them or in what they do; 46 per cent feel that they are not appreciated.

Help make teachers feel that they are a part of your community through activities such as:

1. Writing letters of welcome to newly appointed teachers, in which you offer the help of your organization in such problems as finding adequate living quarters.

2. Arranging for a committee to meet new teachers and their families at trains and buses.

3. Conducting new teachers on orientation tours of the community and area.

4. Inviting new teachers to meetings and to the homes of members.

5. Participating with the P.T.A., the local teachers' association, and school staffs in a reception for new teachers.

6. Inviting new teachers to become members of your organization, and providing opportunities for them to participate in community activities.

RECOGNIZING TEACHER ACHIEVEMENT. Recognition is a powerful incentive for effort. Ask teachers to talk to your group about their accomplishments. Sponsor public exhibits and demonstrations of student work and skills in fields such as art, music, and crafts. In publicizing the outstanding college records and other achievements of graduates, recognize the part that teachers have played. Arrange for a series of "meet your teacher" newspaper articles, and radio or television programs. Publicize the results of student achievement tests employing national standards. Sponsor local grants for further study, based on merit.

IN-SERVICE TRAINING. Objectives and teaching techniques in many fields must be modified to meet changing situations. Encourage the in-service training of teachers. Urge that increments be related to professional improvement. Sponsor extension courses, or establish scholarships and other grants to teachers for training to meet particular community needs.

TEACHING AS A CAREER. Community groups through their national and state organizations, and in projects and programs on the local level, are calling the attention of the nation's youth to the advantages of teaching as a career, and are making such careers possible through teachers' college scholarships.

Other activities to recruit talent include conducting an organization-teacher-youth conference on the opportunities for service and other satisfactions in a teaching career; cooperating with P.T.A.'s and school authorities in sponsoring a visiting day for prospective teachers invited through the placement offices of teachers colleges; presenting interview-type radio or television programs featuring teachers; calling attention to long and distinguished service rendered by teachers through granting awards and holding dinners or other events in their honor; and including teaching in your vocational guidance program.

UTILIZATION OF COMMUNITY RESOURCES

Schools today seek to utilize fully all the educational resources of a community. Indispensable to the realization of this purpose is the cooperation of volunteer groups such as yours.

Many of the chapters of this book suggest the use of membership and community resources, in activities such as helping to plan and publish texts for municipal government and citizenship courses; arranging for work-study programs; providing supplemental planning and supervisory help for field trips; furnishing talent and materials for assemblies; aiding economic education and other essential programs; providing leadership for special-interest groups; helping to maintain guidance, counseling, and job placement services; and encouraging student service activities.

The establishment, maintenance, and administration of scholarship and loan funds have been major interests of most federated organizations since their very beginnings. These awards and funds are incentives for school achievement, publicize the role of schools, and have been of great influence in providing community leadership through the further education and training of hundreds of thousands of American boys and girls. Your organization may serve the youth and the schools by establishing such a grant or by initiating and supporting an intergroup fund administered by representatives of the participating groups, school officials, clergymen, and other youth leaders.

The primary purpose of most organization financial help for students is to encourage development of character, leadership, service to the school and community, as well as academic achievement. However, scholarships and loans may have other important objectives. They may be used to develop student and parent interest in a particular phase of the school program, such as art, music, or literature. They may be designed to provide leadership and trained personnel in a field such as social service, medicine, or nursing.

CITIZEN STUDY, PLANNING, AND ADVISORY GROUPS

Within the last few years thousands of citizen groups have been formed to study the schools of their communities, plan measures to improve them, and serve as advisory bodies to boards of education and school administrations. By 1954, *The New York Times* reported, 9000 were in existence, and several hundreds were being organized each month.

This great "grass roots" movement, sponsored by the National Citizens Commission for the Public Schools, has received the full support of federated organizations such as the National Congress of Parents and Teachers, the United States Junior Chamber of Commerce, and the American Legion.

These citizen groups vary widely in their specific objectives and in the scope of their activities. Some are formed only to give the public a better appreciation of school problems and their responsibilities as parents and citizens. Others are formed to secure needed buildings and facilities. Some have as their purpose the appraisal of school objectives, techniques, and achievements in limited areas such as languages, vocational guidance, and social studies. Many are organized to study the total school program and to make recommendations for its improvement.

In many communities these study groups have become formal organizations with continuing school-support programs. They provide important services such as helping to project enrollment figures, correlating school and community planning, reflecting and interpreting public opinion, providing a sounding board for new school policies, and interpreting school policy and practice.

While no pattern for procedure generally applicable to all communities is practical, the following are characteristic of successful citizen programs:

1. The membership of the initiating organization has a background of knowledge about local problems, and good school relations.

2. At the outset, the sponsors secure the cooperation of the board of education, school officials, the local teachers' professional association, the Council of Parent-Teacher Associations, and other groups with a primary interest in education.

3. Care is taken to make the membership of the study or advisory group representative of all points of view in the community, and to enroll citizens who can rise above neighborhood, occupational, or other narrow interests.

4. In the preliminary stages, the group defines its objectives, its responsibilities, and its relation to the board of education and the community as a whole. The duties and responsibilities of such a committee

must be purely advisory, as boards of education cannot delegate their powers or responsibilities.

5. To maintain the lay status of the group, members of the board of education and school personnel serve as resource persons only.

6. A general school orientation of members is undertaken, no matter how limited the purposes of the group.

7. Objectives finally chosen are specific and concrete, and their attainment is within the capacities and resources of the group.

SOURCES OF AID

Adult Education Association of the U.S.A., 743 North Wabash Ave., Chicago 11, Ill. Formed from the former American Association for Adult Education and the Department of Adult Education of the National Education Association. Publishes *Adult Leadership*, a monthly; *Adult Education*, a professional bimonthly journal; and two occasional pamphlets, *AEA Newsletter* and *Research Reports*.

Advertising Council, Inc., 25 West 45th St., New York 18, N. Y. Maintains a national promotion campaign for better public schools. Cooperates with the National Citizens Commission for the Public Schools. Sponsors the Newspaper Cooperation Plan for public service, participated in by 560 dailies with a total circulation of over 27 million. Will furnish advertising mats, spot announcements, films, recordings, posters, and other promotional aid to local groups.

American Association of University Women, 1634 Eye St., N. W., Washington 6, D. C. Has available pamphlets, bibliographies, and reports of programs of value to groups interested in education.

American School Publishing Corporation, 470 Fourth Ave., New York 16, N. Y. Has available "Citizens Organize for Better Schools," a special issue of *The School Executive*, January, 1952, presenting full coverage of a great national movement, and suggesting organization and action procedures. Publishes *The American School and University*, a basic yearbook devoted to design, construction, equipment, utilization, and maintenance of buildings and grounds. Valuable source material for an organization or intergroup school-study program.

Bureau of Publications, Teachers College, Columbia University, New York 27, N. Y. Offers *Problems and Issues in Public School Finance*, published by the National Conference of Professors and Educational Administrators. Analyzes and summarizes research findings and experiences in public school finance.

Chamber of Commerce of the United States, Committee on Education, 1615 H St., N. W., Washington 6, D. C. Local chambers cooperate with schools, other community organizations, and business concerns in programs for better schools. National headquarters has numerous pamphlets useful in projects and programs: suggestions for organizing and directing an education committee; summaries of national research figures on enrollments, teachers' salaries and training, school costs, population shifts, economic and fiscal trends; facts and figures demonstrating the dollars and cents value of a good school system; charts, posters, and other material to promote better-school campaigns; and suggestions for planning a Business-Education Day.

Congress of Industrial Organizations, 718 Jackson Place, N. W., Washington 6, D. C. *Don't Neglect Our Schools*, a pamphlet emphasizing the need for school improvement, and suggesting a ten-year construction program.

Funke, Harold H., *Community Uses of Public School Facilities*, New York: Columbia University Press, 1951. Covers questions such as what uses may legally be made of playgrounds, laboratories, typewriters, and other facilities and equipment. Discusses problems such as types of groups that should be permitted the use of schools; the scheduling of community group activities; providing for costs; and arranging for joint ownership of facilities.

Hill and Knowlton, Inc., Public Relations Counsel, 350 Fifth Ave., New York 1, N. Y. Distributes industry-sponsored aids for school service programs. Pamphlets and booklets available without cost include the results of research in methods of school-industry cooperation and specific suggestions for using citizens as resource persons in classrooms.

Joint Council on Economic Education, 444 Madison Ave., New York 17, N. Y. Offers pamphlet suggestions for school-community cooperation for the economic education of youth.

National Citizens Commission for the Public Schools, 2 West 45th St., New York 36, N. Y. A nonprofit, nonprofessional organization for the improvement of public schools. Has inspired and given advice and material help to very many of the estimated 9000 volunteer school study and school aid projects carried out in communities in recent years. Offers a series of *Working Guides* to aid in programs of continuing interest. Guides are available in fields such as teaching, school boards, administration, school finance, buildings, philosophies, and goals. Publishes *Citizens and Their Schools*, a monthly report of school improvement projects, and suggestions for group study and procedure.

National Congress of Parents and Teachers, 600 South Michigan Boulevard, Chicago 5, Ill. An organization of over 40,000 local associations, having a membership of almost 6 million, dedicated to the harnessing of the resources of home, school, and community in the interest of children and youth. Has available *Parent-Teacher Publications*, an alphabetical and subject matter index of books, pamphlets, program ideas, and other literature.

National Education Association of the United States, 1201 16th St., N. W., Washington 6, D. C. The professional organization of public school teachers and administrators. Publications include *Lay Advisory Committees*, a 23-page illustrated handbook suggesting patterns of organization and procedure for organization-school improvement committees. Issues a 32-page descriptive listing of publications, many of which are helpful to organizations.

National Institute of Social Relations, 1244 20th St., N. W., Washington 6, D. C. Publishes a series of *Talk It Over* pamphlets for the discussion of school problems.

National Municipal League, 299 Broadway, New York 7, N. Y. Literature includes reports of successful volunteer action in behalf of better schools.

National School Public Relations Association, 1201 16th St., N. W., Washington 6, D. C. Materials include a public relations handbook for teachers, which furnishes a good background for an organization's supporting program.

Office of Education, Department of Health, Education, and Welfare, Washington 25, D. C. Free and low cost pamphlets include subjects such as organization and administration of public schools, education of exceptional children, health and physical education, rural schools, and vocational guidance. Will provide information about films on particular school problems. Film listing available.

Pathfinders of America, Inc., 335 Bulkley Building, Cleveland 15, Ohio. Sponsors moral training programs. Has transcripts of moral education in action in the classrooms of Cleveland.

Progressive Education Association, College of Education, Ohio State University, Columbus 10, Ohio. Seeks to improve education through community planning and action. Has available books, pamphlets, and special reports of value as background material for a membership understanding of modern schools. Publishes *Progressive Education*.

Sumption, Merle R., *How to Conduct a Citizens School Survey*, New York: Prentice-Hall, Inc., 1952. A step by step procedure for organizing citizens, gathering facts, interpreting facts, and developing a long-range education plan. Procedure suggestions based on citizen surveys in 20 Midwest communities.

Superintendent of Documents, United States Government Printing Office, Washington 25, D. C. Offers *United States Office of Education and Other Publications Relating to Education*, a 21-page booklet with items classified under subject matter headings. Also available are lists of publications on separate topics, and of audio-visual aids and other materials.

University of Chicago Press, 5750 Ellis Ave., Chicago 37, Ill. Offers *Lay Professional Cooperation in Public School Education*, the 1953 yearbook of the National Society for the Study of Education. Yearbook presents current education issues, reviews the progress of lay-professional cooperation, and suggests basic principles for further cooperation in communities.

Yauch, Wilbur A., *How Good Is Your School?*, New York: Harper & Brothers, 1951. Explains modern education methods. Includes a check list useful in evaluating your school program.

SOME SOURCES OF FILMS AND FILM INFORMATION

Primary sources of evaluative information about current free loan and low rental films to meet specific local needs are community audio-visual aids centers, state departments of education, state teacher training colleges, professional state teachers' associations, the National Education Association, and the United States Office of Education. Because of the great range and variety of volunteer group interests in school problems, no definitive listing of sources can be offered. The following are representative:

Fish and Wildlife Service, United States Department of the Interior, Section of Visual Education, Washington 25, D. C. Free loan films include *Food for Thought*, illustrating effective planning, purchasing, preparing, displaying, and serving school lunches. Description available.

Ford Motor Company, Film Library, 20 North Wacker Drive, Chicago 6, Ill. Free loan films include the 20-minute *Pride of Workmanship*. Shows how public schools are teaching industrial skills and craftsmanship. Description available.

General Pictures Productions, Inc., 621 Sixth Ave., Des Moines 9, Iowa. Films include *Education Is Good Business*. Contrasts a community in which business and industry actively support the schools, with one in which they are indifferent. Description in general catalogue.

George W. Colburn Laboratory, 164 North Wacker Drive, Chicago 6,

Ill., agency for International Harvester Company. Free loan sound and color films include the two-reel *A Way of Life*, the story of how the whole community of Beaverton, Michigan, participated in a school improvement program. Catalogue available.

Locke Films, Inc., 124 West South St., Kalamazoo 8, Mich. *Learning Democracy Through School Community Projects*, a 20-minute color film suggesting activities appropriate for organization sponsorship. Produced in collaboration with the School of Education, University of Michigan, and the Daughters of the American Revolution of Michigan. Rental. Description available.

McGraw-Hill Book Company, Inc., Text-Film Department, 330 West 42nd St., New York 18, N. Y. Distributor of films about subject matter and methods, child psychology, the recruitment and holding of teachers, and citizens in action for better schools. Of special interest are *Schools March On*, how citizens are working to improve rural schools; and *The Fight for Rural Schools*, volunteer-group action in Virginia, Arkansas, Delaware, and Long Island. Catalogue available.

Museum of Modern Art Film Library, 11 West 53rd St., New York 19, N. Y. Rental films include *New Schools for Old*, a contrast of the little red schoolhouse with a modern school. Description available.

National Education Association, 1201 16th St., N. W., Washington 6, D. C. A primary source of information about films.

State Department of Education, your state capital. Has available without charge *School House in the Red*, sponsored by the W. K. Kellogg Foundation, Battle Creek, Michigan. An effective film presentation of rural education problems. Suggests approaches to their solution. Description available from the Kellogg Foundation.

State University of Iowa, Bureau of Visual Instruction, Extension Division, Iowa City, Iowa. Free loan films include an explanation of how schools may use community resources. Description available.

Superior Coach Corporation, Lima, Ohio. Offers the free loan 17-minute *Priceless Cargo*, the story of the development of school transportation. Description available.

Tennessee Valley Authority, Film Services, Knoxville, Tenn. Free loan sound films include the 20-minute *Wilson Dam School*, the presentation of a typical day in the operation of a modern school. Description available.

Texas Engineering Experiment Station, Supervisor of Publications, College Station, Tex. Free loan films include *Building for Learning*, two reels in sound and color. Produced as a planning aid for community organizations with school expansion programs. Description available.

CHAPTER 16

Vocational Guidance and Rehabilitation

IT IS generally recognized today that an individual's placement and adjustment in a profession or a job for which he is best fitted are matters of community concern. Organizations are helping young people to choose and prepare for careers, or to find permanent jobs. They are aiding adults seeking employment, and those who have failed to become adjusted in their professions or occupations. They are providing guidance for older workers, many of whom are unemployed because of prejudices involving age. They are aiding the physically handicapped to utilize their productive capacities to the fullest extent.

VOCATIONAL GUIDANCE FOR YOUTH

Countless young people leave school to take jobs—any jobs—with little knowledge of their aptitudes, capacities, real interests, or of the opportunities in their communities. Many of them, largely through trial and error, find satisfactory life careers. Others eventually find places in the work world, but at a tremendous cost to themselves, their successive employers, and their communities.

A vocation-choice study in Portland, Oregon, revealed a typical situation. Nine out of ten high school graduates not going to college had no specific vocation plans. Many were aiming at jobs that did not exist and would not exist in Portland in the foreseeable future. Few students had talked to business or professional men about job opportunities.

While many high schools and youth service groups are meeting situations such as this, vocational guidance cannot be handled by these agencies alone. It must be the concern of the community at large, especially of leaders in business, industry, and the professions— the members of influential community organizations.

Hundreds of project and program reports attest to the effectiveness of organization action.

VOCATIONAL GUIDANCE CONFERENCES AND INSTITUTES. In many places community organizations are sponsoring all-day school-community programs in which members and leaders in the professions, business, industry, and public service give students first-hand vocational information and answer their questions. Such "career days," "career determination days," "job conferences," or "vocational clinics" have become traditional annual events. Speakers describe qualifications, employment possibilities, and opportunities for advancement in various careers and jobs.

In other communities, professional and business leaders, with the cooperation of the local Chamber of Commerce, schedule 45-minute individual youth interviews and observation visits to their offices, stores, and plants each week. Young people receive a general description of the profession or business, watch its operation, and learn about its requirements and opportunities.

Another type of activity is the holding of an institute to supplement the work of the public school vocational and guidance staffs. In Grand Rapids over 5000 juniors and seniors from 14 high schools annually enroll in the Chamber of Commerce 30-session Vocational Information Institute. Professional and business leaders describe employment and career opportunities and outline backgrounds essential for success. Subjects include the major professions and a wide variety of employment fields such as accounting, the beautician trade, pharmacy, and auto mechanics.

Efforts in behalf of the vocational guidance of youth are not limited to secondary school students. Many local organizations cooperate with colleges in arranging for talks by national and local business leaders, and for individual student conferences with personnel executives. A discussion of important national trends in business and industry and their effects on employment opportunities is usually featured. Such programs may be open to high school and other students in the area. Evening meetings provide an opportunity for parents to attend.

JOB-GETTING CLINICS. In some communities, organizations cooperate in establishing a job-getting techniques clinic for those about to be graduated from high school. Two or three members, chosen because of their background in personnel work, take the part of employers. Briefed beforehand regarding the nature of the jobs sought, through letters of application written as part of class work, each "employer" interviews several students in the presence of the class.

After each interview, the experts and the students evaluate the applicant's qualifications and criticize the effectiveness of his efforts to sell himself.

JUNIOR ACHIEVEMENT ENTERPRISES. Adult groups are supervising hundreds of Junior Achievement Enterprises, practical projects to bring work and business experience into the lives of boys and girls, and make it possible for them to choose careers realistically. Over 30,000 junior and senior high school students in about 1000 towns and cities are organized into over 2000 companies of from 8 to 16 "employees." Each enterprise plans, finances, and manages its own affairs, under experienced adult supervision.

CAREER CLUBS. Rotary Clubs are forming student career clubs with memberships patterned after their occupational classification system. These "Teenarian" clubs hold a weekly luncheon meeting, elect their own officers and members, and limit their size to that of the Rotary Club sponsor. Each "Teenarian" has the personal sponsorship of a Rotarian, who provides vocational counseling and work experience, and helps him acquire friendships among the community's professional and business leaders.

TEACHER TRAINING. Many organizations sponsor a Business-Industry-Education Day to give teachers a better understanding of how our economic system operates and of the type of training needed by their students. The project calls for visits by teachers to industrial plants and businesses. These visits are not merely sight-seeing tours. Conferences are held with business and industrial managers and supervisors who know the training needed for work in their departments. As a follow-up, executives often visit the schools to determine whether courses of study adequately meet these needs.

VOCATIONAL GUIDANCE AND THE BIG BROTHER MOVEMENT. In other communities, members of business and professional groups serve as big brothers to boys. In almost 50 years of work with over 20,000 boys, big brothers have found that vocational guidance is both a preventive and a curative for juvenile delinquency.

OTHER ACTIVITIES. Other activities that contribute to the vocational guidance of youth include:

1. Furnishing schools, youth service agencies, churches, and other interested groups with information about professional, business, and industrial opportunities.

2. Publicizing youth training or job needs at meetings, and through the newsletter, the public press, radio and television.

3. Supporting youth vocational guidance centers, or encouraging the expansion of guidance services by the schools, youth service agencies, and church groups.

4. Furnishing vocational guidance and counseling for sponsored youth groups; correlating vocational guidance activities with crafts and those programs designed to develop character.

5. Presenting occupational information exhibits in schools, libraries, and meeting places.

6. Providing scholarships and student loans for training in special occupations for which the community or nation has need.

7. Organizing work-study programs in cooperation with schools and colleges.

8. Providing after-school and vacation work experience through members.

9. Arranging visits to industrial and business centers for the youth of rural areas or small neighboring communities.

10. Encouraging the inclusion of formal courses in economic education, as well as vocational training and shop programs, in the public schools.

11. Cooperating with school authorities to keep boys and girls in school until they have been graduated.

12. Helping the school guidance department to organize and administer a graduate counseling and placement service.

VOCATIONAL GUIDANCE FOR ADULTS

Many adults who seek jobs, who are maladjusted in a particular profession, business, or occupation, or who wish to find placement in other fields, need community help. The community, in self-interest, should stand ready to offer it.

Most adult employment problems are intricately related to other problems of living, such as health, personality development, or family relations. Often such problems require the guidance of doctors, psychiatrists, or other counselors. However, a great many opportunities exist for organization service in furnishing occupational information and providing placement service.

As in programs for youth, adult vocational guidance is most effective when undertaken in consultation with experts and organizations with experience in the field, such as family welfare agencies, mental health associations, the Y.M.C.A., Y.M.H.A., the personnel departments of business and industrial concerns, and government agencies.

A review of successful projects suggests activities such as the following:

1. Supporting the vocational guidance services maintained by the United States Employment Service, the Veterans Administration, state agencies, Chambers of Commerce, churches, schools, colleges, and social agencies.

2. Promoting better placement and guidance in local business and industry.

3. Establishing and supporting a community vocational guidance and counseling center.

4. Sponsoring a man-marketing clinic, a business opportunities seminar, or a veterans' guidance forum.

5. Maintaining programs to meet the employment needs of migratory workers, older workers, disabled persons, and minority groups.

6. Promoting establishment of counseling services in the professional associations of the community, such as those in the fields of law, medicine, and education. Such services could offer help in the transition from professional schools to practice; collect and make available information about practice opportunities; and advise about local customs and ethics.

7. Cooperating in measures to direct community man power into defense industry and other essential public service.

8. Helping to provide work experience in local concerns for the faculties of business, technical, vocational education, and other departments of schools and colleges.

9. Aiding convict rehabilitation through establishing prison study and shops courses, and providing occupational information, counseling, and placement service for those about to be released or paroled.

10. Working for community economic development as a prerequisite to satisfactory community employment.

11. Protecting the community against vocational guidance quacks by providing information about counselor's standards and eligibility requirements, and working for regulatory legislation.

GUIDANCE FOR OLDER WORKERS

The increasing number of older workers who are finding it difficult to secure and retain satisfactory employment, because of the erroneous belief that they are unfit, presents a serious social problem.

The Federation Employment Service, a nonprofit vocational guidance and placement organization in New York City, determined that older workers can do a job as well as, and in some instances better than, young persons. In a job performance study, it found that 83 per cent of the older workers equaled or bettered the production record of younger workers. Employers characterized most older workers as better than average and described them as trustworthy and dependable, more reliable, very cooperative, and devoted.

Your organization can give new hope to older people by helping to provide full or part-time employment. Promote their utilization through meeting programs, your newsbulletin, the press, radio, and television.

An opportunity for retraining is a particular need. Cooperate in planning and directing a vocational evening-school program. Urge employment of suitable instructors. Enlist the aid of local business and industry in providing materials with which to work. Promote formation of self-help clubs, or sponsor a special placement service.

GUIDANCE FOR THE PHYSICALLY HANDICAPPED

Organizations have spearheaded national campaigns to utilize more fully the abilities of those who because of physical handicaps have failed to become gainfully employed or have been employed to a limited extent.

Ever since leaders of federated community organizations and representatives of national health and welfare groups met with the President of the United States to plan the program for the first National Employ the Physically Handicapped Week, the record of achievement has been impressive. Well over a half million men and women who would otherwise be wholly or partially dependent have become gainfully employed. These people have earned wages and salaries in excess of $1 billion, and have paid over $250 million in federal, state, county, and municipal taxes.

Millions of handicapped Americans still need medical, surgical, or therapeutic treatment, as well as business and industrial training. They are unable to rehabilitate themselves because of inadequate community facilities and funds, or are barred from gainful employment by public prejudice and lack of knowledge of their potentialities.

A PUBLIC EDUCATION PROGRAM. A community effort to reduce the great social loss represented by failure to employ these individuals is most rewarding. Numerous official and private studies furnish effective ammunition for a sound education program. Among the most comprehensive is one issued by the Bureau of Labor Statistics in cooperation with the Veterans Administration. The study, based on the performance of 11,000 impaired and 18,000 unimpaired workers, revealed these facts:

1. Disabled workers, selectively placed through guidance procedures, were as productive as the able-bodied.
2. There was no appreciable difference in absenteeism. The disabled lost 3.8 days in every 100 working days; the able-bodied, 3.4.
3. The minor, nondisabling injury rate for both groups was exactly the same, 9.9 minor work injuries for every 10,000 exposure hours.
4. The seriousness of work injuries suffered was comparable. In no case could the injury be attributed to an impairment.
5. No injury was suffered by a worker because of the impairment of another worker.

This impressive evidence was confirmed by a survey of company practices jointly conducted by the Chamber of Commerce of the United States and the National Association of Manufacturers.

PRACTICAL ACTIVITIES. With facts such as these as a background, your organization may find practical some of the following activities:

1. Promoting the cause of the physically impaired at meetings; canvassing member employers for opportunities for the placement of handicapped persons.
2. Inviting representatives of business, industry, labor, and government to your meetings for talks, film showings, and demonstrations of the accomplishments of disabled persons.
3. Sponsoring a business-industry-labor committee to map a broad program for promoting employment of disabled persons, including setting up a special placement service.
4. Cooperating with veterans' groups in vocational rehabilitation of disabled servicemen.
5. Sponsoring and supporting a rehabilitation center, or contributing supplementary instruction, equipment, and materials for vocational training.
6. Promoting establishment of special public school classes for the handicapped; urging proper emphasis on vocational training in established classes; and helping to provide transportation, supplementary instruction and supervision, equipment, and materials.
7. Sponsoring establishment of self-help industries; encouraging home self-help by furnishing training, craft, and piecework materials, and markets for homemade products; promoting a Goodwill Week. Over 100

companies organized as the Goodwill Industries of America, Inc., employ about 17,000 persons, earning over $8 million annually.

8. Recognizing with appropriate awards business and industrial concerns that maintain a policy of utilizing the services of the disabled.

9. Presenting exhibits of the work of the blind and other handicapped persons; sponsoring sale of articles made by the handicapped; arranging for demonstrations of the skills of those with major physical impairments.

10. Conducting essay and art contests to stimulate the thinking of students, parents, and teachers about the problem of helping the handicapped become economically useful.

11. Sponsoring the community's observance of National Employ the Physically Handicapped Week, designated by Congress as the first week in October.

12. Promoting legislation, such as laws establishing tax-supported training institutions, schools for seriously handicapped children, and white cane privileges.

SOURCES OF AID

American Association of University Women, 1634 Eye St., N. W., Washington 6, D. C. Has material for use in community guidance programs. Especially useful as a source of aid in planning and carrying out organization-school projects.

American Federation of the Physically Handicapped, 1370 National Press Building, Washington 4, D. C. Information about the problems of the disabled, and suggestions about action to meet them. Current information about legislation in behalf of the physically handicapped. Furnishes plans and materials for local observances of National Employ the Physically Handicapped Week, the first week in October.

American Psychological Association, Inc., 1333 16th St., N. W., Washington 6, D. C. Information about standards, and training and certification or licensing of vocational counselors and other personnel workers. It seeks to eliminate malpractice and to improve consumer judgment in the use of professional services.

American Vocational Association, 1010 Vermont Ave., Washington 5, D. C. A source of information about public school education for occupational efficiency. Film listings available.

Association of Casualty and Surety Executives, 60 John St., New York 7, N. Y. *The Physically Impaired—A Guidebook to Their Employment* presents practical suggestions for full utilization of the handicapped.

Big Brothers of America, 1347 Broad Street Station, Philadelphia 3, Pa. Local units foster vocational guidance and other measures in behalf of boys who are fatherless, delinquent, or for other reasons are in need of adult help.

B'nai B'rith Vocational Service Bureau, 1761 R St., N. W., Washington 6, D. C. Maintains a research department to ascertain the facts of training and employment opportunities, and a community service department to sponsor programs of vocational guidance in the major Jewish population centers. Catalogue of publications, films, and other materials available.

Boston University School and College Relations, 705 Commonwealth Ave., Boston 15, Mass. Offers a series of free and nominally priced reprints in quantity lots. Representative titles: *After High School—What?, Career in Advertising, Finance as a Career, So You Would Like to Break into Radio?, Your Career as a Secretary*, and *Your Career in Law*. Listing available.

Boys' Clubs of America, 381 Fourth Ave., New York 16, N. Y. Maintains a vocational guidance program, using volunteer workers and organization support. Guidance information booklets include *How to Get and Hold a Job* and *How to Get Ahead on a Job*.

Chamber of Commerce of the United States, Department of Manufacture, 1615 H St., N. W., Washington 6, D. C. *Employment of Physically Handicapped and Older Workers* is a summary of a survey of company practices, conducted jointly by the Chamber of Commerce of the United States and the National Association of Manufacturers among member companies. Presents job requirements, selection bases, job performances, and problems in the employment of handicapped and older workers.

Condé Nast Publications, Inc., Glamour Job Department, 420 Lexington Ave., New York 17, N. Y. Has available a series of free fact sheets on selected jobs and how to get them. Representative titles include *Tips on the Technique of Job Hunting, Advertising Agency Jobs, Commercial Art, Medical Secretary, Modeling, Court Reporter, Research Work*, and *Fashion Designing*. Listing available.

Educational Radio Script and Transcription Exchange, Office of Education, Department of Health, Education, and Welfare, Washington 25, D. C. Free loan dramatic recordings, and scripts on vocational themes available to community groups. Useful in arousing membership and public interest in vocational guidance, in providing background information for projects, and in stimulating group discussion. Scripts include dramatic presentations of the role played by the modern vocational counselor; of the use of testing devices in rating intelligence, aptitudes, and interests to particular jobs; and of the importance of planning careers. Recordings dramatize several professional, business, and industrial careers. *Radio Script Catalog* and *Catalog of Radio Recordings* available from Superintendent of Documents, United States Government Printing Office, Washington 25, D. C.

Evansville Manufacturers and Employers Association, 119 Locust St., Evansville 8, Ind. Information about Evansville's vocational guidance program for high school youth. Program includes a ten-week vocational guidance course which uses a 196-page textbook, *Your Career Opportunities in Evansville Industry*, produced by the Association in cooperation with local educators.

Federation Employment Service, 67 West 47th St., New York 36, N. Y. A nonsectarian, nonprofit vocational guidance and employment organization. Interested in utilization of the handicapped and the aged worker. Informational pamphlets available without charge.

General Federation of Women's Clubs, 1734 N St., N. W., Washington 6, D. C. *Guidance Services in the Schools of Today* suggests some of the problems in the fields of vocational guidance. Includes a list of study and program materials, a bibliography of occupational material for group use, and a listing of vocational films for club use.

Goodwill Industries of America, Inc., 1222 New Hampshire Ave., N. W., Washington 6, D. C. An association of over 100 autonomous industries that train and utilize the services of the physically, mentally, and socially handicapped. Literature descriptive of its organization and methods of operation is available. Local Goodwill Industries furnish free loan motion pictures, and free Kodachrome slides.

Junior Achievement, Inc., 345 Madison Ave., New York 17, N. Y. Includes information on what Junior Achievement is, how it operates, and how its program may be sponsored. Describes typical Junior Achievement companies.

Lehigh University, Admissions Office, Bethlehem, Pa. Offers a series of guidance brochures without charge. Representative titles include *What about College?*, *How about a Profession?*, *Brains Aren't Everything*, and *Conservation as a Career*. Listing available.

Manpower Policy Committee, Office of Defense Mobilization, Washington 25, D. C. Offers information about the need for utilizing the productive capacities of handicapped persons, descriptions of programs to train the handicapped, suggestions for further activities on the national and local levels, and a listing of sources of aid for such activities.

Mutual Positions Plan Association, 14 West 45th St., New York 36, N. Y. Offers information about the formation of young businessmen's groups for the purpose of mutual aid in becoming better adjusted to jobs or in finding new ones.

National Association of Manufacturers, 14 West 49th St., New York 20, N. Y. Publishes *Trends in Education-Industry Cooperation; Your Future Is What You Make It*, a 32-page discussion of problems in choosing a career; and *Your Opportunity in Management*. Sponsors free loan films.

National Education Association, 1201 16th St., N. W., Washington 6, D. C. A clearing house of information on education, maintained by the organized teaching profession. Cooperates with community groups interested in improving school programs. List of vocational guidance publications and films available.

National Industrial Conference Board, 247 Park Ave., New York 17, N. Y. Publishes *Management Almanac*, providing information about executive jobs in industry.

National Society for Crippled Children and Adults, 11 South LaSalle St., Chicago 3, Ill. Publishes *Physical Disability: A National Problem*, by Howard A. Rusk, M.D., and Eugene J. Taylor. Presents vital statistics on physical disability. Useful in gaining interest and support for rehabilitation programs.

National Urban League, 1133 Broadway, New York 10, N. Y. Maintains placement services for Negroes; conducts job-getting clinics; sponsors Carver Trade School for Negro training in printing; cooperates with other groups in fostering vocational training through public education services.

National Vocational Guidance Association, 1424 16th St., N. W., Washington 6, D. C. Publishes *Occupations*, a monthly vocational guidance journal. Issues bibliographies, film listings, and other vocational guidance material.

Occupational Planning Committee of the Cleveland Welfare Federation, 1001 Huron Road, Cleveland 15, Ohio. Has available *Occupational Inventory*. Valuable as a pilot study for an organization planning a cooperative inventory.

Office of Vocational Rehabilitation, Department of Health, Education, and Welfare, Washington 25, D. C. Chief source of business and industrial information about the employment of handicapped persons; types of jobs held by impaired workers; an evaluation of the efficiency of impaired workers; comparative absentee, accident, and turnover rates; and other information useful in organization and public education programs and as background for projects. Bibliography available.

Presbyterian Employment Service, 40 East 40th St., New York 16, N. Y. Information about the cooperative vocational counseling and guidance service of the 62 churches in the Presbytery of New York City.

President's Committee on National Employ the Physically Handicapped Week, Department of Labor, Washington 25, D. C. *Program Guide* points out in detail what can be done in the community to carry out the Congressional mandate to enlist public support for the employment of otherwise qualified but physically handicapped workers. Help available includes free loan motion pictures.

School of Commerce, Accounts, and Finance, New York University, Washington Square, New York 3, N. Y. Publications include *Your Job and Your Future* and *Business as a Career. Occupational Index* lists pamphlets, with critical annotations, books on occupations, and articles in current periodicals.

Science Research Associates, 57 West Grand St., Chicago 10, Ill. *Vocational Guide* lists current materials. Offers a series of pamphlets about various occupations and professions.

Superintendent of Documents, United States Government Printing Office, Washington 25, D. C. Publications include *Guide to Occupational Choice and Training*, a bulletin presenting sources and references for those interested in promoting a guidance service for young people; *Homemaking Education in the Secondary Schools of the United States*, an illustrated brochure of the Office of Education, presenting background information useful for organization-school projects; *Job Guide for Young Workers*, information about duties, requirements, opportunities for employment and advancement, and major advantages and disadvantages; *The Occupational Outlook Handbook*, a basic source of information about hundreds of occupations plus relevant information such as trends in populations, industries, and professions; *Occupational Outlook Publications*, a leaflet describing bulletins about employment opportunities in specific fields; *Publications of the United States Employment Service*, listing free and inexpensive materials on occupations, counseling, testing, and the labor market; *Your Community and Its Young People, Their Employment and Educational Opportunities*, a general consideration of the problems to be solved in the field of youth vocational guidance; *After Teen-Agers Quit School*, a report of vocational guidance programs in seven communities in which organizations have participated; *Counseling High School Students during the Defense Period*; and *Workers Are Young Longer*, a report of the results of a special study of the employment problems of older workers in five states. Comprehensive listing available.

United States Civil Service Commission, Washington 25, D. C. Has available a series of pamphlets describing the civil service system: how the merit system works; the functions of the Civil Service Commission; how to apply for a civil service job; requirements for the major job classifications; how to fill out application forms; where to take examinations; hours and wage rates. *Working for the U.S.A.* is a pamphlet of general government employment information. Other sources of information are the regional offices of the Civil Service Commission, and first- and second-class post offices.

Veterans Administration, Washington 25, D. C. The Advisement and Guidance Service of the Veterans Administration, through its field offices throughout the country, will cooperate with officials of any community organization and supply materials to develop vocational guidance and counseling programs. Among booklets available is *Manual of Advisement and Guidance*, describing the procedures and techniques of counseling. Other materials include free loan films and filmstrips. Publications are available from the Superintendent of Documents, United States Government Printing Office, Washington 25, D. C.

Vocational Advisory Service, 432 Fourth Ave., New York 16, N. Y. A nonprofit organization offering free counseling and placement aid to individuals, and consultation service to volunteer groups. Publishes a guidance bulletin twice a month.

W. E. Upjohn Institute for Community Research, 709 South Westnedge Ave., Kalamazoo 44, Mich. Publications include a pamphlet discussion of the utilization of the older worker in industry. Selected bibliography available.

Young Men's Christian Associations of the United States, 291 Broadway, New York 7, N. Y. Information about vocational guidance programs in communities: counseling and placement services; the relation of other youth problems to career problems; and formal courses in vocations.

Young Men's Hebrew Association, 145 East 32nd St., New York 16, N. Y. Information about vocational guidance programs in communities. Descriptions of programs available.

Young Women's Christian Association, 600 Lexington Ave., New York 22, N. Y. Information about vocational guidance programs: counseling, placement, formal courses, vocation and career clubs.

Young Women's Hebrew Association, 145 East 32nd St., New York 16, N. Y. Information about vocational guidance programs.

SOME SOURCES OF FILMS AND FILM INFORMATION

Many of the sources described in the listing above offer free loan and nominal rental films or film information. The following are other representative sources:

American Mutual Alliance, 20 North Wacker Drive, Chicago 11, Ill. Free loan films include an explanation of how volunteer action may help solve the problem of the training and use of handicapped persons. Descriptions available.

Carl F. Mahnke Productions, 215 East 3rd St., Des Moines 9, Iowa. International distributor for Vocational Guidance Films, Inc. Offers free catalogue describing films giving occupational information in many fields. Can supply name of local distributor.

Castle Films, Inc., 1445 Park Ave., New York 22, N. Y. Rental titles include training films produced by the United States Army Signal Corps and other branches of the Armed Forces; films demonstrating the vocational potential of handicapped persons; and several that show the employment of disabled persons as mechanics, cabinetmakers, welders, office workers, and as other skilled and semiskilled employees. Descriptions available.

Coronet Films, Coronet Building, Chicago 1, Ill. Offers a vocational guidance series. Subjects include explanations of fundamental abilities, and how testing and other procedures determine the kinds and degrees of abilities in individuals; descriptions of various employment fields and their requirements; demonstrations of self-appraisal methods; explanations of how to get and hold a job; and dramatizations of personality adjustments to the problems of making a living. Descriptions available.

Film Publishers, Inc., 25 Broad St., New York 4, N. Y. Rental films include The Story of Lucy, which describes how a young woman paraplegic was able to return to full-time employment after a program of rehabilitation. Description available.

McGraw-Hill Book Company, Inc., Text-Film Department, 330 West 42nd St., New York 18, N. Y. Information about films and filmstrips designed to show how communities can provide students with vocational training.

Office of Education, Department of Health, Education, and Welfare, Washington 25, D. C. Information about Community Advisory

Service, a film demonstrating how industrial workers and war veterans overcome physical disabilities and obtain financial assistance, job training, and jobs through a community guidance organization.

United States Department of Agriculture, Office of Information, Motion Picture Service, Washington 25, D. C. *A Decision for Bill* is a 24-minute sound and color dramatization in which a young man learns of career fields in the Department of Agriculture. Free loan. *Motion Pictures of the United States Department of Agriculture and Slide-films of the United States Department of Agriculture* available without charge.

United World Films, Inc., 1445 Park Ave., New York 29, N. Y. Distributor of films issued by United States government agencies. Subjects include vocational opportunities in the Armed Forces, rehabilitation of the disabled, employment opportunities for the disabled, analysis of causes of job maladjustment, methods of effective placement, and the role of the placement specialist. Of special interest is *Businessmen's Service Club*, a film portraying the youth guidance activities of the Kiwanis Club in Waterbury, Connecticut. Shows career conferences with high school students, and arrangements to give students after-school, part-time work experience. Catalogue available.

CHAPTER 17

Labor-Management Cooperation

A NEW era of industrial harmony has its promise in the growing awareness of both labor and management that they have a mutuality of interest. Fear, distrust, old bitternesses are fading, as understanding and appreciation of one another grows, as each tends to accept more fully the responsibilities that complement its rights, and as communism more clearly presents its appalling alternatives.

Evidence of this recognition of a mutuality of interest can be found in the efforts both labor and management are making on a national scale to bring about an awareness of a common stake in our economic system; and to relate freedom of opportunity to our other freedoms, and to vital areas of living such as health, recreation, and cultural growth.

It is in communities that this promise of industrial harmony can be most clearly seen. The concerns and interests of the office, the shop, and the union hall have been extended into other areas. Industry and labor, meeting face to face as people, are finding solutions to their problems in the perspective of community living. In this development, organizations, representing as they do all the major interests of citizens, have an important role to play.

As in other areas of human relations, there is no stock formula for the solution of all problems. Suggestions for action, based on representative community experience, are discussed in this chapter.

FOSTERING ECONOMIC EDUCATION

Basic needs in the field of labor-management relations are for changes in feelings, attitudes, and points of view—to be brought about through increased knowledge and understanding. Foremost among the objectives of your program, therefore, should be public education in the history, structure, principles, and practices of the American economic system, with emphasis upon the interdependence of labor, management, and capital.

Specific goals of such a program might include an understanding and appreciation of subjects such as the material and spiritual stake that each individual worker, employer, investor, professional man, housewife, and student has in the continuing success of our American system; the indivisibility of all the freedoms we cherish, with emphasis on freedom of opportunity as the keystone of the structure; investment and profits as factors important to our economy; the history of the progress of American labor and business toward assumption of community and national responsibility; the cost to the community and the nation of business and industrial strife; problems to be solved in business and industry today; and the human relations attitudes and techniques needed to meet many of these problems.

EDUCATIONAL ACTIVITIES AT MEETINGS. Members, acting in their capacity as either employees or employers, are in positions to improve local labor-management relations. Through meetings, they may receive a better understanding of how our economic system developed, how it operates, and how many of its problems may be solved through labor-management cooperation.

Arouse interest through the presentation of a short, objective quiz on subjects such as the net profit realized from the production of standard products, the contributions of both labor and management to our economy, the open shop and the closed shop, collective bargaining, industry-wide bargaining, and the Taft-Hartley law. Quizzes of the true-false or completion type, short and simple enough to be used and scored during part of a meeting, are interesting features. Misinformation and misconceptions revealed—which are probably community-wide—will impress members with the need for an education program. Have members who are employers discuss the personnel problems they face, and invite others to offer solutions based on their experiences.

Meeting features to satisfy an aroused membership interest include the story of how the growth of the community has been related to the development of a particular business or industry; how local labor has reached its present position of responsible participation in industry, as told by an old-timer from the ranks of labor; talks by labor and management leaders about their arrangements and techniques for better relations; a graphic presentation of the dependence of everyone on industrial harmony in the community; panel, debate, or other types of discussion, using guides and material available from the sources of aid listed at the close of this chapter; formal courses of study; and the presentation of a socio-drama, in which labor and management present local problems and solutions to be discussed.

EDUCATION ACTIVITIES IN THE COMMUNITY. Members with an understanding of how our economic system has developed, how its parts are interrelated, and how the preservation of freedom of opportunity is related to the preservation of all our freedoms may be effective as individuals and as a group in disseminating this knowledge and in influencing the attitudes of other people in the community.

Opportunities for informal education are present in many activities. For example, a program in Americanism might include emphasis on freedom of opportunitiy; labor-union interest in brotherhood programs may be a starting point for an appreciation of the importance of harmony between labor and management groups. Include floats and tableaux with labor-management interdependence as a theme in parades and pageants. Motion pictures primarily intended to attract attendance at organization events might include some of the free-loan or low-rental subjects that effectively combine economic education and entertainment.

More direct methods of fostering economic education include sponsoring labor and management discussions; organizing a speakers' bureau; initiating and supporting formal courses, conferences, and institutes in cooperation with groups such as the Chamber of Commerce, the local department of adult education, local union headquarters, and the extension departments of colleges and universities; arranging for radio and television programs, news articles, and editorials; and cooperating with the library in maintaining special collections of books, pamphlets, and other material.

EDUCATION ACTIVITIES IN COOPERATION WITH SCHOOLS. Schools welcome the interest and cooperation of organizations in developing programs aimed at orienting students in the business and industrial life of the community, and at giving them an appreciation of local and national industrial problems. The special resources of most groups make possible effective cooperative activities such as:

1. Making available discussion guides and background material, and furnishing films and filmstrips for class, assembly, and club programs.

2. Conducting essay, speaking, art, and other contests, and arranging for appropriate school and public recognition of the winners.

3. Inviting students to present discussions and debates on labor-management problems of current interest.

4. Planning and participating in student programs featuring the products of local industry.

5. Encouraging extracurricular activities such as a student merchandising shop, a Junior Achievement venture, and school publications that are organized and operated as student private enterprises.

6. Organizing and participating in "career day" programs.

7. Arranging tours of plants and businesses.

8. Sponsoring work-study plans, providing supervised after-school and vacation employment, and initiating and supporting a part- or full-time placement service in cooperation with the school guidance department.

9. Encouraging labor and management to cooperate in establishing and conducting machinist and other apprenticeship courses.

10. Contributing to the development of study units, or influencing the adoption of formal courses in business and labor history, and labor-management problems and intergroup techniques.

PROVIDING FOR AN EXCHANGE OF IDEAS

Substantial industrial harmony has been experienced in many communities where representatives of labor and management have been brought together in situations that make possible an exchange of ideas and points of view.

Labor-management-citizens committees, for example, operate successfully. In one major city such an organization sponsored group brought an end to a general strike that had threatened to destroy the community's economy. Successful meeting of the strike crisis resulted in a continuing labor-management-citizen program for harmony. The distrust and bitterness developed over the years gave way to a period marked by mutual understanding and cooperative action for better community living.

Citizens in industrial communities should not wait for labor-management crises to develop. Your organization, with no obligation to labor, to business, or to any other special interest, is in a favorable position to provide leadership in the formation of a labor-management-citizens committee.

Such a committee may have as its chief function the exploration of areas of common interest, such as vocational guidance, continuing employment, voluntary fair-employment practices, safety, recreation, and public education.

Existence of a representative body, with a background of successful cooperative action, facilitates mediation, conciliation, or arbitration of labor-management differences that threaten harmony and affect production.

Other appropriate measures are:

1. Including leaders of both labor and management in your membership.

2. Inviting representatives of labor and management to participate in informal, panel, forum, and other meeting discussions.

3. Scheduling special features such as a Bosses and Employees night.

4. Arranging labor-management community and regional conferences and institutes to give leaders a better understanding of how the American economic system works, to identify problems that involve human relations, and to develop the understandings and skills necessary for their solution.

5. Arranging for the inclusion of labor and management personnel on the same team or in the same group in sports, recreation, and cultural activities.

PROMOTING HUMAN RELATIONS PROGRAMS

Essential for the attainment of maximum, profitable production, steady well-paid employment, and the other long-range objectives of labor and management is the maintenance of good relations among workers and managers in business offices and industrial plants.

In many towns and cities the families of the personnel of one or a few plants constitute a major part of the population. Personnel human relations and community human relations are inseparable. Prejudices, habits of thinking, and points of view developed on the job have a direct effect on the way people live together in the community. In turn, the community is the origin of prejudices and attitudes that influence the relations of men and women working together in offices and shops.

Local organizations may make an important contribution to industrial harmony through measures such as:

1. Sponsoring surveys to determine attitudes in the community, or, in cooperation with labor and management, in specific business or industrial concerns.

2. Emphasizing the importance of effective personnel practices through talks and films for members, management, and other groups.

3. Including management personnel in membership courses in leader-

ship training, and group discussion and conference techniques; or sponsoring such courses for particular firms or the public.

4. Sponsoring conferences and institutes to exchange ideas, map programs, and develop techniques of good human relations.

5. Arranging for radio and television programs showing how local firms are developing and maintaining good human relations.

6. Promoting formation of a community or area business-industry council that would encourage adoption and development of human relations programs by member concerns.

PARTICIPATION IN COMMUNITY ACTIVITIES

Leaders of both labor and management recognize that their concern for the physical, mental, and spiritual well-being of personnel must be extended to include the families of employees and the community in which they live.

Is your community one that will attract and hold the kind of supervisory personnel industry desires? Is it one that offers young people the kind of public education designed to fit them to participate intelligently in the American way of life? Do workers find opportunities for the wholesome recreation that results in less absenteeism and greater production efficiency? Can labor find in community living the dignity, security, and recognition that are among its basic needs?

Recognition of the importance of after-work activities can be found in the extensive social, recreation, self-improvement, and other programs carried on by many companies and unions; by the prominence given to the community activities of personnel in company-employee publications; and by the contributions in time and money that both labor and management are making to local welfare agencies.

Organizations with a background of project experience and a tradition of service are in a position to provide many opportunities for community activities. Practical activities include:

1. Inviting leaders of both groups to participate in a conference to determine community needs and plan measures to meet them.

2. Publicizing labor and management contributions to organization projects at meetings and through news releases, the bulletin, and the national magazine.

3. Encouraging the inclusion of labor and management representation on community councils and other intergroup volunteer organizations.

4. Establishing a labor-management organization business-getting team.

LABOR AND MANAGEMENT CONTRIBUTIONS. Service contributions that labor and management can make include supplying speakers, demonstrations, and materials for public education; duplicating and distributing notices to personnel and their families, and through mailing or delivery systems, to all families in the community; providing store, window, office, and plant space for posters, booths, and exhibits; organizing collection depots for clothing and other drives; providing facilities for film showings; duplicating literature in support of welfare drives; earmarking profits of special sales days for fund-raising campaigns; and supplying equipment, articles, materials, and labor for community events and construction or renovation projects.

A community organization may be of great value to management and labor in helping them plan, organize, and carry out their own activities programs. Whether such activities are intended solely for the welfare of workers, for workers and their families, or for the community as a whole, needs and interests to be met parallel or are identical with those described in other chapters of this book.

SOURCES OF AID

American Arbitration Association, 9 Rockefeller Plaza, New York 20, N. Y. A nonprofit membership corporation to advance the knowledge and use of voluntary arbitration. Individuals, firms, corporations, trade associations, and unions are eligible for membership. Provides help in setting up arbitration machinery. Has available pamphlets descriptive of its organization and activity, a code of ethics for arbitrators, voluntary arbitration rules, and procedures in organizing for arbitration.

American Federation of Labor, 1625 Eye St., N. W., Washington 6, D. C. Information about A.F.L. community activities and points of view about industrial problems. Has available study and discussion guides, pamphlets, free loan films, filmstrips, and other material. Publications include *The Federationist*, a monthly; and *Labor's Monthly Survey*.

American Labor Education Service, Inc., 1776 Broadway, New York 19, N. Y. Aids worker education projects through its advisory service, leadership training courses, and various pamphlets and other materials. Publishes *Labor Education Guide* three times a year.

American Management Association, 330 West 42nd St., New York 18, N. Y. Pamphlets on subjects such as employee manuals, employee communications, and employee attitudes.

Association of National Advertisers, 285 Madison Ave., New York 17, N. Y. Offers publications prepared in cooperation with the American Association of Advertising Agencies. Subjects include community relations case histories and how to determine employee opinion.

Chamber of Commerce of the United States, 1615 H St., N. W., Washington 6, D. C. Offers guides to a greater community understanding and appreciation of our economic system. Materials include pamphlets on how to organize plant tours, use the company bulletin board, plan employee meetings, develop business leadership, present radio programs, and use films. *Newsletter on Labor Relations* reports labor-management activities of Chambers of Commerce throughout the country. Includes descriptions of the work of labor-management committees, the Chamber as a mediatory body, the participation of unions in Chamber activities, and Chamber support for other organizations interested in labor-management relations. Pamphlet description of Chamber materials and services is available.

Civic Education Foundation, 5 Chauncy St., Cambridge, Mass. *The Living Democracy Series* of pamphlets for youth group study and activity programs includes an explanation of our business system, and the necessity for labor-management cooperation. Information available.

Committee for Economic Development, 444 Madison Ave., New York 17, N. Y. Pamphlets include *Collective Bargaining—How to Make It More Effective*.

Community Chests and Councils of America, Inc., 155 East 44th St., New York 17, N. Y. Has available pamphlet suggestions for labor participation in community welfare: suggested policies regarding labor representation on boards of directors of agencies, a suggested over-all community welfare program for labor participation, and reports of both C.I.O. and A.F.L. projects.

Council of Profit Sharing Industries, First National Tower, Akron 8, Ohio. *Offers Profit Sharing Manual*, a description of the philosophy, economics, methods, and results of more than 85 profit-sharing plans, such as cash, wage dividend, stock ownership, trust, combined cash and trust, guaranteed annual wage, production sharing, cost-savings sharing, associative, and cooperative. Includes a bibliography. Council has available a list of its affiliated companies.

Institute of Management and Labor Relations, Research Program, Rutgers University, New Brunswick, N. J. Offers a series of low cost study pamphlets on various phases of labor-management relations. Listing available.

International Council of Industrial Editors, National Cash Register Company, Dayton, Ohio. Information about company and employee publications.

International Ladies' Garment Workers' Union, Education Department, 1710 Broadway, New York 19, N. Y. Offers assistance for group labor education. Has available books, pamphlets, periodicals, free loan films, and filmstrips. Arranges visits to garment shops in the New York City area. Furnishes speakers for community group meetings. Offers help to individuals and agencies engaged in labor research. *Report of Educational Department* describes its program. Has available *Labor in America*, a textbook for high school seniors.

Laymen's Movement for a Christian World, Inc., Room 1402, 347 Madison Ave., New York 17, N. Y. Literature includes booklets and reprints suggesting the application of spiritual principles to the solution of labor-management problems.

League of Women Voters of the United States, 1026 17th St., N. W., Washington 6, D. C. Pamphlet material includes ideas for group discussion. Has available a list of materials on labor-management relations selected to present a wide range of points of view.

Louisville Labor-Management Committee, 308 Herburn Building, Louisville 2, Ky. Has available material describing the committee's history, methods of operation, and accomplishments.

McCormick, Charles P., *The Power of People*, New York: Harper & Brothers, 1949. Describes arrangements by which employees participate in the management of McCormick and Company. Brings the multiple management idea up to date. Ideas may be adapted by any company interested in bettering labor-management relations.

National Association of Manufacturers, 14 West 49th St., New York 20, N. Y. Offers aid in interpreting the American opportunity system to the community, correcting public misunderstandings of the facts about business and industry, and setting up and carrying through business public relations programs at the community level. Provides packaged material through a circulating library, and has free loan films and other material. Issues a monthly bulletin, *Exchange*, a clearinghouse for economic education ideas. Operates an Industry Leaders Program through which local groups of businessmen are equipped to tell the story of business to community audiences. Sponsors speakers bureaus. Through a Community Leaders Program it works for cooperation between industry and community organizations. Organizes town hall type community meetings. Publishes three monthly periodicals for community leaders: *Trends*, for teachers and education administrators; *Understanding*, for clergymen; *Program Notes*, for women's club leaders. Other useful publications include *Labor Relations Today and Tomorrow, Employee Communications for Better Understanding, A Guide to Effective Two-Way Information Programs, Management Answers to Some Union Objections to Wage Incentives.*

National C.I.O. Community Services Committee, 1776 Broadway, New York 19, N. Y. *Action for a Better Community* discusses union counseling, labor representation on agency boards, labor's contributions to community health and welfare, C.I.O. blood donor programs, the C.I.O. role in civil defense, and other matters related to labor's participation in volunteer programs.

National Council of Industrial Clubs, an organization associated with the Young Men's Christian Associations of the United States, 347 Madison Ave., New York 17, N. Y. Has available *How to Organize and Conduct a Management Development Group,* a manual for use in training foremen and supervisors in the techniques of group discussion.

National Council of the Churches of Christ in the U.S.A., 297 Fourth Ave., New York 10, N. Y. Sponsors Church and Economic Life Week in January. Offers quantities of *Program Guide to Church and Economic Life Week* without charge. Has available low-cost materials such as *Christian Action in Industrial Relations,* a report of activities in typical communities; *The Christian Attitude Toward Labor,* an informational pamphlet; *Human Relations in Modern Business,* a guide for action sponsored by American business leaders; and a *Program Source Book* of films and other aids. No charge for single copies.

National Foremen's Institute, Inc., 100 Garfield Ave., New London, Conn. Publications include a weekly *Employee Relations Bulletin* of news reports and ideas in the field of labor-management relations.

National Municipal League, 299 Broadway, New York 7, N. Y. November, 1953 issue of its publication, *National Municipal Review,* includes "Industrial Peace in Toledo," the story of the achievements of the city's Labor-Management-Citizens Committee.

National Planning Association, 1606 New Hampshire Ave., N. W., Washington 9, D. C. Offers *The Causes of Industrial Peace under Collective Bargaining,* a series of 15 case studies. Listing available.

New York State School of Industrial and Labor Relations, Cornell University, Ithaca, N. Y. Publishes *Industrial and Labor Relations Review,* a quarterly; *Abstracts and Annotations,* a monthly digest of selected articles on industrial and labor relations from current periodicals. Has available two series of bulletins: one on research and one on information of general public interest. *Guide to A-V Materials in Manpower* and *Industrial Relations* describes films, filmstrips, and recordings available.

Office of Education, Department of Health, Education, and Welfare, Washington 25, D. C. Offers without charge a volume of thirteen 15-minute annotated radio scripts that tell the story of the progress American wage earners have made in attaining security and dignity. Prepared especially for community organization radio programs. Useful as study and discussion aids. Description available.

Purdue University Community Services in Adult Education, 1804 East 10th St., Bloomington, Ind. Interested in encouraging management and labor education and training programs. Publishes *Community Teamwork*, a monthly newsletter.

Rotary International, The Secretariat, 35 East Wacker Drive, Chicago 1, Ill. *Service Is My Business* is source material for conferences on human relationships in business and industry. Includes ideas useful in programs to build confidence in business and industrial leadership, and in planning measures to recognize worker achievement.

Superintendent of Documents, United States Government Printing Office, Washington 25, D. C. Publications include the low cost booklet, *Human Relations in Small Industry*, prepared by the Small Defense Plants Administration.

Teamwork Publications, Inc., 1790 Broadway, New York 19, N. Y. Publishes *Steve Merritt*, a comic book presentation of facts about the American economic system; facts and ideas about subjects such as safety and health; and biographies of successful businessmen.

Toledo Labor-Management-Citizens Committee, 108 Fire and Police Alarm Building, Toledo, Ohio. Has available *The Toledo Plan for Industrial Peace*, a booklet describing the organization and functioning of a successful community mediation committee.

Twentieth Century Fund, 330 West 42nd St., New York 18, N. Y. A nonprofit organization for nonpartisan research and public education in economic and social problems. Its Labor Committee includes representatives of organized labor, economists, and individuals experienced in public affairs. Publishes pamphlets on the need for labor-management harmony and the techniques for achieving that harmony.

United States Department of Labor, Washington 25, D. C. Interested in maintaining full and stable employment, and in programs to bring labor and management together for solution of apprenticeship and other problems. List of publications available from the Superintendent of Documents, United States Government Printing Office, Washington 25, D. C.

University of Pittsburgh, Pittsburgh, Pa. Has available *Current Trends in Industrial Psychology*, a symposium that includes discussions of employee-management relations and the community approach to industrial problems.

Workers Education Bureau, 1625 Eye St., N. W., Washington 6, D. C. An affiliate of the American Federation of Labor. Promotes education through study classes, radio programs, and labor institutes and conferences. Publications include *Labor Unions and the Community*, a discussion of union responsibility.

Yoder, Dale, *You and Unions*, Science Research Associates, Inc., 57 West Grand Ave., Chicago 10, Ill. One of a series of *Life Adjustment* booklets for school use. May be adopted for membership and public education programs. Outlines the important part played by unions in the lives of their members and others. Presents an objective explanation of why and how unions originated and developed, what their aims are, some methods used to achieve these aims, and the relations that exist with the general public.

SOME SOURCES OF FILMS AND FILM INFORMATION

Many business and industrial concerns and associations are important sources of films useful in economic education and other labor-management programs. The following are representative of these and other sources:

Allegheny Ludlum Steel Corporation, Public Relations Department, Oliver Building, Pittsburgh 22, Pa. Free loan films useful for community group presentation include the 28-minute sound film, *The Fifth Freedom*, illustrating what freedom of opportunity means to an American company, a representative plant worker, and investors. Description available.

Civil Service Assembly, 1313 East 60th St., Chicago 37, Ill. *A Selected List of Films for Public Employer Training.* Describes many films which illustrate good human relations techniques. Useful in programs designed to demonstrate effective personnel practices.

Classic Pictures, Inc., 1560 Broadway, New York 19, N. Y. Rental films include *With These Hands*, the history of the International Ladies' Garment Workers' Union, showing a union's successful struggle against communist influence.

Educational Film Library Association, Suite 1000, 1600 Broadway,

New York 19, N. Y. Has available a 30-page mimeographed *Guide to Motion Pictures, Slidefilms, and Recordings for Improving Human Relations and Supervisory Techniques.*

Encyclopaedia Britannica Films, Inc., 1150 Wilmette Ave., Wilmette, Ill. Information about *Working Together*, the story of how industrial harmony was achieved at the American Lead Pencil Company in Hoboken, New Jersey.

Ford Motor Company, Film Library, 3000 Schaefer Road, Dearborn, Mich. Free loan films about the production of automobiles demonstrate the interdependence of labor and management. Catalogue available.

General Mills, Inc., Film Library, 400 Second Ave., South, Minneapolis 1, Minn. Free loan films show management and employees working toward common goals, with reasonable returns for each. Descriptions available.

General Motors Corporation, Department of Public Relations, Film Section, 3044 West Grand Boulevard, Detroit 2, Mich. Free loan films include dramatizations of the need for an understanding of human relations in industry. Descriptions available.

Harding College, Motion Picture Division, Searcy, Ark. Free loan sound and color films include *The American Economics Series* of animated ten-minute cartoons. *Why Play Leapfrog* shows how a worker in a doll factory discovers that making more and better dolls at lower cost is his surest way to an improved living standard. *Meet King Joe* presents the American workingman, who, because of high wages and shorter hours, is king of the world's workers. *Make Mine Freedom* demonstrates that the interest of all groups is best served through harmonious cooperation. *Going Places* explains how the profit motive is the dynamo of American progress. Descriptive brochure available.

Illinois Central Railroad, Library of Audio-Visual Aids, Room 600A, 135 East 11th Place, Chicago 5, Ill. Free loan film describes how employee suggestions are handled by the Illinois Central Joint Labor-Management Suggestions Committee. Description available.

International Film Bureau, Inc., 57 East Jackson Boulevard, Chicago 4, Ill. Rental films include several on labor-management relations: establishment of workers' recreation centers; some of the functions of a labor-management committee within an industry; the role of trade unions; the relation of labor, management, and consumer interests; and others. Films described in general catalogue, available without charge.

Investment Bankers Association of America, 33 South Clark St., Chicago 3, Ill. Offers the 25-minute *Opportunity U.S.A.* on a free loan basis. Film was produced to foster a better understanding of our economic system. Information available.

Modern Talking Picture Service, 45 Rockefeller Plaza, New York 20, N. Y. Has available free of charge an organized program of weekly motion picture showings for employees. Will help find subjects to meet particular group requirements. Subjects include our economic system, consumer education, health and hygiene, homemaking, sports, and travel. Description of service, and film catalogue available.

National Council of Christians and Jews, 381 Fourth Ave., New York 16, N. Y. Rental films include *Chuck Hansen—One Guy*, a story of how workers' attitudes were changed through a positive program of group relations carried out by labor and management in a New Jersey plant. Includes valuable how-to-do-it suggestions. Description available.

New York University Film Library, 26 Washington Place, New York 3, N. Y. Rental films include the 14-minute *Machine: Master or Slave?*, a presentation of the basic problem of reconciling long-term management self-interest with the needs of workers. Filmstrips for sale include *Your Stake in Collective Bargaining*.

Textile Workers Union of America, C.I.O., 99 University Place, New York 3, N. Y. Rental films include *Union at Work*, the official motion picture story of the textile workers union. Information available.

United World Films, Inc., Educational Film Department, 1445 Park Ave., New York 29, N. Y. Information about *Developing Cooperation*, which suggests procedures for both labor and management.

Workers Education Bureau, 1625 Eye St., N. W., Washington 6, D. C. An affiliate of the American Federation of Labor. Maintains a library of loan films, many of which provide backgrounds for an appreciation of labor history, problems, and objectives. *Film for Labor*, a descriptive catalogue, is available.

CHAPTER 18

Conservation

WISE USE of our national resources has become a major concern of thousands of community organizations. There is a growing appreciation of the fact that the well-being of those who live and work in towns and cities, and the well-being of those in rural areas are intimately related, and dependent on cooperative group action to restore, conserve, and develop the wealth that is in our soil, our waters, and our forests.

This interest in conservation has led to a wide range of activities. Worked-out crop, pasture, and wood lands have been restored. Better conservation-conscious farm practices have been introduced. Urban advantages, such as those in education, recreation, and health, have been extended into rural areas, developing among farmers the capacity for a more responsible use of their resources. Our fish life has been preserved through reduction of pollution in streams, lakes, and coastal waters. Establishment of forest preserves and wildlife sanctuaries near urban centers has conserved important recreational, cultural, and spiritual values.

In no other field of community service has an organization such a great variety of kinds of help, and such a wealth of available material. Federal agencies such as those of the Department of Agriculture and the Department of the Interior offer the field services of professional personnel, as well as program guides, informational pamphlets, research conclusions, and free-loan films and filmslides. State agriculture, conservation, and development bodies seek the help of volunteer groups in disseminating information and securing citizen cooperation. Farm organizations, farm equipment manufacturers; processors of farm, fishery, and forest products; and many other business concerns sponsor films which dramatically suggest solutions for conservation problems. National, regional, and local sportsmen's clubs, nature-study groups, garden clubs, recreation and health associations stand ready to help plan and implement local programs.

294

This chapter suggests how, with such help, your organization may make important contributions through activities designed to achieve better urban-rural relations, more prosperous local agriculture, a higher standard of rural living, and conservation of natural resources for their economic, cultural, and spiritual values.

BETTER URBAN-RURAL RELATIONS

In many areas, organizations are establishing better human relations as a basis for effective cooperative action among community groups and those who are in direct control of the use of our natural resources. While better human relations are natural and inevitable by-products of service activities such as those suggested in this chapter, some situations may demand organization action with the primary purpose of bettering relations.

MEMBERSHIP COMPOSITION. Many groups are making special efforts to secure members whose professions, occupations, businesses, or hobbies include a concern for our natural resources. Such individuals have an important influence on an organization's effectiveness in the field of conservation. In addition to making possible closer relations with other conservation-minded individuals and organizations, they help emphasize the conservation aspects of programs in fields such as education and recreation, and provide leadership.

Among such individuals are successful farmers, county agricultural agents, fish and game wardens, foresters, vocational agriculture teachers, officials of farm and farm products trade associations, Grange and Farm Bureau officers, and the heads of sportsmen's, gardening, and other special-interest groups.

In some areas, particularly in the great agriculture and cattle-raising regions, civic organizations exchange honorary and other types of memberships with farm groups, establishing relations that have made possible programs such as those for soil and water conservation and improvement of breeding stock.

MEETING PROGRAMS. Meeting programs can develop good urban-rural relations. Agriculture and conservation committees schedule talks by the county agent, an Audubon representative, and other authorities in local conservation areas; free-loan or low-cost sound and color films; novelty programs such as an agriculture or wildlife quiz; a Farmer's Night, at which each member plays host to a farmer friend; a Recognition or Awards Night for members of 4-H Clubs,

Future Farmers of America, Scout troops, or for adult farmers who have made outstanding achievements in conservation; a dinner or luncheon with a product of the region as the main dish; and joint meetings with farm, sportsmen, gardening, or other conservation-minded group.

PUBLIC EDUCATION PROGRAMS. Perhaps the greatest single influence in developing better urban-rural relations is public education. Care should be taken that those who have a direct interest—those in actual control of natural resources—be adequately represented in the planning of such programs. Representation might be arranged through the formation of a farm-town committee.

Rural relations needs vary so widely that only a few representative public education projects will be mentioned here. Agencies such as those listed at the close of this chapter have many other suggestions. Organizations sponsor public discussions of farm-town problems, present film showings, cooperate in school programs by supplying speakers and films, sponsor farm and wildlife columns in local papers, promote radio and television discussions, publicize the results of conservation surveys, and establish conservation information centers in libraries.

OTHER URBAN-RURAL RELATIONS PROJECTS. Good rural relations may be the primary purpose of some service projects such as a sportsmen's show; a conservation exhibit; a winter fair; hospitality centers for rural visitors; and farmer days, featuring a parade, free parking, baby-sitting arrangements for farm mothers, and movies for children. Excellent relations have resulted from farmer representation on community councils, study and planning committees, and official and quasi-official commissions such as planning groups.

FARM PROSPERITY

Organizations are mobilizing the varied resources of their communities in behalf of a more prosperous agriculture in their areas. They are publicizing the interdependence of town and country, and the need for the wisest possible use of all resources, and are pointing the way to a self-sustaining, conservation-conscious agricultural economy. They are cooperating with official and private agencies in a wide range of practical activities.

SOIL AND WATER CONSERVATION. According to the Soil Conservation Service of the United States Department of Agriculture, over 280 million acres have become useless because of erosion, and another 775 million more have been seriously affected. This waste of soil and water is directly costing the nation's farmers about $400 million annually. The general public, too, must pay many hundreds of millions for removal of silt from reservoirs, ditches, stream beds, and harbors, and for maintenance of highways and roads affected by erosion. To this direct cost must be added higher food costs and a weakened economy generally—a very real threat to our security and well-being.

While soil erosion usually is a technical problem, volunteer groups are contributing to its solution in a very concrete fashion by disseminating information from sources such as those listed at the close of this chapter; by supplementing or furnishing support for official programs often limited because of inadequate personnel or funds; by giving community recognition to the soil and water conservation achievements of individuals and groups; by arranging for lectures and demonstrations in such farm management practices as contour cultivation, use of cover crops, installation of diversion ditches, terracing, watershed planting, and building dams; and by promoting replanting of marginal and other public land.

They have dramatized the need for action by such projects as airplane flights to show farmers the effects of erosion on their own farms, the relation of their farms to the land in the area, and the kind of farm management that must be practiced if erosion is to be checked. School conservation activities include teacher and student field trips, and work projects such as planting cover crops on school grounds, replanting watersheds, and correcting gully conditions.

In many localities, groups have sponsored spectacular farm rehabilitation programs, enlisting the aid of government farm agencies, equipment and supplies dealers, construction and shipping concerns, and others with an interest in farm welfare and rural community relations. Often hundreds of volunteers, using scores of pieces of loaned equipment and thousands of dollars in donated materials, complete in one day operations such as terracing and contour plowing, gully elimination, digging drainage systems, building a farm fishpond, tree planting of marginal land, and construction of a model barn and other buildings. Spectators at such demonstrations have numbered over 25,000.

IMPROVED CROPS AND LIVESTOCK. Farm and community prosperity

is also being achieved through hundreds of organization programs to improve the quality of crops and livestock.

Activities include sponsoring and supporting county and state fairs to acquaint farmers with improved equipment and techniques through exhibits and demonstrations, to raise crop and livestock standards, and to stimulate greater interest and effort through contests and other devices; setting up and operating soil analysis clinics; encouraging wider use of certified seed; supplying improved strains of stock; introducing artificial-insemination programs; distributing free quality chicks; sponsoring crop-planning contests; and offering awards for achievement.

FARM EQUIPMENT. Important to the fullest and wisest use of agricultural resources is adequate mechanization of farm operations. Projects designed to promote extensive use of machines range from sponsorship of equipment shows and performance demonstrations and contests, to arrangements for exchange or part-time use of units, and cooperative purchase of equipment.

In one town, an organization registered practically every piece of heavy equipment available for rent or on a free loan basis. Colored pins on an area map indicated their locations. A card index system included information such as the period when each unit was available, its size or capacity, the rental fee or conditions of loan, and the name and address of the owner.

In another community, an organization was responsible for establishment of a spare parts pool. Its members rounded up abandoned equipment, and salvaged and stocked spare parts for local farmer use at a nominal rental fee. Many farmers were able to keep equipment in full use, and, in some cases, to save perishable crops endangered by breakdowns.

FARM LABOR. Essential to farm prosperity is an adequate and stable labor supply. Organizations are supporting the vocational training programs of the Future Farmers of America and other youth groups, raising the prestige of agriculture as a career, supporting Farm Bureau job-placement measures, and maintaining local guidance services for rural youth.

A practical project is the registration and emergency mobilization of members, high school students, and other citizens for seasonal farm work on a part-time basis. In some towns where there is strong organization support for a program to supply farm labor, merchants close their shops for a day during the planting or harvest season to permit their employees to serve their communities by working on the farms. In other towns, organizations have cooperated with county agents in establishing training schools for boys wishing to work on local farms during their vacations.

MARKETING AND OTHER FACILITIES. While some products, such as wheat and beef, are processed and marketed in far distant places, many farmers depend on markets and marketing facilities in the area.

Organization-supported measures to provide these essentials include farm-industry conferences about marketing problems; surveys to determine the suitability of crops, and area consumer needs; introduction and promotion of new crops; promotion of crop diversification programs; establishment of processing and canning plants; an extended or improved farm-to-market roads system; building facilities such as stockyards and granaries; establishment of stock, poultry, and specialized auction centers; and local auctioning of perishables such as truck and flower crops.

LEGISLATION. Organizations are being of inestimable service to their local farm economy by supporting farm legislation that is clearly in the public interest. They interpret and publicize farm legislative needs through meeting features, a speakers' bureau, and newspaper, radio, and television programs; oppose reduced agricultural appropriations where needs can be demonstrated; promote ordinances to assure better milk and other food supplies; secure legislative support for Bangs and other testing programs, and for better research facilities.

FARM PROSPERITY AND YOUTH PROJECTS. Sponsorship of rural youth groups or youth projects, and encouragement of youth activities through awards and other forms of recognition are usually aimed at developing citizenship and leadership for better rural living. Such activities, however, may be direct and concrete contributions to a more prosperous, sounder agricultural economy. Most projects undertaken by 4-H Clubs or Future Farmers with the support of adult volunteer groups, for example, are business ventures.

Often organizations furnish the best available breeding stock, which over the years may result in greatly increased farm profits or even a completely rejuvenated farm economy. Through the direction of the learning-by-doing programs of rural youth groups, they introduce new techniques for more efficient farm operation. Through scholarships, they help maintain a reservoir of farm leadership. Their education, health, and recreation programs encourage young people to remain in the community and its farm area, making possible continued material progress for both town and country.

RECREATION AREAS. Often completely neglected as a source of income for the farmer and merchants and others in neighboring towns and cities are the sports and recreation potentialities of the region.

Each year the American people spend hundreds of millions of dollars in activities such as fishing, hunting, boating, and skiing. Stock uplands, and streams and lakes. Develop ski and toboggan runs. Guiding, boat livery, tourist accommodations, and other services and facilities may be of economic importance to your area. The members of some organizations have important business and public relations ties, through which they can help develop such attractions.

BETTER RURAL LIVING

Modern highways, rapid transportation and communication, and extension of school, recreation, health, and other services into rural areas have brought to an end the isolation traditionally associated with farm living.

It is impossible to say to what extent the conservation of our natural resources is being influenced by this better rural living. Certain it is that an enlightened, healthy farm population, enjoying the material comforts our American economy makes possible, with the great opportunities brought about by technological and other advances, can be tremendously effective in restoring, preserving, and developing those resources over which it has control.

SERVICE ACTIVITIES. Most of the chapters of this book have activity suggestions adaptable to programs for better rural living. Some include specific recommendations. The following is intended only as a suggestive review.

Organizations are giving rural dwellers the knowledge, skills, and appreciations that make them better producers, consumers, homemakers, and citizens. They are helping to provide better school bus services; encouraging school consolidation where it has demonstrable advantages; providing general education forums, institutes, and study and discussion opportunities through the cooperation of the Extension and Home Demonstration services and other official and private agencies; and establishing such cultural facilities as bookmobiles and book depots.

They are helping to provide recreation opportunities for both farm youth and adults by forming teams, supplying equipment, furnishing transportation, and arranging for inclusion of rural groups in community and regional leagues. Through organization sports and recreation programs, town and country are brought together in a common enjoyment of skiing, tobogganing, skating, and folk dancing. Both town and country have developed participation and spectator interest in harvest festivals, stock and poultry shows, and events that often feature contests, sports, motion pictures, and dancing.

A spectacular rural sports and recreation development in which many community organizations have had a part is the increasing number of Flying Farmers Clubs in Western crop-producing and ranch areas. These clubs are of great service in fields such as pest control, disaster relief, and community and regional promotion.

Organization influence has been brought to bear in many other areas of living. Volunteer groups secured and are supporting visiting nurse services, and are promoting public- and private-agency programs for better farm sanitation, farm safety, and fire prevention and fire-fighting measures. With the cooperation of medical societies, church denominational headquarters, and teacher training schools, they have called the attention of interns, divinity students, and student teachers to the advantages of country living in their areas. Specific projects include inviting such potential rural leaders to meetings; arranging talks by veteran doctors, ministers, and educators before student groups; and establishing scholarships for students who plan careers in farm areas.

Organizations are encouraging higher standards of farm living through a recognition of achievement. In one area, a Centennial Farm Plaque is presented to owners of farms worked by the same familities for 100 years or more. Many communities honor the "farm family of the year." Awards often are given for achievement in electrification, canning, clothing, nutrition, dairy and other production, dress design, safety, forestry, soil and water conservation, health, home grounds beautification, home convenience improvement, leadership, and rural arts.

Some organizations give a very tangible form to their recognition through free trips to cities, or vacations with entertainment and other expenses paid, or through cash awards.

In its efforts to raise the standard of farm living, an organization should, of course, be careful not to duplicate efforts being made by official or private agencies, or by local organizations with traditional programs in this field.

RURAL YOUTH ACTIVITIES. Through cooperating programs and direct financial support, organizations are playing important roles in the success of two great rural youth organizations, the 4-H Club and the Future Farmers of America.

Over two million boys and girls are enrolled in 4-H Clubs, administered jointly by the Extension Service of the United States Department of Agriculture and local volunteer groups. The primary object of the 4-H Club program is to help rural boys and girls develop desirable skills, ideals, and high standards of farming, homemaking, and citizenship.

The Future Farmers of America, with an enrollment of over 350,000 boys, aims to give practical experience in the various fields of farming through work projects carried out under the supervision of high school teachers of vocational agriculture.

Both these great groups welcome the support of community organizations. Your county or home demonstration agent, or the 4-H Club department of the state agriculture extension service will help your group form a 4-H Club, or will furnish information about the needs of established units. Your local high school vocational instructor will welcome support for his Future Farmers chapter. State departments of education and the federal Office of Education have information about rural vocational education needs and how the Future Farmers program helps to meet them. On the national level, business, civic, and educational leaders have formed the National Committee on Boys and Girls Club Work to bring together all community interests to develop education programs for farm youth. The committee, working in close cooperation with federal and state extension services, emphasizes the interdependence of agriculture and industry, and is prepared to give planning and material aid to your program.

Typical youth activities are sponsoring 4-H Clubs and the 4-H Club Foundation; securing and equipping meeting places; organizing and supervising field trips; contributing books and other materials, and visiting vocational agriculture classes; financing visits to agricultural colleges; maintaining scholarships; recognizing youth achievement at organization and public meetings; sponsoring youth leadership training through conferences and institutes; and cosponsoring fairs, demonstrations, shows, contests, and other events in which young people participate.

Boys and girls may be kept from active participation in 4-H Clubs and other groups because of lack of funds. A traditional activity is the financing of projects to raise beef, poultry, potatoes, or other produce important in the area.

Representative of such a project is the following: each member provides a boy or girl with a stake—perhaps a bushel of certified seed potatoes. The sponsor helps the young person plan his venture. He gets to know him and his personal as well as vocational problems. He visits him at his farm home, encourages him as the project develops, and checks his records. Finally he attends the youth's club meeting at which his achievement is to be recognized.

In accepting such aid, the boy or girl agrees to deliver part of his produce to the sponsor, or to dispose of it at his direction. Usually the sponsor's return on his investment is used to give other young people a similar opportunity.

Through this type of project, rural youth is receiving practical business experience, and is developing a strong sense of personal responsibility.

AREA DEVELOPMENT. Organizations are aware of the interdependence of community and area development. The following illustrates the progress that has been realized through their efforts:

The Junior Chamber of Commerce and the Kiwanis, Civitan, Rotary, Exchange, Lions, and Optimist clubs of Knoxville organized the East Tennessee Community Improvement Contest Committee in cooperation with the Agriculture Extension Service of the University of Tennessee. As a result of this program, erosion has been effectively checked and dairying income increased. Communities within the area constructed and remodeled churches and schools, built gymnasiums, established playgrounds, and improved public safety and sanitary facilities. During the first year of the contest, farmers in the area doubled the amount of money spent for home conveniences, sanitation, renovation of homes and barns, installation of furnaces, and new cars, trucks, and farm machinery.

CONSERVATION OF FORESTS

Agencies of the Department of Agriculture and the Department of the Interior, state conservation departments, hunting and fishing commissions, development boards, sportsmen's and nature associations, regional resort associations, trade associations, public utilities, and railroads look to community organizations for support in efforts to conserve our timber, and stand ready to provide valuable help for local projects.

Activities practicable for most organizations include distributing seedlings to be planted on marginal land; surveying timber resources; organizing school and other youth groups to plant public lands; establishing a community forest for both future income and recreation; making available tree-planting equipment for farmers, Scouts, and other conservation-minded groups; and sponsoring tree-planting and tree-care demonstrations.

Organizations are publicizing the need for establishing ground cover in burned-over forest areas to check erosion and permit regrowth. A particularly dramatic project is the Johnny Grass Seed movement initiated by the Izaak Walton League of Grand Junction, Colorado, and adopted by hundreds of groups throughout the country. Members give a packet of grass seed to each hunter and fisherman going into a burned-over area. The sportsman plants the seed where cover is needed. The movement is receiving the support of the United States Forest Service, the United States Conservation Service, and state agencies such as game and fish commissions.

The benefits of forest fire protection ultimately reach the community whose industries use wood products; whose merchants serve the growers, harvesters, and processors of wood; and whose citizens enjoy healthful and recreational use of forests. Organizations in many states participate in Keep the State Green programs sponsored by official forestry and conservation agencies, and state-wide and regional volunteer associations. Their activities include distribution of posters; presentation of window and other exhibits; motion picture showings; and sponsorship of newspaper, radio, and television programs. Many groups sponsor local forest fire protection weeks.

CULTURAL, SPIRITUAL, AND OTHER VALUES

The conservation of the wildlife of our woods, fields, streams and lakes as a source of recreation and health, and cultural and spiritual satisfactions is of paramount importance.

SUPPORT FOR THE PROGRAMS OF OTHER GROUPS. Organizations distribute pamphlets, posters, photographs, and other material supplied by national associations interested in wildlife protection and control, such as the American Camping Association and the National Audubon Society; federal agencies such as the Fish and Wildlife Service; state and county agencies such as fish and game commissions, conservation departments, and the conservation education departments of state boards of education.

They support local sportsmen's groups in measures to free streams and ponds of fish-destroying pollution. They cooperate with garden clubs in campaigns to educate the public to an appreciation of the need for protecting wild flowers threatened with extinction, and encourage the formation of Junior Audubon Clubs.

THE SCHOOL CONSERVATION PROGRAM. Today's children will become tomorrow's custodians of our national resources. Educators accept as an important responsibility the development of an appreciation of the aesthetic and spiritual values inherent in nature, as well as an awareness of the dollars-and-cents importance of natural resources to our economic and social welfare.

Community group activities include providing Audubon and other supplementary course material; presenting wildlife films; encouraging a greater emphasis on conservation in subjects such as social studies; sponsoring essay and art contests; helping to plan and arrange school exhibits and museums; promoting in-service training of teachers; sponsoring seminars, workshops, and summer camps for teachers and students.

CONSERVATION EXHIBITS. Availability of material from sources such as those listed at the close of this chapter makes exhibits a practical and effective type of project. Care should be taken, however, to give them local interest.

A vandalism exhibit has been successful in many communities. Such projects feature, for example, a young dogwood stripped of many of its branches. Placards explain where the tree came from, how it was mutilated, how long it had taken to grow, and what its replacement would cost.

Another dramatic exhibit with a purely local application followed a work project to clean up woodland and streamside public areas near a community. Boy Scouts and other groups had been organized to collect tin cans, paper bags, and other litter. Mounds of such material were displayed in store windows with explanatory posters, pictures of the area before and after, and pleas for more thoughtful use of such facilities.

FIELD TRIPS AND WORK PROJECTS. Organizations sponsoring conservation field trips and work projects are not only opening up great new recreation areas, but are effectively selling the idea that conservation of our natural resources is the responsibility of citizens as well as government officials.

Typical activities include visiting botanical gardens, zoos featuring regional wildlife, fur farms, pheasant-rearing pens, hatcheries, wildlife preserves, the area watershed; organizing members and others for a wildlife count; serving as bird watchers in Audubon or other programs; identifying and listing the flora and fauna of the neighborhood; building and placing birdhouses and feeding stations; planting food patches and constructing wildlife shelters; introducing ducks or other easily controllable wildlife in the community's park ponds; laying out local conservation trails; improving streamside areas; mapping canoe, riding, and hiking trails; serving as forest fire fighters or part-time forest wardens; and planting hedges along roads and farm boundaries as game cover.

SOURCES OF AID

So numerous are the sources of aid in the field of conservation, so extensive the consultant and field services, and so voluminous the material offered by official and volunteer agencies, that no listing or description can be all-inclusive. New services and materials are continually being offered or are in preparation. Your organization might write to appropriate state agencies for information. The Superintendent of Documents publishes *United States Government Manual*, revised annually, which describes the functions and services of all agencies of the United States government departments. The *Manual* is available in most libraries. The following is a partial listing of important sources of aid:

Agricultural and Industrial Exposition Commission, Jackson, Miss. Has pamphlet material on the organization and direction of an agricultural fair.

Agricultural Index, H. W. Wilson Company, 950 University Ave., New York 52, N. Y. Cumulative index of important farm articles since 1916. Available at most public libraries.

American Farm Bureau Federation, Department of Information, 221 North LaSalle St., Chicago 1, Ill. A national association of farmers interested in general agriculture welfare. Promotes research; improved transportation and marketing; and state and county programs in educational, legislative, promotional, and cooperative activities. Maintains a Rural Youth Department. Low cost pamphlets, available in quantity, have education value. Listing offered.

American Forestry Association, 919 17th St., N. W., Washington 6, D. C. Publishes *American Forests*, a monthly. Maintains consultation service for members: how to select trees for cutting, and how to market trees; where to secure information about soil erosion, fish stocking, and game preserves. Offers free program plans and materials for Arbor Day, Forest Week, and Conservation Field Day.

American Humane Association, 135 Washington Ave., Albany 10, N. Y. Has literature and films about humane considerations in shipment and other handling of stock.

American Nature Association, 1214 16th St., N. W., Washington 6, D. C. Awards grants-in-aid for special conservation projects. Issues pamphlet material on conservation subjects. Publishes *Nature Magazine*, a monthly. Catalogue of publications and films available.

Boy Scouts of America, School Service, 2 Park Ave., New York 16, N. Y. Free pamphlet discussions of farm youth and Boy Scout cooperative programs. Information available.

Bureau of Reclamation, United States Department of the Interior, Washington 25, D. C. Offers consultant and field-worker service, and other support for projects to provide water for irrigation, to control floods, and to reclaim land.

Chamber of Commerce of the United States, 1615 H St., N. W., Washington 6, D. C. Promotes community programs in support of agriculture and agricultural products industries. Maintains a natural resources department in the interests of conservation. Local chambers are important sources of information and support. Literature available from the national office.

Community Service, Yellow Springs, Ohio. Interested in the welfare of small communities. *Community Service News*, a bimonthly, includes background material for better rural living.

Countrywomen's League, *The Country Gentleman*, Independence Square, Philadelphia 5, Pa. Free and low cost leaflet material for programs particularly appropriate for rural areas.

Extension Service, United States Department of Agriculture, Washington 25, D. C. The major source of information and material help for all phases of a rural service program. Publishes hundreds of special bulletins of interest to rural dwellers. Through county agents, provides professional personnel help in promoting better rural living. Free publications are available from Extension Service in Washington or from the county office. Welcomes the cooperation of community organizations in sponsoring and carrying out 4-H Club programs.

Fish and Wildlife Service, United States Department of the Interior, Washington 25, D. C. Chief federal agency in the conservation of wildlife. Administers federal wildlife conservation laws. Establishes and maintains game refuges and preserves. Carries on wildlife research. Restocks streams and lakes. Will cooperate with community organizations.

Forest Service, United States Department of Agriculture, Washington 25, D. C. Cooperates in programs for protection and improvement of all forests. Maintains research in forest management, watershed protection, and utilization of forest products. Sponsors forest fire prevention campaigns.

4-H Clubs, United States Department of Agriculture, Extension Service, Washington 25, D. C. Welcomes cooperation of community groups. Pamphlet literature describes the organization, its program, and procedure in sponsoring clubs.

Future Farmers of America, United States Office of Education, Department of Health, Education, and Welfare, Washington 25, D. C. A national organization of farm boys studying vocational agriculture in public secondary schools that operate under the provisions of the National Vocational Education Acts. Local chapters welcome the aid and cooperation of community organizations. The Future Farmers of America Foundation has been established to provide organizations with an opportunity to cooperate in promoting the program and in helping to provide vocational guidance. Pamphlets describing the organization and program are available from national headquarters.

Garden Clubs of America, the Conservation Committee, 15 East 58th St., New York 22, N. Y. Offers a free packet of leaflets and booklets on various conservation problems.

General Federation of Women's Clubs, 1734 N St., N. W., Washington 6, D. C. Study programs and project reports on the conservation of natural resources are available.

International Harvester Company, 180 North Michigan Ave., Chicago 1, Ill. Maintains farm practice research. Offers free illustrated pamphlets about subjects such as erosion control, land classification, soil conservation practices, management of range and pasture land, terracing, strip cropping, contour farming, and farm ponds.

Izaak Walton League of America, 31 North State St., Chicago 2, Ill. Promotes land and water management in the public interest. Sponsors Johnny Grass Seed projects. Publishes *Outdoor America*, six times annually.

J. I. Case Company, Inc., Racine, Wis. *Visual Aids to Modern Farming*, a catalogue of free materials such as films, slide films, booklets, and wall charts on many phases of agriculture.

National Audubon Society, 1130 Fifth Ave., New York 28, N. Y. A major source of low cost wildlife conservation material. Offers study guides, manuals, and other texts; wildlife identification cards; information about wildlife sanctuaries; reprints from Audubon magazines; wall charts; research reports; suggestions for conservation trails and other projects; and many other aids. Welcomes community group cooperation in the sponsorship of nature-study and conservation programs, and the sponsorship of Junior Audubon Clubs.

National Committee on Boys and Girls Club Work, Inc., 59 East Van Buren St., Chicago 5, Ill. An organization of business, civic, education, and other leaders to bring together all community interests to develop education programs for farm youth. Description of program and other literature available.

National Dairy Council, 111 North Canal St., Chicago 6, Ill. The educational and promotional organization of the dairy industry. Sponsors Dairy Month. Furnishes program guides and varied materials.

National Education Association, 1201 16th St., N. W., Washington 6, D. C. Conservation education guides and materials. Pamphlet discussions of rural school problems.

National Farmers Union, 1555 Sherman St., Denver 3, Colo. An organization devoted to the interests of families owning and operating farms. Literature includes pamphlets on various farm problems, and materials for meeting programs featuring farm concerns. Descriptive listing available from local unions or national headquarters.

National Garden Institute, 1368 North High St., Columbus 1, Ohio. Encourages home gardens. Furnishes free *School Gardengram*, a monthly discussion of gardening methods, procedures, and problems useful in youth group programs. Grants awards for special achievement in civic and school gardens.

National Grange, 744 Jackson Place, Washington 6, D. C. An association of farmers interested in agricultural welfare. Sponsors economic, legislative, social, and educational programs. Pamphlet describing a community service project contest includes planning and procedure suggestions, a review of volunteer group achievement, and an extensive listing of project ideas. Literature describing programs is available.

National Recreation Association, 315 Fourth Ave., New York 10, N. Y. Has available low cost manuals on how to develop recreation programs for rural areas.

National Wildlife Federation, 3308 14th St., Washington 10, D. C. A major source of conservation education material. Low cost material includes a series of illustrated leaflets about animals, birds, and fish; reprints, posters, pamphlets, and picture material. Sponsors an annual poster contest. Publishes *Conservation News*, a monthly news digest; and *Conservation Report*, news of legislation affecting conservation. A listing of materials is available.

Office of Education, Department of Health, Education, and Welfare, Washington 25, D. C. Cooperates with official and volunteer agencies and groups interested in conservation education. Conducts research. Maintains advisory and information services. List of publications available. Offers radio recordings and scripts on a free loan basis. Included is a series of recordings about subjects such as the relation between wildlife and community economic and cultural needs, the problem of soil erosion and what can be done about it; and the importance of forest conservation. Recordings have dramatic appeal. Descriptive catalogues with suggestions for use of recordings and scripts are available from the Superintendent of Documents, United States Government Printing Office, Washington 25, D. C.

Soil Conservation Service, United States Department of Agriculture, Washington 25, D. C. Promotes programs for better land use to conserve natural resources; establish a permanent, balanced agriculture; and check soil erosion. Offers education programs and materials for effective conservation. Conducts extensive research, makes land surveys, and furnishes technical help to farmers and ranchers.

Superintendent of Documents, United States Government Printing Office, Washington 25, D. C. Source of publications prepared by the various federal agencies interested in agriculture and conservation. Offers *Conservation*, a free folder with descriptive listings, and prices in fields such as wildlife, animal husbandry, harmful insects, irrigation, drainage, water power, timber resources, grain, soil erosion, conservation, farm credit, marketing, and rural electrification.

Wildlife Management Institute, 709 Wire Building, Washington 5, D. C. Offers free pamphlet literature, such as *The Farmer and Wildlife*. Sponsors the annual North American Wildlife Conference.

Some Sources of Films and Film Information

Allis-Chalmers Manufacturing Company, Tractor Division, Advertising Department, Milwaukee 1, Wis. Free loan color films include subjects such as 4-H Club projects, the 4-H Club National Encampment at Washington, the Agricultural Research Center at Beltsville, Ind., and modern farm machinery in operation.

Association Films, Inc., 347 Madison Ave., New York 17, N. Y. Offers over 40 free loan sound films about farming methods, farm health and safety, and farm financing. Folder, *Free Films for Farm Groups,* available.

Bureau of Reclamation, United States Department of the Interior, Washington 25, D. C., and regional offices. Offers free loan sound and color films, filmstrips, and slides. Descriptive listing available.

Business Screen Magazine, Inc., 7064 North Sheridan St., Chicago 10, Ill. Publishes *Farm Film Guide,* which includes many free loan and low rental films.

California Spray-Chemical Corporation, Advertising Department, Richmond 4, Calif. Free loan color films include how-to-do-it subjects such as how to control livestock pests and how to grow various crops.

Caterpillar Tractor Company, Advertising Department, Peoria 8, Ill. Offers several free loan sound films on soil conservation methods, and demonstrations of the use of machines in many farm operations.

Civil Aeronautics Administration, Audio-Visual Aids, Washington 25, D. C. Information about free loan films available at regional offices. Subjects include weed eradication and pest control through airplane spraying.

DeKalb Agricultural Association, Inc., Educational Division, DeKalb, Ill. Free loan color films about poultry breeding, the development of hybrid seed corn, and good soil management practices. Listing available.

Educational Film Library, Syracuse University, Syracuse, N. Y. Distributor of free loan sound and color films sponsored by the American Potash Institute. Descriptive listing available.

Farm Credit Administration, United States Department of Agriculture, Washington 25, D. C. Information about films available from regional offices. Free loan color films include explanations of better farm financing, farm appraisal demonstrations, cotton and other cooperatives, sheep raising and other operations.

Farm Film Foundation, 1731 Eye St., N. W., Washington 6, D. C. "A nonprofit institution dedicated to the creation of better understanding between rural and urban America through audio-visual education." A major source of free loan farm films especially produced for community organizations. Representative subjects: on-the-farm storage, potato growing, planning and managing a county fair, and land management and conservation. Descriptive listing, *Farm Film Foundation Catalogue of 16 mm. Sound Motion Pictures.*

Fish and Wildlife Service, United States Department of the Interior, Box 128, College Park, Md. Offers a series of free loan films in sound, black and white, and color. Catalogue available.

General Mills, Inc., Film Library, 400 Second Ave., South, Minneapolis 1, Minn. Free loan sound and color films describing General Mills Larro Research Farm, and farm operations such as hog, poultry, and turkey breeding and growing.

George W. Colburn Laboratory, Inc., 164 North Wacker Drive, Chicago 6, Ill. Agency for International Harvester Film Library. Free loan newsreel-type films include an account of a city boy's visit to a modern farm, a visit to Grand Coulee Dam, the Memphis Cotton Festival, and demonstrations of the use of machinery. Descriptive listing available.

Minneapolis-Moline Company, Advertising Department, Box 1050, Minneapolis 1, Minn. Free loan color subjects include a demonstration of the importance of American agriculture to the world's economy, an analysis of American leadership, the development of America from a wilderness, and the conservation of mineral elements in the soil. Descriptive folder available.

National Audubon Society, Photo and Film Department, 1130 Fifth Ave., New York 28, N. Y. Rental films about nature study, wildlife, and conservation. Catalogue available.

National Fertilizer Association, 616 Investment Building, Washington 5, D. C. Free loan sound and color films about soil fertility.

National Garden Bureau, 407 South Dearborn St., Chicago 5, Ill. Offers free loan silent and sound, black and white, and color films. Descriptive listing available.

National Wildlife Federation, 3308 14th St., N. W., Washington 10, D. C. Maintains a conservation film library of low rental titles particularly appropriate for community organization use. Offers about 11 color filmstrips on subjects such as *How Nature Defends Soil, How Man Destroys Soil,* and *Problems of Wildlife Today.* Listing available.

Modern Talking Picture Service, Inc., 45 Rockefeller Plaza, New York

20, N. Y. Free loan industry-sponsored films include many in sound and color about conservation.

Popular Science Publishing Company, Audio-Visual Division, 353 Fourth Ave., New York 10, N. Y. *Conservation Is Everybody's Business*, a series of four color filmstrips.

Princeton Film Center, Inc., Carter Road, Princeton, N. J. Films include the 28-minute *Highways and Byways, U.S.A.*, a dramatization of methods by which rural communities can acquire better farm-to-market roads. Free loan. Sound and color. Full description available.

Reid H. Ray Film Industries, Inc., 2269 Ford Parkway, St. Paul 1, Minn. Distributes free loan films sponsored by John Deere and Co.

Soil Conservation Service, United States Department of Agriculture, Washington 6, D. C. Regional offices are major sources of films on conservation. Representative subjects: methods of combating erosion, flood control, contrast of new and old methods of farming, grasslands, irrigation, exploitation of wildlife resources by hunters and trappers, and steps to restore wildlife.

Swift and Company, Agricultural Research Department, Chicago 9, Ill. A series of free loan films about livestock production and the meat industry of interest to both farmers and consumers. Catalogue available.

Tennessee Valley Authority, Division of Agriculture Relations, Film Services, Knoxville, Tenn. Several free loan sound films dramatizing individual achievement in farm and rural home improvement.

Texas Company, 135 East 42nd St., New York 17, N. Y. Poultry raising, cattle raising, apple growing, laborsaving devices on the farm, and other subjects. Sound. Black and white, and color. Free loan. Catalogue available.

Union Pacific Railroad, Motion Picture Bureau, 1416 Dodge St., Omaha 2, Neb. Dairying and other agriculture subjects. Sound. Black and white, and color. Free loan. Catalogue available.

United Nations Educational, Scientific, and Cultural Organization, New York Office, United Nations Building, New York 17, N. Y. An *International Index on Films on the Conservation and Utilization of Resources*. Free.

United States Department of Agriculture, Office of Information, Motion Picture Service, Washington 25, D. C. *Motion Pictures of the United States Department of Agriculture* and *Slidefilms of the United States Department of Agriculture* describe films and slides and tell where and how they may be secured. Free.

United States Public Health Service, Washington 25, D. C. Information about free loan farm health subjects available from state boards of health and other sources.

United States Rubber Company, Advertising Department, 1230 Avenue of the Americas, New York 20, N. Y. Free loan films include descriptions of farm-modernization programs, and the apprentice farmer program in Arizona.

United States Weather Bureau, United States Department of Commerce, Washington 25, D. C. Relation of weather to forest fires and floods. Sound. Black and white. Free loan. Listing available.

Venard Organization, 702 South Adams St., Peoria 2, Ill. A major distributor of industry-sponsored films. Free loan subjects include dramatizations of 4-H Club achievements, remodeling of farm buildings, better farming through better equipment, vocational agriculture training, and soil conservation. Descriptive listing available.

CHAPTER 19

Government

COMMUNITY ORGANIZATIONS are playing an increasingly important role in an unprecedented revival of nonpartisan interest in municipal, state, and national governments. They are initiating and supporting campaigns to arouse citizens to a realization of their responsibilities as voters. They are identifying and emphasizing the nonpartisan nature of most community issues. They are contributing to successful efforts to bring about municipal reforms such as adoption of the council-manager plan, the short ballot, modern charters, and extended civil service systems. Their representatives serve on citizen planning groups, crime commissions, and other agencies through which citizens are actively participating in their local governments.

Organizations are helping to close the gap between state and national governments and the people in communities. In cooperation with other volunteer associations and agencies, they are an effective influence for greater state and federal economy. Important economic and social advances are being realized through organization support of legislation.

The activity ideas presented in this chapter have been suggested by hundreds of successful programs, ranging from projects for education of members and the general public to sponsorship and support of dramatic, all-out nonpartisan political action to oust selfish and corrupt political machines.

For convenience of treatment, project and program ideas have been grouped rather arbitrarily into types.

AN INFORMED ELECTORATE

Organizations with consistently successful programs in government affairs recognize that effective citizen action often depends on member and public understanding of the organization and function of government, and of specific local, state, or national problems and issues. Some federated groups have as their main purpose the education of their members for leadership and participation in government affairs, through lectures, films, discussions, and other meeting features, and through conferences, institutes, and formal courses of study. Others sponsor similar programs for the community. Some groups have as a major objective the presentation of the information necessary for citizens to cast their votes intelligently in special or general elections. Some others, with government affairs but part of their broad program of service, only occasionally take the responsibility of informing the public about some particular problem or issue. In many instances they restrict their activities in government affairs to those in behalf of a traditional concern such as education, health, or welfare.

EDUCATION FOR YOUTH. Organizations are leading the way in general acceptance of citizen responsibility for participating in planning and directing school and other youth citizenship education programs.

Successful projects to give young people a better knowledge of government and how it works suggest practical activities such as:

1. Scheduling talks by public officials and other experts at school assemblies, class sessions, and youth group meetings.

2. Furnishing films, recordings, pamphlets, charts, and other material of a nonpartisan nature for class and club use.

3. Cooperating with local leaders of political parties in helping to plan a unit in practical politics for senior high school students.

4. Sponsoring the publication of a booklet text in local government suitable for several grade levels, possibly as an organization-teacher-student project.

5. Sponsoring youth debates on local, state, and national issues.

6. Awarding prizes for achievement in the study of government; recognizing essay and other contest winners with appropriate meeting and school assembly ceremonies.

7. Establishing a radio or television "youth town meeting."

Your organization might act as liaison between school authorities or other youth leaders and public officials in providing opportunities for boys and girls to see government in action. The following procedures may suggest worth-while cooperative projects:

1. Schedule and help supervise student group visits to local legislative bodies, municipal departments, courts, and state and national capitals.

2. Urge that academic credit be given for student reports of public meetings and hearings.

3. Sponsor a "youth in government" day or days, in which boys and girls act out duties of town officials, such as countersigning forms, sitting at the judge's bench, and inspecting parks. Student officeholders on their return to school should talk about their experiences in assemblies and classes.

4. Dramatize the study of local government by having a student government body or youth group elect boys and girls to fill municipal posts. Students under organization and teacher guidance might register as youth members of regular parties, hold caucuses, identify real local issues, draw up platforms, and nominate and elect officials. Feature induction ceremonies at which officials talk to their youth counterparts about the responsibilities of their positions.

5. Help stage mock meetings of legislative bodies and political conventions.

EDUCATION FOR ADULTS. Education for citizenship is a continuing process. Organization activities in adult education may have as a longe-range goal a citizenry generally informed about the structure, functions, and persisting problems of government, or they may be designed to meet a need for particular information about specific community, state, or national issues and problems. They may be aimed at the development of a more effective leadership, as well as a better informed citizenry. Kinds of projects range widely from establishment of small formal and informal study groups, to sponsorship of public meetings and use of newspapers, radio, television, direct mail, and other media of mass communication.

The following are suggestions for programs to give citizens a sound general knowledge of how government is organized and administered, to provide them with the special information needed to meet specific problems and issues, and to develop more effective leadership for government.

1. Arrange to have your members attend occasional meetings of the city council or other public bodies.

2. Schedule a mock session of the local council or the state or national legislature as a meeting feature.

3. Urge the local newspaper to feature a series of articles in which town and county officials describe their departments and explain their problems.

4. Urge the publication, and help in the preparation of summaries of

municipal reports and other documents in a style and form that encourage wide reading.

5. Persuade the local radio and television stations that a government forum as a sustaining program is good business.

6. Ask officials to give a series of talks or demonstrations at public meetings or on the air, and feature national authorities in lectures about modern charters, the council-manager plan, primaries, or other matters of current interest.

7. Schedule a series of film showings for your organization and other group meetings. Available free-loan and low-rental films may do a very effective job, for example, of explaining the step-by-step procedure by which a bill becomes law.

8. Ask the library to establish a special government affairs section or shelf.

9. Organize a new voters school for young people and new citizens. Sponsor coming-of-age parties for new voters.

Projects and programs to give citizens the informational background necessary for an understanding of a specific issue or problem are especially valuable in situations in which partisanship may tend to becloud an issue and make a sound solution difficult.

1. Urge your local newspaper to present the issue or problem in an objective fashion. Suggest a series of expository and interpretative articles by nonpartisan authorities. Sponsor a pro and con page in which leaders of opposing points of view may defend their positions.

2. Sponsor a "town meeting" to publicize various points of view.

3. Publish a leaflet objectively presenting the issue or problem.

4. Sponsor a public meeting of candidates for public office. Plan for a question-and-answer period. Ask newspapers and radio and television stations to cooperate in having citizens submit questions. Have candidates who cannot attend answer questions through recordings. Broadcast the meeting.

5. Ask members to volunteer to serve on a speakers' bureau to take the facts to other groups.

6. Utilize the facilities of public and private research agencies in your area, or national organizations such as the National Municipal League. Join with other groups in carrying on research projects and in publicizing findings.

EDUCATION FOR LEADERSHIP. As important as the development of an informed citizenry is the development of individuals with the special knowledge and skills essential for effective official and unofficial leadership in the administration of government affairs. In fostering leadership training in the community your organization might find some of the following suggestions useful:

1. Feature lectures, discussions, and films about government at meetings. Ask officials and other especially interested citizens to attend.

2. Organize a monitor system by which your members and representatives of other groups are assigned, with the cooperation of officials, as observers of the activities of local councils and boards such as those for planning, taxation, health, and education. Feature reports of such observations at organization and other meetings.

3. Sponsor citizen institutes, conferences, study-discussion groups, and forums in government affairs. Suggest a course in practical politics or government as part of the local adult education program, or sponsor university extension courses for citizens and officials.

4. Cooperate in providing political field experience or internships in government administration for students majoring in political science and government. Act as liaison between university political science departments and local political parties.

GREATER EFFICIENCY IN GOVERNMENT

Step by step, American government has moved toward assumption of responsibility for the total welfare of all citizens. Function added to function, service to service has brought into being a complex of federal departments, agencies, bureaus, offices, and commissions. State, county, and local governments continue to try to meet the tremendous population concentrations and the complexities of an industrial civilization with organizations that are often outlandishly obsolete. Inevitable waste, duplication of effort, the avoidance of responsibility, corruption, and a widening gap between public officials and citizens pose a serious threat to American democracy.

Your organization may find the following suggestions helpful in planning unilateral or intergroup action for greater government efficiency:

1. Let officials know your organization is interested in their administration. Invite key officials to luncheon and other meetings. Schedule an Officials' Night. Make officials honorary members.

2. Sponsor a study of the efficiency with which all departments of local government meet community needs. Such a study may be conducted by professional government administration research experts, by a citizens group utilizing the consultant services of a national association

or agency, or by a citizens' group relying wholly on its own resources. Publicize comparative cost data for standard municipal services, and the facts about government functions and services for which no essential need can be established. *The Municipal Year Book*, published by the International City Managers' Association, presents comparative cost figures. Its chapters "How to Use the Year Book" and "Use of Statistical Data" are excellent guides for a study of government costs.

3. Sponsor the formation of a watchdog committee to evaluate fiscal policy, interpret budget documents, and offer proposals for more efficient administration. Publish committee findings and recommendations.

4. Invite key citizens to a series of meetings to hear reports from officials, and talks by tax and other government experts.

5. Study demands for extended government services and facilities often made by special-interest groups in the name of all citizens. Poll members of such groups to determine whether the demands come from the rank and file or from a few "leaders" only. Point out the cost of such services and facilities to the taxpayers as a whole, and the strain often imposed on administrative capacity. Secure expressions of opinion from leaders of other groups. Sponsor a general poll to determine community thinking.

6. Support the programs of taxpayers' associations that are clearly in the public interest. Sponsor the organization of a tax-study committee to determine whether the tax structure is adequate, whether the burden of taxation is equitably distributed, and whether all sources of tax revenue are being considered.

7. Study the relation of your local, county, state, and national governments to discover wasteful duplication or overlapping of functions.

8. Establish awards for municipal appointive personnel who distinguish themselves by special effort in the public interest. Urge the adoption of an incentive system.

9. Urge local better-government organizations to affiliate with county, state, and national associations for an exchange of information and ideas.

10. Schedule a series of showings of free loan or low rental films that dramatize the problems of inflation and the relation of government spending to inflation.

11. Sponsor public meetings to protest unwise spending. Plan such meetings for times when general fiscal policy is being determined, budgets prepared, or major public projects contemplated. Sponsor petitions urging economy. Encourage members and other citizens to write letters to officials and to newspaper editors. Enlist the editorial support of local newspapers. Publicize citizen protests through throwaways, posters, stickers, spot announcements, and other measures.

12. Strengthen inadequate state and local services and support volun-

teer programs in areas such as health, welfare, education, and housing, to counter the extension of federal activities.

In working for more efficient government, however, your group should guard against a wholly negative attitude toward public spending. Your support for expenditures in the public interest, or necessary to realize long-range efficiency or economy, places your group in a strategically strong position to protest against waste and extravagance. Expenditures that often are necessary for long-range economy include those for adequate planning, maintenance of buildings and equipment, and improved facilities for fire protection, health, and education.

Volunteer group study of government efficiency has often led to action for drastic and far-reaching reforms. If major changes are clearly needed in your community, your group should consider the practicability of enlisting the aid of other groups in a concerted effort to bring them about. Many programs for more efficient local government, however, fail to bring about measurable improvement because their objectives are too remote, or involve radical administrative shakeups for which the community is not ready, or are too vague and general to win official or citizen support.

Your program may have greater chance for success with limited, specific objectives such as a central switchboard in the municipal building to eliminate separate, direct telephone lines to departments, agencies, and individuals; consolidation of offices that have closely related or overlapping functions; a personnel selection and supervisory system patterned after best business practice; an adequate retirement system to strengthen employee morale; establishment of a center for maintenance and repair of all equipment; pooling of stenographic help and centralization of duplicating and mailing; a central purchasing agency; consolidation of schools; organization of fire and police auxiliaries to avoid personnel expansion; and utilization of community organizations and other volunteer groups to perform many fringe functions, in fields such as recreation and cultural activities.

INCREASED CITIZEN PARTICIPATION

Essential for democratic government, authorities point out, are a widespread, informed participation in choosing and electing candidates for public office, and establishment and full use of channels of two-way communication and cooperation between government and citizens. Community organizations have been active in providing these essentials.

REGISTER-AND-VOTE ACTIVITIES. A major factor in the record-breaking 1952 presidential election vote was the influence of the thousands of community organizations that initiated and supported register-and-vote activities. One of the greatest services your government affairs committee can perform is to help arouse the citizens of your community to a realization of their grave responsibility for taking an informed part in all primary, special, and general elections.

The extent of your register-and-vote activities depends, of course, on your community situation. Ordinarily, organization efforts consist of educational and promotional activities such as distributing literature and sponsoring intergroup contests. Some volunteer groups, however, have joined with other organizations in ingenious and elaborate register-and-vote campaigns to elect reform administrations, to secure adoption of bond issues, or to bring about other far-reaching changes.

Some of the following procedures, suggested by such campaigns, may help you in selecting activities appropriate for your purposes:

1. Ask the advice and cooperation of other organizations with a traditional interest in citizen participation in government. The League of Women Voters, for example, has a unique background in such an area of service. The General Federation of Women's Clubs, the Junior League, the Parent-Teacher Association, the American Legion, the Chamber of Commerce, the Junior Chamber of Commerce, and other groups have local and national programs to encourage member and other citizen participation.

2. Sponsor an intergroup committee for a register-and-vote campaign.

3. Utilize the campaign organization and direction experience of members of fund-raising committees. Persuade other citizens with organization and management experience to join in the effort. Ask leaders of political parties to help. They may have lists of independent voters, voting maps of the community, campaign organization outlines, and other materials of value. In accepting such aid, however, care should be taken to preserve your nonpartisan approach.

4. Establish a centrally located campaign headquarters. The nonpartisan nature of a program may make it possible to use space in public buildings or the facilities of a church or a community organization such as the Chamber of Commerce. Install telephones; make available the

literature of all parties, as well as nonpartisan information and analyses, demonstration voting machines, district voting maps, and other aids. Brief workers in answers to questions about splitting a ticket, voting a straight ticket, and writing in a vote.

5. Man information booths in department stores, theater lobbies, libraries, and on street corners. Provide registration and party enrollment information and forms.

6. Organize a telephone corps.

7. Mobilize flying squads to visit all factories, stores, and other business places.

8. Arrange with employers for release time for voting and other election-day activities.

9. Ask youth groups to organize a baby-sitter service, and to distribute promotional material.

10. Provide transportation for those who cannot get to the polls.

11. Secure newspaper, radio, and television support. Ask newspapers to feature a polling-place map of the community, and articles and picture explanations about how to register and how to vote.

12. Send citizenship quizzes, informational material, and special appeals to parents through school children.

13. Mobilize publicity resources. Sponsor school and youth group essay and poster contests. Ask the local newspaper to feature a contest for the best cartoon attacking public lethargy. Secure the aid of national organizations such as the American Heritage Foundation and the Advertising Council. Measures successful in many communities include newspaper fillers and prominently displayed boxes announcing the number of days left to register, radio and television spot announcements, stenciled slogans and appeals on sidewalks and curbs, stenciled tracks leading to registration and voting places, sound trucks, loudspeakers in business areas, "vote" stamps for business mailings, and "I have registered" and "I have voted" tags or emblems such as the Gold Feather.

14. Enter your campaign for an American Heritage Award. Publicize your plans to compete as an incentive for special citizen effort.

OTHER PARTICIPATION PROJECTS. Citizen responsibility, however, cannot stop at the polls. Some of the following suggestions may result in a more widespread citizen participation in the government affairs of your community:

1. Draw up and distribute a check list for citizens' self-appraisal. Include items such as "I vote in primaries" and "I am affiliated with a volunteer group for community service."

2. Organize intergroup nonpartisan workshops for development of

plans to facilitate more general and direct public participation. Projects for such a workshop might include a consideration of the extent of party-member participation in policy making and nominating procedures; and the extent to which municipal departments hold hearings, and provide opportunities for supplemental citizen aid in administration.

3. Include professional and other restricted membership organizations in arrangements for community-wide group participation in public affairs. Lawyers, doctors, teachers, and engineers have especially valuable contributions to make.

4. Suggest that officials schedule regular meetings with civic group leaders for discussions of government problems. Urge formation of citizen advisory councils for some of the major departments.

5. Urge members to take an active interest in the policies and programs of the parties of their choice and to accept nomination for public office.

6. Enlist the experience and professional skills of members in support of measures to improve government. Your membership may include personnel and general office managers, statisticians, public relations consultants, and other industrial and business experts with valuable contributions to make to better government. Award citations for effective participation. Have your government affairs committee present a report of members' participation.

7. Initiate and support formation of a permanent nonpartisan association for better government. Many such groups have extensive, inclusive programs such as that suggested by this chapter. Some maintain a salaried director and staff.

8. Enter your citizens participation project in the All-America Cities annual competition sponsored by the National Municipal League and *Look* magazine.

LEGISLATION IN THE PUBLIC INTEREST

Some undesirable situations can be corrected only through legislative action. Better schools may depend on a state law establishing minimum teaching preparation and other standards; control by party bosses, with the inefficiency that frequently accompanies such control, often can be broken only by legislation that liberalizes the nominating procedure; juvenile delinquency and ill health may have their roots in inadequate youth welfare or other services requiring legislative action for their establishment.

Your efforts to arouse interest in needed legislation, to publicize important bills pending, and to secure enactment of legislation clearly in the public interest can lead to far-reaching, permanent results in better community living.

People in communities can be a most effective lobby. Your organization might ask members to start a telephone call or letter chain, or have your government affairs committee organize a community letter-writing campaign. Offer letter writers essential information such as the full names and the addresses of legislators, the proper forms of salutation, the number of the bill being considered, and the committee to which it was referred. Suggest that each citizen make his letter personal, and that he be brief, concrete in his reasons, and courteous. Time the letter with official consideration of the bill. Other practical procedures in behalf of legislation are the following:

1. Ask each service committee to contribute to the program planning of the legislative or government affairs committee. What bills pending contribute to the general objectives of the committee on education, on health, on safety? Are local ordinances and codes in these fields adequate? What other legislation is needed?

2. Seek the aid of the local bar association or the municipal counsel in preparing drafts of legislation in the interest of the community.

3. Arrange for groups of members to observe legislative bodies in session. Ask your representatives to have lunch or dinner with your group to discuss legislation. Appear at committee hearings.

4. Invite legislators to spend a "get-acquainted day" in your community, to meet officials and other civic leaders and to discuss legislation problems.

5. Organize temporary or permanent study-discussion groups on a neighborhood, community, district, or regional basis. Sponsor a conference of organizations in your district or state. Organize an intergroup committee to meet with legislators.

6. Ask those who represent you in national, state, and local legislative bodies to explain their stands on legislation of special interest to your community. Schedule group, intergroup, or general public meetings. Ask permission to distribute the written explanations of lawmakers.

7. Urge your local newspapers to publish a week-by-week report of the status of important legislation, and the voting record of your legislators.

8. Have recordings made of endorsements by prominent citizens, to use as radio spot announcements.

9. Ask your newspaper to serve as a clearinghouse for open letters to legislators, featuring a "Now listen, Councilman . . ." or a "Now listen, Congressman . . ." section.

10. Conduct unofficial community referenda on important local, state, and national legislative issues.

11. Have your delegates to state, regional, or national organization conventions sponsor resolutions or other action in behalf of needed legislation.

12. Sponsor establishment of a community legislative committee or council for consideration of state legislation affecting the community, and for a study of the need for other legislation. In some towns and cities, such legislative committees have a quasi-official status. Their functions include surveying the effects of existing legislation on important areas of community living and publicizing its findings; considering pending legislation and endorsing measures that are in the community's interest; drafting special acts necessary for reorganization or other reform; representing the citizens of the community at legislative committee hearings; reporting on the results of hearings; and publicizing the status of important legislation and the voting records of legislators.

HIGH MORAL AND ETHICAL STANDARDS

Important as is the pressing need to develop an informed electorate, to achieve efficiency in government organization and administration, and to strengthen and supplement the efforts of officials through citizen participation, good government finally must depend on the moral and ethical conduct of men in public life. And if men in public life are insensitive to the obligations their offices impose, tolerant of wrongdoing, susceptible to undue influence, grasping and self-seeking, it can only be because people in communities have failed to insist that the highest moral and ethical standards be maintained by those they elect. It is in the community that the roots of official misconduct lie. Those who go to your state capitals and to Washington have served their internships in towns and cities. Patterns of behavior, attitudes, values—all have been fixed in public office in the communities.

Some of the following suggested procedures may result in a pattern of higher moral and ethical standards:

1. Make a study of the internal organization of political parties to determine just who selects nominees for public office. In many instances a dominant influence is exerted by questionable elements of the population. Work for reform within the parties, or join with others to present candidates answerable to all the community.

2. In cooperation with other organizations, launch a long-range pro-

gram to give politics the prestige it must have to attract the best leadership. Consult schools, churches, and youth service organizations about education programs to counter the all too prevalent attitude that people enter politics for what they can get.

3. Encourage young men and women of character to enter public life.

4. Work for salary schedules that make it possible for your community to compete with business and the professions for the services of able citizens of good character.

5. Sponsor a conference of parents, teachers, clergymen, youth leaders, politicians, and youth to determine what can be done to change attitudes that do not encourage high moral and ethical standards. Encourage youth and adult programs aimed at developing the ideal of service.

6. Sponsor the establishment of a citizens committee for law enforcement. Organization-supported crime commissions in some towns and cities have uncovered an alliance of organized crime and government officials. An aroused public opinion has brought about far-reaching reforms.

7. Ask the assistance of your local bar association, ministerial association, other interested groups, and public officials in drafting a code of ethics for public officials. Give such a code wide distribution.

8. Attack the double standard of morality represented by registration fees for illegal slot machines, gambling fines that are token or solely for the purpose of revenue, and other questionable practices.

SOURCES OF AID

Adult Education Council, 721 Olive St., St. Louis 1, Mo. Leaflets written for an adult political education program in St. Louis may suggest ideas for a similar program in your community. Council has information about other adult government affairs education projects.

American City Magazine, 470 Fourth Ave., New York 16, N. Y. Includes articles about how to improve municipal government and services. Subjects covered include planning, zoning, taxation and finance, public relations, street cleaning, traffic control, water supply, and public safety.

American Council on Public Affairs, 2153 Florida Ave., N. W., Washington 8, D. C. Makes available authoritative facts and significant opinions about contemporary social and economic problems related to government. Publishes numerous books and pamphlets. Listing available.

American Federation of Labor, 1625 Eye St., N. W., Washington 6, D. C. Education program includes government affairs. Has information on government policy and legislation affecting labor interests. Publications include the *AFL Weekly News Service; The Federationist,*

a monthly; and *Labor's Monthly Survey*. All contain news and interpretations of government affairs from labor's point of view.

American Heritage Foundation, 25 West 45th St., New York 19, N. Y.
Offers a series of annual awards to communities, counties, and organizations that conduct outstanding community-wide campaigns to
educate citizens to a sense of responsibility for voting. Has available
a guide for organizing and directing a get-out-the-vote campaign; a
series of one-minute spot radio announcements and other promotional
material.

American Political Science Association, 1785 Massachusetts Ave., N. W.,
Washington 6, D. C. Has information about its Congressional Interne
and other programs, and materials to encourage citizen participation
in politics. Publishes *American Political Science Review*, a quarterly.

Center for Information on America, Washington, Conn. Publishes a
series of *Future Voters Discussion Guides* monthly September through
May. Information about the guides and other services is available.

Chamber of Commerce of the United States, 1615 H St., N. W., Washington 6, D. C. Maintains a staff of national affairs advisors who act
as consultants to business groups interested in better government.
Distributes national legislative information and analyses, and offers
free loan and low rental films, pamphlets, and other material to member and other community groups. Local and state chambers cooperate
with other organizations in community programs for better government. National publications include *Legislative Daily*, a summary of
congressional developments; *Bill Digest*, briefs of major bills, issued
periodically with the *Legislative Daily*; *Legislative Outlook*, published
every two weeks; *Taxpayer's Dollar*, a monthly digest; and *Special
Number*, presenting analyses of selected major legislative proposals.

Chicago Crime Commission, 79 West Monroe St., Chicago 3, Ill. Publications include a manual on how to form a citizens' crime commission, research reports, and reprints of articles on the crime problem.

Childs, Richard S., *Civic Victories*, New York: Harper & Brothers, 1952.
The story of municipal government reform, and what remains to be
accomplished. Describes successful volunteer-action movements for
such measures as the short ballot, the council-manager plan, and civil
service reform.

Christophers, 18 East 48th St., New York 17, N. Y. Among chief objectives is that of arousing the average citizen to a sense of personal responsibility for doing something positive and constructive to strengthen
his government. Publishes inspirational and informative pamphlets giving accounts of individual action.

Citizens Clearing House, New York University Law Center, 40 Washington Square, South, New York 3, N. Y. Sponsors conferences and maintains local citizenship clearinghouses to bring together teachers, college administrators, and political leaders to devise ways to prepare college students for effective participation in political affairs. Literature describes projects for student participation in local party activities.

Citizens Committee for the Hoover Report, 184 East 64th St., New York 21, N. Y. A voluntary, nonprofit, bipartisan committee for public education in behalf of federal reorganization. Furnishes reports on the status of the reorganization program, and proposals for further reorganization measures.

Citizens National Committee, 2844 Connecticut Ave., N. W., Washington 9, D. C. Publishes reports, bulletins, and periodicals about congressional action affecting the national economy.

Congress of Industrial Organizations, 718 Jackson Place, Washington 6, D. C. Maintains a program for citizen political education and action. Will furnish analyses of legislation affecting labor-management relations, collective bargaining, discrimination, housing, and general welfare. Publications include *Union News Service* and *C.I.O. News,* both weeklies.

Congressional Digest, A. G. Robinson, editor and publisher, 726 Jackson Place, N. W., Washington 6, D. C. A monthly which supplies background information useful in education programs.

Council of State Chambers of Commerce, Research Office, 1722 H St., N. W., Washington 6, D. C. Has information about fiscal problems. Publishes bulletins, *Federal Spending Facts* and *Federal Tax Facts.*

Council of State Governments, 1313 East 60th St., Chicago 37, Ill. Publications include the monthly news magazine *State Government. Book of the States,* published biennially, carries authoritative summaries of recent trends in fields such as state-local relations. Supplies statistical and other data useful in a study of local government and its relations with state government. Bibliography included.

Goetz, Rachel Marshall, *Visual Aids for the Public Service,* Public Administration Service, 1313 East 60th St., Chicago 37, Ill. A manual for citizens and officials interested in presenting more effectively the processes of local government and in improving techniques for training personnel. Has to do with such practical matters as designing posters, choosing titles, lettering, use of the feltboard, making charts and graphs, deciding upon a method of reproduction, and choosing and presenting films.

Governmental Research Association, Inc., 684 Park Ave., New York 21, N. Y. Publishes a *Directory* of organizations and individuals professionally engaged in governmental research and related activities on the local, state, and national levels. Local organizations may be valuable sources of information about government, or may be of assistance in community research problems or in the establishment of a community research agency.

Harding College, National Education Program, Searcy, Ark. Aid for better-government programs includes pamphlets and other materials graphically presenting the case for a balanced budget, reduction of taxes through the elimination of waste, and an end to government benefits; and lapel tags and other promotion devices for get-out-the-vote drives.

House Office Building, Washington 25, D. C. Address of your congressman.

International City Managers' Association, 1313 East 60th St., Chicago 37, Ill. Publishes *The Municipal Year Book*, a compilation of statistics and other information indispensable for a consideration of many problems of municipal government. Chief usefulness is that it enables an organization to compare its community facilities and services with those of similar communities. Representative sections include individual municipality data on traffic safety, utilities, revenue, expenditure, debt, zoning and land subdivision, forms of government, methods of choosing officials, pay rates, personnel organization, and retirement systems. Features significant municipal events and trends, model ordinances, and a directory of officials. Its listing of sources of further general and specific information is especially valuable. Other publications include *Check List on How Cities Can Cut Costs*; *Public Management*, a monthly magazine; a semimonthly newsletter; occasional special reports; and a series of textbooks on various phases of municipal administration.

League of Women Voters of the United States, 1026 17th St., N. W., Washington 6, D. C. Promotes political responsibility through the informed and active participation of citizens in government. Affiliated state and local Leagues provide nonpartisan, factual information about registration, voting, candidates, public officials and issues, and promote participation in primaries and general elections. Representative publications include *The National Voter*, issued 16 times a year; *Report from the Hill*, during congressional sessions; *Memos*, background information for a pro-and-con treatment of important issues, with bibliographies and outline guides for discussion leaders; and a series of

Voters Service pamphlets. A complete list of publications is available. State and local Leagues issue periodical and occasional bulletins and reports. Especially useful are *Know Your Town* studies prepared by local Leagues on the basis of a standard outline.

National Americanism Commission, the American Legion, 700 North Pennsylvania St., Indianapolis, Ind. Information about Boys' State and Girls' State, organized in each state to give boys and girls practical training in democratic procedures.

National Association of Manufacturers, 14 West 49th St., New York 20, N. Y. Has available pamphlets, free loan films, and other material about government policy and federal legislation affecting the national economy.

National Civil Service League, 120 East 29th St., New York 16, N. Y. Makes available research results, calls to public attention violations of civil service laws, works for civil service reform, and furnishes patterns for legislation. Encourages organization of local groups interested in government personnel. Will provide speakers on various phases of government personnel problems. Publications include *Special News Service*, a report of developments in the field of government personnel organization and management, and *Good Government*, a bimonthly.

National Education Association, 1201 16th St., N. W., Washington 6, D. C. Publications include many of particular interest to government-affairs committees. Some, such as the *Personal Growth* leaflet series, are available in quantity at low cost. Listing available.

National Foundation for Education in American Citizenship, Butler University, Indianapolis 17, Ind. Makes available to individuals and community organizations inexpensive pamphlets reporting the results of research in economic and social problems. The *Basic American Concepts* series of pamphlets, published in collaboration with the Public Affairs Committee, includes *Political Parties: An American Way*. Explains the individual citizen's role in party affairs, and the importance of the two-party system for our form of government. Written for popular education, this pamphlet is available in quantity at low cost.

National Municipal League, 299 Broadway, New York 7, N. Y. An organization of individuals and local associations interested in better municipal and state government through informed citizen action. Credited by many authorities with being the chief influence, directly or indirectly, in major municipal reforms of the last 50 years. Has encouraged and made possible hundreds of successful citizen efforts to secure the short ballot, nonpartisan elections, proportional representation, city-manager plans, better legislative procedures, modernized city charters and state constitutions, necessary enabling acts, and other reforms. Offers consultant services to community groups, sponsors awards for citizen participation, conducts informal seminars and a national conference. Literature covers the wide field of state, county, and municipal government and citizen organization. Representative subject matter: a guide for charter commissions; a model charter; model fiscal laws; model primary and election systems; the organization of a citizens association; how to direct a nonpartisan campaign; descriptions of arrangements for popular control; trends in municipal government; and reviews of general and specific problems. Publishes *National Municipal Review*, a monthly. Listing of books and pamphlets available.

New Tools for Learning, 280 Madison Ave., New York 16, N. Y. Gathers and makes available information about films, pamphlets, and recordings which are useful for the study and discussion of current issues, many of which involve consideration of legislation and government policy. Catalogue available.

Public Administration Clearing House, 1313 East 60th St., Chicago 37, Ill. Publishes *Public Administration Organizations: A Directory*, describing about 600 unofficial American and Canadian organizations concerned with specialized government matters such as tax administration, traffic control, health, and public utilities.

Public Administration Service, 1313 East 60th St., Chicago 37, Ill. Offers research, consultant, and publications service to government agencies on all levels. *Catalogue of Publications* includes the listings of the Public Administration Service and those of affiliated organizations such as the American Municipal Association, Municipal Finance Officers' Association, American Society of Planning Officials, and the American Public Works Association.

Science Research Associates, Inc., 57 West Grand Ave., Chicago 10, Ill. *Life Adjustment* booklet series includes *Politics for Boys and Girls*, useful in youth education programs; and *Understanding Politics*, a summary especially useful in programs for new voters.

Seckler-Hudson, Catheryn, *Bibliography on Public Administration*, Washington: The American University Press, 1953. Contains over 1100 annotated references to listings and guides, research reports, selected government publications, periodicals, background works, and public relations manuals and studies.

Senate Office Building, Washington 25, D. C. Address of your senator.

Social Legislation Information Service, 1346 Connecticut Ave., N. W., Washington 6, D. C. Nominally priced bulletins include an analysis of the historical background and the program of the Commission on Governmental Operations and the Commission on Intergovernmental Relations, which are continuing the work of the Hoover Commission.

Stewart, Frank Mann, A Half Century of Municipal Reform, Berkeley and Los Angeles: University of California Press, 1950. The history of the National Municipal League. Includes a 29-page bibliography on municipal government.

Superintendent of Documents, United States Government Printing Office, Washington 25, D. C. Publications of interest to organizations maintaining government affairs programs include United States Government Manual, containing comprehensive information about all federal agencies; reports of the many agencies, bureaus, commissions, and other bodies; The Congressional Record; The Federal Budget in Brief, an illustrated pamphlet published annually in February; and catalogues of radio recordings and scripts. List of publications available.

Tax Foundation, Inc., 30 Rockefeller Plaza, New York 20, N. Y. Material especially valuable is a series of booklet guides for appraising the economical administration of the major areas of municipal government, written especially for the layman. Other booklets provide information and procedure ideas for programs aimed especially at government economy. Publishes Tax Outlook, a monthly magazine featuring articles by leading businessmen and economists.

Twentieth Century Fund, 330 West 42nd St., New York 36, N. Y. Conducts research and education projects in current government problems, and aids in formulating nonpartisan policies for their solution. Publishes books, pamphlets, bulletins, study outlines; sponsors radio programs; issues news releases.

United States Conference of Mayors, 730 Jackson Place, N. W., Washington 6, D. C. Has available statistics and other information about the growth of cities; the economic, social, and political significance of such growth; and suggested solutions to political problems brought about by the changing relations of cities, counties, and states.

SOME SOURCES OF FILMS AND FILM INFORMATION

Academy Films, Box 3088, Hollywood, Calif. Low rental films include State Legislature, filmed during an actual session of a state legislature to show the step-by-step procedure by which a bill becomes a law. Description available.

Christophers, 18 East 48th St., New York 17, N. Y. Has a series of low cost films, each of which suggests practical ways by which individuals can contribute to better government. Descriptions available.

Coronet Films, Coronet Building, Chicago 1, Ill. Low rental films include descriptions of the functions of municipal government; how the government of Milwaukee reflects the will of citizens; an explanation of the principles underlying our American system of elections; the role of political parties; and procedures in registering, electioneering, and voting. Catalogue available.

Encyclopaedia Britannica Films, Inc., 1150 Wilmette Ave., Wilmette, Ill. Rental films include subjects such as the election of a President, the structure of government, and the functioning of political parties. Description available.

Farm Film Foundation, 1731 Eye St., N. W., Washington 6, D. C. Free loan sound films include *What Price Government?*, a 20-minute discussion of waste and inefficiency, with specific suggestions for action to eliminate them. Description available.

Film Council of America, 600 Davis St., Evanston, Ill. Has available a list of recommended films about political education.

Ford Motor Company, Film Library, 3000 Schaefer Road, Dearborn, Mich., and local Ford or Lincoln-Mercury dealers. Free loan films include *Ticket to Freedom*, which points out how millions of Americans jeopardize their freedom through failure to vote. Description available.

General Motors Corporation, Department of Public Relations, Film Section, 3044 West Grand Boulevard, Detroit 2, Mich. Free loan sound films include *Joe and His Government*, a 25-minute explanation of the relation of government to a representative worker. Descriptive folder available.

McGraw-Hill Book Company, Inc., Text-Film Department, 330 West 42nd St., New York 18, N. Y. Low cost filmstrips include an *American Government* series of 10 titles giving basic information on the structure and function of the federal government, and *Political Parties and Elections*, 39 frames describing how the constitutional right to vote is restricted in some states. Descriptions available.

National Association of Manufacturers, Motion Picture Department, 14 West 49th St., New York 20, N. Y. Offers a series of free loan government education films for youth and adults. Films emphasize citizen responsibility for good government. Descriptive brochure available.

Pictorial Films, Inc., 1501 Broadway, New York 19, N. Y. Information about *How a Bill Becomes a Law*. Filmed in Washington. A step-by-step procedure, with diagrams.

Princeton Film Center, Inc., Carter Road, Princeton, N. J. Rental films include explanations of the roles of citizens, legislators, the chief executive, and the courts. Catalogue available.

Progressive Pictures, 6351 Thornhill Drive, Oakland 11, Calif. Rental films about the need to modernize the structure of county government, development of municipal government functions, and other subjects useful for government education programs. Catalogue available.

Union Films, 111 West 88th St., New York 24, N. Y. Rental films include *Deadline for Action*, a 40-minute dramatization of the need for citizen interest and participation to counter the influence of special-interest groups in Congress. Description available.

United World Films, Inc., 1445 Park Ave., New York 29, N. Y. Rental and free loan offerings include films dramatizing election-day procedure in a representative American town, and explaining the various functions of state and national governments. Catalogue available.

CHAPTER 20

Community Development

COURAGEOUS LEADERSHIP is needed in every American community to translate into reality the many plans for civic betterment that experts have developed. Community organizations should provide this leadership.

What your organization chooses to try to do depends, of course, on the community's particular physical, economic, and social needs. Many of these may be met through independent, relatively short-term projects. Other needs must be projected into the future, official and citizen support mobilized, and a long-term continuing program maintained to meet them. Many organizations have taken the lead in developing and securing acceptance of a master plan aimed at better living in all areas, within the limits of the community's pocketbook.

The interrelation of needs and problems in general community development makes identification of separate areas of action difficult. Most volunteer group activities, however, may be classified as those primarily in behalf of community planning, housing, traffic control, beautification, or economic welfare.

COMMUNITY PLANNING

It is now generally recognized that communities cannot be allowed to just grow, like Topsy. Their development must be planned for and directed. Planning is a process in which citizens, in cooperation with officials and experts, determine what kind of a community they would like to live and work in, what resources and facilities are available to achieve this ideal, what additional resources and facilities must be acquired, what needs are immediate and what are remote, and finally, by what step-by-step measures needs can be met.

Planning may be in special areas such as traffic, housing, or public works, or it may be general in scope. Volunteer groups typically concern themselves with elimination of slum areas; redevelopment of areas blighted by ribbon zoning and other influences; determination of a general growth pattern for the community to avoid or alleviate undesirable traffic, parking, sewage, and other problems; and maintenance or rehabilitation of downtown areas, a major source of tax revenue in most communities.

Organizations are prominent in development of regional planning. The Lions Club of Mount Kisco, New York, for example, secured the cooperation of five other towns in a joint planning program. Civic leaders and public officials exchanged information and ideas, related their community needs to broader area needs, and by combining their resources secured the necessary technical and other planning assistance.

Successful organization action suggests the following activities to promote better community planning:

1. Scheduling talks by representatives of local businesses and industries about their plans for expansion and how your organization can cooperate to provide greater economic, social, cultural, and other opportunities for the community.

2. Educating the public to a realization that planning affects every individual through taxation; the stability of community investments; opportunities to do business, to find and hold a job, or to have all the satisfactions a good community has to offer.

3. Sponsoring interorganization and interagency conferences to correlate volunteer and official planning programs.

4. Establishing a local workshop or clinic for study of general community problems, or of problems in a specific field such as traffic control.

5. Utilizing the services of state universities and colleges, state agricultural and other development boards, and business and industry in a survey of community needs and resources.

6. Making possible free discussion of controversial development plans through sponsoring forums and discussions, and distributing background information through pamphlets, charts, and graphs.

7. Promoting establishment of a planning council in a specific field such as housing. Maintaining an organization community development planning committee to meet with municipal officials.

8. Promoting establishment of a volunteer-official municipal planning commission, headed by a professional administrator.

HOUSING

Statistical presentations of information about housing seldom succeed in giving an adequate idea of its importance to the development of a community. The health, the moral fiber, the stability of citizens may be seriously affected by inadequate housing. Defense production is affected by availability of housing for workers. Whether or not good teachers and other professionally trained people choose your town or city as their home may depend directly on whether or not good houses may be purchased or rented. Substandard housing—slum areas—breed ill health and crime, arrest the development of many with potential leadership and other contributions to make to society, and impose a heavy burden on the community as a whole.

As in other areas of community development, organizations are taking effective action to help correct undesirable housing conditions, and to provide more dwelling units where there is a demonstrated need.

They cooperate with officials in establishing and supporting volunteer-official housing associations. These council-type associations survey housing conditions, present showings of motion pictures, arrange exhibits, distribute pamphlets and graphic materials, sponsor public meetings and discussions, present radio and television programs, and arrange citizen tours of blighted areas. Often they serve as a clearinghouse for information and ideas about problems. Agencies that cooperate in formation and direction of such groups include the local housing authority, health department, real estate board, and regional offices of state and federal agencies.

SLUM CLEARANCE. In one major city, a citizens' association is maintaining a continuing rehabilitation program that is steadily bringing about the transformation of a blighted area of about 2000 blocks. The public was aroused through an educational campaign that graphically presented startling information such as the fact that this area, 10 per cent of the city's total, was costing the city 40 per cent of its budget; that property assessments in the area had decreased more than $10 million in 12 years; and that the city, in effect, was losing about $14 million a year because of housing conditions in this area. Today, block by block, people are being given new hope, new interests, and are finding a pride in their homes.

In many other towns and cities, volunteer groups are arousing interest in the problem of slum clearance, and are helping to solve that problem, through measures such as these:

1. Sponsoring and supporting a citizens group for the study of the

underlying causes of blighted residential areas, and of measures to correct substandard housing conditions.

2. Providing public officials with a map of the community that graphically relates the incidence of infant mortality, tuberculosis, juvenile delinquency, crime, fires, and other undesirable factors to substandard housing. Information usually is available from sources such as the health department and the juvenile court.

3. Cooperating with municipal officials in campaigns to educate the community to an appreciation of the effect of slum areas upon total community welfare, as for example, the cost in terms of police protection, prisons and other correctional institutions, hospitals, and welfare facilities and services.

4. Urging enforcement of building, fire, and health codes. In many communities centralization of authority to enforce proper standards is needed.

5. Supporting legislation to give local authorities power to act, where necessary, in slum clearance projects.

6. Sponsoring studies and discussions of the feasibility of private-enterprise projects to replace substandard dwellings.

ADDITIONAL HOUSING UNITS. Volunteer groups and municipal agencies are working together to organize and direct public and private resources to meet the housing need. In some communities citizen groups have taken direct action to produce housing units through their own private enterprises.

Illustrative of such direct action was the program of the Junior Chamber of Commerce in Green River, Wyoming. As in so many other communities, industry in Green River suddenly expanded its production to meet defense needs; 25 per cent of the workers could not find housing in or near the city. The Junior Chamber, with the cooperation of the senior Chamber of Commerce, obtained land and constructed 100 housing units within a price range that workers could afford. The success of the project led to further cooperative action to meet industrial expansion with adequate housing facilities.

Those who have a knowledge of the building industry can be particularly helpful in planning and carrying out a community program for more housing. Form an organization building-industry committee, or urge your local Chamber of Commerce to form such a committee composed of developers, architects, contractors, and suppliers. Such a group would be invaluable in efforts to improve building codes, subdivision requirements, zoning ordinances, and other regulations, and to encourage home building through furnishing planning information, arranging for model-home inspections, conducting home planning and design contests, and correlating other building promotion activities.

Other activities include:

1. Helping local officials determine the number of families and individuals who are in need of housing. How many families, for example, are doubling up? How many are living in dwellings that do not meet occupancy standards? How many wage earners in the community are forced to live in other communities?

2. Organizing groups for study and discussion of municipal building, health, and sanitary codes; zoning regulations; mortgage laws and practices; and city planning. Restrictive regulations often discourage housing construction.

3. Encouraging families to rent space or to convert houses into multiple dwellings, where zoning laws permit.

4. Making awards or providing other recognition for achievement in the field of home building.

5. Providing opportunities for a public discussion of the desirability of using federal or other government aid for housing.

6. Promoting legislation to remove unnecessary legal obstacles to a community's building program.

TRAFFIC CONTROL

Many American towns and cities today find not only their economic welfare but the quality of living itself threatened by traffic jammed streets, inadequate parking facilities, street and highway accidents, and accelerating withdrawal of business from areas that people find almost impossible to reach.

Mushrooming suburban shopping centers tax municipal police, fire, sanitation, and other servives. These centers are usually in areas of low land and property assessment. Main Street still supplies a major part of the revenue for these municipal services. This tax base has been seriously weakened by failure of municipalities to control traffic.

GENERAL TRAFFIC CONTROL. Volunteer groups, while recognizing over-all traffic control to be a technical, engineering problem, have made important contributions to its solution. They have called official and public attention to the seriousness of the situation. Their public education programs and other support often have pointed the way to more adequate control.

Successful organization traffic-control activities, many of which may be adaptable to your community, include:

1. Promoting municipal government reforms such as measures fixing responsibility for traffic control.

2. Securing technical assistance in arranging for better traffic control.

3. Initiating and supporting a traffic council or other volunteer organization for continuing study, and support of official measures.

4. Contributing man power and other resources to official or cooperative studies of local traffic-control needs.

5. Publicizing results of traffic surveys through organization and public meetings, radio and television programs, newspaper releases, and other media.

6. Contributing to education and promotion measures to secure public acceptance of necessary changes such as grid systems; walk-light, and other restrictions; staggered store hours; special privileges for delivery truck drivers before peak traffic; and new intersection designs.

7. Providing opportunities for public consideration of important questions such as the desirability of using federal and state aid for urban highways.

PARKING. Organizations have an impressive record of action in behalf of more adequate parking facilities. They have effectively promoted stricter adherence to time limit regulations, secured adoption of parking meter systems, and establishment of nonparking streets. In some communities they have acquired vacant lots and operate parking lot businesses.

Other volunteer group projects which have proved successful include the following:

1. Securing municipal regulation of parking lots and garages: the size and location of entrances and exits, financial responsibility, posting of rates, lighting, and the qualifications of attendants.

2. Distributing maps giving locations, rates, and other information about parking facilities.

3. Organizing volunteer work crews to clear vacant lots or to grade existing parking areas or otherwise make them more serviceable.

4. Arranging for public discussions of controversial questions such as the relative merits of privately and publicly owned and operated parking facilities, and the desirability of assessing benefited property owners to acquire off-street parking space.

TRANSIT. Contributing to the traffic-control problem in many towns and cities is the fact that 60 to 80 per cent of working people and shoppers must be accommodated by public transit. In 1953, over 16 billion passengers were carried on bus and streetcar lines.

Organizations are joining with officials in measures to secure better schedules. They are assisting transit companies in determining routes. They participate in surveys to relocate stops, and are helping to relate routes and stops to the over-all traffic-control problem.

Traffic-control information, and study and promotion material of excellent quality are available from sources such as the Chamber of Commerce of the United States, the American Automobile Association, and the United States Department of Commerce, listed at the close of this chapter.

COMMUNITY BEAUTIFICATION

Important to civic development of any town or city is its physical appearance. A beautiful community draws business from the area and from tourists, attracts new businesses and industries, develops a civic pride that results in greater citizen interest and participation in public affairs, and provides an environment conducive to the fullest possible individual development.

CLEANUP, PAINT-UP, FIX-UP. Among successful measures to make communities more attractive are cleanup, paint-up, and fix-up activities. Some are short-term, individual projects, such as renovation of a public building, undertaken with the man power and other resources of a particular group. Others are organized as community campaigns, with the widest possible citizen participation, during a week usually designated as Cleanup Week.

Most Cleanup Weeks are held in late April or early May. Public interest is aroused through a carefully planned and directed promotion campaign, launched several weeks in advance. Checklists are furnished school children to be used as guides for home improvement.

Cleanup Week often is given a dramatic start. The following measures were used by the Junior Chamber of Commerce of Milwaukee. A Kick-Off Broadcast featured a round-table discussion among city officials and Jaycees. Officials and members donned street cleaners' uniforms to sweep city streets. News photographers made a survey of alleys and backyards, and documented visits of health department and other officials. The razing of an old barn spotlighted the need for the removal of eyesores. A television broadcast demonstrated city sanitation equipment and facilities. Jaycees and other volunteers painted a firehouse. Thirty-five painters blitz painted a house in 35 minutes.

Your group may take advantage of interest aroused during a cleanup drive to urge that a City Beautiful Commission be established to carry out a year-round program.

An excellent single-project beautification effort was carried out by Rotarians in DeSota, Missouri. Ten acres of the local burial ground were covered with weeds, vines, and untrimmed shrubbery. On three successive Tuesdays, volunteers recruited by the Rotary Club cut grass, pruned bushes, and sickled and raked the grounds. Impressed townspeople contributed funds to continue the work, and a citizens' committee was formed to plan and supervise permanent cemetery maintenance.

OTHER PROJECTS. Frequently organizations establish and maintain municipal parks and gardens. In San Jose, California, for example, the Santa Clara Rose Society, with the cooperation of the city government, established a five-acre rose garden. The Rotary Club contributed a reflecting pool. In Westfield, Massachusetts, organizations contribute to the maintenance of a "grandmother's garden." The Junior Chamber of Commerce of Mobile, Alabama, planted azalea growing beds, from which some 40,000 plants each year are distributed to citizens interested in making their homes more attractive. This project resulted in the development of the famous Azalea Trail.

Organization interest in beautifying towns and cities frequently has resulted in very effective community promotion. Ocala, Florida, for example, became known as The Petunia City because of the Garden Club's campaign to popularize the growing of that flower. Smyrna, Georgia, became The Jonquil City of the South when a businessmen's club planted 50,000 bulbs in parks and along streets.

Other beautification projects include conducting service station, store, and yard and garden contests; sponsoring flower shows to encourage flower growing in the community; planting shade trees along streets and highways, in parks, and on submarginal land; promoting legislation to control roadside advertising; landscaping and planting school grounds, bus terminals, and other public areas; cleaning up stream and lake sides; establishing a community forest; renovating railroad stations and landscaping surrounding grounds; and sponsoring the community's participation in programs for the development of regional scenic attractions.

ECONOMIC DEVELOPMENT

All the development activities suggested in this chapter pay dividends in a more prosperous community. Your group, however, may play a more direct role in the economic development of your community and region through programs carried out in cooperation with the Chamber of Commerce and other business and industrial associations.

Organizations primarily interested in economic welfare commonly have general objectives such as the following: to improve the physical facilities of the community as a prerequisite for better business, to control and direct fringe area development and redevelopment of other areas, to promote retail trade, to develop tourist trade, to establish a balanced and stable industry, and to contribute to the growth of the region on which the community depends.

What can your group do to help make possible the achievement of these objectives?

PHYSICAL FACILITIES. A community's physical facilities are directly related to its prosperity and well-being. Business and industry need assured water supply and adequate power. Workers will not take jobs unless they can find homes, and developers cannot supply homes unless sanitation and other services are available. Farmers must have storage and marketing facilities. Prospective newcomers to the community look for good schools, hospitals, fire and police protection, recreation, and other facilities.

Volunteer groups are cooperating with municipal governments to clear up the enormous backlog of public works and to speed renovation projects. They are sponsoring public forums and other education programs. They are helping to measure public attitudes, and to determine public needs. They are supporting bond issues. Their representatives serve on numerous citizens advisory committees on public works.

In addition to this support of public works programs, groups meet many immediate needs through projects carried out with their own resources: building emergency landing strips, air-marking the area, donating public drinking fountains, furnishing street signs, providing public rest rooms, supplying benches and bus-stop shelters, and furnishing wastepaper and trash receptacles. Similar projects are suggested in other chapters.

FRINGE AREAS. Many communities today are facing serious financial problems because of shifts of both population and business to fringe areas. It is estimated that fully 50 per cent of new residential construction, for example, is now outside incorporated limits.

Offer the support of your group to municipal officials, business, industry, and other organizations concerned with suburban planning and development. Join other groups in an education campaign in rural areas to bring about appreciation of planned land use. Promote adoption of realistic, modern zoning ordinances and building codes. Interpret zoning ordinances at organization and public meetings, and through the press, radio, and television.

RETAIL TRADE. The economic health of many communities is directly dependent on maintenance of a high level of retail trade. Promotion of retail trade, therefore, should not be considered the exclusive concern of the Chamber of Commerce or other businessmen's groups.

Frequently organizations participate in celebrations of special occasions that stimulate trade. For example, the Hot Springs' Gift to Its Yule Visitor, an annual Christmas Eve program of pageantry and caroling, is an interorganization event climaxing a week of community activities. It draws tens of thousands of buyers to Hot Springs every year.

Projects carried out for other purposes help promote business. Sponsorship of a summer theater, sports events, water regattas, expositions, carnivals, outdoor fashion shows, and similar events draw large crowds from surrounding areas.

TOURIST PROMOTION. Closely related to the encouragement of retail business are activities to help develop the sports, recreation, scenic, and other resources of communities as attractions for tourists and other visitors.

The record of organization achievement is an impressive one. In Pensacola, Florida, for example, the Junior Chamber of Commerce, the Lions Club, the Anglers Club, and the Chamber of Commerce constructed one of the nation's most beautiful roadside parks, with facilities for over 400 automobiles, a clubhouse, a dance patio, and other attractions.

Another monument to organization interest in making communities and regions more attractive to tourists is the modern concrete highway leading to a magnificent view of Cumberland Falls in Kentucky. The falls were first opened to motorists by hundreds of volunteer workers mobilized by the Kiwanis Club of Corbin, Kentucky. This volunteer effort led to the construction of the modern highway officially named The Kiwanis Trail.

Tourist promotion activities especially appropriate for non-business organizations are those to make communities courtesy conscious. Organizations aid in the planning and direction of panel-discussion meetings of key personnel of hotels, restaurants, service stations, stores, and other establishments serving tourists. Chambers of Commerce and other groups sometimes offer "courtesy" and "service" courses to equip citizens to sell the attractions of their community and region. In some states, these organizations have utilized the services of state vocational education departments in planning and conducting such courses. Interest in a movement to make each citizen a salesman for his community may be aroused by quizzes. The Wenatchee, Washington, Chamber of Commerce distributed such a quiz entitled, "Information or Misinformation—What Do You Serve Our Visitors?"

In some places, awards have been made to policemen, gas station attendants, salespeople, and others who distinguish themselves through acts of courtesy to visitors. In some resort areas, an annual off-season party is given for the employees of concerns catering to tourists. Speeches emphasize the value of courtesy for the tourist trade, and awards are presented to individuals who have shown special consideration to visitors.

Making tourists and new residents feel more at home in the community is another kind of activity appropriate for nonbusiness organizations. Newcomers frequently are invited to meetings. Publicity committees issue releases announcing the presence of visitors in the community. Some groups conduct good-will tours and organize motorcades to points of interest.

In some towns and cities, clubs have been organized to help assimilate new residents. In Caspar, Wyoming, a Newcomers Club has been active for several years. Women members welcome new residents, invite them to meetings, and arrange dessert luncheons, teas, barbecues, pot-luck suppers, dances, and other social events.

Other representative tourist promotion activities include:

1. Establishing and manning a tourists' information center; supplying maps, pictures, and information about accommodations, recreation opportunities, and service facilities.
2. Installing highway signs welcoming visitors.
3. Forming a corps of young ladies for tourist-aid work.
4. Sponsoring fishing derbies, outdoor pageants, song festivals, and other events to attract visitors.

INDUSTRIAL DEVELOPMENT. Despite full production and employment generally, there are areas of surplus labor in America. Many towns and cities, too, are experiencing a need for industrial diversification—for spreading the economic base so that prosperity is not so completely dependent on a single or a very few industries. Other communities are seeking to attract new industries.

Your organization will find ready assistance for study and other industrial development programs from sources such as the Chamber of Commerce of the United States, federal and state employment agencies, state economic development agencies, the United States Department of Commerce, and the United States Department of Labor. Public utilities, railroads, airlines, and other private enterprises frequently offer consultation and material aid to programs to encourage location of new industries or expansion of established concerns.

REGIONAL DEVELOPMENT. Volunteer group interest has given a tremendous impetus to regional, state-wide, and interstate development movements. While such movements often are under the auspices of county and state development boards and state Chambers of Commerce, their planning and implementation is on a local level, dependent for success on groups such as yours.

A spectacular wave of interest in better community living swept through Georgia, Tennessee, Alabama, and Virginia. According to Nation's Business, the movement had its beginnings when community organizations in Knoxville offered awards to farmers for improved farm practices and increased production. The idea was adopted by volunteer groups in other towns and cities. It grew to include general community development, with awards going to neighborhoods, hamlets, towns, and cities as well as to individuals. Municipal departments, newspapers, churches, state agencies for agricultural and industrial development, business, and industry joined civic groups in helping towns and cities make the most of their resources and facilities. Professional field personnel, background material, development guides, and other aids were made available by utilities and other concerns.

Communities underwent amazing transformations. Modern sanitation systems replaced primitive facilities; public water supplies eliminated unsanitary, uncertain shallow wells; recreation programs for youth and adults were introduced; homes were painted; eyesores were torn down; company houses were renovated through labor-management cooperation; schools were repaired and new ones built; volunteer group interest gave new effectiveness to law-enforcement agencies; objectionable roadside resorts were purchased and converted to wholesome recreation use; far-reaching reforms were brought about in the county poor farms and other institutions; and rural roads were made passable at all seasons.

In Georgia, 232 communities entered a Better Home Town contest the first year. Attesting to the lasting effect on long-range community development in that state is the fact that four years later 197 of these towns and cities had continuing programs of action for better facilities and services in fields such as traffic control, housing, community beautification, and economic development.

Industry has been attracted to such areas, bringing a high level of material well-being and lasting security to communities that for generations had been in an economic depression.

COMMUNITY PROMOTION. Many activities initiated and supported by organizations have as their primary purpose the publicizing of the community as a good place in which to live, to work, to do business, to raise families, and to find recreation.

Your group can play an important part in community-wide promotion events such as anniversary celebrations, and special days and weeks such as Oil Day in Nacona, Texas; Dairy Day in Bellefontaine, Ohio; and Farmer Appreciation Week in Effingham, Illinois.

These events require long-term preparation, effective publicity, and a careful scheduling of events. Planning groups usually include municipal officials, church leaders, school heads, industrial management, and labor leaders, as well as the heads of community organizations.

Illustrative of the varied program of such affairs was the Centennial Celebration of Ilion, New York, as reported in the October, 1952, issue of *The American City*. Among the features were a whisker contest, exhibits, parades, special Kids' Day events, special church services, inspection tours of city facilities, plant tours, the Miss Ilion contest, a carnival, a Fun Parade, a pageant, radio and television programs, a block dance, fireworks, street decorations, softball and other games, a band concert, a field day, a family picnic, special theater programs, and special sales days.

Other effective promotion activities include distributing brochures describing your community's attractions through hotels, motels, restaurants, service stations, and other outlets; sponsoring booths at county and regional fairs and expositions; arranging group visits to events in other communities; and sponsoring exhibits and displays at railroad and bus terminals.

SOURCES OF AID

American Automobile Association, Mills Building, 17th St. and Pennsylvania Ave., N. W., Washington 6, D. C. A major source of pamphlets, manuals, and guides in the field of traffic planning and regulation. Offers a model parking lot and garage regulatory ordinance, and a model enabling statute. Description of aids available.

American City Magazine Corporation, 470 Fourth Ave., New York 16, N. Y. Publishes *The American City*, a monthly magazine. Contents include background articles about defense, traffic, parking, lighting, sanitation facilities, and housing; reports of successful community and regional development programs; and reviews of books, municipal reports, catalogues, and other literature in the field of community development.

American Country Life Association, Inc., 800 South Michigan Ave., Chicago 5, Ill. A clearing house for information and ideas for improvement of rural communities. Has pamphlets about such concerns as rural health, economic development, education, the rural church, and government.

American National Theatre and Academy (ANTA), 245 West 52nd St., New York 19, N. Y. Maintains a Department of Community and Industrial Showmanship. Supplies theatrical and technical personnel, and guidance for community celebrations such as anniversaries, expositions, and conventions.

American Planning and Civic Association, 901 Union Trust Building, Washington 5, D. C. Maintains an information and counseling service for communities interested in city planning and improvement programs. Reports of committees on parks, roadside improvement, and other areas are available.

American Public Health Association, Committee on Hygiene of Housing, 1790 Broadway, New York 19, N. Y. Literature includes material on neighborhood planning.

American Society of Planning Officials, 1313 East 60th St., Chicago 37, Ill. Provides technical advice. Publishes reports on subjects such as drive-in theaters, architectural control, municipal auditoriums, urban redevelopment, and off-street parking; background material; and texts for children and youth. ASPO Newsletter, the official monthly publication, includes material of interest to nonprofessional planners. Has Guides to Community Planning, a 40-page booklet, and Motion Pictures on Planning and Housing, a selected, annotated listing.

American Transit Association, 292 Madison Ave., New York 17, N. Y. Free pamphlets about the problem of municipal traffic congestion and the relation of public transit to its solution. List of publications available.

Association of State Planning and Development Agencies, 1313 East 60th St., Chicago 37, Ill. Publishes a mimeographed Directory of State Planning and Development Agencies.

Automotive Safety Foundation, 700 Hill Building, Washington 6, D. C. Pamphlet materials include a study of the financing of parking facilities in 27 towns and cities.

Chamber of Commerce of the United States, 1615 H St., N. W., Washington 6, D. C. The major source of aid for community development programs. Local chambers welcome the cooperation of other volunteer groups, and are important sources of information. Program suggestions and project reports available from local chamber or from national headquarters cover fields such as city planning, utilization of community resources, industrial development and redevelopment, community promotion, community-regional relations, traffic control, zoning and other codes, housing, slum clearance, and public works. Especially useful is Trade Promotion Events, a loose-leaf folder of project reports. Bibliographies of materials and descriptions of chamber programs are available.

Citizens Planning and Housing Association, 319 North Charles St., Baltimore 1, Md. Has available pamphlets describing the Baltimore Plan for slum clearance and enforcement of housing regulations.

Civil Aeronautics Administration, Department of Commerce, Washington 25, D. C. Provides consultation and other aid in planning, designing, constructing, operating, and maintaining community airports. Free loan films, available from regional offices, include *Our Town Builds an Airport*, an explanation of the technical and financial assistance available from the Civil Aeronautics Administration. Listing of publications and free loan films is available.

Committee for Kentucky, 306 South Third St., Louisville 2, Ky. Has pamphlets about how to determine community present and future needs, and how to organize and direct community resources to meet them. Reports of successful action in Kentucky suggest project ideas.

Eno Foundation for Highway Traffic Control, Saugatuck, Conn. Conducts research. Furnishes free monographs on traffic engineering, and a pamphlet on parking authorities. Publishes *Traffic Quarterly.*

General Electric Company, Lamp Division, Nela Park, Cleveland 12, Ohio. Offers a pamphlet, *How Your Community Can Conduct a Christmas Lighting Contest.*

Housing and Home Finance Agency, Washington 25, D. C. Technical and popular manuals and other pamphlets available. Subjects include information on the Housing Act, community responsibility for housing, housing aid for veterans, slum clearance, urban redevelopment, and construction techniques.

Institute for Urban Land Use and Housing Studies, Columbia University, Morningside Heights, New York 27, N. Y. Publishes studies on problems of urban land use and housing.

Institute of Traffic Engineers, 211 Strathcona Hall, New Haven 11, Conn. Conducts research and promotes improvement in street and highway arrangements. Publishes periodic reports, and *Traffic Engineering*, a monthly.

International City Managers' Association, 1313 East 60th St., Chicago 37, Ill. Publishes *The Municipal Year Book*, a major source of statistical and other information about municipal government and activities in areas such as planning and zoning, housing, traffic control, public works, and parks and recreation. Includes extensive and authoritative listings of current sources of information in these areas.

League of Women Voters of the United States, 1026 17th St., N. W., Washington 6, D. C. Has low cost pamphlet discussions of community needs, adequate planning procedures, and how to translate planning into action for better community living.

National Association of Home Builders of the United States, 1028 Connecticut Ave., N. W., Washington 6, D. C. Sponsors a program of community action to check slum development and to rehabilitate substandard areas. Free literature includes a detailed procedure outline, progress reports, and pamphlets useful in public education programs.

National Association of Housing Officials, 1313 East 60th St., Chicago 37, Ill. Maintains research, and offers information and counseling services to public and semipublic agencies and individuals concerned with low rent housing. Description of services and publications available.

National Association of Real Estate Boards, Committee on Rehabilitation, 1737 K St., N. W., Washington 6, D. C. Has available A *Primer on Rehabilitation under Local Law Enforcement*, a low-cost handbook for citizen action.

National Automobile Dealers Association, 1026 17th St., N. W., Washington 6, D. C. Offers pamphlet reviews of pressing traffic and parking problems, and suggestions for their solution.

National Clean Up—Paint Up—Fix Up Bureau, 1500 Rhode Island Ave., N. W., Washington 5, D. C. Offers free manuals on how to organize a clean-up campaign, pamphlet reports of successful projects, publicity aids, and other material.

National Committee on Traffic Law Enforcement, 1704 Judson Ave., Evanston, Ill. Carries on research. Offers field-consultant services to community groups.

National Fire Protection Association, 60 Batterymarch St., Boston 10, Mass. Provides posters and other material for the promotion of clean-up campaigns.

National Planning Association, 1606 New Hampshire Ave., N. W., Washington 9, D. C. Publishes a series of pamphlet reports useful in city planning and improvement programs.

National Public Housing Conference, Inc., 1015 15th St., N. W., Washington 5, D. C. An organization of groups interested in slum clearance and low rent housing. Sponsors forums and conferences. Publishes *Public Housing Progress* monthly, and issues special reports.

National Roadside Council for the Protection and Development of Roadside Beauty, 119 East 19th St., New York 3, N. Y. Promotes restriction of advertising, and rural zoning. Offers the results of state and regional surveys. Publishes a monthly *Roadside Bulletin*, and informational pamphlets.

National Shade Tree Conference, Department of Horticulture, Ohio State University, Columbus, Ohio. Promotes the conservation and wider use of shade trees to beautify communities. Publishes *Arborists News*, a monthly.

New Hampshire State Planning and Development Commission, State House Annex, Concord, N. H. *So—You Want a New Industry?* presents the case histories of 51 communities. Includes a description of industrial foundations, and the organization and operation of a community industrial development program.

Pennsylvania State Chamber of Commerce, 222 North Third St., Harrisburg, Pa. Materials include a practical guide for community development planning.

Public Administration Service, 1313 East 60th St., Chicago 37, Ill. Publications include books and pamphlets relating to housing, urban redevelopment, planning, traffic control, and parking. A catalogue of publications is available.

Public Housing Administration, 1201 Connecticut Ave., N. W., Washington 25, D. C. Offers free eight-page illustrated folder on public housing.

Regional Plan Association, Inc. of New York, 205 East 42nd St., New York 17, N. Y. Bulletins include a description of municipal off-street parking systems in the New York metropolitan area.

Superintendent of Documents, United States Government Printing Office, Washington 25, D. C. Has available *Local Development and Enforcement of Housing Codes*, and suggested land subdivision regulations, published by the Housing and Home Finance Agency; and suggestions for long-range programming of public works prepared by the National Resources Planning Board.

United States Department of Commerce, Washington 25, D. C. Has available model traffic ordinances, a manual on uniform traffic control devices, and information about federal aid for urban highways. Provides background information and survey forms for organizations interested in evaluating community industrial resources, facilities, services, labor supply, and markets.

United States Department of Labor, Washington 25, D. C. Offers technical assistance to community employment and economic development programs. Materials include reports of volunteer group projects. Annotated listing of pamphlets is available.

Urban Land Institute, 1737 K St., N. W., Washington 6, D. C. Booklets about subjects such as subdivision regulations and their relation to land development, and financing street and utility installations in new residential areas.

W. E. Upjohn Institute for Community Research, 709 South Westnedge Ave., Kalamazoo 4, Mich. Publishes pamphlets suggesting community development projects.

SOME SOURCES OF FILMS AND FILM INFORMATION

Allied Chemical and Dye Corporation, 40 Rector St., New York 6, N. Y.
Free loan films include *The Longest Mile*. Shows how a community
group can cooperate with officials in securing better roads. Description
available.

Bailey Films, Inc., 6509 DeLongpre Ave., Hollywood 28, Calif. Rental
films include *What Is a City?* Through pictures, inserts, and anima-
tion, film explains how cities developed to meet needs of people. Provides an understanding of the basic structure of community life. Description available.

Caterpillar Tractor Company, Peoria 8, Ill. Free loan films include a
history of the development of highways in America, and a discussion
of modern sewage-disposal systems. Catalogue available.

Citizens Development Committee, Federal Reserve Bank Building, Cin-
cinnati, Ohio. Has free loan film, *This Is Our City*, that dramatizes
traffic congestion and slum conditions to arouse interest in city planning. Description available.

Encyclopaedia Britannica Films, Inc., 1150 Wilmette Ave., Wilmette,
Ill. Rental films include *Growth of Cities*, an explanation of factors
that influence community development, various types of city plans,
and current trends in city planning; and *The Living City*, a demonstration of what citizens can do to make their communities what they
want them to be. Descriptions available.

General Electric Company, Advertising and Sales Promotion, 1 River
Road, Schenectady 5, N. Y. Free loan films include *Lifestream of the
City*, a demonstration of the importance of transportation to a modern
city; *Going Places*, a review of urban transit problems and some solutions; and others about water and sewage systems. Catalogue available.

Modern Talking Picture Service, Inc., 45 Rockefeller Plaza, New York
20, N. Y. Free loan subjects include *Big Little Things*, a retail-sales
training film; *The Big Kitchen*, a travelogue featuring local civic celebrations; and *Enterprise*, how a Southern ghost town recovered prosperity. Catalogue of free loan films produced especially for community group use is available.

National Motion Picture Company, West Main St., Mooresville, Ind.
Nominal rental films include *Every Drop a Safe One*, an explanation

of how a modern water system safeguards the health of a community. Description available.

Princeton Film Center, Inc., Carter Road, Princeton, N. J. Rental films include *The Cape Ann Story*, a 30-minute sound dramatization of a community's economic and social revival. Full description available.

Purdue University Film Library, Lafayette, Ind. Rental films include the 11-minute *Keep Up with Traffic*, an explanation of how dangerously crowded highways can be made safer by engineering. Description available.

Thomas J. Barbre Motion Picture Productions, 1215 East Virginia Ave., Denver 9, Colo. Films include the low rental *Water and the City*, a detailed explanation of the water system of a representative small town. Description available.

University of Southern California, Audio Visual Services, 3518 University Ave., Los Angeles 7, Calif. Low rental films include *And Ten Thousand More*, a dramatic demonstration of how bad housing affects the whole community. Catalogue available.

Westinghouse Electric Corporation, Film Division, Box 868, 511 Wood St., Pittsburgh 30, Pa. Free loan subjects include home and community planning. Catalogue available.

Wilding Picture Productions, Inc., 1345 Argyle St., Chicago 40, Ill. Information about *By Jupiter!*, which presents the story of how an ordinary man becomes wisely selfish when he learns to be courteous. Sponsored by Marshall Field and Company for use in an employee training program. Useful in tourist trade promotion.

CHAPTER 21

National Security

THE MILLIONS of Americans organized in volunteer groups throughout the nation are of tremendous importance to the nation's security. Community leadership and organization know-how, so effective in meeting local health, safety, education, and other problems, is now being applied to the job of making America secure against foreign aggression.

In both world wars community organizations were of inestimable service in promoting the sale of bonds, collecting scrap material, procuring blood donors, supporting defense organizations such as the Red Cross and U.S.O., aiding in enlistment drives, and organizing community resources and facilities for war production.

Now once again, America is mobilizing its resources to meet the threat of aggression. Your organization, in its own community, has an important contribution to make to this defense effort. It can educate its members for survival, and place its individual member and group resources at the disposal of the director of civil defense. It can help in meeting the needs of the Armed Forces. It can cooperate with the community and command posts in maintaining the morale of Armed Forces in its area. It can promote the sale of Savings Bonds and help furnish blood bank donors. It can cooperate with other groups in meeting the special needs created by the defense effort, and give priority to other projects and programs that directly contribute to a stronger community.

THE UNITED STATES CIVIL DEFENSE CORPS

Civil defense is the mobilization of citizens in communities to minimize the effects of enemy action against people, plants, public facilities, and other installations; to maintain or restore these essentials to civilian life; and to preserve the maximum civilian support of the war effort.

Authorities admit that there can be no complete security for communities in the event of war. The probable effects of an atomic attack strain the imagination. The authoritative *The American City* listed 31 almost certain effects upon a strategic area, any one of which would be catastrophic: hundreds of simultaneous fires, disruption of all utilities and communications, whole populations in panic, thousands of people buried alive in collapsed buildings, and tens of thousands dead and injured.

Millions of citizen volunteers in all the towns and cities of America must be organized, trained, and kept in a state of readiness. New York City alone would require a corps of over one million civil defense workers to cope with the effects of an atomic attack.

The Armed Forces must be free to counter enemy forces in the field and to carry the war to the sources of his military power. The Act of Congress establishing the United States Civil Defense Corps in 1950 placed squarely upon the community the responsibility for its own defense. It must make provisions to minimize the effect of an attack, and restore its facilities. It must be prepared to come to the aid of other communities in critical target areas, through regional and state defense organizations.

With the exception of the Red Cross, no civilian volunteer organization has an official part in the Civil Defense Corps on the national level. The great federated community organizations, however, have played and are playing an important part in its success. They were influential in awakening the nation to a full realization of the danger that faced it, and to the urgent need for defense measures in every town and city. During the civil defense formative period, national officials held 64 conferences with leaders of groups with a combined membership of 60 million in over 200,000 local units. In May, 1951, over 1000 leaders of 286 national organizations attended a two-day conference in Washington to map a program of group support for civil defense. As a result of these conferences, two important assignments have been given organizations such as yours: membership and public education, and participation in and direct support of the Civil Defense Corps. The following are some specific and practical procedures for carrying out these assignments.

MEMBERSHIP EDUCATION. If every volunteer group in your community would adopt a program of membership education for individual survival and for effective participation in the community's organized effort to carry on under disaster conditions, virtually everybody would be reached either directly or indirectly.

In this emergency, the first responsibility of every citizen is to know how to survive and how to help his fellows to survive. Do your members know how to set up and equip a home shelter? Do they know the attack warning system? Has each decided what to do if an attack materializes while he is on the street, in his car, or at his desk or work bench? Can each give first aid or care for casualties in his home? Is each familiar with his community's defense organization and plans?

The following suggestions may be helpful in planning and carrying out your membership education program:

1. Ask your local civil defense director to present a series of talks about your community's problems, and measures taken to meet them; about arrangements with other communities for mutual assistance; and about the role the community is prepared to play in state and regional plans for mobile assistance to critical areas.

2. Make available to members all local materials such as alert cards, manuals, and organization charts, and civil defense literature available from the United States Government Printing Office and other sources listed at the close of this chapter.

3. Schedule meeting and small-group discussions of general and special local defense measures. Feature defense films at meetings. Devote a few minutes of each meeting to civil defense reports and announcements.

4. Ask the Red Cross to provide instructors for a formal course in first aid or home nursing, or urge members to take such courses offered in the community.

5. Have your committees in areas such as health, safety, education, and community development study civil defense needs in their fields.

PUBLIC EDUCATION. Civil defense authorities recognize that no defense organization, however well planned—no corps, however well trained, can do the job without a populace ready to meet their individual responsibilities to themselves, their families and neighbors, and to their community as a whole. There are too many who do not appreciate the dangers or who think it "can't happen here."

Offer the education resources of your group to the director of civil defense. With its background in public affairs, its prestige, and its sound knowledge and appreciation of local defense problems, it can be of immeasurable assistance. Practical activities carried out with the approval and cooperation of official defense authorities might include the following:

1. Sponsoring public meetings featuring civil defense.

2. Maintaining a speakers' bureau as a service to schools, churches, other community organizations, and institutions with lecture and assembly programs.

3. Arranging for exhibits and demonstrations of defense equipment and techniques.

4. Scheduling school, church, and other public showings of defense films.

5. Organizing groups to develop skills needed to make essential repairs, such as stopping leaks in water and gas lines.

6. Establishing a defense information center with the aid of libraries, schools and colleges, and local, state, and federal agencies. Such a center would act as a clearinghouse for educational materials such as books, pamphlets, films, filmstrips, recordings, bibliographies, and lists of speakers.

7. Cooperating with newspapers, and radio and television stations in atomic energy information.

8. Aiding in the publication and distribution of a local civil defense manual, and distributing "survival" booklets available from sources such as those listed at the close of this chapter.

9. Planning and supervising survival education for youth groups.

10. Sponsoring public quiz contests for adults, with local organizations or merchants donating prizes.

PARTICIPATION IN THE CIVIL DEFENSE CORPS. The second general Defense Corps assignment given volunteer organizations is to rally their members to full participation, and to place behind the Corps all their individual and group influence and resources.

Even in communities in which the Corps is well organized and fully manned, there is a continuing need for reserves, for relief personnel, for men, women, and young people to fill unexpected vacancies.

Ask a local or state civil defense official to talk to the members about the qualifications and duties of Civil Defense Corps health and welfare personnel, rescue crews, ground observers, engineering squads, fire fighters, traffic police, switchboard operators, messengers, wardens, truck and car drivers, mechanics, and the many other specialized workers whose efforts are coordinated in the over-all defense strategy.

Conduct a survey of business, professional, technical, crafts, and other experience so that you may be specific in offering the services of your members.

At meetings, feature reports about members' Defense Corps activities, and announcements and news releases by the director's office. Publicize individual member and organization participation through the newsletter, a defense-program scrapbook, and the annual report. Present special citations to those members who are outstanding in local defense activities.

Through letters from the president, or in open letters to the editor of your newspaper, give recognition to the important work the Defense Corps is doing. Invite officials to participate in public discussions of the program. Offer your meeting place for volunteer training programs, and for an emergency shelter area if it is suitable. Let your representatives in the state legislature and municipal government know you are interested in all possible support for the civil defense program.

Your group might initiate an intergroup evaluation of your community defense organization. Use the Federal Civil Defense Administration checklist as a guide for measuring the present adequacy of defense measures and progress toward more complete mobilization. It furnishes an excellent basis for an intergroup study and evaluation of the following aspects of the defense set up: legislation, organization, administration, finance, air-raid warning, shelter protection, engineering, communications, control activities, transportation, evacuation, warden services, law enforcement, health services, defense against special weapons, mutual aid, mobile support, supply services, and plant protection.

SUPPORT FOR THE ARMED FORCES AND RESERVE

Your community responsibility for national security goes beyond that of effectively organizing to meet an all-out attack. Citizens must join with those of other towns and cities in a grass-roots support of the Armed Forces.

The men and women who make up our Armed Forces are conditioned by the communities in which they lived. Their character and general education—whether they consider service in the Armed Forces a privilege, whether the Armed Forces are able to utilize fully their special skills and aptitudes, whether their morale is maintained—all depend to a great extent on community influence.

Your organization can help give the Armed Forces prestige; cooperate with schools, churches, and other youth service agencies in preinduction guidance; help recruiting stations meet special personnel needs; give support to local reserve units; help maintain the morale of servicemen abroad, in posts at home, and in veterans' hospitals; cooperate in the Red Cross blood-donor programs; and facilitate the defense production so essential for the maintenance of forces in the field.

ARMED FORCES PRESTIGE. Strengthening the prestige of the Armed Forces in your community is an important contribution to their support. Feature talks by officers; show documentary and other films. Invite servicemen to attend your meetings. Make them honorary members. Help schools and other youth group agencies plan assemblies to present the opportunities afforded by service in the Armed Forces. Urge newspaper editors, and radio and television managers to feature activities of local men and women in service. Sponsor tours for your members and other groups to military installations in the area.

Ask local recruiting stations for information about the availability of military units for parades in observances of patriotic occasions. Make arrangements for entertainment of such units, and, when necessary, their overnight housing. Sponsor your community's celebration of Armed Forces Day, the third Saturday in May.

YOUTH GUIDANCE. Your organization can help counter the idea, prevalent in many communities, that service in the Armed Forces checks or retards personal development. Enlist the aid of schools, churches, and youth agencies in giving young men and women an understanding of the purposes and functions of various branches of service, and the opportunities afforded by each. Help develop appreciation of the adjustments individuals must make when entering the service, and the threat to our national security that necessitates maintenance of a strong military establishment.

SUPPORT FOR ENLISTMENT PROGRAMS. Community organizations have a background of experience in support of enlistment programs. During World War II and later, when the United Nations intervened in Korea, they sponsored man-power committees, organized preflight and flight-training schools, cooperated with schools in preinduction training, helped recruiting personnel schedule talks to youth groups, compiled prospect lists of those with special training, sponsored radio announcements and newspaper advertisements, arranged for displays, and cooperated with other groups in promoting the Armed Forces through celebration of National Defense Week and Armed Forces Day.

This experience revealed the need to avoid duplication of effort. Your organization, after consulting the nearest recruiting station for information, might consider formation of a committee, made up of representatives from interested community groups, to develop plans for utilizing the special resources of each group.

SUPPORT FOR ARMED FORCES RESERVES. A major factor in the success with which America meets aggression is a civilian readiness developed through the reserve training programs operated by the Army, Navy, Marine Corps, and Air Force.

Your organization can support these reserve units by publicizing their purposes and activities, by securing cooperation of business and industrial management in arranging for training leaves, by cooperating with such units as the National Guard in promoting Open House at the Armory or other training quarters, and by cooperating with high schools and colleges in giving information about the National Guard.

ARMED FORCES MORALE. Those officially charged with developing and maintaining Armed Forces morale in the field, at foreign stations, or in training camps and military installations at home have recognized that service men and women need social activities, and an assurance that they will find places for themselves in their communities when their service is over.

Your organization can make definite contributions to the morale of selectees, of those at distant posts, of those recently separated from the services or hospitalized, and of the thousands who may be stationed at military posts in the area of your community.

Among the more dramatic programs in behalf of the morale of servicemen in overseas posts is the American Legion sponsored Hometown USA, which makes possible an exchange of tape-recorded personal messages between those in communities and the men and women stationed around the world.

Induction into the Armed Forces is a confusing and sometimes frustrating experience for young people. The amount and kind of help they receive prior to induction may determine how quickly they become effective in the Armed Forces, and what attitudes and prejudices they carry with them throughout their service careers.

Community groups have been prominent in going-away ceremonies at railroad stations and bus terminals. Other organization projects to develop morale among those about to enter service include distributing pocket-sized orientation booklets, offering standing invitations to use organization facilities and to attend luncheon and other meetings during leaves, furnishing a list of names and addresses of people who would like to correspond with servicemen, and supplying candy, cigarettes, books, magazines, and subscriptions to the local newspaper.

Recently broader orientation programs have been adopted with important consequences for selectee morale. The United States Junior Chamber of Commerce, with the approval of the Secretary of Defense, established a Salute the Recruit movement to help selectees wind up their civilian affairs and secure articles needed in service, prepare for the processing experience at induction centers, learn about opportunities available in the services, and get the advice of former servicemen.

The Morale of the Returned Serviceman. With selective service and continuing voluntary enlistments a probability for many years, a steady stream of young men will be flowing back into our towns and cities. Most of them will have had little or no work or other adult community-participation experience. They will, however, have special contributions to make to their communities because of their training. The effectiveness of these contributions depends on how quickly and satisfactorily they become readjusted. This is primarily a morale job. The returning serviceman must be made to feel that he belongs. What can volunteer groups do to meet this need?

If there is a veterans' organization in the community with a continuing program, offer to assist it. Enlist the aid of the Veterans Administration, the Red Cross Home Service Department, and other agencies. Collaborate with other interested groups in a Welcome Home program.

Many organizations are helping veterans find jobs. At the weekly luncheon of the Spokane Chamber of Commerce, each member finds at his place a card describing a returning serviceman. Information includes his name, age, military status, education, Army and civilian work experience, and interests. The member is asked to keep the card in his pocket for reference when employment opportunities come to his attention. The project has given hundreds of veterans not only jobs but the assurance that the community is interested in them.

THE MORALE OF HOSPITALIZED VETERANS. Community organizations are contributing to the morale of thousands of hospitalized servicemen. Volunteer workers representing over 300 groups have averaged over 300,000 hours of service each month in behalf of Veterans Administration hospital programs. Over 1000 women's groups affiliated with the General Federation of Women's Clubs have given financial support to morale-building projects ranging from purchase of wheel chairs, television sets, shawls, and other comforts to construction of a $60,000 Hostess House at the State Veterans' Home in Yountville, California, as a memorial to women veterans. Thousands of hours of service in veterans hospitals are given by American Legion and Auxiliary volunteers. Through Legion-sponsored rehabilitation programs, disabled veterans and their families are helped to resume normal lives.

RESPONSIBILITIES OF COMMUNITIES NEAR POSTS. Communities near camps and military installations share with Armed Forces officers the responsibility of developing and strengthening the morale of thousands of men and women.

After V-J Day, there was a tremendous letdown in the morale of servicemen. Everyone seemed concerned only with getting the boys home as quickly as possible. Servicemen's programs became veterans' programs. Then came war again, in a peculiar cold form, and the Korean "police action." Once more a small peacetime military establishment was expanded, and community organizations joined with other agencies in a concerted effort to rebuild morale.

America in peacetime has little precedent for an Armed Force in training that in 1953 was estimated at about 3,700,000 men and women. In 1938 there were only 300,000. In other respects, too, America finds itself with a different military force. Its members are released from duty for longer periods. They have almost four times as much money to spend as those who served in 1938. The range and variety of their interests and needs have increased. Speedy air, sea, and land transport carries them into areas hundreds of miles from their bases. Consequently communities far removed from a military establishment may receive a week-end influx of thousands of servicemen.

Over 70 per cent of these visitors are under 21. They come looking for diversion. Many seek the friendliness and guidance their families, friends, and churches offered them at home. They are lonesome, unsure of their purpose, and vulnerable to all the undesirable influences that would exploit them. If their attitudes, their characters, their spiritual fiber are to be developed for their own sakes and for the sake of a more secure nation, the people of their new communities must be family, friends, and spiritual counselors.

Volunteer organizations in such communities have a great opportunity to contribute to national security through initiating and supporting intergroup morale programs. The following activities suggest some of the ways by which the needs of servicemen can be met.

Encouraging church attendance through contacts with camps, the U.S.O., and other organizations; getting servicemen to become active as members of local church congregations; arranging classes in religious education; having young people's church groups invite servicemen and women to social functions; arranging for interchange of chaplains and community pastors; organizing a program of home entertainment for servicemen; and establishing church-parent and fostering servicemen-parent correspondence.

Arranging for special rates for service personnel at sports contests, dances, shows, and other community events; planning dances; providing hostesses for social affairs; arranging transportation to entertainment and recreation centers; making local club facilities available; and arranging for participation in community group meetings.

Facilitating attendance at lectures, exhibitions, and other cultural activities; conducting Know the Community tours; supplementing military post education programs; and supplying books, films, and other materials through local libraries.

Providing for individual participation in community amateur teams and leagues; including servicemen's teams in league schedules; and making sports equipment available.

Cooperating in suppression of prostitution and prevention of venereal disease; assuring hygienic and safe eating and entertainment places; and considering local regulation of bars and restaurants selling alcoholic beverages.

Helping servicemen find adequate off-post quarters; inspecting and approving "on leave" lodging; working against exploitation by landlords and hotels; finding accommodations for visiting relatives and friends; and encouraging needed housing construction programs.

Maintaining a schedule of talks about servicemen's needs; coordinating military and local police measures; and furnishing the public with information about the services and local military posts.

Establishing a community center to provide information about housing, the school system, churches, clubs, recreation, sports, entertainment events and facilities, historic and other points of interest, hospitals, welfare agencies, and hotel accommodations; supplying chaplains and other post officers with releases concerning community events of interest to servicemen; and providing travel and lounge facilities at railroad and bus terminals for servicemen and their families.

OTHER PROGRAMS CONTRIBUTING TO NATIONAL SECURITY

There is a danger that organizations, anxious to direct all their energies into channels that will lead directly to defense effectiveness, will lose sight of the need for less obviously related though very important security measures, for which their experience, resources, leadership, and committee organization so well qualify them. Projects in health, safety, vocational guidance and rehabilitation, labor-management cooperation, Americanism, and other areas, which have as their objectives a community strong in spiritual and material resources and vigorous in its democratic way of life, become even more important in times of great national emergencies.

Your national security committee might correlate activities in these various fields, urge that community defense be a factor in project selection, and show how many continuing programs may be given a greater national security emphasis.

Representative of the many other projects that contribute to the community's defense potential are: forming an organization or intergroup disaster committee in areas in which floods, storms, forest fires, or other threats periodically present themselves; sponsoring an intergroup labor-management committee to develop industrial harmony; surveying the community's resources, facilities, and man power available for new defense industry; promoting expansion of fire, police, health, and hospital facilities; providing adequate housing, recreation, welfare, day nursery, and other services for defense workers; calling attention to defense considerations in highway, zoning, and other city planning measures.

SOURCES OF AID

American Institute of Architects, 1741 New York Ave., N. W., Washington 6, D. C. Has material explaining some defense aspects of city planning.

American Legion, 1608 K St., N. W., Washington 6, D. C. National security program includes *Hometown USA*, a project to arrange for an exchange of recorded greetings between servicemen and their parents, wives, children, and friends. Description available.

American National Red Cross, 17th & D Sts., N. W., Washington 13, D. C., or local Red Cross chapters. The only volunteer organization officially affiliated with the Civil Defense Corps. Maintains classes in first aid and home nursing. Conducts the blood-donor program. Has pamphlet material to keep first-aid instructors posted on current techniques in civil defense fields. Information about free loan films available.

Boy Scouts of America, 2 Park Ave., New York 16, N. Y. Training-program materials stress individual survival and service to others in civil defense and other emergencies.

Camp Fire Girls, Inc., 16 East 48th St., New York 17, N. Y. Literature describes civil defense programs adaptable to any youth group.

Chamber of Commerce of the United States, 1615 H St., Washington 6, D. C. Suggests specific ways by which community organizations can participate in civil defense, as well as a description of the official national civil defense pattern. Information about programs relating to Armed Forces man power, economic mobilization, stockpiling of strategic and critical materials, location of defense plants, and plant protection. Material includes a selected bibliography.

Department of National Defense, Office of Public Information, Washington 25, D. C. A major source of aid for programs in behalf of national security. Literature describing the services offered by U.S.O. suggests activities appropriate for your organization's morale program. Furnishes program assistance for the celebration of Armed Forces Day. Arranges parade participation by units from area and district headquarters, and Coast Guard stations. Provides radio scripts, spot announcements, posters, and films.

Federal Civil Defense Administration, Public Affairs Office, Washington 25, D. C. The agency charged under the Civil Defense Act of 1950 with developing and furnishing to states and local governments the information, advice, and guidance necessary to organize effectively for defense. Has available an official guide, and other pamphlets and manuals for specific defense problems. Publishes *The Civil Defense Alert*, a monthly. Furnishes official education and training films for local civil defense organizations.

52 Association of New York, Inc., 840 Eighth Ave., New York 19, N. Y. An organization of professional and business men with units in several cities. Has information about unique projects to help disabled servicemen become part of their communities.

Girl Scouts of the United States of America, Program Department, 155 East 44th St., New York 17, N. Y. Civil defense literature suggests activities for your sponsored youth group.

League of Women Voters of the United States, 1027 17th St., N. W., Washington 6, D. C. Has available an inexpensive pamphlet abridgement of the Federal Civil Defense Administration's description of the organization and function of federal, state, and local civil defense organizations.

National C.I.O. Community Services Committee, 1776 Broadway, New York 19, N. Y. Has available pamphlet discussions of labor's role in civil defense, the blood-donor program, and the community effort in behalf of veterans and servicemen.

National Recreation Association, Inc., 315 Fourth Ave., New York 10, N. Y. Offers consultant services to communities planning recreation programs for servicemen. Answers inquiries, conducts studies, and publishes literature. Free pamphlets include *Community Recreation for Defense Workers, Emergency Recreation Service in Civil Defense, Off-Post Recreation for the Armed Forces,* and *What Community Recreation Programs Can Do for Service Women.*

National Social Welfare Assembly, Inc., 345 East 46th St., New York 17, N. Y. A federation of volunteer social agencies with which are affiliated many national organizations such as the A.F.L., C.I.O., National Urban League, Veterans of Foreign Wars, and Y.M.C.A. Through its Conference on Service to the Armed Forces and Veterans it offers aid to communities interested in the welfare and religious problems of servicemen and veterans.

Navy League of the United States, Mills Building, 17th and Pennsylvania Ave., Washington 6, D. C. Encourages community activities that publicize the achievements of the Navy. Literature available.

President's Committee on Religion and Welfare in the Armed Forces, Room 1045, Temporary Building "R," 4th and Jefferson Drive, S. W., Washington 25, D. C. Has available *Report of the National Conference on Community Responsibility to Our Peacetime Servicemen and Women.* Useful to community groups as a guide and checklist for surveying welfare and religious needs in the community; as background material for projects to arouse public interest in local

Armed Forces morale; and as material for speeches and discussion. Discusses the following areas of responsibility: religion, housing, health, family welfare, recreation, and education. *Community Planning for the Peacetime Serviceman* describes the general serviceman morale problem in the community, outlines steps by which the problem can be met, and describes the operation of a community-wide program. The President's Committee will forward requests for assistance to appropriate national organizations and government agencies.

Superintendent of Documents, United States Government Printing Office, Washington 25, D. C. Publishes a leaflet listing of current official government publications on civil defense. Subjects include planning community and state programs; the dangers of fire in an atomic attack; rescue, warden, welfare, and other special defense services; civil defense in the schools; shelter from atomic attack in existing buildings; women in civil defense; and what you should know about biological warfare.

United Defense Fund, Inc., 345 East 46th St., New York 17, N. Y. Organized to raise money more efficiently for Armed Forces and defense-worker welfare. Information about programs, free loan films, and other material is available.

United Service Organization (U.S.O.), 500 Fifth Ave., New York 36, N. Y. A federation of national organizations to encourage and aid local groups in programs to promote the welfare of servicemen. Cooperating agencies are the National Catholic Community Service, the National Jewish Welfare Board, the National Travelers Aid Association, the Salvation Army, Camp Shows, Inc., the Y.M.C.A. and the Y.W.C.A. Description of program may suggest project ideas and procedures.

United States Air Force, Department of Public Information, Washington 25, D. C. Pamphlet aid includes *The Airman and Your Community*, some suggested principles and programs for Air Force-community partnership on behalf of Air Force personnel and their dependents.

United States Treasury Department, Washington 25, D. C. Information about Savings Bonds. Free loan films are available from the Director of U. S. Savings Bonds Division, your state capital.

Valley Forge Foundation, Inc., 1 East 60th St., New York 22, N. Y. Sponsors Alert America convoys, which present a 45-minute show to acquaint communities with the dangers of an atomic attack, and with methods to meet it. Arranges exhibits and demonstrations that include films, dioramas, animated models, fire fighting and other civil defense equipment. Program is sponsored jointly by the Valley Forge

Foundation and the Federal Civil Defense Administration. Information about itineraries is available.

Veterans Administration Voluntary Service, National Advisory Committee, Washington 25, D. C. Helps organize community volunteer aid for hospitalized veterans. Furnishes information about organization representation on local advisory committees.

Women's Bureau, United States Department of Labor, Washington 25, D. C. Background and statistical information for programs to utilize the services of women in defense production. Describes jobs suitable for women. Explains how the Women's Bureau can aid local industry.

SOME SOURCES OF FILMS AND FILM INFORMATION

British Information Services, 30 Rockefeller Plaza, New York 20, N. Y. Has available low rental sound films on British volunteer defense organization experience in World War II, and on current preparation for atomic attack. Free *1954 Roundup of Civil-Defense Films and Film Strips* available.

Civil Aeronautics Administration, Washington 25, D. C. About 100 free loan films, including films on combat training, how air superiority was achieved in World War II, and the history of aviation. Descriptions available.

Cornell Film Company, 1501 Broadway, New York 36, N. Y. Films include *Pattern for Survival*, a detailed explanation of how planned civilian defense can counter fear and panic, and minimize the effects of an atomic attack. Description available.

Coronet Films, Coronet Building, Chicago 1, Ill. Offers a series of *Are You Ready for Service?* films. Subjects covered include similarities and differences between military and civilian life; military discipline; the historical background of the ideal of service to America; how to get ready for military service; the structure and functions of each of the services; and induction and training procedures. Catalogue available.

Department of National Defense, Office of Public Information, Washington 25, D. C. Has available a descriptive catalogue of hundreds of free loan and low rental films sponsored by the Armed Forces. Information includes addresses of Army area commands, Air Force Area Film Exchange Headquarters, and Navy districts, from which films may be obtained. Wide range of subjects includes induction and training procedures, the specialized services for men and women, how men and women may prepare for civilian careers while serving in the Armed Forces, and the Armed Forces in actual combat.

Department of the Air Force, Attention of the Control Film Library, your nearest Area Film Exchange Headquarters. Free loan films include subjects such as Air Force demonstrations; combat training; recreational, educational, and vocational-training activities; the vital part played by women in maintaining our air power; the important role of the Ground Observer Corps; the history of aviation; combat scenes from World War I and II, and the action in Korea; jet-fighter test flights; and morale programs carried out by community groups. Listing available.

Department of the Army, Commanding General, Attention of the Signal Officer, your nearest area command. Free loan films include subjects such as the role played by the Army in national security; training in all branches; recreational, educational, and vocational opportunities; research; demonstrations of the need for whole blood and how easily an individual can contribute; accounts of actual combat in all World War II theaters and in Korea; the story of the development of the American soldier from the beginnings of our nation; views of the United States Military Academy; experimental atomic blasts; aerial views of the bombing of Hiroshima and Nagasaki; views of atomic artillery and other advanced weapons; demonstrations of survival methods during an atomic attack; the role of the Army in disaster; and studies of the Soviet Union. Listing available.

Department of the Navy, Commandant, Attention of the District Public Information Officer, your nearest Naval district. Free loan films include subjects such as the peace-time activities of the Navy; the training of men and women; ships in actual combat in all World War II theaters, and in support of forces in Korea; the history of the Navy; and the Bikini atomic tests. Listing available.

Eastern Air Lines, Inc., Film Division, 10 Rockefeller Plaza, New York 20, N. Y. Free loan films include *Air Power Is Peace Power*, the story of the progress made in organizing an effective striking force to repel aggressor nations. Description available.

Encyclopaedia Britannica Films, Inc., 1150 Wilmette Ave., Wilmette, Ill. Rental films include civil defense subjects such as how a child may best protect himself at home, on the street, or at school, in the event of an atomic attack. Catalogue available.

Federal Civil Defense Administration, Public Affairs Office, Washington 25, D. C. Information about official education and training films for local civil defense programs.

General Electric Company, Advertising and Sales Promotion, 1 River

Road, Schenectady 5, N. Y. Free loan films include *A Is for Atom*, an animated color explanation of atomic energy. Description available.

McGraw-Hill Book Company, Inc., Text-Film Department, 330 West 42nd St., New York 18, N. Y. Information about *You Can Beat the A-Bomb*. Pictures the effect of an atomic explosion, and shows measures to be taken by civilians before, during, and after an attack.

National Film Board of Canada, 1270 Avenue of the Americas, New York 20, N. Y. Offers rental films about civil defense problems and procedures, and filmstrips for the training of civil defense workers. Catalogue available.

United States Coast Guard Headquarters, Public Information Division, Washington 25, D. C. Free loan films include the peacetime and wartime activities of the Coast Guard, enlisted men's training program, and life at the Coast Guard Academy. Listing available.

United States Navy, Motion Picture Section, Office of Public Information, Washington 25, D. C. Has information about free loan films available from district headquarters. Subjects include atomic bomb tests; the Navy's role in transporting, landing, and protecting troops in actual combat; the story of the Naval Reserve Officers Training Corps; the Navy's contribution to peace; life at the United States Naval Academy at Annapolis; naval combat; and a carrier in action off Korea.

United World Films, Inc., 1445 Park Ave., New York 19, N. Y. Free loan films illustrate the role the Red Cross plays in planning for and meeting disasters of all kinds; explain the relation of the Red Cross to the Civil Defense organization; and show volunteer canteen, entertainment, first-aid, blood-bank, transportation and other services. Other national security films include *Self-Preservation in an Atomic Attack*, a demonstration of the effects of blast, heat, and radiation, and what an individual should do to protect himself. Catalogue available.

University of Minnesota, Audio-Visual Education Service, Westbrook Hall, Minneapolis 14, Minn. Rental films include explanations of the training received in the Army, Navy, and Air Force reserve officers' program. Produced to stimulate interest in enrollment in R.O.T.C. programs. Description available.

Veterans Administration, Visual Aids Service, Office of Public Relations, Washington 25, D. C. Free loan sound films explain policies and programs, and report activities in behalf of the physical and spiritual welfare of those hospitalized. Annotated film listing available.

Appendixes

APPENDIX A

Special Days, Weeks, and Months

THE DATES of historic events, the birthdays of men and women who have made important contributions to our way of life, religious and other traditional observances, and special occasions created by proclamation or legislative action do not vary. The dates of other special days, weeks, and months may change from year to year.

Those responsible for planning meeting programs and service activities to be correlated with these observances should write early to the sponsors or sources of information listed to verify dates and to request program guides and materials. The chapters of this book may suggest other activities and sources of additional aid.

JANUARY

First week	Big Brother Week. Big Brothers of America, 1347 Broad Street Station, Philadelphia 3, Pa. To foster measures in behalf of boys who are fatherless, delinquent, or who for other reasons are in need of guidance.
First week	Universal Week of Prayer. National Council of the Churches of Christ in the U.S.A., 297 Fourth Ave., New York 10, N. Y.
2–31	March of Dimes. The National Foundation for Infantile Paralysis, 120 Broadway, New York 5, N. Y. To provide funds for research, education, epidemic aid, and care and treatment of infantile paralysis victims who need financial assistance.
The week that includes the birthday of Benjamin Franklin, January 17	National Thrift Week. National Thrift Committee, 121 West Wacker Drive, Chicago 1, Ill. To encourage prudent spending and regular savings among American families.

Last week, or first week in February	Youth Week (Christian Endeavor Week). United Christian Youth Movement, 79 East Adams St., Chicago 3, Ill. To emphasize the importance of youth to the church.

FEBRUARY

1	National Freedom Day. Presidential proclamation.
First Monday	National Children's Dental Health Day. American Dental Association, 222 East Superior St., Chicago 11, Ill. To educate the community to a sense of responsibility for the dental health of children, and to promote programs to make dental health education and care available to all children.
First or second Sunday	Race Relations Day. National Council of the Churches of Christ in the U.S.A., 297 Fourth Ave., New York 10, N. Y.
12	Abraham Lincoln's Birthday.
The week that includes February 8 and Lincoln's birthday	Boy Scout Week. Boy Scouts of America, 120 West 42nd St., New York 36, N. Y., and over 500 local councils. To celebrate the founding of the Boy Scouts of America on February 8.
11–18	American Heart Week. American Heart Association, Inc., 44 East 23rd St., New York 10, N. Y. To disseminate information about diseases of the heart and circulatory system; to organize support for programs of education, research, prevention, and care.
12–22 (The interval that includes the birthdays of Lincoln and Washington)	Americanism Week. United States Junior Chamber of Commerce, 21st and Main Sts., Tulsa 14, Okla. To give emphasis to the principles and ideals upon which America was founded.
12–22	National Defense Week. Reserve Officers Association of the United States, 2517 Connecticut Ave., Washington 8, D. C. To develop a public awareness of the necessity for adequate national defense.
14	Valentine's Day.

17–23 — Catholic Book Week. Catholic Library Association, Maryknoll Seminary, Glen Ellyn, Ill. To encourage the reading and writing of Catholic books, periodicals, newspapers, and pamphlets.

17–23 — National Crime Prevention Week. National Exchange Club, 335 Superior St., Toledo 4, Ohio. To stress the importance of crime prevention programs.

22 — George Washington's Birthday.

Starts the Sunday preceding Washington's birthday and closes the following Sunday — Brotherhood Week. National Conference of Christians and Jews, 381 Fourth Ave., New York 16, N. Y. To promote justice, amity, understanding, and cooperation among all groups.

MARCH

First week — National Save Your Vision Week. American Optometric Association, 707 Jenkins Building, Pittsburgh 22, Pa. To emphasize the relation of good vision to achievement in school, at work, and in the home.

1–31 — Red Cross Fund Drive. Presidential proclamation. Includes the special occasions of Red Cross Sabbath and Red Cross Sunday. American National Red Cross, 17th and D Sts., N. W., Washington 13, D. C.

16–22 — National Wildlife Restoration Week. National Wildlife Federation, 3308 14th St., Washington 10, D. C. To call attention to the need for conserving our natural resources.

17 — St. Patrick's Day.

17–22 — National Hobby Week. Hobby Guild of America, 550 Fifth Ave., New York 19, N. Y. To encourage hobbies as a worthy use of leisure, and as a measure to combat juvenile delinquency.

Last week — Jewish Youth Week. National Jewish Youth Conference and the National Jewish Welfare Board, 145 East 32nd St., New York 16, N. Y. To focus attention on the needs and problems of Jewish youth, and to encourage their participation in communal affairs.

March–April (The 30 days preceding Easter)	Easter Seal Drive. The National Society for Crippled Children and Adults, 11 South LaSalle St., Chicago 3, Ill. To raise funds for the furthering of the Society's program of education, research, and service.
March, April, or May (Dates determined locally)	Clean-Up, Paint-Up, Fix-Up Week. National Clean-Up—Paint Up—Fix Up Bureau, 1500 Rhode Island Ave., N. W., Washington 5, D. C. To safeguard health, promote safety, prevent fires, and improve property.

April

1–30	Cancer Control Month. Presidential proclamation. American Cancer Society, 47 Beaver St., New York 4, N. Y. To raise funds for furthering the Society's program of research, education, and service.
First week	National Conservation Week. National Life Conservation Society, 2239 Tiebout Ave., New York 57, N. Y. To promote measures to preserve wildlife and other natural resources.
9–15	National Sunday School Week. Laymen's National Committee, Vanderbilt Hotel, New York 16, N. Y. To urge American youth to attend a Sunday school of their own choice.
14	Pan American Day. Presidential proclamation. Organization of American States, General Secretariat, Pan American Union, Washington 6, D. C. Observed on the anniversary of the establishment of the International Union of American Republics by the First Inter-American Conference, in 1890. To publicize the bonds uniting the American republics, and to strengthen those bonds.
The week that includes Pan American Day	Pan American Week. See Pan American Day.
Last Wednesday	National Social Hygiene Day. American Social Hygiene Association, 1790 Broadway, New York 19, N. Y. To develop public appreciation of, and support for, social hygiene programs in the fields of education, venereal-disease control, and law enforcement.

24–30	National Mental Health Week. United States Public Health Service, Division of Mental Hygiene, Washington 25, D. C. To make known the facts about mental health, and to encourage local action.
Last week	Boys' and Girls' Week. Rotary International, 35 East Wacker Drive, Chicago 1, Ill. To arouse community interest in youth problems, and to emphasize the roles played by home, church, and school in youth development.
Last week, or first week in May	United States-Canada Goodwill Week. Kiwanis International, 520 North Michigan Ave., Chicago 11, Ill. To promote continued understanding and good will between the two countries.
Dates depend on date of Easter, during the period March 22–April 25	National Boys' Club Week. Boys' Clubs of America, 381 Fourth Ave., New York 16, N. Y. To publicize Boys' Club activities.

MAY

1	May Day.
1	Child Health Day. Presidential proclamation.
First week	National and Inter-American Music Week. National Recreation Association, 315 Fourth Ave., New York 10, N. Y. To foster music appreciation and participation in the community, and to emphasize its importance in education programs.
First week	National Home Demonstration Week. Extension Service, United States Department of Agriculture, Washington 25, D. C.
First week	National Family Week. National Council of the Churches of Christ in the U.S.A., 297 Fourth Ave., New York 10, N. Y.; Synagogue Council of America, 110 West 42nd St., New York 18, N. Y.; and National Catholic Welfare Conference, 1312 Massachusetts Ave., Washington 5, D. C. To stress the contribution of religion to the family, and of the religious family to society.

Early in month   National Hearing Week. American Hearing Society, 817 14th St., N. W., Washington 5, D. C. To arouse community interest in measures to prevent deafness, conserve hearing, and rehabilitate the hard of hearing.

6–12   Goodwill Week. Goodwill Industries of America, 1222 New Hampshire Ave., N. W., Washington 6, D. C. To promote programs to utilize the services of handicapped persons.

Second Sunday   Mother's Day. Presidential proclamation.

22   National Maritime Day. Presidential proclamation. American Merchant Marine Institute, Inc., 1701 K St., N. W., Washington 6, D. C.

The week that includes National Maritime Day   World Trade Week. Presidential proclamation. Sponsored by many national and local business organizations. Information: The Chamber of Commerce of the United States, 1615 H St., N. W., Washington 6, D. C.

19–25   Letters from America Week. Common Council for American Unity, Inc., 20 West 40th St., New York 18, N. Y. To combat communist propaganda about life in the United States through letters from individual Americans to individual Europeans.

Third Saturday   Armed Forces Day. Presidential proclamation. Military Order of the World Wars, 1700 Eye St., N. W., Washington 6, D. C.; the Navy League of the United States, Mills Building, Washington 6, D. C.; and the Air Force Association, 901 16th St., N. W., Washington 6, D. C. To cooperate with the Secretary of Defense in calling attention to the importance of the Armed Forces, and to develop active support for the Armed Forces.

24   Memorial Poppy Day. American Legion Auxiliary and the American Legion, Indianapolis 7, Ind. To honor the war dead and to aid disabled veterans and their families.

The week that includes Memorial Poppy Day   V.F.W. "Buddy" Poppy Week. Veterans of Foreign Wars of the United States, Broadway at 34th St., Kansas City 2, Mo. To finance aid for needy veterans and their dependents, widows, and orphans.

30   Memorial Day (Decoration Day). Presidential proclamation.

June

1–30   National Ragweed Control Month.

First Sunday   Children's Day. Commission on General Christian Education, the National Council of the Churches of Christ in the U.S.A., 79 East Adams St., Chicago 3, Ill.

14   Flag Day. Presidential proclamation. See National Flag Week.

The week   National Flag Week. Star-Spangled Banner Flag
that includes   House Association, Inc., 844 East Pratt St., Balti-
Flag Day   more 2, Md. To commemorate the anniversary of the birth of the flag.

Third Sunday   National Father's Day.

July

4   Independence Day. Presidential proclamation.

20–26   National Farm Safety Week. Presidential proclamation. National Safety Council, 425 North Michigan Ave., Chicago 11, Ill., and the United States Department of Agriculture, Washington 25, D. C. To call attention to rural accident problems and to encourage accident-prevention measures.

August

First Week   National Cerebral Palsy Week. United Cerebral Palsy Association, 50 West 57th St., New York 19, N. Y. To aid the cerebral-palsied in adjusting to society; to develop public appreciation of their problems; to establish public and private homes, schools, and workshops, and to secure competent staffs.

19   National Aviation Day. Presidential proclamation.

Dates include   National Air Races. Cleveland Air Foundation,
National   Union Commerce Building, Cleveland, Ohio. To
Aviation Day   further aviation interest and development in the United States.

September

First Monday	Labor Day. American Federation of Labor, 1625 Eye St., N. W., Washington 6, D. C.; and Congress of Industrial Organizations, 718 Jackson Place, Washington 6, D. C.
17	Citizenship Day. Presidential proclamation. To foster an appreciation of the privileges and responsibilities of citizenship.
Last week	Christian Education Week. Division of General Christian Education, the National Council of the Churches of Christ in the U.S.A., 79 East Adams St., Chicago 3, Ill. To give impetus to the fall launching of church education programs.
30	Gold Star Mothers Day. American Gold Star Mothers, Inc., 1507 M St., N. W., Washington 5, D. C. To honor mothers whose sons and daughters died in line of duty with the Armed Forces.
Dates set locally	Business-Industry-Education Days. Committee on Education, Chamber of Commerce of the United States, 1615 H St., N. W., Washington 6, D. C.

October

1–31	Red Feather Month (Community Chest Drive). Local Community Chest organizations. Information: Community Chests of America, 155 East 44th St., New York 17, N. Y.
5–11	National Employ the Physically Handicapped Week. Presidential proclamation. American Federation of the Physically Handicapped, National Press Building, Washington 4, D. C.
The week that includes October 9	Fire Prevention Week. Presidential proclamation. National Board of Fire Underwriters, 85 John St., New York 7, N. Y.; National Fire Protection Association, 60 Batterymarch St., Boston 10, Mass.; Chamber of Commerce of the United States of America, 1615 H St., N. W., Washington 6, D. C. To educate the public to an awareness of the seriousness of fires, and to encourage efforts in the fields of fire prevention and protection.

| 12 | Columbus Day. Presidential proclamation. |

19   Laymen's Sunday. Laymen's Movement for a Christian World, Room 1402, 347 Madison Ave., New York 17, N. Y. To encourage lay participation in church services.

20–26   National Bible Week. Laymen's National Committee, Vanderbilt Hotel, New York 16, N. Y. To foster a more widespread study of the Bible.

24   United Nations Day. Presidential proclamation. To commemorate the founding of the United Nations.

The week that includes United Nations Day   United Nations Week. American Association for the United Nations, 45 East 65th St., New York 21, N. Y. To develop public interest in and support for the United Nations.

The week that includes the birthday of Juliette Low, October 28   Girl Scout Week. Girl Scouts of the United States of America, 155 East 44th St., New York 7, N. Y. To celebrate the birthday of Juliette Low, founder of Girl Scouting, and to publicize the Girl Scout program.

31   Hallowe'en.

November

1   National Authors Day. The General Federation of Women's Clubs, 1734 N St., N. W., Washington 6, D. C. To arouse an interest in authors who have influenced the cultural and spiritual growth of America, and to encourage contemporary writers.

First week   American Art Week. American Artists Professional League, Carnegie Hall, 154 West 57th St., New York 19, N. Y. To arouse an interest in contemporary art through exhibits of community arts and crafts.

Varying period prior to Christmas   Christmas Seal Sale. National Tuberculosis Association, 1790 Broadway, New York 19, N. Y. To raise funds to advance the educational, case-finding, rehabilitation, and medical research programs of voluntary tuberculosis associations.

Dates vary | National 4-H Club Achievement Week. Extension Service, United States Department of Agriculture, Washington 25, D. C. To publicize the 4-H Club program, to stimulate further 4-H Club activity, and to relate 4-H Club interests to fields such as international relations.

11 | Armistice Day. Presidential proclamation.

The week that includes Armistice Day | American Education Week. The American Legion, 700 North Pennsylvania St., Indianapolis 6, Ind.; National Congress of Parents and Teachers, 600 South Michigan Boulevard, Chicago 5, Ill.; National Education Association, 1201 16th St., N. W., Washington 6, D. C.; and Office of Education, Department of Health, Education, and Welfare, Washington 25, D. C. To promote better education programs for American youth and to acquaint the public with the history, purposes, achievements, problems, and needs of the public schools.

The second or third week | Children's Book Week. Children's Book Council, 50 West 53rd St., New York 19, N. Y. To foster reading of good books at home, at school, and at the public library.

28 | United Defense Fund Day. United Defense Fund, 345 East 46th St., New York 17, N. Y. To finance national voluntary health and welfare services for members of the Armed Forces, defense production communities, and foreign relief essential for defense.

The fourth Thursday | Thanksgiving Day. Presidential and governors' proclamations.

DECEMBER

10 | Human Rights Day. General Assembly of the United Nations. Information: Department of Mass Communications, New York Office of UNESCO, United Nations Building, New York 17, N. Y.

25 | Christmas Day.

Parliamentary Procedure

THIS SECTION is designed as a concise guide to the language and forms of parliamentary procedure. Following the glossary of terms, the reader will find a brief explanation of how a motion is presented, considered, or amended. The concluding part of this Appendix outlines common steps of parliamentary procedure in the conduct of a meeting from start to finish.

A GLOSSARY OF COMMON TERMS

Adopt: To adopt, approve, or accept a report, resolution, or committee action is an endorsement of the statement or action by the organization. Customarily, minutes are "approved," reports are "accepted," and resolutions are "adopted."

Amend: To change a motion by adding, deleting, or substituting words or provisions.

Appeal: To ask the assembly to decide in a dispute over a decision made by the chairman.

Assembly: The group that has gathered to deliberate.

Chair: The presiding officer. To address the chair means to speak to the chairman. To be recognized by the chair is to receive permission to speak to the assembly.

Committee of the Whole: An assembly sitting as a committee so that it can informally discuss a subject without the usual restrictions limiting debate. When a group resolves itself into a committee of the whole, the formal meeting is discontinued officially, and the presiding officer gives up his position to a temporary chairman.

Debate: To discuss a motion.

Division: A division of the assembly may be requested when a member is uncertain about a vote taken orally or by a show of hands. When a division is called for, the chairman proceeds to take a second vote by having the members stand. When a motion contains several definite parts, a division of the question calls for separate consideration of each part.

Ex Officio: "By virtue of official position." A person who is a member of a committee or board by virtue of his office in an organization is termed an ex-officio member of that committee or board.

Expunge: To delete a motion or resolution or other objectionable matter from the minutes.

Floor: To be given the floor by the presiding officer is to be given the privilege of speaking before the assembly.

Lay on the Table: To set aside a motion or report for future consideration. A motion to lay on the table enjoys the highest priority among subsidiary motions and is neither amendable nor debatable.

Minutes: The official record of meeting proceedings.

Motions:

> *Main Motion:* One which introduces a subject for discussion for the first time.
>
> *Incidental Motion:* One growing out of a question already being considered, to be decided before further consideration of the first question.
>
> *Privileged Motion:* A motion so important that it demands the immediate attention of the group. It has precedence over all other motions. The privileged motions in order of precedence are (1) to adjourn; (2) to recess; (3) to raise a question of privilege; (4) to call for the order of the day.
>
> *Subsidiary Motion:* A motion made for the purpose of disposing of a main motion properly. It need not be decided on prior to the question out of which it arose.

Order of the Day: The regular program of business. A motion calling for the order of the day or to return to the order of business proposes that discussion proceed according to the regular schedule.

Parliamentary Inquiry: To rise to a parliamentary inquiry is to ask for information about the application of parliamentary law.

Point of Order: A subsidiary motion, made whenever violations of parliamentary procedure occur.

Postpone to a Certain Day: To put off action to a specific time.

Postpone Indefinitely: To deter action indefinitely. This motion often is used to avoid a vote on a troublesome issue.

Privilege: A question of privilege relates to matters such as the physical comfort of members, eligibility of those present, and members' conduct. Not to be confused with a privileged motion.

Previous Question: To move the previous question calls for a vote on the pending motion.

Question: A motion becomes a question after it has been placed before the meeting by the chairman.

Quorum: The number of members required before any business can be legally transacted. Unless a different number or proportion of the membership is specified in a bylaw, a majority of the enrolled membership is considered a quorum.

Reconsider: To reconsider places a previously decided matter before the assembly for re-examination.

Rescind: To revoke an adopted main motion.

Resolution: A declaration of fact, purpose, or opinion. It is always a main motion.

Second: To indicate support of a motion proposed by another.

Sine Die: "Without day." Adjournment without fixing the date for a future meeting.

Standing Rules: Rules adopted from time to time as they are needed. They may be adopted or rescinded without advance notice by a majority vote.

Suspension of the Rules: When an assembly anticipates the need for action that would violate the rules, it may suspend the rules that interfere.

Viva Voce: An oral vote.

MOTIONS

Procedure for Presenting and Considering a Motion

1. *Presentation:* A member rises, addresses the chair, is recognized, and makes the motion.

2. *Seconding:* The motion is seconded by another member.

3. *Stating the question:* The presiding official may repeat the motion to the assembly.

4. *Discussion:* The assembly debates and may amend the motion.

5. *Putting the question:* The presiding officer asks the group to vote on the question.

6. *Vote:* The vote is taken and is announced.

AMENDING A MOTION

1. An amendment may be amended only once.
2. It must be voted upon prior to the vote on the original motion. An amendment to an amendment must be disposed of before the original amendment can be considered.
3. If the amendment is passed, a vote on the motion as amended must follow.

BUSINESS MEETING: THE GREENVILLE CITIZENS ASSOCIATION

The following account of a meeting of the fictitious Greenville Citizens Association suggests typical procedure in transacting organization business.

CALL TO ORDER

(The chairman rises and taps his gavel to catch the attention of the members.)

The Chair: The meeting will please come to order. The secretary will read the minutes of the last meeting.

THE MINUTES

Secretary: Mr. President and members: The regular meeting of the Greenville Citizens Association was held in the auditorium of the Greenville High School, January 8th, 1954.

The meeting was called to order by President Boone, at 8.15 P.M. Sixty-one members were present.

The minutes of the regular meeting of December 11th, 1953, were read and approved.

The report of the treasurer was read, accepted, and ordered entered into the minutes.

Mr. Jones, chairman of the Program Committee, reported that many of the members had expressed an interest in international relations, and that after careful study of the various types of programs, and of sources of aid available, the Committee recommended that the Association sponsor a series of public discussion meetings on foreign affairs.

Mr. Clark moved that the report of the Program Committee be accepted, and that the Greenville Citizens Association sponsor a series of public discussion meetings on foreign affairs to be held each Monday evening during the month of March, the total expense not to exceed $100. The motion was seconded by Mr. White.

Mrs. Burns moved to amend the motion by substituting the word "Tuesday" for the word "Monday." The motion was seconded by Mrs. Green. The motion to amend was lost.

The main motion was carried.

President Boone turned the meeting over to the chairman of the Recreation Committee, Mr. Jones. Mr. Jones introduced the speaker, Mr. Harvey, chairman of the Recreation Board, who spoke on the town recreation program. He stated that there was a special need for volunteers to supervise the Huntington Hills Playground. Discussion followed.

Mr. Woods moved that the Greenville Citizens Association offer to assume responsibility for the supervision of the program at the Huntington Hills Playground. Mr. Swallow seconded the motion. Adjournment at 9:45 interrupted discussion.

Respectfully submitted,
William Harris, secretary

The Chair: Are there any additions or corrections to the minutes? (*Pauses.*) There being no additions or corrections, the minutes stand approved as read.

Officer and Committee Reports

The Chair: The treasurer will read his report. (*Report is read.*) You have heard the treasurer's report. If there are no objections, the report is accepted and will be included in the minutes of the meeting. (*Pauses.*) It is so ordered. The chairman of the Youth Activities Committee will read his report.

Adams: Mr. Chairman.

The Chair: Mr. Adams.

Adams: As the members recall, we didn't have time at the last meeting to take action on a motion that the Association offer to assume responsibility for supervising the program of the Huntington Hills Playground. I understand that the report of the Youth Activities Committee is quite lengthy. I move that the report of the

	Youth Activities Committee be made a special order for 9 P.M. at our meeting next month, in order to save time for the unfinished business on this meeting's agenda.
Farley:	I second the motion.
	(The chair repeats the motion and states that it has been seconded.)
Hale:	Mr. Chairman.
The Chair:	Mr. Hale.
Hale:	I believe that we should hear the report now. Many of us feel that the proposed supervision of the playground and our youth activities are closely related.
	(More discussion follows, with many irrelevant and repetitious points made.)
Gay:	Mr. Chairman.
The Chair:	Mr. Gay.
Gay:	I move the previous question.
Brown:	I second the motion.
The Chair:	We are now deciding whether we should go directly to the vote on the motion. Shall the main question be now put? All those in favor say "aye." Opposed, "nay." The "ayes" have it. Now we are ready for the question. It is moved and seconded that the report of the Youth Activities Committee be made a special order for 9 P.M. at next month's meeting. Is there any discussion?
Ottman:	I rise to a parliamentary inquiry.
The Chair:	State your inquiry.
Ottman:	Doesn't a motion to vote immediately on the motion before the assembly require a two-thirds affirmative vote? There were only a few more "ayes" than "nays."
The Chair:	A bare affirmative majority is all that is required. The motion is carried.
Childs:	Mr. Chairman, I appeal from the decision of the chair.

Ottman:	I second the appeal.
The Chair:	The decision of the chair has been appealed from. The chair's action follows the precedent set during meetings last year. Will Mr. Childs please state his grounds for appeal? (*Mr. Childs cites a standard parliamentary-procedure manual.*) Does any other member wish to express his views? (*Members express varying opinions.*)
The Chair:	Shall the decision of the chair be sustained? Those in the affirmative say "aye." Those in the negative say "nay." The "nays" have it and the decision of the chair is reversed. The motion to vote immediately on the motion before the assembly is lost, as it was not carried by a two-thirds vote. Discussion is in order on the motion that the report of the Youth Activities Committee be made a special order for 9 P.M. at our meeting next month. (*Discussion is resumed.*) Are you now ready for the question? The vote is on the motion that the report of the Youth Activities Committee be made a special order for 9 P.M. at the next meeting. Those in favor of the motion say "aye." (*Waits for vote.*) Those opposed? The ayes have it, and the motion is carried.
	(*Other standing and special committee reports follow.*)

Unfinished Business

The Chair:	Unfinished business is now in order. Discussion of the motion to offer to assume responsibility for the supervision of the program of the Huntington Hills Playground was interrupted by the adjournment of last month's meeting. The secretary will please read the motion.
The Secretary:	The motion reads ". . . that the Greenville Citizens Association offer to assume responsibility for the supervision of the program at the Huntington Hills Playground."
Henry:	Mr. Chairman.
The Chair:	Mr. Henry.

Henry:	Mr. Chairman, I wish to offer an amendment.
The Chair:	Mr. Henry, please state your amendment.
Henry:	I move to amend the motion by adding the words "and to supply the necessary equipment."
Davies:	Mr. Chairman, I second the amendment.
White:	Mr. Chairman.
The Chair:	Mr. White.
White:	I wish to amend the amendment by adding "through the public solicitation of funds."
Hall:	Mr. Chairman, I rise to a point of order.
The Chair:	State your point of order.
Hall:	The last motion is an amendment to an amendment and therefore out of order.
The Chair:	Mr. Hall, an amendment to an amendment is in accordance with parliamentary procedure. Is there a second to Mr. White's amendment to the amendment? (Pauses.) Since there is no second, the amendment to the amendment will not be considered. We shall proceed to vote on Mr. Henry's amendment to add the words "and to supply the necessary equipment." Will the secretary read the amendment? (Amendment is read.) All those in favor say "aye." Opposed, "nay." Motion is carried.
Porter:	I call for a division of the house.
The Chair:	A division is called for. Those in favor of the amendment please stand until counted. (Count is taken.) Please be seated. Those opposed? (Count is taken.) Please be seated. The amendment is carried by a vote of 33 to 28. Are you ready for the question? The motion as amended is "that the Greenville Citizens Association offer to assume responsibility for the supervision of the program of the Huntington Hills Playground, and to supply the necessary equipment."
	(The chair puts the question to a vote. The motion is carried.)

Talbot: I move that the president appoint a special committee of three to submit this offer to the Recreation Board, to ask the help of the recreation director in planning the supervision, and to report at the next meeting.

Hall: I second the motion.

(The chair puts the question to a vote. The motion is passed, and three members are appointed to the committee.)

New Business

The Chair: The Association has received an invitation from the Business Women's Club to join other organizations in forming a Community Development Council. Will the secretary read the letter? *(Letter is read.)*

Mrs. Hines: Mr. Chairman.

The Chair: Mrs. Hines.

Mrs. Hines: Mr. Chairman, I move that the secretary be instructed to inform the Business Women's Club that the Greenville Citizens Association will assist in the formation of a Community Development Council.

Mrs. Mott: Mr. Chairman, I second the motion.

(The chair repeats the motion and states that it has been seconded.)

The Chair: Is there any discussion?

Porter: Mr. Chairman!

Gray: Mr. Chairman!

Mrs. Hines: Mr. Chairman!

(Chair must recognize one.)

The Chair: Mr. Porter.

Porter: Like all the members, I'm in favor of cooperating with other groups. But shouldn't we know more about this proposed council? The letter doesn't give any details, nor does it list any other organization participating in its formation. I move that we postpone consideration of this motion until the next meeting.

Gray: I second the motion.

(*The chair repeats the motion and states that it has been seconded.*)

The Chair: Is there any discussion?

Mrs. Hines: Mr. Chairman.

The Chair: Mrs. Hines.

(*Mrs. Hines and others debate motion to postpone.*)

The Chair: Are you ready for the question? We are now voting on the motion to postpone consideration of the motion that the secretary be instructed to inform the Business Women's Club that the Greenville Citizens Association will assist in the formation of a Community Development Council. All those in favor say "aye." Opposed "nay." The motion to postpone has been carried. Is there any other new business?

Holcomb: Mr. Chairman.

The Chair: Mr. Holcomb.

Holcomb: I move that we appropriate $100 for our annual dance.

Mrs. Hines: I second the motion.

Lake: Mr. Chairman.

The Chair: Mr. Lake.

Lake: Do we want to appropriate any funds before we've heard the Entertainment Committee's report? I move that we lay the motion on the table.

Brown: I second the motion.

Smith: Mr. Chairman.

The Chair: Mr. Smith.

Smith: I would like to say a few words about this motion to lay on the table . . .

The Chair: I'm sorry, Mr. Smith, but a motion to lay on the table is not debatable. The members are to vote on the motion. All those in favor say "aye." Those opposed, "nay." The motion is carried. The motion to appropriate $100 is laid on the table. Is there any other new business?

Mrs. Hines:	Mr. Chairman.
The Chair:	Mrs. Hines.
Mrs. Hines:	I move we adjourn.
Smith:	I second the motion.
The Chair:	It is moved and seconded that we adjourn. All those in favor say "aye." Those opposed, "nay." The motion is carried. We stand adjourned.

APPENDIX C

Sources of Films and Film Information

THE SOURCES OF AID section of each chapter includes listings of sources of 16 mm films and film information useful in carrying out the specific activities suggested. The following are standard film guides, selected listings, and sources of films and film information of general interest. Film producers and major distributors often refer requests for films or information to branch offices or local rental outlets.

STANDARD FILM GUIDES AND SELECTED LISTINGS

Blue Book of 16 mm. Films. Revised annually. Includes over 7000 films, many of which are loaned without charge. Contains a classified subject and title index, and an index to producers and distributors. The Educational Screen, Inc., 64 East Lake St., Chicago, Ill.

Catalogue of Films for Church and Community Use. Ninety-six pages. Lists many films of general interest. Describes film service available without charge. Representative subject matter classifications: the life of Christ, Bible stories, Christian achievement, Christian life problems and responsibilities, family-life education, leadership education, other peoples of the world, interfaith and interrace relations, economic problems, and recreation. Broadcasting and Film Commission, 220 Fifth Ave., New York 1, N. Y.

Directory of Public Service Training Films. Lists free loan and rental films. Many, such as those on safety, public health, public relations, and public works are of interest to community organizations. Civil Service Assembly, 1313 East 60th St., Chicago 37, Ill.

Directory of 16 mm. Film Services. Describes and gives sources of selected films in five subject categories: special interest, general interest, entertainment, religious, and educational. Has a cross-reference index to those films which are available on a free loan basis. Sixty-four pages. The Radiant Manufacturing Corporation, 2627 West Roosevelt Ave., Chicago 8, Ill.

Directory of 2,660 16 mm. Film Libraries. Prepared by the Visual Education Service of the Department of Health, Education, and Welfare. Arranged by states and cities. Annotated. An aid to finding sources of films for special program needs. Available from Superintendent of Documents, United States Government Printing Office, Washington 25, D. C.

Educational Film Guide, 1953. Supplements scheduled to be published semiannually through spring, 1957. Lists over 11,000 16 mm films arranged in subject matter classifications, and indexed by subject matter and title. Includes more than 3000 free loan films sponsored by business, industry, national organizations and agencies, and government. Contains "Directory of Main Sources and of Local Distributors." H. W. Wilson Company, 950–972 University Ave., New York 52, N. Y.

Educators Guide to Free Films. Revised annually. Complete information about thousands of educational and entertainment films sponsored by business, industry, national agencies and associations, and government. Indexed by subject matter and title. Educators Progress Service, Randolph, Wis.

Educators Guide to Free Slidefilms. Revised annually. Thousands of filmstrips and slides from government, business, industry, and national organizations. Representative subject categories: applied arts, fine arts, health education, language arts, science, and social studies. Educators Progress Service, Randolph, Wis.

Handbook of Free Films. Lists films especially appropriate for film forums, and their sources. Allanan Associates, 509 Fifth Ave., New York 17, N. Y.

Index and Guide to Free Educational and Classroom Films from Industry. Complete information. Many films suitable for adult showing. Free loan and nominal rental. Modern Talking Picture Service, Inc., 45 Rockefeller Plaza, New York 20, N. Y.

Index to Selected Film Lists. Eastman Kodak Company, Rochester 4, N. Y.

Index to Training Films. A guide to motion pictures and slidefilms for industrial training. Business Screen Magazines, Inc., 7064 North Sheridan St., Chicago 26, Ill.

Listing of important documentary and experimental films. Cinema 16, 175 Lexington Ave., New York 16, N. Y.

Listing of libraries offering film services. American Library Association, 50 East Huron St., Chicago 11, Ill.

Listing of over 200 related film libraries. *The Saturday Review*, Film Editor, 25 West 45th St., New York 19, N. Y.

Listing of scientific films. Restricted to special groups. Information available. Psychological Cinema Register, Pennsylvania State College, State College, Pa.

Listing of selected film libraries in schools, universities, colleges, and public libraries. Educational Film Library Association, 345 East 46th St., New York 17, N. Y.

Selected Films for Adult Education. Bureau of Audio-Visual Instruction, Extension Division, State University of Iowa, Iowa City, Iowa.

Sound Slidefilm Guide. Includes over 600 sound slidefilm programs, many suitable for community-organization use. Operadio Manufacturing Company, Visual Aids Division, St. Charles, Ill.

Sources of Educational Films. National Education Association, Research Division, 1201 16th St., N. W., Washington 6, D. C.

United States Government Films. Describes over 3000 motion pictures, filmstrips, and sets of slides that may be borrowed, rented, or purchased by organizations; explains how and where to get them; includes a listing of United States government and other film libraries and sales sources. Many audio-visual aids produced by government agencies are available on a free loan basis. Superintendent of Documents, United States Government Printing Office, Washington 25, D. C.

SOME SOURCES OF 16 MM FILMS AND FILM INFORMATION OF GENERAL INTEREST

Adventure Films, Inc., 1560 Broadway, New York 19, N. Y. Travel, exploration, and foreign lands. Sound and silent. Black and white, and color. Sale, rental. Listing available.

Aetna Life Affiliated Companies, Public Education Department, Hartford 15, Conn. The United States Secret Service, sports, highway and home safety, and entertainment features. Sound. Black and white. Free loan. Catalogue available.

Air France, Advertising Department, 683 Fifth Ave., New York 22, N. Y. *Flight to Israel* and other travel films. Sound. Color. Free loan. Descriptive pamphlets available.

Alan Shilin Productions, 450 West 56th St., New York 19, N. Y. *Mirage on the Mesa, Pueblo Heritage, Seminoles of the Everglades,* and other entertainment and education films. Sound. Black and white, and color. Free loan. Catalogue available.

Aluminum Company of America, Motion Picture Section, 818 Alcoa Building, Pittsburgh 19, Pa. Films dramatizing the development of aluminum. Entertainment value. Sound. Black and white, and color. Free loan. Catalogue has suggestions for the effective showing of films.

American Air Lines, branch offices. Southwest and Mexican vacation areas. Sound. Color. Free loan. Descriptive folders available.

American Gas Association, 420 Lexington Ave., New York 17, N. Y. Films useful in homemaking programs. Sound. Black and white, and color. Free loan. Listing available.

American Humane Association, 135 Washington Ave., Albany 10, N. Y. Selected bird, animal, and insect pictures; and animal training and handling. Sound and silent. Black and white, and color. Free loan. Catalogue and lists of bird and animal films from other sources are available.

American Museum of Natural History, 79th St. and Central Park West, New York 24, N. Y. About 400 films on natural history, travel, social studies, biology, general science, and other subjects of educational and entertainment value. Sound. Black and white. Rental. Catalogue available.

American Society of Bakery Engineers, Department of Visual Education, 208 Third Ave., S. E., Minneapolis 14, Minn. Cooking, nutrition, food production and processing; home safety; the American standard of living and how it was achieved. Sound. Black and white, and color. Free loan. Catalogue available.

Armour and Company, Consumer Service Department, U. S. Yards, West 43rd and South Racine, Chicago 9, Ill. Cattle and poultry raising, dairy products, meat processing, cooking and food serving. Sound. Black and white, and color. Free loan. Catalogue available.

Associated Bulb Growers of Holland, 29 Broadway, New York 4, N. Y. Views of flower production, flower exhibitions, and other Dutch subjects. Sound. Color. Free loan. Descriptions available.

Association Films (Y.M.C.A. Motion Picture Bureau), 347 Madison Ave., New York 17, N. Y. A large collection of films in fields such as adventure, agriculture, arts and crafts, aviation, biography, the employment of the handicapped, entertainment, geography, health, government, history, industry, homemaking, literature, music, nature study, religion, and science. Sound and silent. Black and white, and color. Sale, rental, and free loan. A 64-page annotated, indexed catalogue available.

Association of American Railroads, Transportation Building, Washington 6, D. C. Large collection with a wide range of themes: scenic, travel, biography, Armed Forces training, agriculture, safety, regions of the United States, industry, aviation, Alaska, sports, and many others. Sound and silent. Black and white, and color. Free loan. A 64-page catalogue—annotated, indexed by subject classification and title, with sources of films listed.

Bermuda Trade Development Board, 620 Fifth Ave., New York 20, N. Y. Bermuda travelogues. Sound. Color. Free loan. Description available.

Bethlehem Steel Company, Inc., Publications Department, Bethlehem, Pa. Shipbuilding, building the Golden Gate Bridge, and the story of steel. Sound. Black and white. Free loan. Descriptions available.

Bituminous Coal Institute, Education Film Department, 320 Southern Building, Washington 5, D. C. Films about coal-mining operations and the training of youth in the industry. Sound. Black and white. Free loan. Descriptions available.

Brandon Films, Inc., 200 West 57th St., New York 19, N. Y. General education, painting, sculpture, crafts, literature, music, and entertainment. Sound. Black and white, and color. Sale, rental. Catalogue available.

British Information Services, Film Division, 30 Rockefeller Plaza, New York 20, N. Y. Documentaries, art, agriculture, education, health, social planning, and travel. With British settings, but of interest to Americans. Sound. Black and white, and color. Sale, rental. Catalogue available.

Canadian National Railways, 630 Fifth Ave., New York 20, N. Y. Travel in Canada: Canadian scenery, National Parks, sports, peoples, cities, industries, and other subjects. Sound. Color. Free loan. Catalogue available.

Canadian Pacific Railway Co., 581 Fifth Ave., New York 17, N. Y. Scenic Canada, Canadian travel, vacation areas, sports, cities, and many other subjects. Sound. Color. Free loan. Catalogue available.

Canadian Travel Film Libraries, 1270 Avenue of the Americas, New York 20, N. Y. About 75 films on subjects such as travel in Canada, life in Canadian provinces, sports, industry, agriculture, fisheries, and the Arctic. Filmstrips suitable for meeting programs. Sound and silent. Color. Rental, free loan. Catalogue available.

Castle Films, Division of United World Films, Inc., 1445 Park Ave., New York 29, N. Y. Safety, disaster relief, home economics, foods, good grooming, history, hobbies, and many others. Sound and silent. Black and white, and color. Sale, rental, free loan. Catalogue available.

Chicago Tribune, Public Service Office, Tribune Tower, Chicago 11, Ill. The making of a newspaper, and sports. Sound. Black and white, and color. Free loan. Descriptions available.

Coronet Films, Coronet Building, Chicago 1, Ill. Travel, music, home-making, sports, health, science, nature study, literature, industry, vocational guidance, and children's themes. Sound. Black and white, and color. Sale, rental. Catalogue available.

Douglas D. Rothacker, 729 Seventh Ave., New York 19, N. Y. A series of films about production of nickel. Sound. Black and white, and color. Free loan. Listing available.

Eastin Pictures Company, 707 Putnam Building, Davenport, Iowa. Over 2400 features and short subjects. General interest and entertainment. Sound. Black and white, and color. Sale, rental. Catalogue available.

Eastman Kodak Stores, Inc., Kodascope Libraries Division, 347 Madison Ave., New York 17, N. Y. Features, travelogues, sports, cartoons, comedies, and travel. About 1500 titles. Sound and silent. Black and white, and color. Rental. Catalogue available.

E. I. duPont de Nemours and Company, Motion Picture Distribution, Wilmington 98, Del. Films include a Hollywood-produced story of the DuPont Company; subjects such as nylon, color fastness in yarns and fabrics, rayon, and others useful in homemaking or consumer education programs. Sound. Black and white, and color. Free loan. Catalogue available.

Employers Mutual Liability Insurance Co., Engineering Department, Wausau, Wis. First aid, fire-fighting methods, and World War II action pictures. Sound. Black and white. Free loan. Catalogue available.

Encyclopaedia Britannica Films, Inc., 1150 Wilmette Ave., Wilmette, Ill. Catalogue describes more than 600 films and filmstrips, many of which are useful in carrying out meeting and public education programs suggested in this book. Subjects include arts and crafts, music, literature, recreation, safety, health, international relations, Americanism, public schools, conservation, government, and community development. Black and white, and color. Sale, rental.

Esso Standard Oil Company, 15 West 51st St., New York 19, N. Y. Four series: films about Eastern states, *Meet North Carolina*, *New England Calling*, and others; films about foreign lands, India, Iran, Africa, Peru, and others; films about modern farming in America; special instructional and other technical films. If the audience warrants it, division offices may supply an operator and equipment at no cost to the sponsoring community organization. Sound. Color. Free loan. Catalogue available.

Ethyl Corporation, Chrysler Building, 100 Park Ave., New York 17, N. Y. Gasoline engines, farm chemurgy, soil conservation, travel, and scenic. Sound. Color. Free loan. Catalogue available.

Father Hubbard Educational Films, University of Santa Clara, Santa Clara, Calif. Over 200 travelogues: Africa, Alaska, Asia, Central and South America, West Indies, the United States, and other areas. Sound. Black and white, and color. Rental. Catalogue available.

Film Center, 38 West 32nd St., New York 1, N. Y. A collection of about 2500 features: cartoons, comedies, sports, serials, and other types. Sound and silent. Black and white, and color. Sale, rental. Catalogue available.

Film Images, Inc., 18 East 60th St., New York 22, N. Y. About 22 films about France, adapted for use in America. Sound. Black and white. Sale, rental. Catalogue available.

Films, Incorporated, 202 East 44th St., New York 17, N. Y. Over 3000 entertainment, informational, and educational films. Sound. Black and white, and color. Sale, rental. Catalogue available.

Ford Motor Company, Film Library, 3000 Schaefer Road, Dearborn, Mich. Supplies information about Ford films available through local Ford and Lincoln-Mercury dealers. Film subjects include automobile production, the free-enterprise system, the interdependence of American industry, foundry operations, racing at Indianapolis Speedway, ranch life in the American West, other regions of America, American Indians, and American vacation centers. About 80 titles available. Sound. Color. Free loan. Catalogue available.

Franco-American Audio-Visual Distribution Center, Inc., 972 Fifth Ave., New York 21, N. Y. Over 200 films with French and English dialogue: Paris, skiing, famous rivers, sailing, youth hostels, architecture, and scenic. Sound. Black and white, and color. Free loan. Sale, rental. Listing available.

General Electric Company, Advertising and Sales Promotion Division, 1 River Road, Schenectady 5, N. Y. About 50 films, and glass slides and filmslides. Subject classifications include aviation, television, the sciences, biography, amateur photography, medicine, transportation, city planning, farm problems, and homemaking. Sound. Black and white, and color. Free loan. Catalogue available.

General Mills, Inc., Film Department, 400 Second Ave., South, Minneapolis 1, Minn. Nutrition, employee training, and sports. Sound. Black and white, and color. Free loan. Catalogue available.

General Motors Corporation, Department of Public Relations, Film Section, 3044 West Grand Boulevard, Detroit 2, Mich. Over 40 films. Representative subjects: mass production, the story of General Motors Institute, modern industrial medicine, scenic, transportation, aircraft, television, sports, home and job efficiency, employer-employee relationships, motors, homemaking, safety, and the All-American Soap Box Derby. Sound. Color. Free loan. Catalogue available.

Goodyear Tire and Rubber Company, Inc., Motion Picture Department, Akron, Ohio. Lighter-than-air craft in production and flight, synthetic rubber, balloon racing, Scout pictures, motorcycle racing, the Cleveland Air Races, and others, Sound and silent. Black and white, and color. Free loan. Catalogue available.

Government of India Information Services, 2107 Massachusetts Ave., N. W., Washington, D. C. Indian arts and crafts, fine art, dances, music; current political, social, and economic themes; and travelogues. Sound and silent. Black and white, and color. Sale, rental. Catalogue available.

Hercules Powder Company, Inc., 900 Market St., Wilmington 99, Del. The manufacture of lacquers, plastics, paper, and other products; road building; and agriculture. Sound. Color. Free loan. Listing available.

Humble Oil and Refining Co., Film Library, P. O. Box 2180, Houston, Tex. A series of pictures about operations in the oil industry. Sound. Color. Free loan. Catalogue available.

Ideal Picture Corporation, 65 East South Water St., Chicago 15, Ill. Comparison of American industry with that of other countries, the story of nickel and other products, auto racing, home economics, fabrics, and other education and entertainment subjects. Sound. Black and white, and color. Free loan. Catalogue available.

Illinois Central Library of Audio-Visual Aids, 135 East 11th Place, Chicago 5, Ill. Economic education, courtesy, history, safety, labor-management cooperation, and musicals. Sound. Black and white, and color. Free loan. Catalogue available.

Institute of Visual Training, 40 East 49th St., New York 17, N. Y. Offers about 15 titles. Subjects include travel, health, physical culture, science, and entertainment. Sound. Black and white, and color. Free loan. Catalogue available.

International Film Bureau, Inc., 57 East Jackson Boulevard, Chicago 4, Ill. Distributes the films of hundreds of producers. Fifty-six page catalogue, annotated, arranged in subject-matter classification, indexed by subject and title. Has selected listings of educational and entertainment films for community organizations. Sound and silent. Black and white, and color. Sale, rental, and free loan.

International Geographic Pictures, 1776 Broadway, New York 19, N. Y. American history: territorial expansion, territorial possessions, causes and effects of World War I, and others. Sound. Black and white. Sale, rental. Catalogue available.

International Harvester Company, 180 North Michigan Ave., Chicago 1, Ill. Subjects include agriculture, Boulder Dam, and rural school problems. Black and white, and color. Free loan. Catalogue available.

McGraw-Hill Book Company, Text-Film Department, 330 West 42nd St., New York 36, N. Y. Distributors for International Film Foundation, March of Time, National Film Board of Canada, RKO-Pathe, British Information Services, the United Nations, and others. Entertainment, education, and social problems. Sale, rental, and free loan. Catalogue available.

Minneapolis-Moline Company, Advertising Department, Minneapolis 1, Minn. Agriculture; travel in the United States, Central and South America, the West Indies, the Island of Guernsey, France, and other areas; and documentaries. Sound. Color. Free loan. Catalogue available.

Modern Talking Picture Service, Inc., 45 Rockefeller Plaza, New York 20, N. Y. Lists free loan films from more than 100 leading business and industrial concerns, educational foundations, and national associations. Many others for sale or rent. Subjects of free loan films include sports, travel, homemaking, nutrition, safety, health, and economic education. Arranges a "Film of the Month" program service for organizations, without cost. Sound and silent. Has a catalogue *Industry Presents Free Motion Pictures for Adult Audiences*, and other listings.

National Film Board of Canada, 400 West Madison St., Chicago 6, Ill. Health, agriculture, arts, social planning, travel, industry, resources, and many other subjects in Canadian, American, and British settings. Sound. Black and white, and color. Sale, rental. Catalogue available.

National Garden Bureau, 210 South Desplaines St., Chicago 6, Ill. Five films on gardening. Black and white, and color. Sound and silent. Free loan. Descriptive listing available.

New Mexico State Tourist Bureau, Box 1716, Santa Fe, N. M. Four films about New Mexican Indians, rodeos, cattle raising, and fiestas. Sound. Color. Free loan. Descriptions available.

Oil Industry Information Committee, 50 West 50th St., New York 20, N. Y. Subjects related to petroleum: agriculture, aviation, travel, foreign countries, building the West, safety, transportation, and history. Sound. Black and white, and color. Free loan. Catalogue available.

Pan American World Airways, Educational Director, 135 East 42nd St., New York 17, N. Y. Travel films: the Caribbean, Bermuda, Cuba, Ireland, Latin America, Mexico, Guatemala, and Alaska. Sound. Color. Free loan. Furnishes program aids with each film: synopsis of film, background information about the region, suggestions for introducing the film, discussion guide, suggestions for further activities, and a selected bibliography. Catalogue available.

Pix Film Service, 34 East Putnam Ave., Greenwich, Conn. Features, travelogues, sports, cartoons, comedies, and travel. About 2300 titles. Rental. Catalogue available.

Princeton Film Center, Carter Road, Princeton, N. J. Helicopter development and use, jet fighters and bombers, the coal industry, agriculture, lumbering, the agricultural and industrial growth of the South, rail transportation, and others. Sound. Black and white, and color. Rental, free loan. Catalogue available.

Program Bureau, New York Telephone Company, 140 West St., New York 7, N. Y. Offers several free loan sound films to supplement lecture programs. In limited area, supplies equipment and projectionist without charge. Descriptions available.

Santa Fe Film Bureau, Oklahoma City 2, Okla. The production of citrus fruit, running the rapids of the Colorado River, Pueblo Indians, Chicago, National Parks, Armed Forces training, and transportation. Sound. Black and white, and color. Free loan. Catalogue available.

Shell Oil Company, 50 West 50th St., New York 20, N. Y. Plane design, principles of flight, principles of hydraulics, and petroleum products. Sound. Color. Free loan. Catalogue available.

Swift and Company, Agricultural Research Department, Union Stock Yards, Chicago 9, Ill. Sixteen films about meat raising, processing, cooking and serving. Sound. Black and white. Free loan. Catalogue available.

Tennessee Valley Authority, Film Services, Knoxville, Tenn. The story of T.V.A. dramatized, the operation of a progressive school, timber growing, forest-fire prevention, shell mounds in the Tennessee Valley, Norris Dam construction, other semitechnical subjects, farm and home improvement, and others. Sound. Black and white. Free loan. Catalogue available.

Texas Company, 135 East 42nd St., New York 17, N. Y. Poultry raising, labor saving devices on the farm, cattle raising, apple growing, Saudi Arabia, petroleum production, and petroleum research. Pictures have scenic and dramatic value. Sound. Black and white, and color. Free loan. Catalogue available.

Union Pacific Railroad, Motion Picture Bureau, 1416 Dodge St., Omaha 2, Neb. Agriculture, dairying, Sun Valley, National Parks, sports, and safety. Sound. Black and white, and color. Free loan. Catalogue available.

United Israel Appeal, Inc., 41 East 42nd St., New York 17, N. Y. Representative titles: *Israel Reborn, The Song of the Negev, Israel in Action, Voyage of the Unafraid, Flight to Freedom,* and *Tent City.* Sound. Black and white, and color. Free loan. Catalogue available.

United States Bureau of Mines, Experiment Station, 4800 Forbes St., Pittsburgh 13, Pa. Seventy-five films about production, fabrication, and utilization of metals and mineral substances in the United States. Sound and silent. Black and white, and color. Free loan. Catalogue available.

United States Rubber Company, Advertising Department, 1230 Avenue of the Americas, New York 20, N. Y. General interest, education, and entertainment films. Sound. Black and white. Free loan. Catalogue available.

United States Steel, Film Distribution Center, 71 Broadway, New York 6, N. Y. A series on the making of steel, building the San Francisco-Oakland Bay Bridge, and other education and entertainment features. Sound. Color. Free loan. Catalogue available.

United World Films, Inc., 1445 Park Ave., New York 29, N. Y. Offers over 1000 entertainment, recreational, instructional, character building, health, religious, and other types of films. Depository for government films. Sound and silent. Black and white, and color. Sale, rental, and free loan. Catalogue available.

Venard Organization, 702 South Adams St., Peoria 2, Ill. Has available many films sponsored by business and industry. Dramatizations of American history, newsreels, nature, successful farm practices, economic education, adventure, cartoon and other entertainment features. Sound and silent. Black and white, and color. Free loan. Catalogue available.

Virginia Conservation and Development Department, Division of Publicity and Advertising, Richmond 19, Va. A series of films about Virginia's shrines and colonial mansions, scenic, and travel. Sound and silent. Black and white, and color. Free loan. Catalogue available.

Westinghouse Electric Corporation, Film Division, Box 868, 511 Wood St., Pittsburgh 30, Pa. About 75 films. Representative subjects: home planning, community planning, rural programs, farm problems, home repairs, health, safety, and television. Sound. Black and white, and color. Free loan. Some titles in 35 mm. Slidefilms 35 mm only. Scripts available. Films and slidefilm program aids supplied. Catalogue available.

Wool Bureau, Inc., Educational Department, 16 West 46th St., New York 36, N. Y. Scenes of Scotland, Australia, South Africa, and animal husbandry and wool manufacturing. Sound. Black and white, and color. Free loan. Catalogue available.

Young America Films, Inc., 18 East 41st St., New York 17, N. Y. Many teaching films suitable for adult meeting programs or study groups. Teaching guides supplied. Agriculture, chess fundamentals, kitchen safety, cooking, food, racial and religious tolerance, sewing, speech, and many others. Sound and silent. Black and white, and color. Rental. Catalogue available.

Some Magazines Featuring 16 mm Film Reviews
Audio-Visual Guide, 1630 Springfield Ave., Maplewood, N. J.
Business Screen, 7064 North Sheridan Road, Chicago 10, Ill.
Educational Screen, 64 East Lake St., Chicago, Ill.
Film News, 444 Central Park West, New York 35, N. Y.
Film World and A-V World, 1159 North Highland, Hollywood 38, Calif.
See and Hear, 7064 North Sheridan Road, Chicago 10, Ill.
Saturday Review, 25 West 45th St., New York 36, N. Y.

A Course in Effective Speech

A FORMAL course in effective speech meets an important organization need. Many individuals possess qualities of leadership, but lacking the ability to express themselves easily and effectively, they cannot take their proper places in the group or the community.

While it is important that as many members as possible participate in a speech improvement program, enrollment must be limited, as the value of an organized course depends on the practice opportunities it affords the individual. Experience has shown that a group not larger than 25 furnishes opportunity at each session for formal instruction, at least one short practice talk by each member, and adequate time for group discussion and evaluation of everyone's work.

To maintain continuity and sustain interest, classes should meet in two- to three-hour sessions, preferably once a week. The number of meetings depends on the needs and interests of the group. Usually such a program has about 15 sessions, although the subject is so complex and varied that an indefinite number of meetings is possible and profitable.

The meeting place should be large enough to permit seating arrangements appropriate for formal speaking, informal group discussion, and panel forums. Large auditoriums are undesirable for most practice sessions.

An important part of course planning is a marshaling of the assistance that may be found in the community. The local librarian might be asked to help collect materials. The advice and assistance of well-known public speakers should be sought. Many schools have speech specialists. Adult education departments are usually cooperative in providing competent instructors and helpful materials. Many colleges and universities have extension departments that offer courses, without academic credit, for community groups.

The cost of securing a trained instructor, shared by 20 or more individuals, is slight. A member's payment of a fee is an assurance of his seriousness of purpose, and gives him a vested interest in the success of the project. Expert assistance, however, is not essential. It is possible to organize and conduct a formal speech course using only the talent and resources of the oganization itself. In such a project a leader or coordinator is needed to make the meeting arrangements, conduct the sessions, and see that the course outline is followed carefully.

The emphasis in speech training should be on the individual. Each member should be helped to make a self-analysis. Suggest that he list the weaknesses or shortcomings revealed through group criticism of his performances. Part of the job of the permament leader or chairman should be keeping notes on each member's speeches, to be used in briefing the individual and the group about such special personal objectives. To help the practicing speaker keep specific goals in mind, and to make possible group observation of his progress toward these goals, the speaker should be encouraged at some sessions to comment briefly on the faults he is trying to correct.

In addition to learning by doing, individuals learn through critical observation of others. The extent of such learning depends largely on how well the chairman trains the group in the techniques of observation.

Another important part of a leader's job is to instill in each member an interest in, and responsibility for, the development of other members, so that the improvement of one is felt to be an achievement of the whole group. This coming out of oneself in a concern for others is the best antidote for self-consciousness. If the group does not build this attitude, there will be no real audience, but only a collection of individuals, each isolated in his self-concern. The attitude that permits each to participate with confidence that he is not exposing himself to ridicule, certain that he has the friendly, sympathetic support of the others, must be developed.

A member's evaluation of another's performance should be in terms of what the speaker tried to do. What was the purpose of the speech? To what extent was that purpose realized? What unusually good devices were used in achieving that purpose?

No general statements unsupported by specific reference to a speech should be permitted. General comments like "That was well done," or "I don't think his posture was good" are of limited value. Specifically, what made it "well done"? Just what about his posture distracted the observer? Remember that there can be no talk so poor that something complimentary cannot be said of it. Recital of lists of relatively minor errors or slips of the tongue should be discouraged. No criticism should be recognized that is not accompanied by a "how to do it better" suggestion. Criticism in this spirit can be most valuable in building good human relations as well as in developing speaking skills.

Each of the 16 sessions in the following suggested course in effective speech has two general purposes: to provide practice in speaking, and to help the members prepare for the next session. Each session depends on the preceding one, giving the series a continuity that should be maintained.

As part of each preparation it is suggested that a 10-minute talk cover the principles and techniques to be used at the next session. In the absence of a speech expert, each member might be asked to study one particular phase of speaking and report on it. The chairman should then take the responsibility for directing its practice in the following session. Such speeches should be scheduled in advance for the whole series. At the first meeting, this part of the preparation may be eliminated or handled by the chairman, or a film may be shown.

An early choice of a topic for the final, competition speech, "A Better Community Through. . .," to be delivered in Practice Session Fifteen, is desirable. At the first session, explain that each member, before the seventh meeting, is to have chosen some phase of community betterment as his subject matter. Point out that each chapter in this book is a guide for a survey of community needs, a manual for planning measures to meet those needs, and a source of information about how they have been met in other communities. A chapter title can be used to complete the individual topic: "A Better Community Through Better Health Facilities," for example. Early choices of areas of community living are necessary so that duplications can be avoided, broad coverage achieved, and adequate time for research and other preparation assured.

PRACTICE SESSION ONE

ALL IN THE SAME BOAT. In addition to the ordinary business of organization, the first meeting should have as a major objective the establishing of a group "We're all in the same boat" attitude, essential to the success of the course.

PROCEDURE SUGGESTIONS

1. Have the chairman, instructor, or an officer give a short talk about the importance of speech to leadership success, the specific goals of the course, the "learning by doing" emphasis to be maintained, and the fact that everyone is present because he feels need for improvement.

2. Ask each member of the group to break the ice by standing up to explain briefly his reasons for joining the class.

3. Fix the time and place of future meetings.

4. Ask each member to choose one of the chapters in this book as his subject field for the final competition speech to be given at Practice Session Fifteen. Fix Practice Session Seven as a deadline for announcing choices.

5. Stimulate a general discussion of speech difficulties. Show the film *Speech: Stage Fright and What to Do About It*, or play a recording such as Lesson One of Dr. Walter Robinson's *Course in Effective Speaking*, "Why Fear Cannot Stop You from Speaking Well."

6. For Practice Session Two, assign a speech of definition.

PRACTICE SESSION TWO

DEVELOPING DIRECTNESS. The speaker must be in direct, personal contact with his listeners. He should talk *with* his audience, not *at* them. One of the best ways of achieving a sense of communication is through direct eye contact with the individuals in the group. This practice gives each listener a feeling that the speaker is talking to him. Moreover, the speaker can judge, by observing facial expressions and other reactions, the extent to which he is reaching his audience.

PREPARATION SUGGESTIONS

1. Select a technical word or phrase used in your particular vocation, one not understood by people generally, the meaning of which you can make clear and precise.

2. In addition to the dictionary definition, use one or more of the following special methods to develop your meaning: (a) definition by synonym, (b) definition by classification and differentiation, (c) definition by gradation, (d) definition by negation, (e) definition by etymology, (f) definition by illustration, (g) definition by context, and (h) definition by using visual aids.

PROCEDURE SUGGESTIONS

1. Have a member of the group count the number of times each speaker looks away from his audience, at the ceiling, at the floor, or into space.

2. After each speech of definition, ask the group to consider whether the speaker had a genuine contact with his audience; a friendly, intimate manner; and clear and interesting methods of definition.

3. For Practice Session Three, assign a three-minute talk on a "topic of your own choosing."

4. Present the scheduled 10-minute preparatory talk, "The Effective Use of Voice," or show Your Tell-Tale Voice, a 20-minute film about how people judge others, often unfairly, by the sound of their voices; or Speech: Using Your Voice, which stresses the fact that a good speaking voice can be achieved; or play a recording such as Lesson Two of Dr. Walter Robinson's Course in Effective Speaking, "How Your Voice Instrument Works."

PRACTICE SESSION THREE

EFFECTIVE USE OF THE VOICE. How something is said may be as important as what is said. In fact the "what" and the "how" can be said to be inseparable. Through control of the sound of the voice alone the speaker gives information, suggests ideas, reflects states of mind, creates feeling, implies, and emphasizes. Practice this control.

PREPARATION SUGGESTIONS

1. Choose a topic from a field in which you have experience and in which you and the audience have some interest. Be sure it can be adequately handled in the three-minute time limit.

2. Choose details that are important, unusual, concrete and specific, picture-making or dramatic.

3. Listen to speakers, noting the methods they use in achieving their purpose.

4. Practice the assignment with attention to expressing your meaning by your voice. If possible, listen to yourself on a tape recording or ask a friend to criticize.

PROCEDURE SUGGESTIONS

1. After each three-minute talk, ask the group to consider whether the speaker conveyed meaning through control of volume, inflection, and timing; and spoke clearly and distinctly.

2. Where remedial practice is necessary, ask members to see how many different shades of meaning they can give a rather commonplace statement, or read or speak passages the sense of which demands a slow down or speed up, or repeat part or all of some speeches with attention to faults noted.

3. For Practice Session Four, assign a three-minute special purpose talk in which each member pleads a cause or informs or entertains or persuades or arouses to action.

4. Present the scheduled ten-minute preparatory talk, "Effective Platform Manner," or show the film, *Speech: Platform Posture and Appearance.*

PRACTICE SESSION FOUR

It is important to remember that an audience is looking as well as hearing. The reaction that the audience has to a speaker—from his appearance and mannerisms—is as important, in many respects, as what he says.

Preparation Suggestions

1. Observe the posture and actions of speakers you admire; make note of those whose posture and actions appear to be naturally motivated.

2. Avoid unnatural and artificial gestures. Such gestures call attention to themselves and detract from the idea being presented.

Procedure Suggestions

1. After each "special purpose" talk, ask the group to note whether the speaker's general bearing suggested his purpose; facial expressions reflected changes in thought or feeling; gestures supported his words; attention was given to many individuals in the audience; and posture was natural.

2. Plan interruptions and distractions, such as two or more in the audience suddenly and noisily leaving the room, whispered conversations, mild heckling in the form of questions, and fits of coughing. Discuss the speaker's reaction, and the general problem of interruptions and distractions.

3. To correct platform shortcomings revealed in the talks, ask an athlete to demonstrate a "readiness for action" stance in his sport; have members without words express wonder, surprise, consternation, or delight; assign simple situations or incidents to be told in pantomime: "The Car Won't Start," "The One That Got Away."

4. Remind members of the Practice Session Seven deadline for a choice of a final speech topic.

5. Have the group choose a topic or topics for informal discussion at Practice Session Five.

6. Present the scheduled talk, "The Roles of the Chairman and Participants in Informal Discussion."

PRACTICE SESSION FIVE

INFORMAL DISCUSSION. The informal discussion group is the most common public-speaking situation, and an important leadership opportunity. Each individual who speaks assumes, for the time being, the role of leader.

PREPARATION SUGGESTIONS

1. Learn all you can about the subject chosen; tentatively make up your mind about controversial points; and gather data.

2. Become familiar with the duties of a chairman: he should provide background for the subject, ask leading questions, give as many as possible an opportunity to speak, tactfully check talk that is irrelevant, withhold personal opinion, help the group to relate opinions expressed, and recognize the possibility of a consensus.

3. Listen to radio and television discussion groups.

4. Observe and practice the techniques of good conversation.

PROCEDURE SUGGESTIONS

1. Record the discussion. After the playback, discuss the techniques used by the chairman and the effectiveness of each person's participation. Were there violations of the following rules? Do not take more than your share of the time. Never phrase a statement as a flat, unqualified contradiction of another's statement—word it as another possible consideration. Preface disagreement by all possible concessions to those having opposing ideas. Use the question form in expressing opposition or contradiction. Permit the chairman to steer the discussion. Never interrupt with comments while another is speaking. Avoid addressing remarks to particular individuals.

2. For Practice Session Six, divide the members into panel discussion groups of five, two on a side and one to act as chairman. Assign each panel a controversial subject, preferably with but one or two clear-cut issues. Have each panel meet to decide what debate position each member is to take, the order of speaking, and the time limits for main speeches and rebuttals.

3. Present the scheduled talk, "The Panel Discussion: Roles Played by the Chairman, the Panel Members, and the Audience." Supplement the talk with the 10-minute film *Learn to Argue Effectively.*

PRACTICE SESSION SIX

THE PANEL DISCUSSION. The panel type of discussion of controversial issues is taking the place of the debate, with its formalized structure and style.

PREPARATION SUGGESTIONS

1. Review the principles and techniques of discussion brought out in Practice Session Four—"How You Look to the Audience."
2. Become familiar with various aspects of the subject, not merely those that support your particular position.
3. Know the responsibilities of a panel chairman. They include opening the meeting by giving the background for the discussion, arousing interest by relating subject matter to the lives of the people in the audience, naming the panel members, establishing the authority of each to speak on the subject, and identifying the position each is to take; keeping each speaker to the subject and within the time limit; stimulating discussion by provocative questions; and recognizing members of the audience, deciding upon the relevancy of their questions or comments, and keeping order.

PROCEDURE SUGGESTIONS

1. Have those not speaking on the panel act as an audience, very briefly joining in at the close of the discussion.
2. Ask the group to evaluate the panel chairman's introductory speech.
3. Have the group note how effectively each panel member presented his arguments, anticipated and answered the arguments of his opponent, and met challenging questions from the audience.
4. For Practice Session Seven, assign a three-minute sales talk about a product or service of each member's choosing.
5. Present the scheduled talk, "Salesmanship," or use a film available from sources listed at the close of this chapter.

PRACTICE SESSION SEVEN

SALESMANSHIP. Every successful man owes his success to his ability to sell: his product, his service, his skills, his ideas, his personality. This ability depends for the most part on the effective communication of information, ideas, and feelings through speech.

PREPARATION SUGGESTIONS

1. Be sure you know the product or service you are selling.

2. Have with you the product to demonstrate, or evidence of the quality of the service you are offering.

3. Consider the prospect's probable buying motives.

4. Plan the steps to the sale: attention—interest—desire—action.

5. Study the sales talk and demonstration techniques used in presenting products on television.

6. Review the selling suggestions made in the preparation talk or the salesmanship film.

PROCEDURE SUGGESTIONS

1. Divide the members into two-man teams. Have each man sell the other a product or service.

2. Ask salesmen to criticize performances.

3. Suggest that the prospect offer sales resistance.

4. Have the group note whether or not each seller permitted the prospect to participate in the demonstration, recognized indications that the buyer had been convinced or persuaded, and guarded against terminating the talk prematurely.

5. Have each member announce his choice of an area of community living as his subject matter for the final speech to be given in Practice Session Fifteen. Avoid duplication.

6. For Practice Session Eight, assign a formal speech for an occasion of public significance. Determine its length by the number of speakers to be heard in the time limit of the session.

7. Present the scheduled talk, "The Formal Speech." Supplement the talk with the film, *Speech: The Function of Gestures*, or play a recording such as Lesson Seven of Dr. Walter Robinson's *Course in Effective Speaking*, "How to Give Your Speech Forcefulness."

PRACTICE SESSION EIGHT

PUBLIC OBSERVANCES AND OTHER SPECIAL OCCASIONS. Speeches for public observances and other special occasions usually are presented before relatively large audiences. They have to do with ideals, concepts, and sentiments that are part of the nation's traditions, and that are of such deep significance that they call for an especially formal speech organization, language, and platform manner. Organization and community leadership require an ability to meet these situations.

PREPARATION SUGGESTIONS

1. Choose an occasion such as the Fourth of July, National Citizenship Day, or the dedication of a public building or war memorial. Find out all you can about the background and history of the occasion.

2. Determine the type of audience you would probably face: its politics, its general age level, and its social and economic status.

3. Review all that has been said about adapting material, approach, language, voice, and platform manner to the speaking situation.

4. Read some classic speeches.

PROCEDURE SUGGESTIONS

1. Have the members of the audience evaluate each speech, using a checklist form permitting short, personal, unsigned comments about such matters as content, vocabulary, voice, and platform manner. If duplication of a form is impracticable, use a sheet of notepaper with the speaker's name written at the top.

2. For Practice Session Nine, assign to each member two other common speech forms.

3. Present the scheduled talk, "Common Speech Forms."

PRACTICE SESSION NINE

OTHER COMMON SPEECH FORMS. While no two occasions, in membership meetings or in the community, are ever exactly alike, many are similar enough to permit use of forms that are more or less set. Leadership demands a knowledge of these forms and the ability to adapt them to particular situations.

PREPARATION SUGGESTIONS

1. Fix in mind the patterns suggested in the preparatory talk given at Practice Session Eight.

2. Be careful about such important matters as the full names of people involved and their pronunciation, the exact wording of a citation, and such information, for example, as the experience and background of a speaker being introduced.

3. Do not use the speech to further any purpose other than that demanded by the occasion.

4. Study specimen talks in a good public-speaking handbook.

5. Review the principles and techniques brought out in Practice Sessions Two, Three, and Four.

PROCEDURE SUGGESTIONS

1. To give the practice an air of reality, have each member team up with another to act out such situations as welcome-response and presentation-acceptance.

2. Have members demonstrate speech forms such as introduction,

welcome, response, nomination, presentation, acceptance, farewell, and eulogy.

3. As a preface to each talk or set of talks, describe the occasion.

4. Announce that Practice Session Ten will be a formal business meeting of the group, conducted in strict accordance with parliamentary law. Ask the group to study the material on parliamentary procedure in Appendix B.

5. Present the scheduled talk, "The Essentials of Parliamentary Procedure."

PRACTICE SESSION TEN

PARLIAMENTARY PROCEDURE. An individual who lacks knowledge of the essentials of parliamentary procedure finds participation in formal meetings difficult. This session is designed to provide parliamentary practice in a realistic setting.

PREPARATION SUGGESTIONS

1. Participate in drawing up an agenda for a regular business meeting. Help decide on an order of business. Among the items on which formal action might be taken are the method of choosing the winners in the speech contest in Practice Session Fifteen; the form the awards are to take; the recognition of other kinds of speech achievement; Recognition Night plans, including a dinner, guests, entertainment, and the method of choosing a toastmaster.

2. Prepare to take part in the formal discussion and action by developing some ideas about the business of the meeting, and by fixing in mind the parliamentary procedures by which you can introduce them.

PROCEDURE SUGGESTIONS

1. Invite someone familiar with parliamentary law to act as parliamentarian.

2. Create situations requiring the use of such procedures as making main motions; subsidiary motions, such as those to refer the business to a committee or to lay on the table; incidental motions, such as those to withdraw a motion or to appeal from the decision of the chair; and privileged motions, such as those to take a recess or call for the order of business.

3. Provide time for the parliamentarian to review proceedings from the standpoint of correctness.

4. Arrange a question-and-answer period.

5. For Practice Session Eleven, give each member two assignments: a

three-minute speech in which humor has an important part, and a short humorous story.

6. Present the scheduled talk, "The Use of Humor in Public Speaking."

PRACTICE SESSION ELEVEN

HUMOR IN PUBLIC SPEAKING. Humor, important for its own sake, is a major device for making an audience receptive to ideas. Its effective use in public speaking requires practice.

PREPARATION SUGGESTIONS

1. Give stories fresh detail or application.
2. Adapt your story to the occasion and to your audience.
3. Respect the intelligence of your audience—avoid explaining the point of the story.

PROCEDURE SUGGESTIONS

1. During the first part of the session, schedule the three-minute speeches in which humor is an integral part.
2. During the second part, perhaps a half-hour long, have each member tell a joke or a funny story.
3. Guests or members might be asked to serve as a panel of judges to choose the funniest joke, the humorous story with the most surprising ending, and the best adaptation of an old story.
4. For Practice Session Twelve, ask each member to be prepared to read aloud two passages from material of contrasting content and style.
5. Present the scheduled talk, "Reading Techniques."

PRACTICE SESSION TWELVE

READING ALOUD. Some speeches involve reading reports or quotations that are too long to be given from memory, or that must be presented verbatim. Speeches are often read because they embody matters of policy, the careful wording of which is important. Material usually read includes minutes of meetings, resolutions, treasurer's reports, legislation, historic documents, poetry, and the Bible.

PREPARATION SUGGESTIONS

1. Practice reading aloud a wide variety of materials.
2. Avoid single-word attention. Develop the ability to read in logical blocks of words.
3. Work for maximum eye contact with the audience when reading.

4. Hold the reading matter so that all the audience has a full view of your face. Keep your head up.

5. Pronounce and enunciate as in normal, proper speech.

6. Develop the ability to grasp the concept back of the word while pronouncing it.

PROCEDURE SUGGESTIONS

1. Ask some members to repeat their readings after criticism.

2. Present material to be read at sight.

3. After each reading, ask the group to indicate by a show of hands how many felt the reader maintained a direct contact with them, as suggested in Practice Session Two.

4. Ask some members to read a passage, giving it several shades of meaning through variations in volume, inflection, and pauses.

5. Announce that Practice Session Thirteen will be held at the local radio or television station.

6. For Practice Session Thirteen, schedule some members to prepare a short radio talk, and other members to prepare to partipicate in an interview-type program.

7. Present the scheduled talk, "Radio and Television Techniques."

PRACTICE SESSION THIRTEEN

THE RADIO OR TELEVISION TALK. The basic principles of good speech hold for radio and television. These media, however, impose special limitations and conditions that demand particular emphases in preparation and delivery. A mastery of radio and television speech skills extends the range of leadership influence. It should be an important objective of the course.

PREPARATION SUGGESTIONS

1. Although radio speeches are usually read from manuscript, write and practice reading the speech as though you were talking.

2. Review the points brought out in Practice Sessions Five and Twelve.

3. Practice a radio presentation with attention to the fact that sound alone must convey the full meaning; you cannot have the support of gestures or facial expression.

4. Observe television speakers, and consult recent texts on television techniques.

5. Keep in mind not thousands of listeners but the individual or family group in the living room.

6. Rehearse your speech for timing.

PROCEDURE SUGGESTIONS

1. Have a station official demonstrate the proper position to take before the microphone and how to discard pages of manuscript to avoid the rustle of paper. If broadcasting from one studio room to another is possible, ask him to show the group the effects of faulty techniques: sudden withdrawal from or approach to the microphone, heavy breathing, uneven voice volume. Observe a telecast. Ask the station director to conduct a coaching session for your group.

2. If possible, have members, unseen in another room, formally but briefly "broadcast" to the group, or have a recording made.

3. Record the discussion-interviews; have the group note violations of the informal discussion principles practiced in Session Five.

4. Present the scheduled talk, "Helps in Speaking Extemporaneously."

PRACTICE SESSION FOURTEEN

THINKING ON YOUR FEET. The individual who can think on his feet has an asset of incalculable value. Only through practice can this be acquired.

PREPARATION SUGGESTIONS

1. Fix a reasonable achievement goal: the impromptu talk is not expected to be finished.

2. Be prepared to concentrate on ideas.

3. Be prepared to take the audience into your confidence. If the right word escapes you, or if you realize your argument is incomplete, by manner and words ask the group to help. Speaker-audience collaboration is a perfect solution to the problems of impromptu speeches.

PROCEDURE SUGGESTIONS

1. Divide the session time into two parts. In the first half allow two minutes for preparation of a two-minute speech. Give the first speaker a slip on which his topic is written. He may prepare while the chairman is explaining the situation and reviewing the previous session's preparatory talk. Give the second speaker his topic at the opening of the first speaker's talk. In this fashion, preparation and speaking may be arranged for all in the session's time. In the second half, hand out one topic at a time for a speech to be given without any preparation. In both sets of talks the subjects assigned should be within the experience of everyone, but should not permit speakers to use material with which they are too familiar.

2. Announce again each member's topic for the "A Better Community Through . . ." contest to be held at Practice Session Fifteen.

3. Present the scheduled talk, "The Finished Speaker," as a résumé of the course.

PRACTICE SESSION FIFTEEN

THE FINISHED SPEAKER. In other sessions, attention was given to the separate aspects of public speaking as the group practiced for specific skills, or as individuals tried to remedy particular defects. Emphasis at this session should be on each member's demonstration of all the skills that make a finished speaker. Attention should be given not only to the techniques of public speaking but also to the thoroughness of each member's community study and the value of his suggestions for betterment in the field of his choice.

PREPARATION SUGGESTIONS

1. Use the wording of the chapter titles in this book to complete topics such as "Community Betterment through Sports and Recreation" and "Community Betterment through Safety."

2. Study your community through news articles, editorials, municipal reports, and interviews with municipal department heads and community leaders.

3. Review the principles and techniques emphasized during the course, with special attention to individual shortcomings.

4. Remember the two "musts" of any speaking situation: You must attract attention and interest at the very outset; you must relate your subject matter to the interests of the audience.

PROCEDURE SUGGESTIONS

1. Invite community public speakers of note to act as judges in choosing three "best" speakers for Recognition Night.

2. Have the group choose by secret ballot the member who proved most versatile, the member who showed the greatest improvement, the member who was most helpful to the group through his constructive criticism, the member who contributed most to the fun of the course. Withhold announcement of the choices until Recognition Night.

3. Urge all members to attend the Recognition Night dinner.

4. Present as scheduled talks, the "Report of the Committee for Recognition Night Arrangements" and "After-Dinner Speeches."

SESSION SIXTEEN

RECOGNITION NIGHT. While the primary purpose of this last session is to recognize group and individual achievement, it should have a social atmosphere, with no suggestion of study or practice in the proceedings.

PREPARATION SUGGESTIONS

1. Serve on an awards, program, or guests committee.
2. Be prepared to act as toastmaster.
3. Anticipate the speaking demands the situation might make. How would you respond to an introduction? How would you accept an award? How would you offer a toast? Do you have a few jokes you could adapt to the situation? Could you substitute for the toastmaster?

PROCEDURE SUGGESTIONS

1. Invite husbands or wives, friends, and those who contributed to the success of the course.
2. Appoint a member as toastmaster in recognition of achievement.
3. Ask each member to introduce his guest.
4. Present appropriate gifts as awards to winners of the "Better Community" contest and to others chosen by the group as having excelled.
5. Feature five-minute speeches by the contest winners.
6. Make the presentation of a diploma or a certificate of achievement in speech an occasion for each member's introduction to the guests.

SOME SOURCES OF SUGGESTED MATERIALS AND OTHER AIDS

American Telephone and Telegraph Company, 195 Broadway, New York 7, N. Y. Free loan films include *Your Telltale Voice*, showing how voice inflections reflect the mood of the person talking; and films on good telephone usage. Descriptions available.

Chamber of Commerce of the United States, 1615 H St., N. W., Washington 6, D. C. Offers single or quantity copies of speeches on such timely topics as "It's Your Money They're Spending" and "How High Can Taxes Go?" Useful as material for individual or group analysis of the speech form that effectively pleads a cause in a vigorous, forthright manner. Has information about Chamber-sponsored clinics and institutes.

City News Publishing Company, 33 West 42nd St., New York 36, N. Y. Publishes *Vital Speeches*, a bimonthly carrying the text of important addresses by recognized national and international leaders of public opinion. Speeches are excellent examples of good expression.

Coronet Films, Coronet Building, Chicago 1, Ill. Rental films include

Fundamentals of Public Speaking, Learn to Argue Effectively, and *Parliamentary Procedure.* Good introductions to a course in speech. Descriptions available.

Dale Carnegie Institute, 285 Madison Ave., New York 16, N. Y. Organizes formal leadership training courses frequently sponsored by organizations.

Dictaphone Corporation. Apply to district offices in major cities. Free loan films include *Two Salesmen in Search of an Order,* a demonstration of right and wrong techniques.

Duerr, Edwin, *Radio and Television Acting,* New York: Rinehart & Company, Inc., 1950. Describes microphone and camera techniques useful to the student of effective speech.

Harper & Brothers, 49 East 33rd St., New York 16, N. Y. Offers a series of five double-sided records of the Dr. Walter O. Robinson *Course in Effective Speaking.* Narration is by Milton Cross. Ten lessons are (1) Why Fear Cannot Stop You from Speaking Well, (2) How Your Voice Instrument Works, (3) Now Let's Stop Being Lip Lazy, (4) How the Vowels Are Formed, (5) Learn to Be Your Own Audience, (6) How to Give Your Speech Variety, (7) How to Give Your Speech Forcefulness, (8) Don't Let Words Fool Your Ear!, (9) It's Time to Test Your Progress, and (10) Now Relax, Let Yourself Go—and Practice!

Modern Talking Picture Service, 45 Rockefeller Plaza, New York 20, N. Y. Free loan films include *On the Air,* a 20-minute explanation of the production of a radio show: how radio programs are written, rehearsed, timed, and transmitted. Description available.

Nash-Kelvinator Corporation, Kelvinator Division, Film Section, 14250 Plymouth Road, Detroit 32, Mich. Free loan films in sound and color cover the basic techniques of selling. Description available.

Prochnow, Herbert V., *The Toastmaster's Handbook,* New York: Prentice-Hall, Inc., 1949. Outlines the responsibilities of the chairman and toastmaster; describes many precise techniques used by successful chairmen; offers a fund of illustrative material—over 400 epigrams and witticisms, numerous quotations, and many humorous stories with suggestions for their use.

Toastmasters International, 1104 West 8th St., Santa Ana, Calif. A nonprofit, noncommercial association of local groups interested in speech education. Offers information about how to form a Toastmasters Club.

Westinghouse School Service, Box 1017, 306 Fourth Ave., Pittsburgh 30,

Pa. Free loan films include several about the basic principles of sales-manship. Descriptions available.

Young America Films, Inc., 18 East 41st St., New York 17, N. Y. The source of the rental films suggested for use in "A Course in Effective Speech": *Planning Your Talk, Stage Fright and What to Do About It, Platform Posture and Appearance, Using Your Voice,* and *The Functions of Gestures.* Descriptive brochure available.

INDEX